SCIENCE AND RELI

ERA OF WILLIAM JAMES

PAUL JEROME CROCE

Science and Religion in the Era of William James

VOLUME I

Eclipse of Certainty,

1820–1880

The University of North Carolina Press

Chapel Hill and London

© 1995 The University of North Carolina Press

All rights reserved

Manufactured in the United States of America

The paper in this book meets the guidelines for permanence and
durability of the Committee on Production Guidelines for
Book Longevity of the Council on Library Resources.

Library of Congress Cataloging-in-Publication Data

Croce, Paul Jerome.

Science and religion in the era of William James: Volume 1, Eclipse of certainty,
1820–1880 / Paul Jerome Croce.

p. cm.

Includes bibliographical references and index.

ISBN 0-8078-2200-0 (alk. paper). — ISBN 0-8078-4506-X (pbk. : alk. paper)

1. Religion and science—United States—History—19th century. 2. James, William,
1842–1910—Friends and associates. 3. James, William, 1842–1910—Contributions in
philosophy of relation of science and religion. I. Title.

BL245.C76   1995

215'.0973'09034—dc20   94-29749

CIP

99 98 97 96 95   5 4 3 2 1

To A. W. C. and A. P. C.

for planting the seeds

and to A. J. C.

for helping me see

the forest from the trees

CONTENTS

Preface: Science and Religion in the Era of William James   ix

Acknowledgments   xv

Chronology   xix

Introduction: The Erosion of Certainty   1

PART I. OUT OF THE JAMES HOUSEHOLD   23

1. A Native of the James Family   27

2. Science and the Spirit according to the Elder Henry James   49

3. Groping toward Science   67

PART II. AN EDUCATION IN SCIENCE   83

4. The Shock of Darwin   87

5. Darwinian Debates   111

PART III. THE SCIENTIFIC PERSUASION   149

6. Chauncey Wright and the Aim of Pure Science   157

7. Charles Sanders Peirce and the Elusive Certainty of Science   177

Conclusion: William James and the Culture of Uncertainty   225

Notes   233   Bibliography   299   Index   339

A section of illustrations follows page 110.

PREFACE

Science and Religion in the Era of William James

[William James] found an eager audience waiting.

JOHN DEWEY, 1910

I will never forget the response of a fellow graduate student when I enthusiastically announced my intention to embark on researching William James for my dissertation more than ten years ago: "At least everyone will have heard of him." The comment was a many-layered text. My friend was recognizing the fact that the subject was yet another white male from the cultural canon. But the comment also offered backhanded consolation that William James was universally known within the academy and broadly familiar outside. Familiarity has not often bred contempt, and, in fact, James's prominent status has not even bred neglect. Since his own time, James has been an increasingly towering figure in a dizzying array of cultural arenas, from the popular to the professional.

William James appears as a founding father in many theoretical fields whose very diversity testifies to his cultural importance, even if he is not central to any one discipline in the late twentieth century.[1] In addition, he is no less a familiar presence in historical and cultural studies, although these fields have not yet devoted as much attention to him.[2] James is widely recognized, generally admired, and frequently studied, but his canonization has often portrayed him as a charming avuncular presence, rather than a potent cultural player and an intellectual who readily crossed disciplinary boundaries. Most important, analyses of James's theories have paid little attention to his youth, and studies of his development toward maturity have put little emphasis on his intellectual life.

This book focuses on the intellectual and cultural context of James's early development, and in telling that story, it is also an interpretation of the way James became a central figure in a far-reaching cultural trend away from certainty in science and religion. While there were many other pressing questions and prominent cultural arbiters during this time, I propose that on issues relating to the intersection of science and religion, the middle to late nineteenth century is the era of William James.

It is not that his was a name on everyone's lips or that he persuaded all listeners and readers to his views of nature and the divine. Instead, his significance is that his life and thoughts were at the center of debate on the relation between science and religion. He experienced firsthand some of the most influential figures on this issue, and he was one of the first to become aware of the erosion of certainty in each field, which seeped into their theoretical roots despite the growing social authority of science and the ability of most religious believers to generate convictions. He was directly affected, personally and in his work, by this intellectual and cultural change, and his response to this problem performed cultural work by offering a widely popular way of coping with uncertainty without sacrificing either scientific authority or religious belief. He gradually formulated, for himself and then in his speaking and writing for a wide segment of the public, a belief that science and religion are both fallible human inquiries into the structure of the world; they can each offer plausible and persuasive explanations, but in their paths of constant investigation, they are never justified in resting comfortably with objective proof or dogmatic faith. Despite the high profile of conflict between science and religion, James argued that they are actually distinct yet parallel in their approaches to the truth of the world's architecture.

This book is about the first part of the era of William James, before he had authored the compromise and, in part, even prior to his birth—a period that would culminate in his learning from the challenges to certainty that were becoming gradually more apparent from the 1820s to the 1870s. In this volume, James is at the center of many clusters of people who felt concern over the changing relation between science and religion, including his family, the educated public, his teachers, and his friends. This book is in part a story of James's personal confrontation with the growth of uncertainty in science and religion, especially in relation to his father, but it is also a study of his context; more precisely, it is a study of those circles of people surrounding him, observed from the point of view of this centrally significant figure who was keenly attuned to the problems in his milieu and who eventually formulated persuasive responses to them.

By the 1860s and 1870s this cultural shift left gnawing questions about ways to understand and cope with uncertainty. I intend to write a companion volume that will directly evaluate James's gradual molding of a revised vision of science and religion based on the inability to know or believe with certainty. The two projects are related in sequence: the present volume raises cultural questions that the second volume will show James answering. This is why he himself is a minor presence in many of the chapters of this volume: with James at the eye of this emerging cultural system, much of this book is devoted to charting out the contexts and players of the storms over declining certainty that pervaded James's education and that he would address as he grew up. Therefore, Volume 1 is about James and his circle in the context of certainty just entering an eclipse; Volume 2 will cover James's early adulthood and his formulation of answers to uncertainty—and of a template for twentieth-century intellectual life. The two-volume project is about James at the center of groups of intellectuals who gradually steered scientific and religious understanding, often unintentionally, away from proclamations of certainty.[3]

I began this book as a study of James's scientific education. My research to understand what he learned led me to an inquiry into the context of shifting attitudes toward religion and science in general during the mid-nineteenth century. This investigation in turn trained my attention on the theme of declining certainty—and transformed my work into what might be called a cultural biography, a study of a cultural trend from the point of view of a key figure in that context. Although I have felt the pulse of a new discovery, no new line of inquiry emerges wholly new and unconnected to previous scholarship. I am deeply grateful to the historians of science, of religion, and of philosophy who taught me the contours and fine points of figures and movements in James's circle. Too numerous to mention here, their works and my debt to them appear in the notes of every chapter. Of course, I do not agree with every commentator, but I view the different perspectives as an opportunity to broaden and deepen my own argument. Like Charles Sanders Peirce's community of inquiry, or even like the mythical blindfolded persons feeling the parts of an elephant, we are all groping for a fuller understanding that we hope to approach but will likely never decisively reach. As a scholar shaped by the cultural turn of the intellectuals I study, I offer my conclusions and my gleanings from other commentators in a spirit of fallibility rather than as conclusive certainties.

This book begins with an introduction describing the erosion of certainty as a cultural player both in the history of scientific and religious thinking in the nineteenth century and in the historiography of American cultural and intellectual history. While the introduction lays out a map, sketching scenes in broad strokes, the other chapters focus very specifically on James's youth, his contexts, and the figures and ideas he encountered. Part I includes three chapters on James's earliest encounters with science, religion, and their relation to each other. Chapter 1 portrays young William James in his family, with a particular eye for tensions between openness to new experience and conformity to family expectations. Chapter 2 deals with the relation between science and religion as his father expounded it, which was the son's personal introduction to early-nineteenth-century assumptions of certainty from science and religion. Chapter 3 depicts James's halting steps toward his career in science, freighted with his father's hopes for spiritual science and his own admiration for the rising authority of empirical investigations of nature.

Part II follows the history of methodological and religious reflections on science as they surrounded James's experience through young adulthood. Chapter 4 takes up the wider canvas, describing the evolution in scientific practice from the 1820s, which set the stage for the reception of Darwinism and its ironic establishment as a model of both scientific authority and methodological uncertainty. Chapter 5 brings the focus back down to James's context in Cambridge, where he learned science from teachers who debated the merits of the content of Darwin's theory and the new, probabilistic method of science that it represented. In particular, James witnessed Louis Agassiz's religious and scientific assault on Darwinism and Asa Gray's defense based on probabilism, naturalism, and natural theology. The young scholar worked even more closely with Charles Eliot, Jeffries Wyman, and Oliver Wendell Holmes, Sr., who taught him the importance of professional techniques and encouraged his moderate but confirmed Darwinism.

Part III explores James's closest peers during the 1860s and 1870s in the Metaphysical Club discussion group, which served as a crucible for coming to terms with the theoretical uncertainty of scientific inquiry. James, Chauncey Wright, and Charles Peirce shared an enthusiasm for science and an eagerness to retain traditional morality despite modern changes. Chapter 6 depicts Wright carrying his excitement about science into an aggressively agnostic positivism. Chapter 7 is an analysis of Peirce's ironic combination of confidence in science's ability to find truth and the fallibilist assumption that truth is ever elusive. James learned from the tensions in these men's thought and gradually veered away from their confidence in scientific truth and method.

At the turn of the century, Peirce looked back at the history of his lifetime and concluded triumphantly, "The glory of the nineteenth century has been its science." James disagreed only in degree and was attentive to the nature and implications of Peirce's argument. The more enthusiastically scientific philosopher maintained that "the word 'science' . . . did not mean . . . 'systematized knowledge,' as former ages had defined it, nor anything set down in a book; but, on the contrary, a mode of life." More specifically, Peirce continued, science is "devotion to the truth that the man is not yet able to see but is striving to obtain."[4]

The prevalent view at the time and in the conventional wisdom ever since has been that the nineteenth-century scientific outlook was full of confidence and certainty. But revolutions in the methods and practice of science were dissolving beliefs in scientific certainty from within. Peirce offered a more humble emphasis on process in science, in which the methods of inquiry would be more important than the results. In the 1860s and 1870s William James learned the tools of scientific inquiry and began to wonder if they could apply to science itself. James went one step further in noticing the virtually religious character of such scientific investigations and the way religious belief had similarities to scientific theories. James's scientific education did not lead him to doubt religion, but it exposed him to the possibility of uncertainty at the root of both scientific method and religious belief. James was one of the first to raise doubts about the imperial claims of scientific certainty that swirled around the public reputation of science. If Peirce opened the door for a reconstruction of scientific and religious beliefs, James more fully walked through to where the scientifically committed Peirce refused to tread. Unintentionally, William James stumbled onto this hidden history of scientific progress in the nineteenth century.

ACKNOWLEDGMENTS

One unimpeachable certainty remains upon completing this book: I am very much in the debt of many friends, colleagues, and family members for their insights, help, and support.

Although this work has evolved into a wholly new species since I wrote my dissertation, I still lean on the excellent education I received at Georgetown and Brown Universities. My intellectual preparation as an undergraduate and my professional training as a graduate student complemented each other as did the institutions' contrasting cultural traditions. I would particularly like to thank Emmett Curran for his patience and sterling example during my first steps in intellectual and cultural history. Joan Richards introduced me to the "Darwin industry" and continues to be an excellent guide to the history of science and professional life in general. John E. Smith, of Yale's philosophy department, welcomed a graduate student from a neighboring school and a different discipline, giving generously of his time and vast stores of knowledge in teaching me about James's own works. The late William G. McLoughlin was a paragon of integrity and energy, and his model of moral commitment and rigorous scholarship continues to inspire. Most important, John L. Thomas, who could be tough, kind, and enthusiastic all at once, pushed me with his youthful exuberance always to think about the broadest cultural trends and to write with storytelling drama.

I am also pleased to thank the many people who have helped this project by reading my work or offering critical suggestions: Catherine Albanese, Andrea Birch, Priscilla Brewer, Andrew Carlson, Vincent Colapietro, Deborah Coon, P. Todd Davis, William Dean, Steve Gillon, Kenneth Everett, Mark Franklin, Mary Gluck, John Hague, David Hollinger, Davis Jerome, James Kloppenberg, Jack Lane, Paul Lauritzen, Phillip Lucas, Michael McFarland, Jay Mechling, Don Musser, Robert Perkins, Lewis Perry, Theodore Porter, Dorothy Ross, Marc Rothenberg, Charlene Haddock Seigfried, Jeff Simpson, Zeno Swijtink, Eugene Taylor, Sumner Twiss, Jane Williams-Hogan, Bill Woodward, and Leila Zenderland. In addition, Paul Boyer, George Cotkin, and Jon Roberts have read all of the manuscript in earlier drafts—often more than once—and I can only hope that this final fallible draft makes use of their criticism and lives up to their standards.

I thank all of my students for listening (usually!) to the things I find so very important, for giving me daily reminders of the relation between scholarship and popularization, and for constantly challenging me with their questions and surprising me with their sharp insights. A few deserve special thanks for teaching the teacher: Tracy Boisseau, Rob Carbonneau, Joyce Nailling, and Ryan Smith.

Librarians are behind the scenes of every book. I thank those great organizers of information and texts at Brown University's Rockefeller, Sciences, and Hay Libraries; at Georgetown's Lauinger Library; at the Library of Congress; at Harvard's Houghton and Pusey Libraries; at Rollins's Olin Library; at the Smithsonian Archives; and especially at Stetson's DuPont-Ball Library. And for his searching skills and untiring zeal, I especially thank David Everett.

I am delighted to thank the National Endowment for the Humanities and Stetson University for providing me with the funds to buy time for travel, research, and concentration on this project.

I am very much in the debt of many individuals and institutions for permission to quote from manuscript material. Use of manuscript material by William James and Henry James, Sr., is by permission of Alexander R. James and the Houghton Library, Harvard University; use of manuscript material by Charles Sanders Peirce is by permission of the Department of Philosophy, Harvard University; use of Ralph Waldo Emerson material is by permission of the Ralph Waldo Emerson Memorial Association and the Houghton Library, Harvard University; use of the Faculty Records of the Lawrence Scientific School is by permission of the Harvard University Archives; and use of the Joseph Henry material is by permission of the Smithsonian Institution Archives.

Previous portions of much earlier drafts of this book appeared in *New York History*, *Swedenborg and His Influence*, *Intellectual History Newsletter*, and *History of Human Science*. I thank the editors of each for permission to use the published materials.

The University of North Carolina Press has been a delight to work with. People in every department are professional and efficient—even when I was not on time. I especially appreciate Barbara Hanrahan, who has a special talent for combining rigor and good sense.

It is conventional to thank parents. But thanks do not seem enough for such parents with unconventional capacities for generosity and support. I offer them this book as partial payment for first getting me hooked on reading. I also thank my uncle John Wilson for his constant interest in my work.

My prime directive during the long cultivation of this book was that I would only write it if doing so would not disrupt my family. I generally succeeded well enough—until the last few weeks. For their longstanding love and support and for their patience at the crunch I have the deepest thanks. I hope these last few peak moments have been creative; I know they have produced some immortal words. When asked, "What is Daddy working on?" with a toddler's unintended wisdom, Elizabeth responded tersely, pointing to the computer discs: "This." Fair enough. And four-year-old Peter delivered an unimpeachable line manifesting a belief that surpasseth all understanding: "But Daddy's book will never be finished." So it seemed. Still, he never lost faith in me—as long as I took along his "imaginary friend who knows how to write." Every book should have one.

Finally, my deepest thanks go to my wife, Ann Jerome Croce, who not only offered extra child care at the bitter end, but also was my first best reader, offering sharply insightful commentary and suggestions. She took the text to heart and made it a better read. And that's just the past month. Through the years, she has always been a force pushing me to see the big picture, personally, professionally, and intellectually. Her kindness is golden; her judgment is sound; her logic is impeccable. For all this and for being my intellectual colleague and partner in life, I dedicate this book to her.

CHRONOLOGY

1771	William James [the first American William James, who would become known as "William of Albany"] born
1789	William of Albany immigrates to the United States
1807	Louis Agassiz born
1809	Charles Darwin born
	Benjamin Peirce born
	Oliver Wendell Holmes, Sr., born
1810	Asa Gray born
1811	Henry James, Sr., born
1814	Jeffries Wyman born
1830	Henry James, Sr., graduates from Union College
	Chauncey Wright born
1832	William of Albany dies
1834	Charles Eliot born
1839	Charles Sanders Peirce born
	Lowell Institute lectures inaugurated
1840	Henry James marries Mary Walsh
1842	William James born
1843	Henry James, Jr., born
1843–45	James family travels in Europe
1844	Robert Chambers publishes *The Vestiges of Creation* anonymously
	Henry James's spiritual crisis and discovery of Swedenborg
1845	Garth Wilkinson James born
1846	Louis Agassiz arrives in the United States
	Robertson James born
1847	Lawrence Scientific School founded at Harvard
1848	Louis Agassiz accepts position in zoology and geology at the Lawrence Scientific School
	Alice James born
1852	Chauncey Wright graduates from Harvard

1855	Saturday Club founded
1855–58	James family travels in Europe
1857	William James attends his first science class in Boulogne, France
1858	William James studies art in Newport with William Morris Hunt
1859	Charles Sanders Peirce graduates from Harvard
	Charles Darwin publishes *The Origin of Species*
	Building of the Museum of Comparative Zoology begun at Harvard University
1859–60	James family travels in Europe
	William James studies at the Geneva Academy, Switzerland
1860–61	William James studies art in Newport with William Morris Hunt
1861	William James enrolls at Lawrence Scientific School to study chemistry with Charles Eliot
1863	Henry James, Sr., is elected to the Saturday Club
	Charles Sanders Peirce graduates summa cum laude from Lawrence Scientific School
1864	James family moves to Boston
1865–66	William James travels with Louis Agassiz to Brazil
1869	William James receives Doctor of Medicine degree from Harvard University
1872	William James appointed Instructor in Physiology at Harvard University
1873	Louis Agassiz dies
1874	Jeffries Wyman dies
1875	Chauncey Wright dies
1877–78	Charles Sanders Peirce publishes "Illustrations of the Logic of Science" series in *Popular Science Monthly*
1878	William James delivers Lowell Institute lectures on "The Brain and the Mind"
1880	Benjamin Peirce dies
1882	Charles Darwin dies
	Henry James, Sr., dies

1888	Asa Gray dies
1890	William James publishes *The Principles of Psychology*, 2 vols.
1894	Oliver Wendell Holmes, Sr., dies
1895	William James delivers "The Will to Believe" lecture
1901–2	William James delivers the Gifford Lectures on Natural Religion, which would become *The Varieties of Religious Experience*
1907	William James delivers Lowell Institute lectures, which would become *Pragmatism*
1910	William James dies
1914	Charles Sanders Peirce dies
1926	Charles Eliot dies

SCIENCE AND RELIGION IN THE

ERA OF WILLIAM JAMES

INTRODUCTION

The Erosion of Certainty

For just as necessity *and search for a* single *all-comprehensive* law *was typical of the intellectual atmosphere of the forties of the last century, so* probability *and* pluralism *are the characteristics of the present state of science.*

JOHN DEWEY, 1939

This philosophy denies nothing of orthodoxy except its confidence.

CHAUNCEY WRIGHT, 1867

While William James was still a young boy, Edgar Allan Poe tried to teach his contemporaries a lesson in perceiving and understanding the world around them. His character, C. Auguste Dupin, shows the unsuspecting reader of "The Purloined Letter" that sometimes the best way to hide something is to put it in an obvious spot. The Parisian police are perplexed by a deceptively simple mystery: a letter, with contents embarrassing and therefore politically potent, has been stolen; they know that a certain government minister has the letter still in his possession. But an investigation of his person and his premises has turned up no letter. The police then search in more elusive parts of his apartment, including a secret "cavity . . . [in a] piece of furniture," and "the rung[s] of every chair"; they even use "the aid of a most powerful microscope" for trace evidence, but all of this sophistication is to no avail. Dupin smiles at their exploits; the police, after all, are "persevering, ingenious, cunning, and thoroughly versed in the knowledge which their duties seem chiefly to demand."

Dupin, by contrast, thinks outside habitual channels. When first hearing the story, he tantalizes the dutiful prefect of police by suggesting that "perhaps it is the very simplicity of the thing which puts you at fault." Dupin surmises that "the Minister has resorted to the comprehensive and sagacious expedient of not attempting to conceal it at all." And sure enough, on entering the sly politician's rooms, he finds the letter openly but inconspicuously displayed. All other investigators had walked past the open secret. The canny Dupin explains that "the Minister had deposited the letter immediately beneath the nose of the whole world, by way of best preventing any portion of that world from perceiving it."[1] Poe's playful rendering of the elusive relationships between physical signs and subjective knowledge is an important cultural marker on the road to understanding the changing epistemologies of the nineteenth century.[2] In Poe's day, when William James was born, most people expected that confidence, assurance, and certainty would increase in direct relation to increases in knowledge. Dupin's lesson in the importance of simple, profound insights that shape the path of inquiry is also a good one for historians and cultural commentators trying to understand the forces that have shaped the course of American culture.

In the last generation of scholarship, women's studies has provided a prime example of this kind of discovery. Despite the deceptive familiarity of gender relations, historians have revealed a whole world of women's lives that had previously been considered too simple or too obvious or too unimportant to be the subject of historical inquiry. These recognitions have set the stage for a reconstruction of historical knowledge with gender relations knit into the fabric of the past.[3] In a different historical field, demographic and environmental historians have added a whole new dimension to the story of Europeans' encounter with Native Americans in the New World by investigating the long-known fact of the natives' precipitous population decline in the first generations after contact. For years observations about the devastating influence of European-based diseases had passed through writings on colonial history without much influence on their explanation of European cultures' triumph in the Americas. Recent scholarship has shown that European microbes were at least as effective as European technology and expansionist energy in conquering the New World.[4] Poe has not been alone in observing that people can easily overlook major issues. And William James himself recounted and documented the powerful influence of prior knowledge and entrenched habit on perception.[5] Like Dupin, so too would James have understood these twists and turns of scholarship: the most obvious factors sometimes seem wholly hidden from view.

Introduction 3

The Dawn of Uncertainty

This book makes no further inquiry into the works of Poe. But I do take Dupin's lesson and James's introspective psychology seriously: I trace the frequently elusive or simply assumed growth of uncertainty in religion and science through the nineteenth century by evaluating its place in relation to James and his circle. I use the term "certainty" not as a philosopher's abstract theory, nor even as a synonym of truth, but rather as a cultural category indicating confidence or assurance in any particular idea or belief.[6] We are used to thinking of cultural forms as a rather humble lot, including standards of cleanliness or civility, or nonintellectual feelings, such as a sense of honor.[7] But ideas also perform a cultural role in shaping values and worldviews, and they cannot be left solely to the abstract treatment of philosophers. Students of theory may object to the inevitable limits on nuance of such a definition, but they will gain an overview perspective, a recognition of patterns, and broad insights about context from the student of culture.

Early in the nineteenth century most Americans, for all their range of differences, felt fully certain about their scientific and religious outlooks on the world. Scientific pronouncements benefited from the rising authority of the scientific method, and, despite the warnings of Immanuel Kant about the uncertainty of the noumenal realm, most religious believers bypassed such philosophical inquiry in their own convictions. Those who relied more on reason than on emotions or faith looked to the confirming proof of rationality and empirical fact; even Kant assumed the certainty of science and provided an outlet from the starkness of religious uncertainty by positing the effective certainty of the "practical reason."[8] Yet by the end of the century, such certainty was almost completely routed. Although many popular believers retained confidence in the certainty of science or the absolute truth of religious beliefs, serious professional and intellectual inquiry in these fields had almost totally abandoned certainty. By the twentieth century, religious doubt is so widespread that it has become a major concern of religious leaders, and, as Clifford Geertz notes, professional science has become "an institutionalized scepticism which dissolves the world's givenness into a swirl of probabilistic hypotheses."[9] While no generalization dealing with large issues and large numbers of people is universal, it is fair to say that during the nineteenth century epistemic certainty largely disappeared from the intellectual and cultural landscape in America and throughout the European world as well.

In the cauldron of nineteenth-century culture, new scientific discoveries, the ebb and flow of religious debates, and the coexistence of sharply differing beliefs, theories, and ideologies left seeds of doubt that could not even be dreamt of in earlier cultures with less scientific inquiry, less diversity of peoples, and more respect for authority. Moreover, the anxiety produced by the turbulence of market competition, geographic expansion, and changing social roles was trickling down to the inner recesses of people's minds and hearts. The prescient Alexis de Tocqueville was one of the first to notice that the freedom, equality, and ceaseless agitation of democratic capitalist culture left the average citizen prone to confusion and uncertainty about philosophical and religious questions.[10] When change became accepted as more the rule than the exception in the nineteenth century, it brought doubt about the stability of any one theoretical proposition concerning the nature of the world or humanity's place in it. Sometimes the more these doubts gnawed, the more people conducted their lives with confidence to cast away the restlessness of uncertainty. Beneath the surefootedness of every rugged individual's social role was an emerging uncertainty about his or her place in the universe, about the truths of religion, the divine, and morality, and about the ability to understand the natural world with assurance. Although the growth of socially confident professionalism, the robust pronouncements of positivist readings of science, and the publicly zealous convictions of some religious leaders often masked their changes, science and religion evolved in the direction of uncertainty at their theoretical roots and in their cultural roles throughout the century.

Most attention to the erosion of certainty in the nineteenth century has emphasized the rise of religious doubt, but this does not do full justice to the depth of the cultural and theoretical shifts toward uncertainty. The growing apparent certainty of science, which gained wide currency with the popularization of positivism, did contribute greatly to the erosion of confidence in religious beliefs. Yet positivism was more a belief of science watchers than of scientists, and this philosophy could not stem the tide of new professional insights about the conditioned and relational quality of all knowledge.[11] As the last great burst of confidence in scientific knowledge, positivism would retain a popular appeal while probabilism, relativity, and hypothetical methodologies firmly established the fundamental uncertainty of modern science.

The social location of most of these theoretical shifts was among the rising professional classes, who have most often been evaluated in terms of their growing social authority and public confidence.[12] Yet the turn to professionalism, which ostensibly would bring a stream of definite answers to perplexing questions, would ironically contribute to the underlying uncertainty because of the path of ceaseless inquiry of intellectual endeavors. An examination of the theoretical construction of professionalism shows that beneath this robust social power was an ever-deepening well of intellectual uncertainty about the ultimate truth of the topics under inquiry. In 1929 the philosopher John Dewey even took up the expectation that inquiry could produce certainty as a point of ridicule in his lectures on *The Quest for Certainty*. Paradoxically, the more people knew of religion or science, the less certain they felt. Uncertainty shifted from being a synonym for falsehood to becoming a path on the way toward truth.[13]

This development is one chapter in the story of the split between popular and professional discourses. Average citizens had been accustomed to turning to religious leaders and scientists for assurance about fundamental truths and ultimate meaning, but as the century wore on, religion and science watchers found less final assurance from intellectual leaders and more frank inquiry among multiple viewpoints. An expanding base of knowledge seemed to the public to offer ever more definitive answers, but when experts knew more, they simply multiplied the questions to be asked. Disappointed by the decline of certainty and intimidated by professional methods, many nonexperts exercised their democratic right to reject the best and the brightest intellectual insights and cling willfully to conviction and simple commonsense facts. And so, most people, when they thought about scientific or religious truths, simply ignored the growing mountains of professional research and instead looked to nonintellectual justifications of their beliefs and convictions and to uncomplicated expressions of information. For example, religious modernists are ready to adapt their beliefs to the latest research, while fundamentalists hold firm despite the fruits of inquiry; medical doctors take educated guesses, while patients ask for definite answers about their maladies; teachers present multiple interpretations, while students puzzle over which one is the true fact. Professionals, therefore, have developed a Janus-face: an edifice of certainty turned toward the public, and a private posture of steady unceasing scrutiny, with constantly multiplying questions to their fellows within their disciplinary circle.[14] Despite the inevitable presence of doubt produced by constant professional inquiry, experts can present facsimiles of traditional certainty with research programs based on probabilistic near certainties.

The gradually emerging culture of uncertainty in science and religion is the deep context for this book. With this cultural landscape in the background, this volume is devoted to examination of the set of characters on the American scene in the middle of the nineteenth century who were among the most devoted to trying to understand these questions of certainty and uncertainty. The philosophers, scientists, and religious thinkers in this book, in addition to engaging in their abstract and professional tasks, also performed the cultural work of producing usable theories.

While the story that follows this introduction is primarily about intellectuals struggling with an erosion of certainty, popular perspectives and issues of popularization shadow the central tale throughout. Not only did the intellectuals in this story have constant interaction with a broader public; their ideas also became key cultural factors, which attracted supporters, adapters, and detractors from their audience of intellectuals and educated observers as well. As a consequence, while this book makes no claim to identify a culture of uncertainty for America as a whole, I do propose that one cultural group set the terms of debate on science and religion for years to come. While this study focuses on a privileged group of New England philosophers and scientists with an influence disproportionate to their numbers, similar examinations of intellectuals and cultural leaders in other regions could enlarge and adapt the thesis. The evolution of James's circle away from certainty had a deep influence on American cultural elites and on their relation with other groups who would ask less probing questions of science and religion.

By the late twentieth century, the rejection of certainty has become such a frequent feature of the intellectual's outlook—and a point of annoyance to nonintellectuals—that the origin of this sea change in the nineteenth century is frequently overlooked. It is also a treacherous and embarrassing fact because it suggests a chink in the armor of experts' social authority and reputation for providing much-needed answers. Exposing the uncertainty embedded in professional inquiry may contribute in some small ways toward the democratic purpose of bridging the cultural gulf between professional and popular thinking, a chasm that has widened dangerously since the erosion of certainty in the last century. Two separate streams of scholarship have already touched on this theme: historians of science have uncovered a "probabilistic revolution," and cultural and intellectual historians have revived the concept of secularism for study of the nineteenth century.

The Probabilistic Revolution

The discovery of the probabilistic revolution has sent an exciting current through the field of the history of science in the last decade. Somewhat like Auguste Dupin's notice of the purloined letter or political and cultural historians' discovery of the pervasive ideology of republicanism in the 1960s and 1970s,[15] historians of science since the 1980s have enthusiastically assembled familiar facts around a new organizing principle. The recent flowering of scholarship on the probabilistic revolution has emphasized the increasing recognition of chance operations in the natural and social sciences throughout the nineteenth century in Europe and North America and the establishment of probabilistic laws, often expressed with statistics, to explain patterns or even make predictions amid the uncertainty of individual events. While observations of chance date back thousands of years and the study of probabilities began in the seventeenth century, the probabilistic revolution itself is a product of the nineteenth century.[16] In particular, while it was common practice in the late eighteenth century to express the truth of a social generalization or a physical phenomenon in deterministic terms with an air of absolute certainty, by the twentieth century, the language of tentative but plausible probabilities and the notion of predicting likelihood based on chance had, in the words of historian of science Lorraine Daston, "unseated the ideal of determinism shared by almost all European thinkers in 1800."[17] Historians of science have uncovered the way probability theory found wider applications among diverse theoretical questions, scientific inquiries, and social problems.

The first such application of probability was not motivated by an embrace of uncertainty but, on the contrary, by an enthusiasm for finding certainty within uncertainty. Probabilists in the nineteenth century relished the order which seemed to lurk beneath chance-filled occurrences in a variety of fields ranging from random biological species variation, to the personal choices for marriage and suicide, to the chaotic movement of gases. As historian of science Theodore Porter notes, the statistical manipulation of chance events "stemmed not from the weakness of science, but from its strength—or rather, its aggressive imperialism, the drive to extend scientific determinism into a domain that had previously been seen by most as the realm of inscrutable whimsy."[18] As science extended its explanatory reach and built up its confidence with probabilistic patterns, this very set of outlooks had already let out the genie of uncertainty into the practice of its method. Scientific probability theorists might be able to "tame chance," to use Ian Hacking's evocative phrase, but first they had to recognize it and assume its role in natural and social phenomena. These two sides to chance parallel the Janus faces of professionalism: in theory, the recognition of chance assumed more uncertainty; in practice, the use of chance involved an increase of certainty through the manipulation and control of more of the natural and social world. The most recent manifestation of this dual demeanor of chance is in the science of chaos, which involves the discovery of patterns in seemingly disordered systems.[19] Once probabilistic thinking set in, no social or scientific theory could go back to the brand of certainty that dominated European-centered thinking before the nineteenth century, just as no other philosophical outlook could blithely assume certainty as a starting point or working principle.

Historians of science maintain a view of the certainty of nineteenth-century probabilistic science that is similar to Kant's view of certainty in religious belief. Although Kant cautioned prospective religious believers that their "truths" can never be epistemologically certain, he also said that religious beliefs should be approached as practical and effective certainties. Similarly, historians of the probabilistic revolution have paid more attention to the probabilistic near certainties of new scientific theories in the nineteenth century than to the intellectual role or cultural impact of these assumptions about underlying uncertainty. The difference between scientific outlooks and the intellectual and cultural perceptions of them is readily apparent in the current heated debate over the spread of AIDS. Scientists argue plausibly and with great confidence that the disease cannot spread through casual contact because the chance of contracting it from touch or saliva is uncountably remote and undocumented in current research. The public listening to these scientific pronouncements asks a simple question: "Are you sure?" Scientists respond with extreme probabilities rather than with certainty. The gap between those two kinds of answers is often filled with anger and fear—generated by the anxiety, as the telling popular phrase goes, that the person on the receiving end of the improbable contraction of the disease "might become a statistic."[20] The public is more concerned with the consequences of uncertainty than with the experts' nuance on this point. Although popular uncertainty and scientific near certainty stand theoretically close together, they are culturally far apart.

Any day's dip into the sea of popular culture can produce similar demands for certainty in popular cultural forms. An unsolicited flyer arrived in my mail recently from a group eager to save my soul. Its headline reads searchingly: "DO YOU KNOW FOR SURE . . . that you are going to be with God in heaven?" Few academics, theologians, or even most educated people with spiritual interests would frame religious questions that way. Answering the question with an assumption of its unknowability, and our at best probabilistic ability to know about the afterlife, they would ask about doctrine, cultural traditions, the power of stories and their impact on human feelings, moral work, or even about models of God; the authors and intended readers of this flyer would find those issues to be mere obfuscation. To them, faith is a kind of verifiable knowledge, and a more sophisticated inquiry constitutes a sheer distraction from their quest for certainty.[21]

Nonsophisticated religion is not the only site for popular demands for certainty. A recent episode of *Nova* on public television showed the preparations before the eruption of Mount Pinatubo in the Philippines. With Clark Air Force Base and many hundreds of thousands of people nearby, predictions about the volcano's timing and intensity would have enormous consequences. The volcanologists offered predictions about when the big explosion would come and how big it would be, but the residents just wanted a directive: "Should I evacuate and, if so, when?" Untrained in the nuances of geology, the average resident did not care about the professionals' mountain of knowledge, and their percentages of likelihood were just so many tantalizing rumblings; they simply wanted some certainty about what to do next. In fact, the episode showed that when volcanologists elsewhere had predicted eruptions that did not in fact come, they were sued by the affected communities for the loss of business and the damaged reputation.[22]

The complications of modern life demand more and more people to be educated with professional understandings of their fields, but they leave a cultural tension in the wake of their educational progress. As these examples demonstrate, misunderstanding and antagonism occur as readily in science and religion as in any other field of keen intellectual inquiry. By contrast, William James's perspective on science and religion bridged the work of professionals in those fields and the popular audiences who followed their work. He himself was an intellectual, trained in nuance, familiar with probabilistic expressions of ideas, and comfortable with a tentative balancing of philosophies rather than the expression of absolute truths. Yet he was also culturally sensitive enough to sympathize with lay people whose eyes glazed at probabilistic chances and who longed for the confidence and assurance that come with certainty.

James's interest in religion and his tendency to be more a watcher and user of science—albeit often an avid one—than a scientist himself explain why he has earned virtually no mention in writings on the probabilistic revolution. He played a major role in advocating the rejection of deterministic certainty, and his writings are peppered with direct and indirect negotiations with chance, but, from the point of view of historians of science, his work is on the soft underbelly of the probabilistic revolution. He relates to this historical trend through his careful attention to scientific method and the epistemology of belief and through his attention to their intellectual and cultural consequences. But where scientists of the probabilistic revolution opened the door to uncertainty only to close it with the force of science claiming even more certainty, James kept the door open and attended to the uncertainty itself as an issue to be fully addressed, recognized, sometimes lamented, and eventually embraced. As he matured he gradually formulated a philosophy, born in the swirling maelstrom of religion's relation to science, that would use probabilistic thinking not to deride the uncertainties of beliefs but to legitimate belief without certainty.[23]

In this book the probabilistic revolution serves as a deep background to the more immediate context of the science, religion, and philosophy surrounding James's early years. This discovery in the history of science has alerted me to the widespread nineteenth-century concern with chance and uncertainty. Most notably for James's context, this theme appears in recent studies of Darwinism. Before the last generation of scholarship, and still in most popular descriptions, the radical new science of species development has often been viewed as a harbinger of the scientific certainties of positivism.[24] Although historians of science frequently intended their discovery of the probabilistic revolution to illuminate only scientific issues, their research has opened up the possibility for general recognition of science as a major subject for intellectual and cultural history and for the theme of discovering and taming uncertainty to become an important element in historical scholarship in general.

The Rise of Secularism

While historians of science have given the most enthusiastic recent attention to the role of uncertainty in nineteenth-century thought, intellectual and religious historians have for years shown a broad awareness of the emerging culture of uncertainty. Attention has focused on the role of secularism, which has been seen sometimes as the decline of a public role for religion and sometimes as the increasing strength of religion due to its spillover to other fields.[25] The term has generally remained mired in the murkiness generated by such a variety of definitions; moreover, it has often been adopted by conservatives to label all that is religiously modernist, criticized by social historians for its irrelevance in the face of steady or rising church attendance in the last two hundred years, and even dismissed by intellectual historians in the face of evidence for an ongoing strength of religion in harmony with science.[26] Despite batterings, the term "secularism" still has historical viability, because, I maintain, even in its many definitional roles, it suggests the declining certainty that most intellectuals have felt for their religious beliefs at least since the nineteenth century. Pared down to this core, secularism has cropped up in the work of a handful of recent cultural and intellectual historians, although each has pursued different arguments for different purposes.

While references to secularism are rare in recent historical work, a few generations ago it made frequent appearances in intellectual history and in consensus perspectives on the American past generally. Many traditional and generalist historians have made secularism a central theme of their explanations of the origins of modern American culture in the late nineteenth century. For example, Henry Steele Commager acknowledged the rise of church attendance in the nineteenth and twentieth centuries but found increasingly thin convictions among religious adherents and steadily lessening influences on public life and institutions. Paul Carter depicted religion confronting a crisis of faith, slowly retreating during modern times in the face of scientific doubt, industrial materialism, unholy church scandal, and the relativizing impact of comparative religions. The avowedly Christian historian Gary Scott Smith cites the "strong challenges . . . mounted to the traditional biblical basis" of American society and culture since the late nineteenth century.[27]

A problem with these general treatments, however, is that they have kept a fairly loose definition of the term, and their research has rarely intersected with the work of historians of religion and of science. In addition, they confined secularism to a phenomenon of the intellectual life, so when intellectual history declined in the 1960s and 1970s, the historiography of secularism virtually disappeared. Like Yogi Berra describing a restaurant he no longer liked to frequent, many young historians and cultural critics, feeling the excitement of social history and recognizing the dominance of intellectual history in previous generations, looked at the older field and declared, "Nobody goes there any more. It's too crowded."[28] Older histories involving secularism offer tantalizing suggestions about the cultural implications of their intellectual history accounts, which were largely ignored until the recent resurgence of intellectual and cultural history.[29]

In the last decade attention to secularism has revived, thanks to the new layers of sophistication and cultural awareness that intellectual and cultural historians have added to the term and to issues of science and religion in general.[30] David Hollinger has been a major advocate for the inquiry into the ideas surrounding nineteenth-century challenges to religious beliefs. In a 1989 essay he breathed new life into the old term "secularism" when he used it "to refer to the growth in size and in cultural authority of de-Christianized academic elites, and to the corresponding decline in the role played by churches in public life."[31] Distancing himself from recent scholarship emphasizing harmony between science and religion, Hollinger argues that advocates for science were in fact forceful agents for antireligious outlooks, but the partisans for science ironically maintained their positions with a religious zeal. His evangelicals for science had serious doubts about religion, but Hollinger does not discuss the place of uncertainty within their science.

In an earlier essay Hollinger had suggested a place for uncertainty in science, when he distinguished between science as practiced and "'science'" as advocated by the likes of W. K. Clifford, T. H. Huxley, Herbert Spencer, and John Tyndall. These zealots of "science" held a "quaint conceit" in the "transcendent objectivity" of science, which James among others boldly punctured by the late nineteenth century. Hollinger succeeds in identifying James's embrace of the "contingency in all beliefs," including the religious and the scientific, in his mature theories, but he does not show James responding to scientific and religious reflections that were themselves moving toward uncertainty, nor does he examine young James developing his ideas prior to the bold declarations of his later years. While Hollinger portrays James criticizing those who were "so infatuated [with] 'science,'" this volume will examine the science itself that James would learn during his early years.[32] In that setting, James gleaned messages of uncertainty from the heart of science itself, as I plan to show in the follow-up volume to this book.

Even the scientific thinkers of the mid-nineteenth century who are included in the present volume veered away from certainty in the methods and results of their inquiries. One broad implication of all of my work on James is that for all of pragmatism's use in philosophical and literary circles,[33] it was originally conceived and used as a scientific way of thinking. This brings me to a final important contribution of Hollinger to my development of the themes of this book: his new historicist declaration that "an accurate reading of James requires that we not screen out as an irrelevant curiosity the anxiety about the fate of religion in an age of science."[34] The relation between religion and science and the resulting rise of uncertainty in those fields are the most important context and theme of this volume.

James Kloppenberg's analysis of the emergence and widespread political use of ideas of uncertainty is contemporary with the scholarship of the probabilistic revolution. He begins his study of turn-of-the-twentieth-century political theorists and policy advocates with an account of the gradual shift among European and American intellectuals during the nineteenth century from an enlightenment urge to know the truth to a chastened recognition of the impossibility of knowing with certainty. Like the historians of science, Kloppenberg recognizes this pattern in the nineteenth century and spends most of his study on the intellectual responses to this changed context; where others have analyzed scientists' development of probabilistic laws, he evaluates political thinkers' formulations of progressive and pragmatic theories for explaining and controlling the "blooming, buzzing" chaos of modern industrial society.[35] Although in different fields and rarely in direct contact, the scientists and political intellectuals of the late nineteenth century were performing similar cultural work with their ideas: both probabilistic theories and Progressive reform policies sought to achieve greater certainty in the face of growing uncertainty. While the proponents of these movements were primarily concerned with expanding the domain of understanding and control for their fields, their intellectual roots reach to the more generalized recognition of the uncertainty that would make their enterprises necessary.

This book's treatment of the emergence of uncertainty addresses an earlier time than Kloppenberg's and covers the subjects of science and religion rather than political theory and public policy, but I found hearty endorsement of my project in his acknowledgment of so much importance in the "[earlier] generation raised in the mid-nineteenth century and preoccupied with the relation of religion and science" and in his description of "a later generation that sought solutions to social and economic problems by rethinking political activity according to the radical conceptions of knowledge and responsibility they derived from their predecessors." Kloppenberg traces the origins of turn-of-the-century uncertainty to "the question that gnawed at this generation, the question whether science and reason were compatible with religion and belief." In particular, he argues, the uncertainty emerged because "scientists demolished [the] arguments [of] religion." This view dominated historiographical interpretations until the last generation but, in fact, it accurately describes only one faction of the relation between religion and science in the middle to late nineteenth century. The argument does not recognize the continuing power of the sentiment for harmony between the fields, which would encourage a creative range of accommodations; many of these did indeed embed uncertainty into their religious beliefs, not because religion had been slain by science, but because of the growing importance of change and uncertainty in both fields.

In addition, while Kloppenberg observes that "by 1900 [scientists'] own presuppositions appeared equally unsteady" because of questions about "not only specific findings but [also] the fundamental legitimacy of claims to certainty based on science," he does not notice the growing uncertainty gradually emerging in science as early as the 1830s, especially in methodological practices and reflections. These observations do not take anything away from his argument about the character and importance of a more fully mature uncertainty in the late nineteenth century; at that point many intellectuals who would be important to Progressives and Social Democrats came to believe that "truth must be cut free from notions of eternity and necessity and grounded instead in human experience, never definite and subject always to revision."[36]

This is uncertainty bold and confident; this book covers an earlier period when the moves toward uncertainty were more tentative.

James Turner explicitly addresses uncertainty in religion. He argues that secularism is not so much an antireligious outlook as a drift away from belief and toward an indifference about religion. Hence his dominant concern is not the rise of atheism, but the breakdown of the assumption that God exists. The important issue for Turner is that the doubting of religion became a plausible and respectable intellectual option in late-nineteenth-century America. This topic leads him to a notoriously elusive subject matter: a history of assumptions, the core beliefs and intellectual frameworks that often remain unarticulated or expressed only in passing.

Turner prefaces his study of the emergence of religious unbelief in the late nineteenth century with an extensive inquiry into the roots of this intellectual and cultural trend going back to the European sixteenth century and even earlier. Turner divides these centuries into three periods that differed on the question of certainty's place in belief. He begins with the centuries up through the sixteenth: with still strong medieval assumptions, religious belief was an unreflective assurance that was expressed in behavior and ritual rather than in doctrine as knowledge or certainty.[37] During the second period, Reformation divisions brought an increased attention to doctrine, and the scientific revolution encouraged greater confidence in humanity's ability to know the natural world. So, beginning somewhat in the sixteenth century and accelerating in the next two centuries, religious belief was maintained and proclaimed with more avowed certainty;[38] this trend culminated in the first half of the nineteenth century when religious leaders self-consciously modeled their beliefs on scientific propositions in the hopes of earning the same authority and certainty for religion that science had come to assume.[39] The third period emerged by the late nineteenth century, when religious belief was so tied to the quest for certainty that it could no longer be treated as an unquestioned assumption; once a subject for reflection and rational inquiry, it inevitably fell short of scientific certainty and became subject to widespread and corrosive doubt.

Turner's argument addresses the European-American or more precisely the Anglo-American world. Because the empirical and scientific thinking that play such large parts in his study are European phenomena, then, implicitly, the trend away from medieval assumptions about religion should also measure the distance between the religious styles of modernizing Europeans and those of peoples from around the world with whom they came into contact during the era of European expansion and domination. Especially since the age of exploration and empire building coincides exactly in time with Turner's analysis of belief in God, a comparative study of religious assumptions of both Europeans and non-Europeans would make a welcome complement to Turner's book and would be a path-breaking synthesis of contact studies and intellectual history.[40]

One hint of what could be discovered in such a study is reflected in the experience of Spanish missionary Father Juan Nentuig. At a site in northern Mexico in 1763 he encouraged the Opata Indians to farm and raise cattle and also preached Christianity to them. The Opata adopted more of the missionary economy than the missionary religion because "to everything they hear," Nentuig wrote, "(no matter from whom), . . . they say: *Sepore ma de ni thui.* Perhaps thou speakest truth." This suggests that the Opata had no interest in the European assumption that religion was specific doctrine to be known and believed with certainty. Nentuig goes on to point out sternly that they will never acquire true religion unless "the ministering Father is able to banish this phrase from his neophytes."[41] The Christian religious tradition, with the increased demand for certainty that Turner chronicles, was also becoming distinct from other world religions and worldviews.

Turner's own main purpose in painting his broad canvas is to argue that by the nineteenth century religious believers themselves encouraged the decline of belief. By dismissing ancient unreflective certainties and tying their fate to the rising authority of science, they invited a loss of respect for religion. Religion became less transcendent and, in trying to gain some of the worldly authority of science, it lost the basis for its own authority.[42] This trend happened in both overt and subtle ways. Some forms of religion, such as the "reasonable faith" of natural theology, explicitly imitated science in treating nature as a series of "proof-texts." Less overt imitations of scientific ways of thinking included the insistence on demonstrable principles that underlay the emotion and sentimentality of evangelical religion and even the transcendentalist exaltation of intuition as a "private knowledge of God." In 1830 the minister Orville Dewey provided a dramatic example of science-shaped religion; he beckoned: "It is not enough to say, in the general, that God is wise good, and merciful. . . . We want statement, specifications, facts, details, that will illustrate the wonderful perfections of the infinite Creator."[43] The respect for science spanned the religious spectrum, from liberals who looked at the Bible as history to be examined for accurate proof to conservatives who used biblical literalism as a way to make religious belief more comprehensible and certain.[44] In short, religion let the Trojan horse of science into the citadel of faith, and the warriors of science did not so much slay religion as attract so much attention and respect that a large number of people simply deserted to their side, ultimately ignoring religion in the widespread modern phenomenon known as secularism.

Turner's historical narrative is helpful in organizing the "prehistory" of uncertainty before it emerged as a key historical factor in the nineteenth century. His discussion of the growth of nineteenth-century doubt is limited, however, by its exclusion of history of science perspectives on the very science which he credits with luring religion into the spiritual deserts of rational certainty. Throughout the nineteenth century, scientific theories became less statements of proof and certainty and more propositions concerning explanation and plausibility. Darwinism was a major step in this direction, but other scientific theories followed a similar path, as the scholarship on the probabilistic revolution amply testifies. A key distinction from the history of science can put Turner's view in perspective: Throughout the century a gulf gradually widened between the science practiced by professionals and the popularization of science. Where professional science included a commitment to constant inquiry, explanatory hypotheses, and tentative conclusions, popular science had a more exalted picture of the certainties that science could determine.[45] Turner's thesis is best suited to explaining the relationship of religion to popular science, with his portrait of believers imitating science in order to gain more certainty. Yet the science they were imitating was disappearing from professional practice beginning in the second third of the nineteenth century. Attention to popularized—and very boldly confident—science has tended to cloak this historical trend.[46] The professional practice of science and philosophical questions about religion set the stage for the central issue of this book: the emergence of a culture of uncertainty when intellectuals of religion and even of science came to a recognition that wholesale certainty could not be achieved.

For all of their assumptions about the growth of uncertainty in science and religion, Hollinger, Kloppenberg, and Turner are more concerned with the fact of cultural and intellectual uncertainty in the late nineteenth century than with its emergence in the early to middle part of the century. The search to uncover the roots of modern uncertainty leads to the historical moment just before secularism bloomed publicly in the late nineteenth century, bringing great excitement and alarm; and it requires an inquiry into the specific histories of religion and science because these realms of life are the ones that most fundamentally tell us who we are and define our relationship with the rest of the world.[47] Uncertainties in other departments of cultural and intellectual life may come and go, but religious and scientific uncertainty is doubt at its most profound.

William James as Focal Point

William James is a particularly apt focal point for the search to understand the emergence of scientific and religious uncertainty. The span of his life (1842–1910) coincides with the most crucial years of this cultural shift, and his relationship to the figures that influenced him in his early years, including his family, teachers, and peers, place James at the center of a circle that witnessed and struggled with the major issues of this cultural emergence. Moreover, religion and science were the most important factors of his own cultural and intellectual life. In particular, his father offered intensive home-based instruction that centered on his own eccentric and impassioned religious beliefs; and as young James grew to adulthood, his formal education was in science and most of his informal education was based on scientific concerns. As an adult, the psychologist James offered the autobiographical theory that most people's outlooks on life are fundamentally shaped by the time they are thirty; his own early years were dominated by questions about the relations between, and the respective truths of, science and religion.[48]

Because of this background, he felt the shifts and tugs of the emerging intellectual culture of uncertainty on a personal as well as a philosophical level. Being a reflective and sensitive soul, James was able to articulate a way to understand and cope with uncertainties in science and religion. John Dewey credited James with developing a "*via media* between natural science and the ideal interests of morals and religion"—a path between the two that was based on the ultimate uncertainty of human inquiry in each field. Many of James's mature writings partake of this balance between science and religion with an assumption of widespread epistemological uncertainty. But Dewey himself pointed out that, as a pioneer in the culture of uncertainty, James at first "stood practically alone—a voice crying in the wilderness."[49] In James's youth, the densest wilderness was his own lack of confidence that the freedom, choices, and risks of uncertainty could survive in the godless naturalistic picture of a world made of matter. His recognition of the surprising uncertainty lurking within the deterministic scientific perspective, and then his strength and confidence in the face of uncertainty, would come only gradually.

Historical generalizations and theoretical statements about the emergence of uncertainty in science and religion can be expressed in retrospect much more simply and clearly than they were felt in the lives of James and his circle as they experienced these changes. The story of their experience is full of ambiguities and ambivalences, of steps taken along the same path as the general cultural pattern, intersecting with switchbacks and related trends. The theme of this book is the erosion of certainty in science and religion, but cultural context and biography are rarely as clear as that formulation. While this introduction summarizes the significance of this book with the neatness of argument, the book itself is a story whose message lies embedded in the gropings of experience. In particular, the frame of this story is William James's early education and his search for a career and a philosophy to live by. These topics are intricately interwoven with the cultural context featured in the following chapters. To be authentic to the characters' lives as lived, the thematic generalizations retreat to the background in the body of this text. The theme of uncertainty is the skeleton of the story, but the experiences of James and his circle are the flesh and blood that give the story drama.

William James and Contemporary Scholarship

No one following historical and cultural scholarship during these last ten years when I have been researching William James could ignore the issues of gender, race, ethnicity, and class that have become crucially important in the field. These multicultural concerns have at times tempted me to abandon work on a hero of the monoculture of white male intellectual elites. Significantly, even James was taken in by the lure of this establishment: although he himself was of Irish descent, he readily identified with elite Anglo-Saxon culture. Although he did not remain captive to the worst prejudices of those in power, his understanding of pluralism would never have the radical edge of later voices for diversity.[50]

I am keenly aware that while he grew up with educational advantages and expectations, he never questioned why his sister Alice and other women grew up with less privilege and with separated, subordinate power; that while James gradually, reflectively examined the implications of science in relative leisure and comfort, slaves were being whipped and beaten with increased intensity as Southerners hardened their grip on their human chattel; that in the year when James published his psychological masterwork, hundreds of Native Americans were massacred at Wounded Knee.

In this context, despite his heroic fight against imperialism,[51] his work can seem irrelevant or insensitive—or worse. Walter Benjamin once said, "There is no document of civilization which is not at the same time a document of barbarism," and perhaps the very focus of James's concern with science and religion made him guilty of barbarism by reason of indifference to what would later be called multicultural issues. As the heavy demands for classroom teaching in a wide range of subjects distracted me from research on this book, the materials I learned for class also told my conscience that the intellectual and cultural contexts of William James were moral backwaters to the sweep of American history and the purposes of scholarship.

But my wide reading for teaching, as well as my awareness of recent scholarship in journals and books and at conferences, did more than distract or humiliate; it also put my research on James, science, and religion in a very broad context. In particular, it helped me to understand that the intellectual works of James and his circle were part of the many interacting layers of culture.[52] This perspective helped shape my appreciation of the difference between professional and popular views of certainty. If my analysis were applied to broader fields, it would speak to the tensions between, for example, the educated and anthropologically curious Friends of the Indian who accepted pluralistic uncertainty in their comparative inquiries into the cultures of Native Americans and the Native Americans of different nations who felt comfortable with the convictions of their own groups and puzzled by the inquiries and help of their philanthropists.[53]

The cultural and intellectual issues of this book do not speak to this particular subject matter, but they do address the tensions of these groups and of many others who grappled with questions that grew from the gradual emergence of uncertainty in science and religion during the nineteenth century. Even my own professional role as a researcher at a liberal arts college pointed to the theme of this book. If I had been teaching graduate students, who are adopting the outlooks and assumptions of professional life, I might not have paid as much attention to the nonprofessional's demand for certainty. Undergraduate students are more like the general public in expecting definite answers to emerge readily from learning. Charles Sanders Peirce understood this distinction. "In order that a man's whole heart may be in teaching he must be thoroughly imbued with the vital importance and absolute truth of what he has to teach." By contrast, he continued, such certainty actually interferes with the process of research, because "in order that he may have any measure of success in learning he must be permeated with a sense of the unsatisfactoriness of his present conditions of knowledge." Perhaps in grudging recognition that he could never get a teaching position, he concluded grandly: "The two attitudes are almost irreconcilable."[54] While I cannot agree with such an absolute division, Peirce does capture the crucial differences over certainty of the pedagogical and investigative frame of mind.

Bringing a researcher's questions to a broad range of cultural topics for teaching brought my attention to connections between multicultural issues and James's circle. Multicultural scholarship tends to notice painful experiences in its turn away from triumphal history. So, on the most simple human level, I redoubled my attention to the emotional and intellectual traumas associated with the sea change from certainty to uncertainty in science and religion. While it was of a wholly different order from the suppression and torment of women, African-Americans, and Native Americans, it nonetheless brought many traumas. In addition, the intellectual troubles in science and religion set trends in the culture, not just because these seekers were leaders, but also because the fruit of their inquiries would influence policies, outlooks, values, and tastes throughout the culture. Multicultural lines of inquiry have themselves evolved from studies of outsiders to the analysis of all parts of culture, with attention to how different individuals and groups have constructed American culture in relation to each other. "In that sense," as Alice Kessler-Harris says, "we are all 'other.'" From this point of view, James and his circle are not presented here as a blueprint of all American minds, but as one revealing facet of a diverse culture.[55]

An even more direct connection between mid-nineteenth-century concerns over science and religion and late-twentieth-century scholarly assumptions is James's role as a grandfather to our embrace of diversity. The attention to difference did not emerge just from the variety of disfranchised groups in American culture;[56] it also grew from within the citadels of intellectual power, from intellectuals such as James who made overtures to minorities and who astutely noticed the implosion of philosophies of certainty and self-consciously worked to construct outlooks based on uncertainty. While the alliances were never complete, philosophical certainty generally had cultural correlations to dominance by elites and rationalizations of mastery by upper-class European males. James was a pioneer of the shift away from the power of those ideas of certainty and their cultural manifestations; in addition, he often served to encourage and act as mentor to people who were frequently ignored for being powerless or eccentric.[57] Although James did not himself represent a disempowered or underprivileged class of people, he was a major player in the intellectual trend that would make openness and acceptance of difference not only tolerated by intellectuals, but demanded as part of their teaching and research agendas. Insights such as James's served as theoretical preconditions to the more forceful and sensitive pluralism that emerged two generations after James's life. Recognition of the formative status of James (and the history of pragmatism in general) in contemporary cultural analysis is coinciding with a renewed attention to this history itself in the construction of theoretical methods based on pragmatism.[58]

Finally, although most treatments of intellectuals who contribute to debates on science and religion either assume their socially elite status or ignore social class altogether, I found this issue to be centrally important to my analysis, especially of James, Chauncey Wright, and Charles Peirce. Knitted together with their theoretical questions about the decline of certainty in religion and morality was a strong commitment to their identity as part of the New England cultural elite. Their intellectual critiques were radical, but they expected little disruption of their social standing or of the religious and moral beliefs they felt to be a major part of their culture. In fact, their secure status actually contributed to the intensity of their criticism. They were privileged enough to be bold.[59] Much of their critique of the certainties of traditional religion was an attempt not to repudiate religion but to defend it on an alternative basis, relying on uncertainty rather than certainty. So the class factor, far from being irrelevant, is actually woven into the theoretical and cultural questions.

For all the connections to issues of gender, race, and class, this is not fundamentally a book on multiculturalism and makes no attempt to be what it is not. It is a book about intellectuals and their contexts. It uses the figures and issues surrounding the early life of William James to flash light on the changing contours of religion and science in the middle of the nineteenth century. James was at once at the center of much of this discussion and personally a cauldron of inquiry on their nature and implications. Moreover, scholarship on James has reached a level of maturity which allows broader discussion of the implications of his work and its relation to the culture as a whole. So beneath the story that follows, of James learning science and religion and of his familial, institutional, and cultural contexts, is a steady concern with cultural epistemology, that is, the study of how cultures, including their nonexpert citizens, understand, appropriate, transform, or even distort the knowledge and belief that intellectuals and professionals produce.[60] The intellectuals in James's circle searched for true knowledge and genuine belief, but from those epistemological inquiries, the cultural questions of certainty keep leaking out. What would the world feel like without the confirmations of science and the assurances of religion? If modern trends encouraged a separation of science and religion, how strict could the boundaries remain before professionals and the public would ask religious questions of science and scientific questions of religion? Could theories be expounded and religious values believed without the assurances of certainty? When citizens in the public at large demand secure answers to their questions in science and religion, how should experts respond? The place to begin answering these questions is in the first half of the nineteenth century, in a culture committed to the certainties of science and religion and in a family acutely devoted to confirming their spiritual harmony.

PART I

Out of the James Household

By the time he had reached the age of eighteen, William James could look back at an unusual childhood. The household of Henry and Mary James was an intellectually active setting. Reading, learning, intense talk, and deep reflection on philosophical and religious issues had been his daily fare. The enthusiastic leader of the household was the independent-minded, intensely religious philosopher, Henry James, who, in an idiosyncratic departure from nineteenth-century conventions of domesticity and gender roles, took an active part in the instruction and moral development of his children. Since his own father had been one of the wealthiest men in New York state, he and his children grew up with the material freedoms that wealth can purchase. Henry James reinforced this atmosphere of freedom through a program of unstructured education for his children. He pulled his children in and out of schools, constantly searching for the ideal setting that he never found, and he often kept them out of school altogether.

In this energetic and chaotic setting, the parents often literally served as their children's teachers, and the five children, William (born 1842), Henry (1843), Garth Wilkinson (1845), Robertson (1846), and Alice (1848), became each other's closest playmates, rivals, and intellectual companions. Remembering his youth, Henry James, Jr., said, "We were, to my sense, the blest group of us, such a company of characters and such a picture of differences, and withal so fused and united and interlocked." While the cheerful glow of this description is typical of many of the James children's memories from adulthood,[1] their constant close proximity led to many submerged tensions, and the parents' intense care and devotion bloomed into forceful expectations for the children's vocational choices. In particular, the parents destined the youngest boys for careers in business even from their childhood, supported

Henry's passion for writing only after their failed attempt to interest him in law school, subtly encouraged Alice to stay at home with them, and were certain that William should be a scientist.

As a child, William James did not, of course, notice the intellectual currents that would erode the certainties of science and religion. However, his father did direct his education with a degree of freedom unprecedented even in his cultural circle. While Henry James viewed the lack of structure as a sure route to spiritual truth, William experienced his early education as his first encounters with uncertainty, especially when his father's spiritual truths did not present themselves obviously or clearly. Years later, when he encountered intellectual forms of uncertainty, his education in freedom would serve as a storehouse of sympathy for unstructured, provisional, and probabilistic forms of thinking. While William approached adulthood, however, his father's tides of love and expectation threatened to wash away the freedom that he had grown so accustomed to. Pulling away from those family plans would be difficult, as William discovered during his brief but bold attempt to become an artist. All of these forces and freedoms, along with the father's eccentric philosophy, meant that the children would feel what William said of his brother Henry when he christened him "a native of the James family [who] has no other country."[2] The intense family setting contributed to the children's realization that being a James meant growing up with a distinct identity, with wide-ranging freedoms and strong feelings about the deepest workings of the universe. Father made sure of it with the insistence of enthusiasm.

CHAPTER 1

A Native of the James Family

The early life of William James . . . in his setting, his

immediate native and domestic air.

HENRY JAMES, JR., 1913

The elder Henry James took great pride in his philosophic enthusiasm and eccentricities, in part because they were so hard won. As he grew up, he maintained a stiff resistance to his own parents' way of life. The elder James set the tone for describing the independent path he took in his career when he began the first part of his autobiography by claiming not to know the date of his birth. It must have been before 1815, he surmised, because he remembered the fireworks in the night sky, lit to mark the 1815 Peace Treaty with Great Britain that ended the War of 1812. But to the child's mind, "this municipal illumination in honor of peace" only served to highlight "the contrast of the awful dark of the sky with the feeble glitter of the streets." His description is symbolic of his relation with his family, who wanted him to follow his father on the glittering road to business success and community leadership, while he steadily gravitated toward the more murky and mysterious, yet more broadly alluring path of personal religious questing and philosophical inquiry.[1]

The Money and Morality of the First William James

Henry James's father, the first American William James (1771–1832), known as "William of Albany," would never have understood or even imagined the intellectual and religious world of his descendants.[2] His successful business career was so strikingly different from the work of his more famous progeny that grandson Henry James once wryly observed that "the rupture with my grandfather's tradition and attitude was complete; we were never in a single case, I think, for two generations, guilty of a stroke of business."[3] Grandfather James was an extremely successful businessman who viewed his religion as an aspect of his role as a wealthy and upright pillar of the community in Albany, New York. An immigrant from County Cavan, Ireland, at the age of eighteen in 1789, James took on the republican values of his adopted country with the zeal of a convert.[4]

The life of William of Albany is an American success story of mythic proportions. Perhaps already with an eye toward catching the main chance, he moved to the small but strategically located town of Albany shortly after his arrival in America. He began his career of enterprise and uplift in 1793 as a store clerk. Two years later he went into business for himself selling "tobacco and segars." Shortly thereafter he opened a store to buy produce from the back country and sell dry goods and groceries. In 1798 the merchant James became the owner of a tobacco factory.[5] James expanded his interests so dramatically that by 1818 he turned the daily operations over to his business-minded son Robert and retired to the life of investor, speculator, money lender, and manager of his extensive holdings that ranged from prime New York real estate to frontier "wild land" in Illinois. He demonstrated his business acumen by acquiring land that was then under water from the city of New York in exchange for building streets and wharves.[6] As his holdings and his wealth grew, so too did his status: he served on numerous boards and commissions, including the board of trustees of the Albany Academy and of Union College in nearby Schenectady and the chairmanship of the Albany commission celebrating the building of the Erie Canal. His contemporaries called him "untiring in his efforts to advance the interests of his place of abode." By mid-career, James had become one of the "gentlemen of property and standing," an American facsimile of European nobility who, although without title, served many of the social functions of aristocrats, due to their wealth and community-mindedness and because of the deference they expected from fellow citizens. This social position of high status, community leadership, and social responsibility would inspire his descendants, despite the rebelliousness of his son, to feel intimately a part of Northeastern upper-crust culture, and it would serve as a starting point for much of their thinking.[7]

The elder William James's own way of identifying with his culture, unleavened by his progeny's intellectual nuances, was with an unabashed glorification of capitalistic republicanism. James was an avid booster of the transformation of revolutionary era republicanism to a republicanism that endorsed the profit-oriented liberal capitalism of the early republic.[8] He showed no embarrassment or hesitation in the turn to marketplace concerns, as his unreserved pride in the canal amply demonstrates: "What palpitations! What excited hopes!" The canal opened up the landlocked backcountry of New York state, James noted exultantly, giving "a solid value to the products of their soil, by enabling [farmers and merchants] to transport [their goods] to the best markets at a trifling expense." The acceleration of commerce from the interior Great Lakes region to the Atlantic coast will "pour wealth into the lap of industry," he added frankly but with a full conviction that all classes would benefit from such business growth. More specifically, of course, the canal raised the value of James's land and increased demand on his various businesses.[9] His excitement mingled his acquisitive passion for improved business opportunities with real enthusiasm for the general social improvement that would result from the completed transportation artery between the Great Lakes and the Atlantic.

To William of Albany, the Erie Canal was more than good business; it also promoted good politics—the virtuous but fragile freedom of the American republic. By expanding lines of transportation and creating a "union of the lakes with the ocean," the canal established "durable ties of interest and indissoluble affinities" among the widely scattered citizens of the United States. Patriot James, like many of his countrymen in the early republic, admired the "republican spirit" of America but felt that the young nation was vulnerable to internal discord and external challenge. He argued that economic growth and success were necessary to offset those weaknesses so that while "Independence and the Constitution are the pillars of our Liberty," he declared, "the great work we this day celebrate is the splendid arch which gives elegance, durability and strength to our temple of freedom." James was fully committed to republicanism, geographic expansion, and business opportunities, and to the canal that in his mind symbolized their interconnection. He called the canal "a work which sheds additional lustre on the United States, bearing the stamp of the enterprising spirit and resolution which declared our independence and wisdom that cemented the union of different republics by the adoption of the federal constitution."

To James the uniting threads of his economic and political ideas lay with the uniquely American "republican energy and free institutions." His experience as an immigrant reinforced his conviction that, by contrast, "the old world" was "a perpetual example of despotism and wretchedness, . . . dogmas and prerogatives." He had higher hopes for his adopted homeland: "Was an empire such as ours to be established, the only emigrants fitted to do it were those who abhorred the profligacy, bigotry and slavery of European governments." The Erie Canal embodied William of Albany's highest hopes for economic advancement, for the improvement of the Albany region, and for American republicanism.[10]

The public words of William of Albany also reveal the unquestionable place and unquestioning character of religion in his ideology. He urged that "Americans ought to rejoice with gratitude to heaven" for the blessings and promises of national growth. Then he grew more harsh in summoning a holy sanction for the national purpose: "Nothing but the torpid stupidity of atheism can prevent the reflecting mind from perceiving the special interposition of providence, in protecting and advancing our national honor and greatness."[11] Here was a conventional religion that justified a public role in building the local community and guiding the nation's manifest destiny—a destiny that included both private profit and public order. The religion of William of Albany was not consciously self-serving but instead flowed from a sense of the importance of good works. He helped many of his immigrant Irish relatives establish themselves in businesses and careers.[12] In addition, he was charitable in the community at large. His son Henry later wrote: "I remember that my father was in the habit of having a great quantity of beef and pork and potatoes laid by in the beginning of winter for the needy poor. . . ; and no sooner was the original stock exhausted than the supply was renewed with ungrudging hand." The conventionality of his steadfast and traditional morals extended into his marriage as well; his wife embraced the same social values, and Henry remembered that "my mother regulated . . . the distribution" of the family's abundant charity.[13] Good works were the centerpiece of William of Albany's religious life, the product of moralism and an emphasis on achieving good—and increasing his moral status—in this world through material means.

The James family patriarch's churchgoing and even his charity reflected the conventionality and sense of duty in his religion, which, as demonstrated in his public role as community leader, was based on moral commitment rather than spiritual conviction. He was a close friend and patron of the clergy, especially at Albany's First Presbyterian Church and Union College. In fact, the president of the college during James's years of patronage was the Reverend Eliphalet Nott, who had been pastor of the First Presbyterian Church for six years. As James's son remembered from his childhood, "the clergy . . . used to frequent my father's house, which offered the freest hospitality to any number of the cloth."[14] Complementing this social side of his religious involvement, he readily linked his religious beliefs to the business world. For example, when his church sponsored Sabbath Day measures, James was probably one of the first of those to sign a pledge promising to "use their best endeavors to dissuade the owners of steamboats, canal boats, stages and hacks, from travelling on the sabbath, and to encourage and patronize such of them as should cease running on that day."[15] Such measures reflected religious sanctions but also helped to maintain order in the community. His son Henry would later criticize the worldliness of his religion and renounce it as devoid of spirituality. But his grandson, William James the philosopher, would revolt in his own way from *his* father's religion and would search in a more sophisticated and unorthodox way for his own worldly religion of morality.

William of Albany's religion of good works and public order received strong support from the mainstream republicanism of his political beliefs but not without imbibing some of its ambiguities.[16] He maintained strong hopes that freedom and equality of opportunity would lead ultimately to a classless society in which distinction would be based on individual merit, the private accumulation of property, and public-spirited devotion to the local community rather than on the artifice of aristocratic privilege. These beliefs were reinforced with the zeal of an immigrant convert. But the republican ideology of William of Albany contained the seeds of its own transformation in his life and especially in the lives of his descendants. Republican freedom encouraged the growth of wealth, which, in the large quantities that James held, created a privileged status for himself and his family. Ironically for the James family and, to a certain extent, for American society in general, the egalitarian ideology of republicanism had contributed to the development of massive inequality and privilege. William of Albany's republican ideology was formed while he was becoming a self-made man. Once established as a republican aristocrat, he lived the irony of his status by maintaining the ideology of republicanism even as he embraced his aristocratic place in his society.

The elder Henry James's recollection of his mother exemplifies the family's republican attitude toward its wealth and success. Never pretentious, "she was the most democratic person I ever knew . . . [with] the frankest sympathy with every one conventionally beneath her." Grandmother James also blended her republican sensibilities with a conventional perception of her public role in Albany society. "She felt a tacit quarrel with the fortunes of her life in that they had sought to make her a flower or a shrub, when she herself would so willingly have remained mere lowly grass."[17] Wealth may have made the Jameses a local aristocracy, but their democratic sensibilities further reinforced their commitment to republicanism and its moralistic values, because these leading Albany citizens retained the charitable public-spiritedness, the commitment to stratified class and gender roles, and the belief in social mobility that were central to the republican outlook. This family of Jameses lived their lives without a whiff of science, and they believed their religion without considering challenges to the unreflective certainty of their beliefs, but their social position and ideology would set the stage for the religious and scientific inquiries of the next generation.

The First Henry James: Growing Up Irreverent

For all his public prominence, wealth, and morality, William James's social status had little appeal to his reflective and spiritually restless son. Finding little spiritual food in this setting, Henry James later caustically suggested that his father was religious because "it was eminently respectable to belong to the church."[18] As a consequence, he remembered a "family righteousness" but no "spiritual Divine leaven."[19] Even in his childhood the son rebelled against the family moralism: he ridiculed the First Presbyterian Church of Albany, which the Jameses attended, and he took great pride in his mischievous play during services. He dramatically equated routine and solemn attendance at church with "Herod's . . . slaughter of the innocents," because of its "wanton outrage to nature," especially the "natural delights" of childhood.[20] When he grew up, what he remembered from the family church was its strictness and sobriety, which restricted his spontaneity and spiritual longing. While his father was satisfied with a religion of good works and respectability, young Henry James anguished over spiritual questions: "It was very seldom that I lay down at night without a present thought of God." Moreover, he viewed his small childhood sins as "instances of youthful depravity" that led him to "acute contrition, amounting at times to anguish."[21]

The profound guilt Henry James felt for his youthful misdeeds encouraged his spiritual originality: as this guilt and spiritual questing made him feel estranged from the God of Presbyterianism, he turned to different forms of religious awareness. Most important, he began to explore the contrast between spirituality and moralism. Henry James's spiritualism was a Protestant's Protestantism, a personal reformation of his moralistic Presbyterian heritage, which by the early nineteenth century had lost much of the original spiritual fire of the Reformation. He characterized moralism as a "self-conscious, or distinctively human experience," considering it mundane and materialistic—and the touchstone of his father's life. Like that of many religious seekers of the second quarter of the nineteenth century, his spirituality involved a distaste for the merely human structures of religion and the worldly rules of morality; also, like many during this romantic era, he felt a hunger for more direct contact with the divine, or even for seeking potential divinity in humanity itself.[22] The laws of morality that were so important to his father's religion could not match the freedom and spontaneity he sought in a more spiritual approach to religion. The James family generation gap was a microcosm of the emergence of the romantic religious sensibility in the second quarter of the nineteenth century.[23]

In addition to his fundamentally different philosophical outlook, Henry James gave his parents other causes for concern. Frustrated by his differences with his family and unable to do anything about them, he turned to devious and often rebellious behavior. He enjoyed socializing with the household servants and with workers in town. He admitted that these more spontaneous, less moralistic people "sacrificed occasionally to Bacchus," and he hinted that they probably shared their alcohol with their young admirer. James would, in turn, steal food and wine from his home for "feasts" at the artisans' shop.[24] He suffered pangs of guilt for his misdeeds, and his parents grew increasingly frustrated with him. They felt even more serious concern when tragedy struck. At the age of thirteen Henry James accidentally burned his right leg so severely that he was confined to bed for two years and underwent first one and then a second surgery on his thigh—agonizing experiences in the days before anesthetics. Unfortunately, the injury to his leg further cultivated his taste for alcohol. To relieve his pain his parents and doctors gave him "all manner of stimulants." Years later in a letter to his son Robertson, who suffered from alcoholism, Henry James wrote, "I emerged from my sick-room, and went to college . . . hopelessly addicted to the vice."[25]

Union College was the natural place for the Jameses to send their son. They had known the president of the college, Eliphalet Nott, as their minister at the First Presbyterian Church. Furthermore, the Reverend Nott was known as a liberal educator with a special ability to handle difficult, strong-willed boys.[26] In addition, Nott owed the elder James more than a small favor for the loans that kept Union College afloat. By 1822 William James became, in effect, the college's banker, lending the young institution large sums of money and holding most of its land and buildings as collateral.[27] Once enrolled at Union in 1828, Henry James was not a very serious student. He joined a fraternity within a month after his arrival on campus, and he ran up bills on his father's account without his consent, for such luxuries as oysters, fine clothes, good cigars, and books. Being the product of a generation that expected, as Benjamin Rush said, that "the most useful citizens have been formed from those youth who have never known or felt their own wills till they were one and twenty years of age,"[28] William James was furious. The fact that he had made a significant portion of his fortune selling tobacco did not make him any more tolerant of his son's profligate smoking of it. He had his lawyer write to the son that he was engaged in a "career of folly" that was leading him to "the verge of ruin." The father wanted his son to conform to his wishes and to the morality he valued; he even directed his lawyer to say that "If you do not, you will lose all respectability, all support, independence, everything valuable in life."[29] With his sights set on spiritual questions and with his youthful rebelliousness, Henry regarded such demands for social status and respectability as paltry and boring.

Despite the threat of disinheritance, Henry James left Union with his bills unpaid and his parents and the Reverend Nott uncertain of his destination. He went to Boston where he found work in a publishing house and relished his freedom from the influence of his parents. In a statement that would also characterize his lifelong taste for independent action and righteous crusading, he asserted, "The great step has been taken and I am alone in my pilgrimage."[30] Yet despite his enthusiasm he did not stay long in Boston. He returned to Union and graduated with the class of 1830. He spent the next few years in an undirected way, fitfully sampling a number of professions, including law, newspaper editing, and the ministry. While he was searching for a vocation, his father died suddenly in 1832. This precipitated Henry James's mightiest conflict with William of Albany, one more impassioned and with greater implications than any struggle he had had with him in his lifetime.

In July 1832, shortly before his death in December, William James of Albany wrote his last will and testament. The document reflected the sixty-one-year-old businessman's dominating personality, his concern for the character of his descendants, and his worries about the future of his hard-earned money.[31] The stakes were high: by 1832 he had amassed a fortune of over $3 million—an enormous sum in early-nineteenth-century America. Such great wealth left the republican patriarch in an ideological bind: while William James the businessman had earned his wealth for his family according to republican ideals, his children had merely been born to wealth and enjoyed an unearned privilege that violated the principle of equality of opportunity. As a true republican, he scorned unearned wealth and attempted to use his will as an instrument to lessen the harmful effects of inheritance. He directed that his estate should not pass simply or directly to his dependents. Even if they would not earn their wealth as he had, his children would be forced, he determined, to show that they deserved it by being held to the highest standards of morality and republican social thought.

The will, a series of forty-eight commandments weaving together detailed instructions and didactic advice, sought to delay the division of the estate and restrict the size of his children's inheritance, which he hoped would encourage his family to live "prudently and circumspectly." He was especially concerned about the future of his estate because of the size of his family: he was survived by Catherine James (his third wife), ten children, and numerous grandchildren.[32] Despite his bold and moralistic plans, the document was so stingy that even his wife contested it. Catherine James won the court case easily because the will violated a recent New York state law which allowed "the widow . . . to take her dower in the real estate of the testator, instead of the provision which was made for her in the will."[33] Catherine James's success in 1833 broke the authority of her husband's will, and others, including the rebellious son Henry James, soon entered the breach. Within a few years, and after a series of cases, the court ruled that "the *real estate of the testator [should] descend . . . to his heirs at law* free, and discharged of all conditions, devises, directions, authority, *power or control* of the trustees."[34] After a series of court cases, the estate of William James of Albany was supplying the idiosyncratic Henry James with a large and steady income, which he used to finance his own intellectual pursuits and, soon thereafter, the intensive education of his children.[35]

The conditions surrounding William of Albany's death offer another connection to the life of his descendants. Although he died of a stroke, the cholera epidemic that terrorized Americans during his last few months suggests a parable in miniature of some themes in nineteenth-century science and religion. William of Albany's wealth did improve his chances of avoiding the disease because cholera spread most readily among the poor, who lived in less sanitary conditions and who could not as easily travel to gain refuge from the disease. Still, since the pathogen had first appeared outside of Asia less than two decades before, and because medical knowledge and public health provisions were so unprepared for its outbreak, cholera did claim a significant percentage even of the affluent.

Scientific and religious responses to the plague encapsulate the movement toward uncertainty in science and religion that would be so important in the grandson's lifetime. In 1832 some religious leaders charged that "God is chastening us"; scoffing at this stern belief, mainstream scientists and liberal religious believers proposed that the outbreaks were another example of the divine operating through secondary causes. Most religious leaders maintained a middle ground, by referring to God's punishment and also seeking the help of physicians. The elder Henry James did not comment on the cholera epidemic, but we can infer that his theory of the correspondence between the spiritual and natural world and his openness to scientific innovations would have put him in the mainstream. Despite their differences, all of the commentators shared an assumption that religion and the natural world operate in harmony—even if nature's facts in the cholera epidemic were particularly horrific.

By the time of the cholera epidemics in 1849 and 1866, however, that consensus was shattering; the scientific and religious disagreements became even more stark, with nonreligious naturalistic interpretations gaining public authority. As the younger William James grew up, explanations about the spread of fatal diseases took on less certainty. The dogmatic assurance of declaring the disease a punishment became implausible, especially in his cultural circle, while the alternative religious explanation positing God's operation through natural forces took a small step toward secularism by distancing divine operations from everyday events. Similarly, scientific arguments about natural laws or the causes of diseases, although gaining in social authority, were grounded not in certainty but in probabilistic considerations, from the chances of contagion, to the inferences used in diagnosis and treatment, to the hypotheses brought forth to identify the disease and its course. The history of cholera's scientific and religious reception provides a window to the issues that would frame the decline of certainty and that became live topics in the younger James's circle.[36]

Ironically, from the point of view of the grandson William James, his moralistic Presbyterian grandfather and his idealistic father were not so very different: they were both absolutely sure of their outlooks on the world. The younger William James would never replicate their feelings of confidence. In their stark opposition to each other, William of Albany and the elder Henry James remained on the common ground of certainty for their respective positions. Meanwhile, winning his inheritance in court allowed Henry James the material means to continue the spiritual questing that had begun with his childhood differences with his family. His youthful musings met no material check, since he never had to wrench himself away from reflective philosophical problems in order to earn a living. Throughout the 1830s he remained undecided about his profession and vocation. Even after that he never really settled down vocationally; he just gradually decided to continue in the life of thinker, student, and writer to which he had always gravitated, and which was made possible by his father's wealth and his own inquisitive stamina.

Transcendent Gender Roles

In 1840 Henry James married Mary Walsh, who was an encouraging, nourishing, and stabilizing force for this exuberant and eccentric man. Although he relished unconventionality, much of his relationship with his wife was true to the contemporary cultural standards of gender roles in marriage.[37] Yet, where the average wife of their time provided her husband with a comforting and inspirational asylum from his worldly working cares and troubles, Mary James's role in her unemployed, independent husband's life was to offer an affectionate antidote to his other-worldly, philosophical struggles. James was concerned that his own spiritual quest was itself selfish because it was too personally focused.[38] In response to that anxiety, he recalled, "she really did arouse my heart, early in our married life, from its selfish torpor." Where he probed for knowledge and sought understanding, Mary James did not treat spiritual questions in a theoretical way; as her husband remembered, "She was not to me 'a liberal education,' intellectually speaking." Instead, she served him as an emotional anchor, "altogether unconsciously, without the most cursory thought of doing so, but solely by the presentation of her womanly sweetness and purity, which she herself had no recognition of."[39] With financial security and a personal relationship worked out whereby Henry probed the spiritual universe while Mary brought comfort and intuitive wisdom, they decided to have a family.

Within six years, the Jameses had their five children. By the late 1840s the father had slipped into a double vocation. In addition to his continuing philosophical work, he dedicated himself to the education and moral development of his children. In its partial challenge to the contemporary conventions of women's moral role in the household, this commitment required Mary James to do some adjusting, and it encouraged Henry James to delve into the "woman's work" of educating children. Although he experimented with social change and idealistic philosophy much like many reformers of his time, James never conceived of wholesale revolutions in cultural conventions.[40]

Henry James's enthusiasm for child rearing did not eliminate his wife's place in the household, but what role she did retain is difficult to determine because she left so much less written evidence than her husband.[41] However, the records made by and about her do indicate that, while the father was full of ideas, the mother was the person of action and often the implementer of those ideas; father was the dreamer, while mother was the dependable worker. In the James family division of labor, Henry was more interested in the raising of his children than was conventional for fathers; he himself recognized the difference, noting that "in ancient days, ... the parental bond was then predominantly paternal," while he hoped to be part of a trend toward parents "becoming predominantly maternal."[42] Despite these brave declarations and his devotion to the children's education, reading, and discussion, he did not play a fully active role in parenting them.

While William James's father was content with his cerebral role, his mother took on the more material and emotional responsibilities of handling physical needs, finances, and general nurturing of the children. Henry James wrote to a friend that although he was "the head of a family," he was "indebted to [his] wife's greater presence of mind for some needful help." Lucky for him with his spiritual concerns, Mary James matched his stereotype of women's intellectual orientation; he wrote condescendingly that "worldly considerations have ever too much weight, I regret to say, oftentimes with the feminine mind."[43] Similarly, in their letters to the children, father dealt with intellectual concerns, leaving mother with the less interesting and often touchy financial questions.

Mary James was no more engaged by the rise of the women's rights movement than was young William, who thought of her in sentimental and purely domestic terms. For example, while traveling in Europe a few years after her death, he saw "old wrinkled peasant women ... dragging their carts or lugging their baskets ... but belonging far away, to something better and purer." They made him think of "all the mystery of womanhood" as he cried out "the Mothers! the Mothers! Ye are all one!" and in particular they also reminded him, "My own dear Mother is one with these." All the James children remembered their mother for both her hard work and her gentle emotional support. In one image of the childhood household, William remembers her "raking out the garret-room like a little buffalo." His brother said that "she was to us the sweetest, gentlest, most natural embodiment of maternity and our protecting spirit, our household genius."[44] Beneath these familiarly teasing and glowing comments, the children also revealed a submerged tension about the anxiety beneath their mother's helpfulness and her tendency to judge them harshly when they did not live out her expectations.[45] The children had extra reason to feel resentment toward her, because, with the parents' unusual division of labor, the mother took charge of most of the onerous and least glamorous parts of dealing with practical problems, without the compensating pleasure of educating her children, which was the chief source of status for most women of her time.

Instilling Spiritual Assumptions

With Mary James's steadfast work and constant support, her husband could afford to take on the task of instructing his children according to his own spiritual outlook on life. In the education of his children, Henry James developed a thoroughly planned philosophy of child rearing which he proudly discussed in his autobiography. Because the idealistic philosopher wrote this account late in life, his statements on child rearing cannot be taken as a literally accurate account of the way he raised his children. It does serve as a good record of the way he translated his spiritual philosophy into an educational theory. There are, of course, differences between ideal and reality: he professed to raise his children in complete freedom, but when they began to commit themselves to personal choices, he chafed at their turn from wide-ranging freedom. Then, ironically, Henry James acted more like his insistent and absolutist father. This often confused the children, especially William, who was dutiful to his father but also had been exposed early in life to philosophies and vocations strikingly different from his father's wishes for him.

The elder Henry James declared that "The parent . . . should be the . . . medium of the Divine communion with the child."[46] In the education of his children James attempted to nurture innocence, foster spontaneity, and allow for the unrestrained development of natural impulses. For the children these goals remained vague and highly abstract, as Henry James, Jr., confirmed when he described his upbringing with the coy comment that "the literal played in our education as small a part as it perhaps ever played in any."[47] To the philosopher father child rearing was founded in his belief in the natural divinity within humanity, a reflection of the romantic view of childhood goodness that was popular in early-nineteenth-century theories of education and child rearing, especially in James's reform circles.[48] James shared with these approaches a great faith in the potential educational power of childhood spontaneity and a great disgust for any restrictions on it. In his own upbringing in the Presbyterian church, he felt that "the entire strain of the Orthodox faith . . . restricted the motions of the divine life" in him as a child. Moreover, he declared, the required "paralytic Sunday routine" actually restricted his "training in the divine life."[49]

When James raised his own children, he hoped to maintain their natural innocence for as long as possible. He insisted that their unencumbered development would be more important than any formal instruction. He therefore maintained that "the great worth of one's childhood to his future manhood consists in its being a storehouse of innocent natural emotions and affections."

In place of conveying knowledge, he hoped to foster spontaneous, natural feelings "based upon ignorance," in hopes of purging his children of as much worldly affiliation as possible. These untutored feelings, he maintained with a stark imposition of his own religious beliefs on the freedom that he planned for his children, "offer themselves as an admirable Divine mould or anchorage to the subsequent development of [the child's] spiritual life or freedom." Just as the benefits of this unstructured approach were great, so too were the dangers of ignoring the spontaneous charm of childhood, because "in so far as you inconsiderately shorten this period of infantile innocence and ignorance in the child, you weaken his chances of a future manly character."[50] Henry James bathed his children in freedom and enforced nothing on them, except of course his insistence on freedom itself—a commitment that could become aggressive when the children began to make specific personal career choices.[51]

William James began his adulthood with a double inheritance from his father: he cherished freedom and the flexible thinking it encouraged, and he internalized his father's religious and scientific goals. One of his biographers, Gay Wilson Allen, calls this "the paternal grip," which had an ironic hold on the children: although they were overtly free, "their knowledge of his wishes did more to curb them than overt opposition" to their ambitions.[52] Still, once the elder James's ideas settled inside William's head, these spiritual goals began to look rashly overconfident compared to the scientific and religious ideas he would start learning outside the James household in his young adulthood.

The elder Henry James even conveyed his zeal in advice to friends about the rearing of their children. For example, he wrote to Ralph Waldo Emerson about his son Edward: "I thought . . . I would take the liberty of this one word about Eddy"; James warned that the child "is not near so robust as he ought to be, because he is allowed to study too hard, in order that he may enter college one year rather than another." He went on to say that too often parents subject their children to "the snubbing of their innocent natural delights, which of course at that age are delights of sense."[53] This advice explains Henry James's rationale for the unstructured, noninstitutional character of his children's education and points to the loose nature of William James's early educational experience. Young William was not forced to learn, but rather he followed his intellectual appetites, and then, as an adult, he used the same approach as he explored a wide range of intellectual fields.[54]

Although Henry James maintained that childhood innocence is more important than the lessons of strict moral instruction, he also argued that this blissful state should not be an end in itself. Innocence should be the means to achieving maturity and excellence of character, not by compunction but by natural attraction. James held to this educational philosophy with great conviction. He maintained this permissive, nurturing approach even in 1855 when he was living with five children, ages seven to thirteen. He asserted: "I desire my child to become an upright man, a man in whom goodness shall be induced not by mercenary motives as brute goodness is induced, but by love for it or a sympathetic delight in it." He realized that "inasmuch as I know that this character or disposition cannot be forcibly imposed upon him, but must be freely assumed, I surround him as far as possible with an atmosphere of freedom."[55] Through freedom, Henry James hoped to foster rather than force his spiritually ambitious goal of raising his children to his degree of religious awareness and conviction. This then was an underlying design in Henry James's educational program: through fostered freedom and deliberately maintained innocence, the James children were to become disciples of his idiosyncratic brand of religion.

The educational freedom in which Henry James indulged his children was of two kinds. One involved his educational approach and his religious philosophy. He never imposed rules or duties on his children; rather, he asked "What sensible parent now thinks it a good thing to repress the natural instincts of childhood, and not rather diligently to utilize them as so many divinely endowed educational forces?" His own early rejection of moralism suggested to Henry James that children were by nature spiritual rather than moral; he therefore assumed he could use these "natural instincts of childhood" to preach his spiritualism. The other freedom for the James children was a freedom from most worldly want and free access to great worldly educational opportunities. They enjoyed this economic freedom because of their grandfather's wealth and their own father's generosity: "When I became a father in my turn," Henry James said, "I felt that I could freely sacrifice property and life to save my children from unhappiness."[56] With his wealth, James did not have to sacrifice much, but he did indulge his children as much with material benefits as with spiritual freedom.

Because of his commitment to freedom in his children's education and his conviction that childhood innocence should be maintained for as long as possible, the elder James disapproved of his children specializing, or even gaining a strong particular interest too early. The father viewed any hints at such specialization as a potential threat to his children's freedom. This conviction further explains the constant change of schools: the father moved his children as soon as they started making real progress in rigorous learning and before they could establish roots in any one discipline. The father deliberately obstructed the vocational choices of his children as too "narrowing" in hopes of delaying their decisions for as long as possible. Confused by their father's glib but insistent instructions, the children realized that "what we were to do instead was just to *be something*, something unconnected with specific doing, something free and uncommitted."[57] His wealth allowed, and his religious philosophy demanded, an emphasis on being rather than doing.

Henry James's parental freedom extended even to the choice of religious worship. The family belonged to no church, except perhaps to the father's eccentric religion of one. This ambiguous situation, which son Henry James called "our pewless state," prompted indignant and perplexed questions from the children's peers. Henry James, Jr., remembered them asking, " 'What church do you go to?'—the challenge took in childish circles that searching form." His father's gleeful reply was in keeping with his desire to foster a cosmopolitan spirituality: "We could plead nothing less than the whole privilege of Christendom." The father hoped that the openness would encourage exploring; therefore, "there was no communion, even that of the Catholics, even that of the Jews, even that of the Swedenborgians, from which we need find ourselves excluded." The elder James recognized that this variety perplexed the children, but he trusted that it would have a salutary and maturing effect by allowing his children to be "small unprejudiced inquirers obeying their inspiration." This process was exactly what his educational method was intended to foster; as the son added, "With the freedom we enjoyed[,] our dilemma clearly amused him." The children's moments of religious confusion, along with other perplexing episodes of their youth, provided the father with an educational opportunity that suited childhood's "comparatively primal innocence" and the intellectual freedom that became the rule of the household.[58]

With all their freedom of choice, the son Henry explained, although "our young liberty in respect to church-going was absolute," the children most often ignored all the churches. With so much freedom and so little reverence for religious traditions coming from the James household, they tended to treat churches more as museums than as houses of worship. Along with the other children, William James experienced little influence from churches or contemporary religious movements outside the household. During the 1840s and 1850s, while established American churches went through fundamental changes brought on by rapid growth and democratization, while evangelical movements and new religions swelled in numbers and influence, and while a religious spirit animated much of the politics of the time, especially the reform politics, the James children experienced the religion of their day mainly through the filter of their father's spirituality.[59] Ironically, by allowing his children free exposure to all the diversity of American religion, the elder Henry James effectively barred them from any particular features of it. Instead, the young Henry James confirmed that from their father, "we had plenty . . . of religious instruction . . . of the most charming and familiar" kind.[60] Because of the father's influence, the children, according to William's sister Alice James, came to view traditional religion as full of "ignoble superstitions," and she was grateful that her parents had not tried "to fill our minds with the dry husks" of religious institutions. Preferring not to have been exposed to conventional religion, she explained that in place of the husks, they were left with intellectual "*tabulae rasae* to receive whatever stamp our individual experience was to give them, so that we had not the bore of wasting our energy in raking over and sweeping out the rubbish."[61] Of course, such an upbringing could not leave the slates completely blank. Their peculiar education in religion gave the children a familiarity with uncertainty, a taste for private and personal approaches to religion, and a set of assumptions about the life of the spirit rooted in the thought of the elder Henry James.

The rest of the James children's education followed similar patterns of non-institutionalized and broad freedom. The lack of definition extended to every part of their education, with which Henry James never stopped experimenting. The education of the James children included many trips to Europe, so many that Gay Wilson Allen has aptly called the youth of William James a "transatlantic infancy."[62] The James family departed for Europe three times before William was twenty-one, and they settled there for at least a year each time: 1843–45, 1855–58, and 1859–60. In Europe, James hoped, his children would "absorb French and German and get a better sensuous education than they are likely to get here."[63] Despite its lack of discipline, the children's early education exposed them to a broad range of ideas, cultures, and languages.

If freedom was the central theme of Henry James's educational program, the central content of the children's instruction was the study of foreign languages. This reflected a deeply felt conviction of Henry James. When he ran away to Boston, one of his major goals was that "I now go on with the study of languages much more thoroughly than I should have found it necessary should I [have] remained at home." He always associated language learning with high achievement and was determined that his children would not be as "slighted" as he had been in his education.[64] By his eighteenth year, William James had acquired some Latin, a good knowledge of German, and excellent speaking and writing fluency in French. In a sense, language learning was the ideal education to suit the elder James's unstructured program. To learn a language was not to enforce particular points of view, but to gain access to another realm of culture and thought; to be fluent was to see the world from another perspective. Languages have traditionally been the basis of a liberal education, and to the elder Henry James they had the added appeal of cultivating the freedom he insisted on. The father's promotion of language learning found fertile ground in the mind of young William James, who took up the task with great gusto. During his few months in Germany in 1860, he said, for example, "I ought to devote myself to acquiring the language during the few weeks that remain."[65] Within a few years James had learned a little Greek and attained a reading knowledge of Italian as well as a thorough command of German.

The education of the James children also included a great variety of schools and tutors and, at times, no formal instruction because Henry James so disliked institutions. For almost the first decade of his life, William James rarely attended school or even studied with tutors. In the next few years his father was literally his children's teacher, especially when they were between teachers or schools. For example, William noted in 1856 that on days when their tutor could not come, "we have History, geography, &c. . . . with father."[66] Ralph Barton Perry reported that one "surviving witness" remembered Henry James's loose-reined but deliberate educational approach: "The father would propound some provocative idea, and throw it into the midst of his brood in order that they might sharpen their teeth on it and, in their eagerness to refute him or one another, exercise themselves in the art of combative thinking."[67] Ralph Waldo Emerson's son Edward, after visiting the James family for dinner some time in the 1850s, described a charming and revealing situation:

> "The adipose and affectionate Wilkie," as his father called him, would say something and be instantly corrected or disputed by the little cock-sparrow Bob, the youngest, but good-naturedly defend his statement, and then, Henry [Jr.] would emerge from his silence in defence of Wilkie. Then Bob would be more impertinently insistent, and Mr. James would advance as moderator, and William, the eldest, join in. The voice of the moderator presently would be drowned by the combatants and he soon came down vigorously into the arena, and when, in the excited argument, the dinner knives might not be absent from eagerly gesticulating hands, dear Mrs. James, more conventional, but bright as well as motherly, would look at me, laughingly reassuring, saying, "Don't be disturbed, Edward; they won't stab each other. This is usual when the boys come home."

Significantly, Alice remained silent during this incident: "And the quiet little sister ate her dinner, smiling, close to the combatants."[68] In the spirited family circle, although the parents' educational goals were a constant presence, they preferred that the children—or at least "the boys"—generate and pursue their own interests.

According to Henry James's theories of education, the things that the children thought to do spontaneously, of their own volition, were the most important ingredients of their education. The junior Henry James recalled that when the children played comedies in the attic, it was the "vividly bright" William who composed them and played the leading roles. Because of the children's constant closeness in their early years, such companionship and playfulness was very important. As the oldest of the five children, William was always their leader, being also the most outgoing, charismatic, and impulsive. Henry remembers his older brother as the most humorous person he knew: "In fact, almost no one but W. J. himself, who flowered in every waste, seems to have struck me as funny in those years."[69] At age eighteen William James was fond of "composing odes to all the family," especially to sister Alice. For example, Wilkie paused while writing a letter to his father to insert, "Willie interrupts me here and wants me to go into the parlor with him to hear him deliver a little sonnate [sic] on Alice which he has just composed and which he means to perform with much gusto." And he promises, "I will tell you its success when it is finished." After the letter trails off, he resumes, "Song went off very well, and excited a good deal of laughter among the audience assembled." William once even drew a sketch of himself as a troubadour singing to Alice.[70]

When William James finally did receive institutionalized instruction, it was very haphazard, in the spirit of the parental goal of freedom. Henry James approached the education of his children in the same way as he conceived of his philosophy: the constant change of schools was a repeated attempt to achieve the ideal education that he always sought but never attained. In 1851, while the Jameses were living in New York City, William and Henry were tutored by a series of "educative ladies." The following year, they attended the Institution Vergnes on lower Broadway, a small school that emphasized an international atmosphere and the learning of foreign languages. But they did not stay there long. Before leaving for Europe in 1855, the boys attended two different schools, including the academy of Mr. Richard Pulling Jenks, where the drawing master, Mr. Coe, first excited William's interest in art, and the school of Forest and Quackenboss.[71] The pattern continued as the James family traveled in Europe that year. They landed in Liverpool and made their way to Geneva, Switzerland, within six weeks, after stops in London and Paris. The reason for this move, the father explained, was to "go to foreign parts . . . and educate the babies in strange lingoes."[72] Henry James had decided "to put his boys in school in Switzerland"[73] not only because of its multilingual culture, but also because of its promise of liberal education. Within a week of their arrival, "the boys [were] all nicely established at school at Mr. Roediger's." The school promised to be a "polyglot pensionnat," and at first, the family seemed to have found its desired ideal educational institution. Henry James exclaimed: "We liked Mr. Roediger and his family extremely. . . . The children have been there now a week, and are getting very fond of the place." The father had planned for his children to stay at this school all winter, but by October they were on the move again. The elder James was again disappointed with his children's education: "We had fared across the sea, under the glamour of the Swiss school in the abstract, but the Swiss school in the concrete soon turned stale on our hands."[74]

The family returned to London, where the children were put in the charge of a series of French governesses. Then they were turned over to the formal instruction of Robert Thompson, who had once been the teacher of Robert Louis Stevenson. They stayed in London until June 1856, when they returned to Paris and came under the tutelage of a M. Lerambert, whom brother Henry remembered as "spare and tightly black-coated, spectacled, pale and prominently intellectual." But by the winter, following a "rupture" with Lerambert, the elder James enrolled his children in the Institution Fezandie, a Fourierist school "inspired, or at any rate enriched, by a bold idealism."[75] Even though James was a great admirer of Charles Fourier's theories of social perfectibility, he had withdrawn his children from this school by the summer of 1857. This example of impetuosity may have been due as much to material reasons as to idealistic ones. The financial panic of 1857 reduced the family income, forcing them to move from Paris to the less expensive nearby town of Boulogne. This move proved to be important for William James, who received his first formal training in science at the Collège Impérial, which the children attended during the summer of 1857.

Throughout their early years, the James children were educated with a bewildering freedom and range of experiences. William James's childhood was a kaleidoscope of ever-changing schools, tutors, cities, museums, churches, and playmates. Unable to understand his father's larger but cryptic purposes, young William James often disliked this constant uprooting. After leaving one school, he wrote poignantly to a friend: "I find myself compelled to leave at the very moment when I have begun to make friends—to take root, in short. That's the great inconvenience of being always *en passage*."[76] The only thing that remained constant in his changing life was his family: his spiritually intense and insistent father, his devoted and often judgmental mother, and his siblings who served as friends, schoolmates, and traveling companions. Reflecting on the variety of their schools and the complexity of their father's teaching, Henry James, Jr., remembered: "We wholesomely breathed inconsistency and ate and drank contradictions."[77]

The style of child rearing with which Henry James and other romantics experimented in the middle of the nineteenth century became increasingly prevalent in middle-class households in ensuing decades. The James family was an unintended prototype for increasing freedom in children's development—and for the increased qualms about vocational choice within that freer setting. Households like the Jameses' produced a battery of well-educated, inquisitive young adults who had no clear idea of what to do with their training and intellect. Complementing this vocational indecision was the emergence of an outlook on life that emphasized openness and uncertainty. As William James's own life shows, freedom-oriented child rearing encouraged new patterns in both culture and philosophy.[78] Although he could not have known it at the time, William James was building up a fund of experiences that would orient him toward the philosophical commitments of his adulthood. It was just a few steps from an education in freedom to a mature embrace of uncertainty, even if those steps would be neither swift nor sure. He first had to formulate his own vocation and outlook in the face of his father's designs.

Henry James's educational program directly reflected the way he lived his own life. He once said of himself that "the bent of my nature is towards affection and thought rather than action."[79] Thanks to his wife and his large inheritance, he could afford to pursue without interruption his own impulsive drive for spiritual awareness. His lack of any outside employment often perplexed his own children, who did not know how to answer their playmates' questions about his occupation. Pleased with this lesson in freedom from definition, he responded, "Say I'm a philosopher, say I'm a seeker for truth, say I'm a lover of my kind, say I'm an author of books if you like; or, best of all, just say I'm a Student."[80] In his educational policy of discouraging specialization in his children, Henry James actually sought to replicate his own life experience.

Given his dedication to his role as a father, Henry James would have been surprised to find that his policies actually helped to produce his children's inaction and vocational frustration. He did not fully advocate open inquiry, but he inculcated a specific brand of spontaneity and spirituality that nurtured his own religious orientation. Despite all of his emphasis on freedom, Henry

James's spiritual enthusiasms and convictions kept his educational program from appearing fully free to his children. Ironically, his very spiritual convictions produced a striking likeness to his own father's insistence and certainties. Such checks on freedom would be most apparent in retrospect, but the children gradually noticed them as they set out to establish their own identities. Young William became so used to the constant uncertainty of his "rootless and accidental childhood," as his sister called it,[81] that when his father's brand of freedom turned to insistence and revealed its uncompromising certainties, he was left truly confused.

Among the children, William James had the most difficulty deciding what to do with his life, living primarily with his family until his mid-thirties.[82] The paternal direction away from "narrowing" decisions was a constant presence throughout William James's childhood, but before his late teens, when serious questions about his vocational directions in adulthood first began to bother him, he actually relished the family freedoms. Although he would soon be beset by many private doubts and open conflicts with his father, young William flourished in this atmosphere, learning widely and coping easily, at least at first, with freedom and uncertainty. During his childhood, as William James developed in the unsystematic way his father intended, he slowly and unintentionally absorbed the assumptions of Henry James's outlook. As a native of the James family, he would have to cope with the ambiguous legacy of his father's philosophy.

CHAPTER 2

Science and the Spirit according to the Elder Henry James

The various orders which we behold in nature, the distribution of her

kingdoms and her tribes and families, the succession of her seasons, and the

grand choral procession of her forces out of brute chaos and confusion

into exact scientific symmetry and adjustment, do but typify

the invisible things of man's spirit.

HENRY JAMES, SR., 1852

For all of his parental concern and intellectual commitment to romantic child rearing, Henry James could not resist a deeply felt hope that William would keep the family faith. In his educational plans the senior James harbored an earnest desire for his eldest son to become a scientist, because he felt that the field would complement his own intense religious convictions. While in other times and different contexts, religion could find little life, nor even a warm reception, in the works of science, Henry James firmly believed that an education in science would be the best way for young William to maintain interest in and enthusiasm for a spiritual outlook on the world.

The elder James sometimes wondered if he himself should "learn science and bring myself first into men's respect, that thus I may the better speak to them."[1] He never did follow his scientific ambitions, except to place them vicariously on his son. He hoped that scientific training would gain for William James a wider acceptance than he had received with his own unorthodox philosophy. When his son was considering other fields, the elder James admitted, "I had always counted upon a scientific career for Willy, and I hope the day may even yet come when my calculations may be realized in this regard."[2] The father readily believed, along with most people in the early to middle nineteenth century, that honest inquiry into the natural world would readily confirm the certainties of his spiritual faith. Henry James's tendency to look for religion in science had deep roots in his own spiritual development and in the philosophy he clung to as his lifeblood by the time William was old enough to look for a career.

Spiritual Seeking

From his own childhood in a devoutly Presbyterian household, Henry James wrestled with his family's religious traditions. His quarrel with mainstream religion did not grow from religious doubting, but rather from an earnest desire to secure more certainty in his faith. As he actively sought further spiritual truths, the conventional and worldly concerns of the Presbyterians began to seem more and more brittle or even irrelevant to questions about his relationship with God and his place in the universe. Highly sensitive about his spiritual state, young James kept a close account of his misdeeds and felt "heartbroken with dread of being estranged from God." His introspection defined the shape of his religious goals in decidedly spiritual form. "For what after all is spiritual life in sum?" In answer to his own searching question, James provided an adamant declaration of human dependence on the divine: "It is the heartfelt discovery by man that God his creator is alone good, and that he himself, the creature, is by necessary contrast evil."[3] This intense antinomian emphasis on spiritualism encouraged him to trust only in the power of faith in the struggle to attain spiritual worth, and it made him very skeptical of all human attempts to assert religious truth, including institutional churches and their traditions, rituals, organizations, and hierarchy—and even, eventually, his own seeking. In short, he put great stock in Reformation Protestant ways of thinking, maintaining these outlooks to an extreme degree.[4]

As a young man, James tried briefly to find a place for his spiritual interests within his own Presbyterian tradition. At the age of twenty-four, he enrolled at Princeton Theological Seminary but he soon became disenchanted.[5] Within a few years he came to dread the thought of becoming a minister, who, he scornfully declared, "is personally mortgaged to an *institution*—that of the pulpit—which is reputed sacred." Having gained this professional status in the eyes of his peers, the minister, according to James's spiritual standards, "become[s] simply servile to convention."[6] With these high standards for religious truth, Henry James would think carefully and thoroughly before bowing his head in religious worship; at the same time his intensity promised wholehearted belief if he could only find genuine spiritual truth. At the age of twenty-six, financially secure from his inheritance and intellectually restless, he left the seminary and embarked on his own lifelong search for spiritual truth. He began with a careful study of the Christian Scriptures, looking for their spiritual message, but he soon became frustrated by their lack of striking revelations.

Starting what would become a pattern in his family at times of unease and confusion, Henry James went to Europe. In this case travel became more than a metaphor for his inner journey; while in Britain he became attracted to the thought of Robert Sandeman, an advocate of primitive Christianity.[7] Sandemanianism, a radical religious movement originating in Scotland in the late eighteenth century, was dedicated to independence from the established national Presbyterian church, a position that particularly attracted James, who was still reeling in alienation from the religious tradition of his family and his recent seminary experience. The small movement attempted to recreate the customs of the early Christian religious communities, with no pay for clergy, bans on the accumulation of wealth, and a communal sense of spiritual fellowship and shared property. Although they did not generally emphasize the intellect in their religion of simplicity, they did stress one theological position with vehemence: justification by faith alone. Sandemanians sought a more strict adherence to the Reformation emphasis on faith as the only means for gaining salvation, and they viewed church establishments and moral righteousness as feeble human endeavors to curry favor with God. Sandemanianism appealed to James because he himself was searching for truths outside the Christian traditions, spiritual gems which he also fervently hoped to find in the simplicity of everyday things and actions.[8] While in England in 1837, James met Michael Faraday, the famous scientist and adherent of Sandemanianism. Unfortunately, little is known of this meeting beyond the attraction of James the religious seeker to the renowned scientist who was also a pious Christian. His friend, the scientist Joseph Henry, wrote a letter of introduction for him in 1838 which shows an early indication of the practice of science veering away from religious belief: "Mr. James has devoted himself more to moral and literary subjects than to science and will therefore want one community of feeling with you; you will find in him qualities of head and heart sufficient to make ample amends for this." Along with most of their contemporaries, James and Faraday shared more of a hope for the mutual interaction of spiritual truth and natural investigations than Henry could muster. Their encounter provided James with an alluring picture of science in harmony with spiritual goals.[9]

Beginning with his interest in Sandemanianism, James's religious wandering had taken on a new urgency in his search for a philosophy of life. While his rebellion from his family traditions and his initial religious quests during his twenties would establish the predominant questions and concerns of his life work, in the next decade he discovered, at least in outline, answers to his deepest spiritual concerns. His responses to the new ideas and philosophies he encountered in the 1840s established patterns of thought that he would live with for the rest of his life.[10] William often playfully ridiculed the intense focus of his father's thought, calling it a "monotonous elaboration of one single bundle of truths," and he even designed a cover for one of his books showing a man beating a dead horse.[11] When his father died, however, William expressed the same idea more reverently, declaring that his father's life was "like one cry or sentence" urging a spiritual reading of the world.[12]

His religious beliefs, as well as his wealth, cultural standing, and exuberance for ideas and ideals, inexorably attracted the senior James to the transcendentalist thinkers of his day. During these years, James first met Ralph Waldo Emerson. The friendship began in 1842, when James attended a lecture Emerson gave in New York City. Impressed with the New England sage at first sight, he immediately wrote a letter to his "fellow-pilgrim" in which he declared that "this evening . . . I beheld a man who in very truth was seeking the reality of things."[13] Soon after they met, James, with pride and hope for setting a standard of spiritual influence on his children, took Emerson to "give his blessing" to the newborn William James.[14] The nursery room encounter may not have insured William's adoption of spiritual ideas, but Emerson and the elder James soon developed a lifelong friendship born of mutual admiration and common interest in unorthodox and idealistic thought.

Although he found Emerson's thought heartening, the seeker James still hoped for a spirituality that he had not yet found. His first access to a truth that would stay with him all his life came to him in 1844. While on another trip to Europe and still "absorbed in the study of Scriptures," Henry James experienced a spiritual crisis. His account of the event indicates the profound spiritual impact it had on his thought. He begins by recounting, "Having eaten a comfortable dinner, I remained sitting at the table after the family had dispersed, idly gazing at the embers in the grate, thinking of nothing and feeling only the exhilaration incident to a good digestion." Without warning, dark thoughts invaded his mind:

> Suddenly—in a lightening-flash as it were—'fear came upon me, and trembling, which made all my bones to shake.' To all appearance it was a

perfectly insane and abject terror, without ostensible cause, and only to be accounted for, to my perplexed imagination, by some damned shape squatting invisible to me within the precincts of the room, and raying out from his fetid personality influences fatal to life. The thing had not lasted ten seconds before I felt myself a wreck; that is, reduced from a state of firm, vigorous, joyful manhood to one of almost helpless infancy.[15]

As was not uncommon in men's narratives of conversion experiences at the time, James felt his prideful "manhood" crumble. But unlike that of most men of the 1840s, his male sense of personal power was not wrapped up in his enterprising skills or physical strength; rather, it was linked to his spiritual investigations.[16] The intensity of this crisis convinced him that all his previous spiritual paths had been barren.

For years the spiritual seeker had felt that slowly, through his study of the Scriptures, he had begun "to contribute a not insignificant mite to the sum of man's highest knowledge."[17] But now he wrote,

> I felt sure I had never caught a glimpse of truth. My present consciousness was exactly that of an utter and plenary destitution of truth. Indeed, an ugly suspicion had more than once forced itself upon me that I had never really wished the truth, but only to ventilate my own ability in discovering it. I was getting sick to death in fact with a sense of my downright intellectual poverty and dishonesty.[18]

The character and extent of his self-mortification is a measure of his intellectual orientation and an indication of the spiritual zeal that this experience generated. As Henry James raised his children, he would share his convictions and ambitions with them, especially with his son William. Significantly, when the son was a young man, he too experienced a personal crisis which filled him with fear and rocked his previous assumptions and beliefs. At this point, however, the similarities end: many of the assumptions that the son questioned were those that he had adopted from his father.[19]

Discovery of Swedenborg

This crisis of 1844 opened up a new spiritual vista to Henry James. If his previous researches had been in vain, perhaps it was vanity itself that was the barrier to his spiritual awareness. Soon after his moment of great fear, James made this connection and underscored it vehemently:

The curse of mankind, that which keeps our manhood so little and so depraved, is its sense of selfhood, and the absurd, abominable opinionativeness it engenders. How sweet it would be to find oneself no longer man, but one of those innocent and ignorant sheep pasturing upon that placid hillside, and drinking in eternal dew and freshness from Nature's lavish bosom![20]

Soon the writings of the Swedish mystic Emanuel Swedenborg[21] confirmed and reinforced these private realizations of the evils of selfhood. After James told a friend about his fearful experience, she said to him: "It is, then, very much as I had ventured from two or three previous things you have said, to suspect: you are undergoing what Swedenborg calls a *vastation*; and though, naturally enough, you yourself are despondent or even despairing about the issue, I cannot help taking an altogether hopeful view of your prospects."[22]

It was on this tantalizing suggestion that James began to read Swedenborg's numerous and voluminous writings, and he found in them the spiritual truth for which he longed. The elder James constantly read and referred to them. The books, stored in a large trunk, "inveterately [became] part of our luggage" during the family's numerous trips, as the junior Henry James recalled. The children did not fully understand the large, arcane, and dignified volumes, but they were a constant presence, "forming even for short journeys the base of our father's travelling library."[23] From these books James joyfully gleaned Swedenborg's hopeful message for his spiritual questing.

When he read that Swedenborg proclaimed that "a new birth for man, both in the individual and the universal realm, is the secret of the Divine creation and providence," James began to experience his crisis as more an opportunity than a problem. He was especially satisfied to hear "that the other world, according to Swedenborg, furnishes the true sphere of man's spiritual or individual being, the real and immortal being he has in God." This message conformed to his spiritual hopes and idealistic leanings. And most important, it allowed him to maintain that God "represents *this* world, consequently, as furnishing only a preliminary theatre of his natural formation or existence." Swedenborg provided James with a conceptual map of the nature and interworking of the spiritual and physical worlds. Understanding the world in these terms would involve, James declared grandly and with a sense of personal mission, answering "the question of human regeneration." In fact, "one of the stages of [his own] regenerative process" after his "vastation" would flow from that insight to become a template for instructing his children, for writing his essays to reform religion and society, and for the adamantine confidence that would sustain his spiritual faith.[24]

Henry James's vastation and discovery of Swedenborg had a profound impact on his thought. These events marked the substantial starting point of his mature philosophy. From this point James began his lifelong project of constructing his own spiritual outlook. His religious thought began in his antinomian awareness of the limits of religious institutions and his spiritual urge to get closer to the divine. Both of these impulses, his rejection of human effort and his spiritual longing, impelled him to reject all previous religious constructions and to develop his own religious philosophy. Despite their eccentricity and their eclectic blend of traditional concerns and contemporary unorthodox outlooks, James's ideas satisfied his own scrupulous demands. He was one of those rare and lucky human beings who developed a philosophy of life that gave him certainty and happiness.

The philosophy of the elder James is very difficult to understand because he writes with more passion than clarity and because his cosmic subject is inherently elusive. His style was invariably forceful and often even brilliant, but usually his meaning remained cloudily obscure. The novelist William Dean Howells, remembering James's exposition designed to communicate the spiritual importance of Swedenborg, quipped slyly that he "wrote the *Secret of Swedenborg* and kept it." His wife Mary reported with more loving empathy about his discouragements after his frequent lectures: "All that he has to say seems so good and glorious, and easily understood to him, but it falls so dead upon the dull or skeptical ears who come to hear him."[25] The difficulties of expression always frustrated him; William remembers hearing his father groan: "Oh, that I might thunder it out in a single interjection that would tell the *whole* of it, and never speak a word again!"[26]

Like his fellow romantics, James pushed the limits of language's ability to describe the spirit. His religious philosophy included an idealistic belief in the reality of the spirit, a millennialist hope for a society based on spontaneity rather than legalistic morality, and a vision of creation and redemption that anticipated the ultimate merging of human life with the divine. His oldest son eloquently summarized his father's spiritualism in a letter written to his brother Henry shortly after their father's death. This statement offers perhaps the best "single interjection" about Henry James's philosophy: "As life closes, all a man has done seems like one cry or sentence. Father's cry was the single one that religion is real."[27]

Despite his intensely religious focus, science played a central role in James's metaphysical grand scheme of God, humanity, and nature, because he regarded it as a weapon in the arsenal of spiritual truth. James was not alone in his faith in the potential harmony of religion and science. Romanticism and the direction of scientific investigation before 1860 encouraged a widespread faith that science could be an agent of religious truth.[28] An underlying assumption that religious truths would inevitably harmonize with the findings of science made strange bedfellows of a wide range of early- to mid-nineteenth-century American thinkers. Orthodox Christians were fond of referring to the book of nature and the Holy Bible as God's complementary forms of revelation.[29] Students of natural theology further refined this position by pointing to the "marvelous mechanism" of providential design in nature as evidence of God's existence and of His loving construction of our world. According to the argument from design, each human discovery of a natural law revealed a portion of God's will.[30] Even as natural theology declined in the face of the romantic upsurge, moralistic mainstream educators never questioned that science, in the words of Greek scholar and Yale president Theodore Dwight Woolsey, "is man's arrangement of the thought of the infinite God."[31]

Although their cultural descendants would scorn the work of science, even evangelicals of this period believed that science would reinforce religion. Charles Grandison Finney, for instance, maintained that "studying science is studying the works of God." As for other evangelicals, science was not a major concern for Finney, and so he leaned on Paley's comforting argument in urging investigators of nature to "go out into every department of science, to find the proofs of *design*, and in this way to learn the existence of God."[32] While the transcendentalists, with the exception of Henry David Thoreau, were generally ignorant of experimental science, they shared the assumption that scientific investigation into nature would continually point to spiritual truth.[33] Ralph Waldo Emerson's famous dictum that "every natural fact is a symbol of some spiritual fact" revealed a faith that spiritual truths are at the unshakable core of nature. He declared, "How calmly and genially the mind apprehends one after another the laws of physics!" and quickly added, "Therefore is Nature ever the ally of Religion. . . . This ethical character so penetrates the bone and marrow of nature, as to seem the end for which it was made."[34] The popular brand of science discussed in Christian homes and public schools and published in primers and general introductions for the nonspecialist readily coincided with religious belief.[35] This range of thinkers shared little in their intellectual outlooks—least of all their religious views—but they all displayed a conviction that scientific investigation into the natural world would invariably yield a harmonious relationship between science and religion.

Henry James never spared criticism of those who did not share his eccentric religious outlook, yet he likewise partook of their assumptions about the ultimate harmony of religion and science. He regarded organized churches as lifeless relics of religion which "imprison" the spirit in ritual and professional requirements.³⁶ He criticized natural theology for submitting to the materialistic implications of science and molding religious belief to fit its mundane demands, leading to the conclusion that "everything really is as finite as it seems." Even his good friend Emerson did not meet his spiritual standards, although on the spectrum of his contemporaries' ideas of science and religion, the transcendentalist viewpoint came closest to his own. Emerson's fault, the gadfly James teasingly pointed out, was an excess of spirituality without the rigor of scientific laws: "I am led to seek the *laws* of these appearances that swim round us in God's great museum . . . [while] you," James wrote to Emerson, "continually dishearten me by your apparent indifference to such laws."³⁷ James was an eccentric in his day not because he disagreed with the conventional wisdom on the relation between science and religion, but because he believed in their harmony and sought their certainty to an extreme degree. He was seeking but not finding in his own generation a combination of the two fields that would not make religion either wholly material or purely idealized. James found more spiritual food in the thought of Swedenborg, who envisioned religious truths as empirical facts and who claimed a direct correspondence between nature and spirit.

Henry James was searching at about the same age at which his son, a generation later, was deciding his career and philosophy of life. While William would remain in the grip of uncertainty, the elder James's encounter with Swedenborg left him instantly enthralled, and the mystic's thought became the permanent core of his own thinking. "I was glad to discover that any human being," James said in explanation of his enthusiasm, had "shed the light of positive knowledge upon the soul's history."³⁸ Here at last, James believed, was a thinker who did more than speculate about spirituality; instead, Swedenborg offered calm, factual proof. James found particular encouragement in Swedenborg's belief that the physical world possesses a deeper spirituality which is here and now merely clothed in matter. James admired the evolution of Swedenborg's work from prominent scientist to enlightened mystic, and he enthusiastically noticed that he carried much of his scientific method and outlook into his religious thought. The absence in Swedenborg's writings of ecstatic rapture or of brief extranatural union with the divine appealed to James, who likewise sought an empirical and rational brand of mysticism. Although James found reading Swedenborg's works a "tedious" experience and assessed his writings as "these artless books,"[39] James actually felt that the artlessness of this scientific mystic was an indication of his spiritual worth—a genuine and precious authenticity based on the scientific quality and accuracy of his spirituality: "His books are a dry, unimpassioned, unexaggerated exposition of things he daily saw and heard in the world of spirits, and of the spiritual laws which these things illustrate."[40]

Upon reading Swedenborg, James felt he had discovered the key to understanding natural and human mysteries, but he did not so much adopt Swedenborgianism as use the mystic's thought to inaugurate his own philosophy. The first step in James's scheme of thought was Swedenborg's theory of correspondence.[41] If nature is viewed according to that "science of sciences . . . the science of correspondence," then, James argued in resonance with Swedenborg's beliefs, we can see the true spiritual reality of nature. James returned to this basic belief repeatedly in his writing and speaking. Nature in itself, he wrote in 1857, has no "absolute or independent existence." Nature "is not a substance," he explained in 1863, "but the shadow of a substance whose reality is altogether spiritual." He declared again in 1865, "At best, Nature is but a subjective correspondence of eternal Truth, as realized by our infirm understanding." James boasted of the truth of the theory of correspondence, an opinion which he said was shared by "men of the profoundest scientific culture." For James, correspondence revealed the true and proper way of regarding nature, and it enlisted science as "God's great minister."[42]

James took pains to point out that his spiritualism had no occult qualities; instead, it reflected an awareness of the purpose of physical things, that which makes them more than the sum of their material parts. "In short the spirit of a thing," James wrote, "is the end or use for which it exists." In 1863 he explained his interpretation by recounting an analogy he used in teaching his children—an example typical of the directed religious instruction he gave them. In it he explains the spiritual truth that the science of correspondence can reveal, but which conventional scientific empiricism cannot. The "material constitution" of a coat, he reasoned, is its phenomenality, namely its cloth and buttons, which are necessary for its existence, but they are only a part of its spiritual existence. "But obviously the coat is not merely a visible existence, it possesses also an invisible or spiritual BEING in that distinctive use or power which it exerts over other existence." This being involves the cut of the cloth, the placement of the buttons, and our naming and using the resulting object for particular purposes and in relation to other objects. These qualities "constitute its true individuality, its distinctive personality or discrimination from all other things."[43] Thoroughly resisting occult or mystical meanings for spirituality, James defined the spirit in ways that show a marked similarity to the future pragmatic philosophy of his son William, as the intention or purpose of things as they are used. The son's theory is a secular version of his father's outlook, with psychological rather than spiritual explanation of larger purpose; yet, in concert with his father's work, William's pragmatism is also a rejection of the strictly factual orientation of traditional empiricism in favor of a focus on practical application and an awareness of the way relations influence perception and meaning.[44]

Henry James was an enthusiastic but not wholly devoted follower of Swedenborg. Yet when he criticized Swedenborg and tried to move beyond him, he invariably did so with a view, like Swedenborg's, toward carrying spiritual principles to new terrain. For example, he warned that "before getting the slightest scientific aid from Swedenborg, [the reader] will be obliged first of all intellectually to harvest his spiritual principles."[45] Characteristically, James framed his intellectual goals as scientific enterprises that would begin with spiritual insights. James devoted much of his life to an idealized brand of social reform and to construction of a cosmology that would explain humanity's relation to the divine. Both of these lifelong projects display a solid root in his spiritual beliefs, and they reveal the depth of James's commitment to science as he came to define it.

In Henry James's philosophical system, explanations of the cosmos and creation precede theories of social reform—an order of priority that well suited a thinker who maintained spirituality as the taproot of his thought. Creation, like the theory of correspondence, has a role in between the spiritual and the physical, and partaking of both. He distinguishes "formation" of the natural world, which is a physical event, from "creation," which takes place only on the level of the spirit. According to the elder James, creation is the establishment of relations between physical things and the investment of purpose in their actions. Physical formation is the prerequisite for creation and the arena in which it takes place. Empirical formation is a separation from God. Created humans, however, develop a rudimentary spiritual character by adopting a personal identity, following their physical desires, and living according to the laws and ethics of human making. These hallmarks of conventional morality and religion, James argued, are limited but vital first steps in spiritual creation which demand their own complete transcendence: religious seekers must resign their moral conscience and realize their vanity and limitations before a more complete spirituality can be achieved. R. W. B. Lewis describes James's paradoxical theory as the doctrine of "the fortunate fall" from innocence and self-striving toward the salvation of spiritual understanding and social connectedness.[46]

While physical creation was a single event at the beginning of time, spiritual creation, by James's reckoning, is an ongoing process of human progress. The key to spiritual creation is the abandonment of selfishness, a position he first developed in the heat of his crisis of 1844. His disgust with selfishness was a keynote to his philosophy and a constant presence in his daily life. For example, he wrote to Charles Eliot Norton, the editor at the *North American Review*, that he feared some of his racy style had offended Emerson, although Emerson often responded gamely, as when he wrote, "I am glad to get your note to cavil at its brave vituperative" tone. But James confessed to Norton that "one writes a thing at a heat, . . . but when the heat is over one is very apt to fear—at least I am—that there was a good deal of the unconscious fire of self-love at the bottom of it."[47]

In his philosophy James described selfishness as mankind's original sin, implanted at physical formation and since then serving as the "origin of all the evils that desolate humanity."[48] The path to spiritual creation lay in weaning humanity away from its prideful focus on self in favor of a redemptive union with the divine. On this path Christ served as a spiritual role model of total selflessness. James also drew inspiration from Swedenborg, who, as he notes, called Christ the "Divine Natural man."[49] For both thinkers Christ's dual divine-human nature was crucial to their theological hopes. For James, the path to such divine aspiration lay with cultivation of the self's opposite, mankind's social nature. This turn of thought encouraged James to introduce a zeal for social reform into his Christian and Swedenborgian ideas.

Spiritual Science

James saw social reform, especially the idealistic schemes of the utopian socialists, as the most exciting prospect for mankind's abandonment of selfishness. He was particularly enthusiastic about the meticulous and messianic social scientific plans of Charles Fourier, whose planned communities and visions of a perfected society promised that all could act with social-minded selflessness.[50] Spontaneity not duty, social spiritedness not selfishness would shape the ideal future society. While Fourier and other communitarian reformers presented plans to transform society, James saw in their schemes the potential realization of man's cosmic destiny through the spiritual awakening of society.⁵¹ A perfected community would encourage each individual to develop a spiritual spontaneity without the inhibitions of selfishness. Human salvation could not be an individual event, James claimed, because only in society could "the redeemed form of man" exist.⁵²

In the second third of the nineteenth century, "science" was contested intellectual territory. In addition to debates over which fields could claim to be scientific, a wide variety of intellectuals vied over the very definition of science. The term still had a glow of meaning remaining from its medieval identification with philosophical inquiry in general; even through the seventeenth-century scientific revolution, the experimental practices that have been called "science" in recent history were called "natural philosophy" and were conducted along with a variety of theoretical inquiries. By the middle of the nineteenth century, many groups competed for the label and its positive associations with sober inquiry and truth. Groups of amateurs and proto-professionals engaged in study of the physical universe—fields that would be called "the natural sciences" in the twentieth century—were only one group of scientists. Other groups included reformers of society and serious scholars of history, language, theology, and biblical texts, each of whom also laid claim to the mantle of science. The reformers themselves were philanthropically minded people, with either religious or secular motivations, who constructed plans for the right ordering of human interaction; they proposed schemes for utopian prototypes, crusades for renovations of personal and social life, and theories for eliminating social maladies. This last group produced the most varied descendants. Some of their outlooks, when chastened by professionalism and a more thorough modeling on natural science, fed into the modern social or human sciences. But these idealistic reformers also anticipated the emergence of many new religious impulses and unorthodox secular therapies. Fourier, James, and many of their contemporaries claimed to be speaking of science with meanings that would be clearly unorthodox in the next few generations.⁵³

James was glad that scientists of society had developed their plans, which he equated with the hand of divine Providence, because they would be the human means of perfecting society and thus gaining union with God. James asserted that humanity's redemption could be achieved only in "the organization of the whole race in perfect fellowship, an organization not by human legislation, not by police, not by contention, but by God's legislation which is SCIENCE."⁵⁴ He felt an enthusiasm for science because he saw it as the agent for achieving a spiritual millennium. The plans of the socialists use "scientific methods" to remove the temptation to selfishness "by reconciling the interests of every individual, with the interests of all men."[55] James cheered the success of these scientists of society's ills, and he hoped "that all our futile old rulers, civil and religious, will grow so bewildered as to abandon their thrones and leave the coast clear to scientific men."[56]

Despite his enthusiasm for a science of society, James made clear the priority of spiritualism in his brand of social reform. He was attracted to science that had a spiritual purpose, not to positivism or religiously neutral natural science. He had little respect for or understanding of experimental science, and he abhorred the positivistic exaltation of the scientific method as the standard criterion of philosophical knowledge. In fact, he chided Fourier, Auguste Comte, and many of the supporters of Charles Darwin for their positivism. James believed that, without a spiritual awareness, they tended to view society as a "purely physical phenomenon . . . subject exclusively to natural laws."[57] James believed that such positivistic science was a prideful assertion of individual potential that exacerbated the spiritual problem of human pride and selfishness. He welcomed science, in other words, only when it was treated according to his belief in the spiritual essence of material things.[58]

Although his convictions for a spiritual approach to science remained strong, James realized the direction of intellectual change toward a positivistic, naturalistic, and experimental science that would ignore spirituality.[59] He lamented this development, which he called "rank with earthiness," yet he maintained a steady interest in scientific developments.[60] His interest was at two levels: one was an enthusiasm for scientific social reform, while the other was a wary recognition of the importance of experimental science and the scientific method in the study of nature. Although he wistfully contemplated learning such science as a means to understanding his times better and as a way to increase his audience to include people persuaded by naturalistic explanations, the closest he came to such training was in encouraging and witnessing the scientific education of his son William. The elder James maintained a constant suspicion that naturalistic perceptions of the methods and assumptions of science would undermine respect for his spiritual outlook on the world. Throughout his own life, Henry James embraced science only so long as it remained in subordination to spirituality.

James expressed the depth of his hope for a science guided by spirituality in a series of letters to his friend, the scientist Joseph Henry. Henry had been his teacher in Albany during his youth and had since developed a great proficiency in modern experimental scientific methods. He became one of the leading American physicists of the nineteenth century and the first Secretary of the Smithsonian Institution.[61] James's letters to Henry illustrate his interest in science and his curiosity about its current direction; they also display the poignancy of a man who felt increasingly alienated from current intellectual trends. In one particularly revealing letter, James wrote, "Again and again I am forced by scriptural philosophy to the conviction that all the phenomena of physics are to be explained and grouped under laws *exclusively* spiritual—that they are in fact only the material expression of spiritual truth, or, as Paul says, the visible forms of invisible substance (Heb. ii. 3)." When faced with the developments of modern science, James reverted to his intellectual starting point, the Swedenborgian conviction that nature is spirit clothed in matter.

Despite his own spiritual conviction, James could never find treatments of science written from his religious perspective. Complaining in the same letter about the technicality of most science and its lack of a larger vision, James lamented:

> I am perplexed by the barrenness of . . . scientific books . . . which give one nothing but bewildering heaps of facts peculiar to one branch of science, and never attempt to shew [sic] the brotherhood of these facts to every other fact of nature. . . . How can a man separate one branch of science from another without perceiving that he is in so far belittling and dishonouring it, and that it is only by making it connect itself in some manner with *all* other sciences that it becomes worthy of his pursuit?

Although a late-twentieth-century reader may find kinship with this critique of modern scientific specialization, James was even more thoroughly alienated from professional science. The unifying chord that he sought among the sciences was the spiritualism that he so readily perceived, but that, he lamented, was lacking in most scientific investigations. Full of spiritual demands for scientific inquiry, he asked the scientist Joseph Henry for advice: "I have wanted to know from you whether some book did not exist exhibiting the *fundamental* unity of the different sciences; that is, exhibiting the presence and operation in *all* the sciences of great leading and fundamental principles which make all *one* at bottom, in spite of their superficial diversities." Although James expressed his concerns to Joseph Henry about his admitted ignorance of "preliminary science," such lack of technical knowledge was not his major concern.[62] James searched anxiously for a unity among the sciences that would reflect the spirituality that he maintained with utter conviction.

Joseph Henry replied with a letter that was at once full of friendship and of recognition of the differences between his career and that of his former pupil. He hardly knew what to say because the spiritually minded James asked such different questions than those he encountered in his work; still he lamented that "I cannot give you within the compass of a letter an idea of my views of the connexion of the different branches of physical science with each other and with truths of a higher nature." Despite their differences, the experimentalist and the spiritual seeker shared some general outlooks and long-range goals for science. Like most scientific workers at the time, Joseph Henry maintained religious beliefs, but they were more like assumptions than active beliefs. Religion had little to do with the practice of science, even if it still made an appearance in philosophical speculations about science. Although he notes that "the book you enquire after has not yet been written," he does frame the nature of his scientific work in ways that would satisfy the spiritual longings of Henry James. The physicist Henry conjectured about the ultimate spiritual potential of his work: "The tendency of science is to higher and higher, or rather I should say wider and wider, generalizations, and could we be possessed of sufficient intelligence we would probably see all the phenomena of the external universe, and perhaps all those of the spiritual, reduced to the operation of a single and simple law of the *Divine* will. I cannot think that any fact relative to mind or matter is isolated."[63] Henry does not dismiss these spiritual concerns, but his tone and his qualifying words indicate that they are peripheral to his scientific work: his divinity was pushed to a wider and wider distance from scientific work here and now. And, of course, a scientist's spiritual asides could not answer all of James's longings, but they did encourage him to maintain belief that science could be a road to spiritual truth.

Joseph Henry's gently phrased disagreements did not break his friendship with Henry James nor sway the spiritual philosopher's hopes for science. James maintained these convictions through the time, nearly two decades later, when his son took up the study of science at Harvard's Lawrence Scientific School, but he gradually despaired of communicating them to scientists—including his own son and Joseph Henry. After completing a work on the relation between science and religion, James sent a copy to Henry, but the gesture was more "a token of my personal esteem and affection" than a bid for intellectual solidarity. In his note accompanying the gift, James wrote "I have just been putting out a book which remembering your interest in Philosophy, I take the liberty of sending you herewith, and beg your acceptance of." The book was likely *Substance and Shadow*, which James called "an essay upon the physics of creation." His approach to physics could hardly have been more alien from that of the practicing physicist, so James apologized: "I think it may conflict with some of your conclusions"; and he added in a spirit of confusion about "this day of most Providential chaos," that their different views presented "a circumstance I am neither proud nor pleased to contemplate."[64]

James's exchange of letters with Joseph Henry reveals the limits of the place of science in his thought: he never crossed the boundary to the methods of modern experimental science and instead remained faithful to the ideal of empirical certainty through scientific spirituality. The ideas of Emanuel Swedenborg, especially his theory of correspondence, initiated James into a lifetime of devotion to the reality of the spirit. He worked to extend the life of the spirit into religion, social reform, and even the natural sciences, and he promoted a similar vocation for his eldest son. Henry James's spiritualism, including his view of science, had much of its origin in the saga of his personal development and intellectual commitments. These distinctive and forceful ideas became part of William James's intellectual makeup, as assumptions, concerns, and problems that he carried with him as a foil to the science he encountered in the 1860s. Henry James was not a representative mid-Victorian in most of his beliefs and values, both because his philosophy was outside the mainstream and because he was not able to persuade many people to agree with him or even to read his works. Yet in his views of science, especially in the way science and religion reinforced each other in his mind, he was typical of intellectuals in his day. Many things seemed uncertain to the elder James and his peers, but religion and science did not. Comforted and pleased by his son's decision to study science, the elder James regarded such an education as the crown of his educational program and as a way to gain intellectual status within the current cultural climate.

By the 1860s, the elder James could proudly point to many similarities between his and his son's outlooks and experience. Father and son shared a sensitivity for religious issues, a deep yet discriminating respect for science, and a personal introspective intensity. Moreover, a decade after he started his scientific education, William James experienced a personal crisis of a strikingly similar character to the one that shook his father in 1844. These crises and their responses to them show that they also shared as young men a sense that they "had never caught a glimpse of truth"[65] from their previous intellectual work. From the time of his crisis, the elder James became disgusted with his previous religious inquiries and embarked on intensive spiritual investigations that he pursued for the rest of his life. William's education in science, begun with his father's blessing and his vicarious religious ambitions, soon spurred the younger James to doubt his father's beliefs about the proper relation between religion and science. William James's crisis not only paralleled his father's; it was also in large part a reaction to the unflinching fervor of the elder James's mature thought. While Henry James associated the spirit with freedom, William James found his father's spirituality constraining, overconfident, and unsuited to the intellectual challenges of his generation, especially in the culture he encountered in his scientific education. The spiritual liberation of the father became the intellectual shackles of the son.

CHAPTER 3

Groping toward Science

William, charged with learning—I thought of him inveterately from our younger time as charged with learning.

HENRY JAMES, JR., 1913

William James was a dutiful son. When his father encouraged him to avoid specialization and postpone any decisions about his career choice, he readily obliged by experimenting with a host of vocational possibilities. His own temperament reinforced his tendency to follow the outlook and assumptions of the elder Henry James. With an active and exuberant but undirected mind, William pursued interests in a wide variety of areas before he was even nineteen years old. He briefly considered business, he felt a strong urge toward medicine and engineering, he had always enjoyed drawing and spent his nineteenth year studying painting, and throughout his early years he was attracted to the work of scientific research. Except for the time studying art, which he took up with definite but briefly held zeal, all of his vocational indecision must surely have pleased his father. After all, his eldest son approached adulthood avoiding specialization by developing a range of interests; in addition, without direct pressure, William was gravitating toward work in science. While the elder James wanted to take up his spiritual interests in scientific investigation vicariously through his son, his educational philosophy dictated that William grasp this interest of his own free will. In addition, of course, the eager father was always ready to encourage his scientific tastes. William James groped toward science by sorting through his own interests in the field, his attractions to art, and his father's eccentric but fervent desires.[1]

As a child William James exhibited a desire for exact and certain knowledge of the things around him, a trait that often annoyed those around him. During the family's stay in Paris in 1856–57, according to his brother Henry's account, "the wonderful Mlle. Danse" had charge of the children. He reports that she was bright eyed and generous, and that she was a patient and cheerful guide to the beautiful and romantic city. With an easygoing temper, she loved the James children, but, the junior Henry James pointedly notes, she took little interest in William because he so enjoyed flaunting his scientific knowledge and testing the others' analytical powers. The kindly governess soon became exasperated with young William's insistence on exact and scientific answers about everything the children saw in the grand city.[2] The elder James, however, delighted in these early indications of William's intellectual interests and personality. Confident, keenly curious, and downright jaunty or even aggressive about his talents, William James was the apple of his father's eye. Until doubt and disagreement brought a change of mind, he found no reason—and hardly even any motive—to dissent from his father's plans.

For the elder Henry James, William's early scientific inclinations were a source of pleasure, especially when he exhibited real scientific talent as well as interest. In the summer of 1857, when the family moved from Paris to Boulogne, William James received his first taste of formal scientific training. There, his parents and teachers strongly encouraged him to pursue scientific studies, as the elder Henry James confessed in a letter to his own mother: "Willy is very devoted to scientific pursuits, and I hope will turn out a most respectable scholar." After the young James had been attending the local preparatory college for only a few months, his father proudly reported, "One of his professors told me the other day 'that he was an admirable student, and that all the advantages of a first-rate scientific education which Paris affords ought to be accorded him.'"[3] Of all the comments that parents hear about their children, this one found a particularly attentive audience in the elder James because it coincided with some of his deepest ambitions for his son.

Encouraged by the Boulogne teacher's assessment, Mary and Henry James gave William, age fifteen, a microscope for Christmas in 1857, much to the delight of the eager young investigator.[4] His brother Henry remembers William playing with it and other scientific instruments very seriously, and he noted William's scientific interests in his autobiographical writings: "As certain as that he had been all the while 'artistic' did it thus appear that he had been at the same time quite otherwise inquiring too." By 1857 William took up the study of science in earnest, and the more fastidious younger brother did not much enjoy his scientific investigations, especially when he brought his soiled hands and clothes and his "addict[ion] to 'experiments'" into "the room I for a while shared with him at Boulogne." Henry impatiently catalogued a series of his older brother's enthusiastic experiments: "The consumption of chemicals, the transfusion of mysterious liquids from glass to glass under exposure to lambent flame, the cultivation of stained fingers, the establishment and the transport, in our wanderings, of galvanic batteries, the administration to all he could persuade of electric shocks, the maintenance of marine animals in splashy aquaria, the practice of photography." His brother, the future novelist, could not understand most of William's gadgets or his "interest in the 'queer' or the incalculable effects of things."[5]

This interest and enthusiasm for investigation were not lost on the father, who harbored hopes for harnessing William's interest in science for spiritual ends. Before the rise of professional science, and especially in the perspective of the romantic elder James, curiosity about the natural world was a "philosophical" interest that complemented a desire for religious understanding. Henry James, Jr., later remembered of his older brother, "There was apparently for him no possible effect whatever that might n't be more or less rejoiced in as . . . merely knowing."[6] Until his young adulthood, when his desire to learn pushed him beyond the bounds of his father's plans, William gave every indication that he would accede to his father's wishes; soon the indecision and the expectations of his father would lead to crisis, but in his teens he felt little vocational or intellectual conflict. Even more significant from his father's point of view, he was developing these appetites on his own.

The First Questions of "What to Be"

In his teens William James tended to imbibe his father's wishes and intellectual assumptions uncritically. He even adopted his father's point of view in discussing philosophical and social issues with his friends. As questions of vocation began to torment him with troubles that would haunt him for over a decade, James at age sixteen framed even these personal questions in terms of his father's spiritual, reformist philosophy. In one of a series of remarkably frank and detailed letters to his friend Edgar Van Winkle from 1856 to 1859, he admitted that "the choice of a profession torments everyone who begins life" but then added that "there is no reason why it should . . . if society was decently ordered." Young William even echoed particular items in Henry James's platform for renovating society. He asked rhetorically, "What ought to be everyone's object in life?" and answered with shades of his father's idealistic philosophy: a person's goal is "to be as much use as possible." He goes on to imagine a utopian society in which people working to be useful enable "food and clothing and shelter [to be] *assured* to everyone." In his enthusiasm for this ideal image, William declares another feature of his father's philosophy: "In such a state of society (which will soon come, I hope)," in which basic physical needs are readily met, "every man would follow out his own tastes" and thus be of most use "by excel[ling] as much as possible in the particular line for which he was created."[7] This sentiment echoes the father's enthusiasm for Fourier's utopias and his attempt to create such an idealized society in microcosm within the James family: innocent of material want, the children would be free to pursue their natural impulses.

In his young adulthood, William James not only expressed his father's hopes and ideals but also shared some of his father's favorite antagonisms. For example, with words that echo Henry James's fiery antinomianism, he once wrote, "All the evil in the world comes from the law and the priests and the sooner these two things are abolished the better."[8] Although many of his words could well have been taken from the books, lectures, or conversations of Henry James, Sr., William stated them without attribution, taking on his father's thought as his own. While these idealistic musings did not directly help the son decide on a vocation, Henry James could be pleased that at least William was thinking in ways sympathetic to his father's thought.

For a young man in William James's position in the 1850s, operating by his father's philosophy presented some problems. In the years after the prominence of romantic thought, the idealistic hopes of the elder James's generation began to seem implausible to most in his son's circle. In addition, the wealth—steadily being drained—that kept Henry James from having to work could not sustain the five children of the next generation in leisure. While the idealistic father kept urging a focus on being rather than doing, the more practical mother, Mary James, insisted the children find useful work. Saddled with those intellectual, economic, and familial burdens, William realized that no particular vocation suggested itself as both a mission to mankind and a career that would yield practical results. For years, James would repeat his lament of 1858: "The question of 'what to be' has been tormenting me." He was certain only about what he would not do; he repeatedly declared, "Trade I detest." His uncertainty raised many career possibilities, including his pursuit of painting. But, throughout his youth, as his brother had repeatedly noticed with perplexed amazement, James maintained a steady interest in science. He was still not sure, however, which particular area within science to pursue. He was ambivalent about medicine, but he indicated early on that he "would like to be a doctor." When James realized that his friend Van Winkle would be studying engineering at Union College, he asked elaborate and probing questions about his courses and about the field. He sensed vaguely that engineering would fulfill his interest in science and his need for practicality but added, "I have not as yet got a very definite idea of an engineer's duties." James conveyed a deep concern and a demand for detailed explanation: "Please . . . tell me precisely what your duties are going to be, and in what manner you expect to enter upon them." He concluded his requests with a tone of urgency: "Please write soon. . . . I am sure you would write willingly if you knew how much I wanted an answer."[9]

When Van Winkle's answers left James with lingering curiosity and anxiety about the profession of engineering and the way to prepare for it, he implored his friend, "Please write immediately, . . . and tell me what to study." In other letters his pleading turned to searching for his own vocational direction; still in his teens, James mentally modeled his friend's profession to test its fit on his as yet untried intellectual and vocational identity. He said, for example, "I have no doubt were I an engineer, I could succeed as well or better than most of those who embrace that profession." Although in that same letter he declared, "I don't think I am specially cut out for an engineer," five weeks later he wrote, "I am not yet decided about being an engineer, but at all events an engineer's education will do me no harm."[10]

Engineering appealed to both young James's interests in science and his sense of duty about doing something practical, but still the field never fully excited him. His enthusiasm soared, however, when he contemplated the more theoretical pursuits of scientific research. He must have appreciated his family's Christmas present, because in describing the kind of work that "was most agreeable to me," he recalled, "I would get a microscope and go out into the country, into the dear old woods and fields and ponds. There I would try to make as many discoveries as possible." With this expression of scientific ambition and of admiration for the truth-finding virtues of science, he renounced his earlier attraction to engineering: "I'll be kicked if I would not be more useful than if I'd laid out railroads by rules which others had made and which I have learned from them." He concluded his youthful forecasting with a prediction that proved somewhat accurate about his training in the next decade: "I'll . . . do as much good in the natural history line as I can."[11] His efforts would lead to a thorough training in science, which in turn would provide the matrix and starting points for much of his mature thought.

In his late teens, while his father was still shuttling the children across the Atlantic and among various schools, William James was already beginning to take his scientific education seriously. In a letter of early 1858 to Van Winkle, he was particularly intent on reporting his extensive study of mathematics and science. He listed a broad curriculum of study in geometry and algebra, and he was proud that he was "already pretty well grounded in natural philosophy."

He even boasted, "I like mathematics and am one of the 3 head boys of my class" at Boulogne. One of his major attractions to this field was his mathematics teacher, whom James considered "the best man in the College." While there, James also found his early intellectual and professional attractions with ringing clarity: "I liked the Scientific Classes," but "As for the inflated, pompous, pedantic literary Professors in their magisterial robes, the less said of them the better."[12] Ironically, for a person whose work would become most famous in humanities and philosophy circles and who himself would become a respected professor, during the first half of his career, he disdained those intellectual and vocational directions as being too theoretical. His education and most of his intellectual explorations began with scientific inquiry.

Because of the family's constant movement, William did not have the benefit of systematic classroom study. Later in life, he regretted the spottiness of his knowledge in the basics of mathematics and science created by the lack of structure in his early education. With characteristic exaggeration, the adult William James dismissed his childhood education, saying he "never had any." To overcome this handicap, he often took the initiative in his education. While at the Geneva Academy in 1859, for example, young James began to study anatomy, but, because of the academy's limited instruction, he took up the subject for study on his own. He borrowed an anatomy textbook and obtained permission to visit the museum to examine human skeletons by himself.[13] In addition, he showed enough interest in his own education to keep "busy teaching [him]self Mathematics" and related fields. Moreover, he took advantage of the family's travels to learn foreign languages. Characteristically, he thought of this learning in terms of his ongoing interest in science: "Nothing could be more advantageous for a scientific man . . . than a knowledge of French and German."[14] Between moments of despair and uncertainty about his vocation, he felt currents of optimism that his broad education was building a firm and general foundation for his scientific interests. For all of his independence and self-motivation, which had become essential elements for surviving in his family, James realized the limitations of constructing his own education and hoped to go to college.

Even when he was fifteen his first college of choice was Union College, his father's alma mater, although he never mentioned that connection. His preference may be a measure of his dutiful relationship to his father, or perhaps he simply wanted to join his friend Van Winkle, who was already enrolled there. He visited Van Winkle in Schenectady and toured the campus, and he eagerly wrote to him that he felt "almost certain" that "in a few months" he would become "a fellow 'man' with you at Union College." With that expectation, he probed his friend with as many questions about the college as he had asked about the engineering profession. Indicating his preference for scientific study, James asked, "I would . . . like to know if it is necessary to study the classics at Union College or if one can merely go through a mathematical course." Hoping that his independent study would prepare him for college, James asked in early 1858, "Do you think then that I could enter Union College in the fall after studying hard in the summer?" A few months later, however, he felt that his self-directed study was not allowing him to "master the subjects."[15]

Despite all these personal plans, William James was dismayed to discover, much to his surprise, that his father disapproved of his going to Union. In fact, the always idiosyncratic elder James "would not hear of my going to any College whatsoever." The son was stunned at this overt assertion of his father's educational designs, which as a child he had not been able to perceive. True to his fiercely independent temperament and anti-institutional philosophy, Henry James explained that "Colleges are hot beds of corruption, where it [is] *impossible* to learn anything." Still the very dutiful son, William did not argue, but merely complained to his friend, "I think this opinion very unjust, but of course, much as I should like, myself, to go to Union, I must abide by his decision." But William could not get this issue out of his mind, and in the same letter, he lamented, "I am very sorry not to go to Union which I think wd. be by far the best place for me."[16]

Although he abided by his father's decisions, he sometimes defied them with argument or anger. For example, when his pleading to go to Union proved fruitless, he took up one of Van Winkle's letters describing the college and his courses and "showed it to Father." The elder James read it and "admitted its truth," but then snapped back to his initial position without further explanation by simply declaring, "'The moral atmosphere of College was very debasing.'" In the midst of these tensions William, who was frustrated and powerless to persuade his father on the college question, sometimes lashed out in anger on other issues. Although he was enjoying Newport in 1858 and just starting to take some painting lessons, William stated bluntly, "Father took it into his head the other day that it was absolutely neccessary [sic] for our moral and intellectual welfare to return immediately to Europe." Thoroughly disappointed, he could not mask his anger, as he cried out to his friend, "I suppose your lively imagination could hardly have conceived such turpitude on the part of a being endowed with a human heart."[17]

These disagreements with his father about college and travel seem to have gone so deep that they colored even small, everyday family interactions. For example, after reporting that the family had not gone to Europe that year after all, because "we repented just in time," William told Van Winkle about a family argument about ways to discipline their pet dog. As the disagreement escalated, the son blanched with amazement that "I have become an object of contempt to my Father." The incident raged into a major controversy, with the elder James scolding his son "with tears in his eyes: 'Never, never before did I so clearly see the utter & lamentable . . . worthlessness of your character; never before have I been so struck with your perfect inability to do anything manly or . . . good.' "[18] The idealistic elder Henry James rarely became angry, but when he did, he could be fiercely righteous.

Having reached a stalemate at home over his desire to go to college, William James felt confused about his vocation and "innocent of future plans." In the fall of 1858, he felt profound regret that he would not be seeing "the palatial walls of Union, where I might now be distinguishing myself" but for the opposition of his father. When he told his friend in 1858 that "I am very sorry not to go to Union," he continued disappointedly, "I think it probable that I shall go to the Scientific School at Harvard," where his father knew the teachers enough to know that its science would be spiritually safe. Not fully understanding his father's designs, William added dutifully, "At any rate I must make the best of it."[19] Having grown comfortable with freedom, he would take a while to warm to his father's choice of schools. He had many reasons to embrace the prospect of attending the scientific school, but a combination of defiance of his father's insistence and a world of options conspired to encourage his consideration of other career paths. Most important, even as he thought about a scientific career, he became thoroughly attracted to an artistic vocation while taking painting lessons with William Morris Hunt during one of the family's stays in Newport. Despite his anger at his father, young James was approaching his career questions in just the uncommitted and open way that the elder James had intended. Growing up with and dealing with the ideas of Henry James was full of such subtlety and intricacy. By his early adulthood, the ideas of the elder Henry James were not only a family treasure but also a personal burden in William James's development of his own thought and career.

Until 1858 William James had found few difficulties in his education. The freedoms of the James household had coincided closely with his own interests, and they fostered a buoyant confidence that was a trademark of his childhood. But as he approached his late teens he felt increasingly confused and frustrated, especially with the looming necessity to make definite decisions about his future and with his father's new and surprising insistence on guiding his plans. He had always believed, as part of the assumptions he had learned from his father's philosophy, that "everyone has his own particular use, and . . . he would be a traitor were he to abandon it for something else for which he had little taste."[20] After his sixteenth year, because of his disagreements with his father over particular career plans, he felt for the first time a tension between his tastes and his duties. These differences were just the beginning of a long struggle to find his mature path and his personal identity among the strong forces in the James family. By 1858 William James's troubled quest for vocation had just begun. His indecision about his life's particular professional work would last about two decades, but the mental habits of this context of uncertainty would last for his whole lifetime.

In at least one James family trait William never wavered: even when he suffered from personal indecision, he usually did so with pen in hand. In a diary written in 1859, which fortunately has been preserved, young James records a scattered range of ideas that demonstrate some of his private hopes and fears about a variety of interests. In the notebook he shifts quickly and readily across a wide range of topics—a characteristic that would make the mind of the mature William James so impressive, but also contributed to agonizing vocational indecision in his young adulthood. James recorded some aphoristic poems that serve as inspirational sayings and express his deepest fears about his search for a vocation. In these lines about fate, for example, he found encouragement to make choices in the face of uncertainty: "T'is writ on Paradise's gate / Wo to the dupe who yields to fate."[21] Despite this declaration, the issue of fate still presented a vexing personal and philosophical problem. In his essay, "The Dilemma of Determinism," first published in 1884, James placed "the ideas of fate and of free-will" among the most important of philosophical questions.[22] No mere academic issue, the dilemma of free will was already palpably real and troubling to the young William James in 1859. Despite his bold words about resisting determinism, another entry in the same notebook reveals his fear about fate. Relinquishing his earlier tone of defiance, James wrote somberly: "The mind of man naturally yields to necessity & our wishes soon subside when we see the impossibility of their being gratified."[23] In the face of stubborn forces, he felt his will grow weak, he acknowledges, and perhaps he even imagined the inevitability of resigning his will to the predetermined path of his father's choices. The entries also display characteristically middle-class Victorian values, stressing the importance of morality, duty, and hard work as well as anxiety about personal choice.[24]

These diary statements indicate an ambivalence over vocational decisions in that they involve both a recognition of a necessity that would deny choice, and the making of personal choices even though necessity loomed. Despite all, James resolved: "Having determined your aim, think not to shirk the means of attaining it, nor grumble if by neglecting them you reach it not." Although James had not yet decided the issue between freedom and fate, he had found an expedient to help him mediate the choice. On the same page he wrote, "Nothing can be done without work." All enterprises, those free and those fated, require work, so if he could not decide the ultimate philosophical dilemma, at least he could start acting in a practical way. Work was a central theme for James not only in his later philosophy of action but also during his period of maturation in the James household. Reports of members of the family and his friends, as well as his own book lists and his numerous diaries and notebooks filled with a wide range of notes and ideas, indicate that, despite his often melodramatic statements to the contrary, he worked very hard. He even worked hard during periods of indecision and depression—perhaps especially then because he searched so avidly for answers to his vocational and intellectual questions.[25]

Much of William James's hard work and worry about fate was part of the universal youthful concern with discerning one's own capacities. One diary entry emphasizes just this aspect of work: "The differences of intellect which appear in men depend more upon the early habit of *cultivating the attention* than upon the disparity between the powers of individuals." But another earnest entry indicates the inescapable limits of fated talents and capacities: "The man who has well studied the operations of nature in mind as well as matter, will acquire a certain moderation and equity in his claims upon Providence; he will never be disappointed in himself or in others; he will act with precision and expect that effect & that alone from his *efforts* which they are naturally adapted to produce."[26] Considering himself to some degree a product of fate, James was humble about his own capacities, yet he maintained a steady motivation to keep working and searching. Perhaps inspired by his father, who had met Michael Faraday in the 1830s, he read and invoked the great British scientist on the intricacy of the human mind and the delicate balance between given talent and acquired capacity: "Moderate ability on a mere mechanical instrument, ought not to be discouraged by the irksomeness inevitable in the learning to use that far more delicate & perfect instrument the mind."[27] This quotation provides an early example of his interest in psychology, especially from the philosophical perspective of the nature of the mind and the importance of moral choice. But before he turned to the field of psychology, James was to follow a long difficult path on which he discovered some of the range and depth of his own mind.

His first stop on that path was a short-lived decision to become a painter. A year after writing his earliest preserved diary, William James packed up his assorted private doubts and vocational musings and, in 1860, publicly declared his choice for his lifelong career. As he approached adulthood, no one in his family was very surprised to hear of William's interest in becoming a painter. He had shown an early artistic talent and a steady taste for the field. As his father had started to shut off some career possibilities and coax him into others, young James's decision for art was an act of defiance because it was a career choice that was wholly his own. In addition, with its romantic and impractical associations, painting matched the creativity his childhood freedom had nurtured, and the boldness of his decision suited the independent temperament he had developed as a child and adolescent.

The End of Childhood and the Lure of Art

In the fall of 1858, at the apex of his shock and disappointment in his father over his college plans, young James began to study drawing and painting with the American painter William Morris Hunt. James had been interested in art throughout his childhood, with a strong enthusiasm for visiting museums and studying artwork and a genuine talent for drawing. His brother Henry recognized his fascination with great art and his desire to learn from it directly: "I remember his repeatedly laying his hand on Delacroix, whom he found always and everywhere interesting—to the point of trying effects, with charcoal and crayon, in his manner."[28] In 1857, while the family was living in Paris, fifteen-year-old William took some lessons with the French painter Leon Cogniet, whose "Marius among the Ruins of Carthage" (1824) he had seen exhibited at the Luxembourg Palace. He took his lessons seriously and practiced diligently, as his brother recalled: "As I catch W. J.'s image, from far back, at its most characteristic, he sits drawing and drawing, always drawing, . . . to see him at all was so to see him." Moreover, his talent and steady practice produced in him a sure hand and great drawing skill; his brother continues his description with the comment that he worked "not . . . with a plodding patience, which I think would less have affected me, but easily, freely, and, as who should say, infallibly: always at the stage of finishing off, his head dropped from side to side and his tongue rubbing his lower lip."[29] Far removed from the interests of his father, art was a welcome respite for a young man testing his freedom and independence.

Although William had given many early indications of his tendency toward this career choice, his father was strangely disturbed by it, so much so that he attempted to veto the idea abruptly. In 1859, while William was becoming increasingly excited about his lessons in Hunt's Newport painting studio, the elder Henry James tried to block his career choice by taking the extraordinary step of moving the family abroad. This was not, of course, the family's first international excursion; the Jameses had traveled to Europe twice before, but when they set sail again on October 8, 1859, the father explained their most recent decision by admitting the reason for the move: "Willy especially felt, we thought, a little too much attraction to painting—as I suppose, from the contiguity to Mr. Hunt; let us break that up, we said, at all events."[30] Despite his affinities with Hunt, which would later become apparent, Henry James was adamantly opposed to his son's study of art.

The elder James maintained deep-seated philosophical objections to the field of art because, like Plato,[31] he did not associate it with essential creativity nor perceive how the product of human artifice could be connected with the transcendent ideals of his philosophical truths. The antinomian elder James derived his ideas from religious truth unmediated, as he perceived it, by any human constructions. By contrast, he argued, "Art is not the gush of God's life into every form of spontaneous speech and act; it is the talent of successfully imitating nature."[32] Although this perspective encouraged the idealistic elder James to deride the field of painting as a "spiritual danger," understandably, the vigor of this denunciation alarmed young William. Having grown up in an atmosphere of educational freedom with all his interests and appetites encouraged, he was indignant that his career decision proved to be so "repugnant" to his father.[33]

The elder James's philosophical view of art left William thoroughly confused. Ironically, Henry James actually declared an admiration for "the aesthetic man, or Artist," yet in character with the rest of his highly abstract philosophy, the elder James, while lauding artists in general, scorned any particular manifestation: "When I speak of the aesthetic man or Artist, I do not mean the man of any specific function, as the poet [or] painter." His ideal artist was the worker in any field who performed from natural inspiration rather than from "necessity or duty."[34]

When the family moved from Newport to avoid William's decision to specialize in painting, they went to Geneva, Switzerland, where William enrolled in the academy. There, the father hoped, he would pursue intellectual and scientific subjects and language study—while presumably forgetting the world of painting. By the summer of the following year, the family moved to Bonn, where the children could concentrate on learning the German language. According to the father's pedagogical plan, a general education in this international setting would keep the children from specializing too soon. Yet, despite his father, William, with renewed boldness, had decided on his vocation. He wrote in July of 1860: "I have fully decided to try the career of a painter." In fact, his father reported that "he felt the vocation of a painter so strongly that he did not think it worth my while to expend any more time or money on his scientific education!"[35] This bold decision marks William James's first significant attempt to gain independence from his father's control and forge his own intellectual and vocational identity.

Despite his antipathy to particular artistic work and his reluctance to encourage specialization, Henry James let indulgence win out over educational design: he resigned himself to his eldest son's career choice and moved the family back to Newport. William's interest in art had survived the move to Europe, and his father now realized how important it was to him. Henry James was so dedicated to his children's education (or at least William's) that he was willing to move the family to satisfy his oldest son's vocational interest.[36] Another reason for the father's acquiescence in his son's career choice was William's choice of art teacher. He noted before leaving Europe that "we are glad enough to turn homewards, and let him begin at once with Mr. Hunt."[37] William Morris Hunt's ideas of painting and his practice of teaching in his studio appealed to the elder James, even if he had his doubts about the field in general.

Hunt had set up his studio in Newport four years before the Jameses returned from Europe in 1860. The quieter younger brother Henry, in trying to understand this latest family move, noted the irony of leaving Paris to study art: "Never surely had so odd a motive operated for a break with the spell of Paris." Their attraction to Newport was not patriotism, but the studio of Hunt, who was "distinguished, charming, kind, and known to us."[38] The artist and the father knew each other through their common dealings with Boston intellectuals and social leaders. Hunt had strong connections with these circles because he was a well-established artist, and also because he was from a wealthy and prominent Vermont family and his wife was the daughter of one of the wealthiest merchants on Boston's Back Bay.[39] In addition, Henry James, through his friendship with Ralph Waldo Emerson, had met many intellectuals in the Boston area. In particular, they both regularly attended the Saturday Club, a discussion group composed of the intellectual elite of Boston society, including Emerson, many other transcendentalists and writers, and a number of Harvard scientists, including Louis Agassiz.[40] After Henry James finally moved to Boston, he was elected to the club in 1863. In a talk to the club that may have persuaded the elder James of Hunt's virtues as an artist and teacher, the painter discussed the theme that he and his contemporaries lived in a period of great art, and he implored these cultural leaders to promote this valuable impulse.[41]

As a father who took such a keen interest in educating his children and maintaining an atmosphere of freedom for them, Henry James appreciated Hunt's approach to teaching art. Hunt shared James's distaste for institutions, especially educational institutions. For example, Hunt felt that in his college education "there was nothing to stimulate or develop the perceptions and everything to suppress instinct and enthusiasm."[42] Here was an artist who embodied the outlook and values that Henry James lived by. Hunt declared to his students that "painting is a great joy.... Take it as such, and don't make a labor and duty out of it." He even chided moralists who objected to his painting on the Sabbath, because to him, painting was "one sort of prayer."[43] Hunt used a line of argument in sympathy with James's ideals when criticizing fellow artists for "the mechanical and soulless practice of the profession" and asserted that "truth only is of value in art."[44] In his artistic career Hunt was known as much for his teaching as for his artwork itself, and his students gushed with praise for "the inestimable value of his instruction" and especially for stimulating his students with "a great deal of personal magnetism."[45] Not only was Hunt a good teacher, but also like James he believed in teaching on the basis of the student's freedom. John La Farge, the painter and fellow student with William James in Hunt's studio, praised Hunt's loose reins of instruction and his ability to inspire his students: "The Master would occasionally walk [into the studio], inquiring as to what I had done or would do, but bearing on the question with an easy lightness, a friendliness of tact, a neglect of conclusion, which it touches me still to remember."[46]

Henry James must also have been attracted to the religious aspects of Hunt's art. Hunt had studied for five years with the French painter Jean-François Millet in the town of Barbizon in southern France. The two painters worked so closely together that they became good friends. From Millet, Hunt learned a sensitivity to the simplicity, gentleness, and quiet of the Barbizon countryside and people. Millet's paintings are often called biblical, and, in fact, Hunt commented on the role of religion in Millet's work: "It was marvelous to hear him read the Bible.... He is the only man since the Bible was written who has expressed things in a Biblical way."[47] As the elder James resigned himself to his son's specialization in painting, he was pleased that at least William's teacher would be an artist who made a "religion of art," and who "taught the doctrines of this religion with the zeal of a born propagandist."[48] Hunt gave the elder James reason to hope that William's study of painting could be part of his educational goals for reaching spiritual truths, but Henry James could not yet realize that his concession to his son's artistic interests would lead to a series of intellectual and vocational steps away from the father's educational designs.

The move back to Newport marked the beginning of another form of education: the attempt to settle on a vocation, which would prove for him a search almost as undirected and confusing as his previous studies. Also, in his eighteenth year, young James for the first time sought education outside the James household. The influence of his father had dominated his early years, but now he began to learn primarily from other sources. The change was not sudden or complete, but the decision for a career in painting was a turning point in the education of William James. After years of the uncertainty of educational freedom, William finally started making his own decisions about himself and his future. He would still have a wide range of interests and many uncertainties about his future, but his uncertainties would be his own, not his father's imposition. This self-possession, however, was only the beginning of his attempts at asserting his own intellectual and vocational identity; his dynamic father still held a great power of persuasion over his sensitive oldest son.

Within a year of his study at Hunt's studio, William James decided to abandon his chosen career as an artist, and he almost never again mentioned his Newport experience.[49] Despite his genuine artistic promise and the affinity for the artistic outlook he retained for the rest of his life, he seemed to grow frustrated with the practice of painting and his progress in the craft. Although his fellow student John La Farge, who went on to become a prominent artist, said that he "drew beautifully," James declared with typical overstatement that "there is nothing on earth more deplorable than a bad artist."[50] To fill the vocational void, he turned to a profession that his father had long advocated for him; in 1861 William again expressed an interest in pursuing a scientific education. With this, Henry James felt he could rest content: after a brief foray into the career of painting, his son had finally chosen a field of study that would encourage him to keep learning what his father had taught at home. Henry James maintained this hope for his son's education because he assumed that scientific knowledge would inevitably support religion. Although such a position was becoming increasingly implausible by the 1860s, he maintained it with the conviction of a religious faith. William's homegrown interests in science and his father's views would little prepare him, however, for the bold new ideas he would discover in his scientific education.

PART II

An Education in Science

As William James became increasingly frustrated with his first career choice, he decided to take up the field that his father had urged all along. In September 1861 he began his formal education in science by enrolling as a chemistry student at the Lawrence Scientific School of Harvard University. The possibility of having William study science satisfied longstanding hopes in the father, and the fact that William chose this direction himself after exploring the world of art gratified Henry's expectations for his children's unstructured education. To the father William's education in science was the logical culmination of his religious education from within the James household. A scientific training would give young William the means for true and certain knowledge of the spiritual world. Because the elder James sought scientific legitimacy for his spiritual ideas, he supported his son's education in science with enthusiasm.

His father's thought gave William James an appetite for religious issues and a hope for their harmony with science, but his scientific education sharply challenged the religious assumptions that the elder James had taught. Although Henry James viewed his son's scientific education as the crown of his educational program, William James experienced the Lawrence Scientific School and his new life of increasing intellectual independence at Harvard and in Cambridge, Massachusetts, as a decisive break with his earlier education and the first step toward new ways of thinking about religion and science.

Before the 1860s Henry James could gain support from most scientists in his hope for harmony between science and religion based on an expectation of mutually supporting certainty in each field. The publication of Charles Darwin's *On the Origin of Species* in 1859 drove a decisive wedge between the approaches to science and religion with which the elder James could sympathize and the new approaches in these fields that did not assume or expect certainty. Darwin's naturalistic scientific explanations ignored the claims of religion, especially the assertions of a spiritual science, and relied more on the plausibility of explanation than on the certainty of proof. Darwin created equal controversy in religious and scientific circles for both the content and the method of his science. The intellectual drama of these changes in science and religion, which took shape in the 1860s after Darwin's decisive naturalistic statement, divided both the faculty at Harvard's scientific school and the intellectual community in Cambridge. More often than not this division manifested itself as a generational conflict. The shock of Darwin's ideas repelled Henry James and many of William's teachers even as it attracted William James and his peers to a new world of thought in science and religion. Their differences were a microcosm of the cultural divisions Darwin generated.

CHAPTER 4

The Shock of Darwin

Darwin ... has brought to the discussion a vast amount of well-arranged information, a convincing cogency of argument, and a captivating charm of presentation. His doctrine appealed the more powerfully to the scientific world because he maintained it at first not upon metaphysical ground but upon observation. Indeed it might be said that he treated his subject according to the best scientific methods, had he not frequently overstepped the boundaries of actual knowledge and allowed his imagination to supply the links which science does not furnish.

LOUIS AGASSIZ, 1874

The disagreements between Henry and William James over the nature and purpose of science went much deeper than a family misunderstanding. The conflict that split father and son in the James household also polarized many other popular and elite observers of scientific and religious developments in the mid-nineteenth century. Almost immediately after its publication, Darwin's theory became an object of conversation and controversy. Popular reaction focused on the possibility of the animal origins of human nature. For example, while waiting for a battle in 1863, weary infantry troops in the Confederate Army hotly debated the *Origin of Species*, but the exchange was cut short by the persuasiveness of one soldier's loyalty to Robert E. Lee: "Well boys, the rest of us may have developed from monkeys; but I tell you none less than God could have made such a man as 'Marse Robert.'"[1]

Among intellectuals Darwinism had even more points of controversy. It was the flash point between the generations, between Henry, Sr., and William

James, and between the older and newer views of science. Pressure surrounding these tensions within science and religion had been building for decades, but, like the contemporaneous issue of slavery in American politics, Darwinism became the symbolic vehicle for a host of issues that divided the intellectual world. Science practiced under the star of Darwinism represented the displacement of the cultured amateur by professional experts and the divorce of science from moral purpose and religious conviction. Most important, the new science, operating according to probabilities, removed its findings from expectations of certainty in either science or religion. This methodological challenge to scientific certainty is the true Darwinian revolution, far more than the supposed triumph of science over religion or even the dominance of Darwin's particular insights about evolution. The Darwinian revolution epitomized a sea change away from the assumption that scientific research can provide certainty and toward a brand of science that found plausible, persuasive explanations as patterns in the midst of indeterminate events.[2] The disagreements over Darwinism after 1859 put an identifiable label on a trend in science and religion that had been quietly emerging for decades; as journalist and editor Charles Godfrey Leland said of his education in the 1830s to 1850s, "I was advancing rapidly to pure science, though Evolution was as yet unknown."[3]

The Divorce of Science and Religion, 1815–1860

Darwinism may have been the most prominent and important agent of changing attitudes toward science, but its impact became revolutionary because it was the culmination of decades of evolution in approaches to science. After 1815 the aggressive confidence toward geographic and economic expansion spurred a blossoming of interest in science in the new republic, although there were some grumblings from Federalist elites who feared its associations with the radicalism of the French Revolution and from some Democratic-Republican party members who suspected the sophistications of science would produce an aristocratic and manipulative social caste.[4] Despite these worries, "natural history" or "natural philosophy" in the early republic earned the hope of combining enlightened learning with broad democratic appeal. Scientific knowledge became a point of national pride, a tool to facilitate growth, and a popular topic in books, magazines, and lectures. And so science could appear less dangerously radical or elitist if communicated to the public. The minister Orville Dewey enthused over this work of science: "It is indeed one of the peculiar and great undertakings of the age, to communicate scientific knowledge to the whole intelligent portion of the mass of society.... *Diffusion* is the watchword of the age."[5]

There were few scientists available to take up this task. By the 1820s the small American scientific community had begun to take on a distinct professional identity. The process would be slow, however, because there were few opportunities for scientific education, even fewer jobs for working scientists, and, in a telling conceptual indication of the uncertain social standing of the field, the very term "scientist" was not coined until 1840.[6] Individual sciences had little professional cohesion and the general cultural role of science was not clearly defined, so it was fully plausible for Henry James to expect science to enforce spirituality and for William James to enter scientific school with that assumption intact.

Beginning in the second and third decades of the nineteenth century, many Americans traveled abroad to study at European universities and to learn from European philosophers and writers. Scientists were part of this intellectual migration designed to lift American standards of thought.[7] In addition, within the United States, the zeal and thoroughness of professional standards were beginning to make their mark; the establishment of new colleges increased the demand for teachers, and learned and scientific societies and journals, most notably the *American Journal of Science*, emerged as outlets for new research. Although clearly in transition to modern professionalism,[8] these preliminary trends encouraged not only a stronger standing for the scientific worker, but also a great increase in scientific knowledge and a tendency toward specialization, which strained the ability of natural history and natural philosophy to generate popular appeal. These changes would reach a critical milestone in the work of Charles Darwin and in the education of young scientists in William James's generation who adopted professional practices in their intellectual inquiries. Whereas earlier scientific research was within the reach of the average lyceum-goer, by the middle of the nineteenth century the growth in knowledge and its greater sophistication made science much less accessible to the popular audience. Science began to grow at odds with its public, because, while the emerging professionals emphasized research, the average person took an interest in specific and practical results. By the 1830s scientific research was beginning to work up an esoteric body of knowledge that was relevant to business and government, but that the public could appreciate only indirectly. At the same time, however, the growing influence of German-inspired idealistic thought softened the blow of esoteric science by fostering the view that complex findings were part of the wonders of nature and the mysteries of the divine.[9]

While scientific knowledge became more complicated, its avowed methods remained simple and within the understanding of nonscientists. The orthodox yet enlightened approach to science took the scientific method of seventeenth-century British philosopher Francis Bacon as its guiding principle. The general practice of science involved a thorough commitment to Baconian fact gathering, with the assumption that simple assemblage of information about the physical world would point with certainty to its true and unambiguous nature. This use of Bacon as a model for exclusively inductive investigations was generally an exaggeration of the scientific philosopher's own method, which allowed a more definite place for hypothesis than his later reputation would allow.[10] The nineteenth-century Baconian outlook included a strict commitment to the empiricist proposition that the senses are the only source of true knowledge, a distaste for theory because it involves going beyond that which can be directly observed, and an identification of science with the description and classification of taxonomy.[11]

Baconianism was particularly popular in the United States because it coincided so readily with the natural theology of most Protestant churches and with the Scottish Common Sense school of philosophy.[12] Also, with relatively recent settlement by Europeans and vast tracts of territory as yet remote from systematic analysis, the North American continent had an abundance of natural facts still awaiting scientific identification and description. Baconianism also tended to be more popular among nonscientists, who appreciated its simplicity and directness, than among scientists, who often professed Baconianism but then enlisted the use of theories to organize and conceptualize their research. This was often troubling to scientists like the astronomer and chemist Lewis Gibbes, who was clearly disturbed by the difficulty of explaining the dynamics of light, heat, and electricity from the observed facts of research. Straying from facts to theories, he wrote hesitantly to Joseph Henry, "It appears unphilosophical to assume the existence of fluids whose presence we are totally unable to prove, and yet . . . the hypothesis itself serves so admirably to fix our ideas, to direct thought, and to connect facts, and in so many cases wonderfully consistent with facts that I know not whether to decide for or against it."[13]

In this era Bacon's method still had a solid reputation, but the practice of science had begun to stray from strict fact-finding. Often scientists simply threw Baconian scruples aside, as Joseph Henry himself did when he reported, "I have adopted the hypothesis of an electric plenum believing that some of my late results cannot be explained without this hypothesis." He bluntly stated, "No working man of science advocates Bacon's method."[14] Most scientists found that Baconian fact gathering was best suited to the early stages of scientific exploration—for any individual investigation or for the orientation of American science as a whole before the 1830s. From that time on scientists began to grow dissatisfied with simple empiricism. The deluge of facts that the Baconian system produced, often with the religious zeal of investigators hoping to demonstrate the glory of God's creation, cried out for organization, and a range of different interpretations belied the claim that description alone would reveal truth.[15]

Some observers of science, such as the popularizer Samuel Tyler, maintained their commitment to Baconianism and even claimed that scientists should more strictly limit their practice to fact gathering, while others, notably the institutional organizers Louis Agassiz, Alexander Bache, and Joseph Henry, boldly called out for more theories and generalizations.[16] In 1831 moral philosopher Francis Wayland offered a creative compromise by enlisting the method of analogy, which allowed for an explanation beyond the observed facts, but on the basis of facts that have already been described. This did not require a substantial break with the Baconian outlook because it focused scientific thinking on the level of effects without the inquiry into causes that hypotheses and theories invite. Whether defended, criticized, or compromised, Baconianism remained the reigning philosophy of science in the early to middle nineteenth century because it coincided so readily with the values of theoretical directness and common sense that most Americans held dear.[17]

Throughout these debates over science and its methods, one set of convictions remained constant: traditional scientists and emerging professionals, Baconians and their critics, professed with virtual unanimity that their work did not conflict with the essential tenets of religious belief. The humbly pious declarations of scientists even calmed the worries of elites and democrats about the dire social implications of increased scientific knowledge. During the first half of the nineteenth century, most scientists, like most religious believers, readily announced that their researches into the natural world pointed with certainty to the reality and benevolence of God. An exception can help demonstrate the general rule of American belief in the harmony of science and religion.

In 1796 the French astronomer and mathematician Pierre-Simon Laplace proposed the nebular hypothesis, a theory of the origin of the solar system in purely natural terms, without the intervention of the divine. His naturalistic science gained some support in the United States in the next few generations, but most Americans before the 1850s, including scientists, regarded the atheistic theory as an unfortunate anticlerical exaggeration or adapted it to their religious perspective. Still, the nebular hypothesis, along with new geological investigations, research in the fossil record, and other scientific discoveries of nature operating without direct divine actions, was a potent reminder that the European Enlightenment had produced the seeds of an antireligious science. When the nebular hypothesis became widely accepted by the 1850s, it was understood by most Americans as one more scene in the picture of God as a designer, even if a distant one, but these religious assimilations of the hypothesis still ushered in enough naturalistic interpretation to make religious believers cautious. Before 1850 such an interpretation of natural processes was viewed even more frankly as a warning of the dangerous potential of science unguided by religious truths, and rarely became a weapon in American scientific attacks on religion.[18]

Common Sense philosophy was also a product of the Enlightenment, but without its incipient atheism. This moderate religious philosophy served as a potent and widespread inoculation against the irreligious potentials of naturalistic science. Common Sense reinforced confidence in the alliance of science and religion, with its pictures of God as a force outside of nature that assured its harmonious operation, and of science as a pool of commonsense proofs for religious beliefs. As idealism gradually displaced Common Sense thought among many academics and intellectuals, it enlisted different reasons for maintaining a similar harmony of science and religion. By mid-century, Common Sense propositions mingled with idealism in most declarations on the mutually reinforcing relation between science and religion.[19] In this context it was perfectly respectable and reasonable for the idealistic elder Henry James to find confirmation of his religious views in the work of scientists in his day. The geologist Edward Hitchcock's pious expression that "the proper study of nature begets devout affections" and mineralogist and geologist James Dwight Dana's fervent declaration that scientific investigators are "pupils of the infinite God" were wholly typical scientific statements from this era. Religious leaders welcomed these statements and spoke of science with a similar spirit of harmony and with relief for its support of faith; for example, theologian James Henley Thornwell said, "That science which at its early dawn was hailed as the handmaid of infidelity and skepticism . . . has turned the whole strength of its resources against the fundamental principle of Rationalism. . . . The earth can never turn traitor to its God."[20]

The religious claims of Hitchcock, Dana, and other scientists honestly reflected their own religious beliefs and their hopes and expectations for science's relations with religion. Although Henry James fully endorsed such religiously inspired scientific work, neither he nor most scientists could understand that their religion was becoming increasingly irrelevant to the work of science. Tacit assumptions emerged in scientific circles that religious belief, while welcome, should have no necessary or crucial place in scientific research.[21] As with the professional trends, these changes came gradually, and, in fact, when these implications were taken to their antireligious conclusions, most scientists reacted angrily in defense of scientific harmony with religion. Robert Chambers's 1844 argument for the evolution of species in *The Vestiges of Creation* is a case in point. Chambers published the book anonymously because he anticipated the scorn it would receive for proposing a purely naturalistic account of species development. The book's hostile reception contributed to Darwin's delay in announcing his own theory of evolution through natural selection. Many criticized the lack of rigor in *Vestiges*, but most detested the book for its overt disruption of the widely accepted harmony of science and religion.[22] Even later supporters of Darwinism, such as Asa Gray, who taught at Harvard during William James's student days, had dismissed Chambers's arguments. Scientists and nonscientists alike harbored small, quiet worries over potential threats to scientific reinforcement of religion, but most preferred to ignore the problem.

The elaborate and intricate design of nature, especially the multispecied array of living things, had traditionally been one of the most powerful elements of science used to support religious belief. God had designed the world, created each species of animal and plant, and maintained them in majestic permanence. By the time William James was born in 1842, and especially by the 1850s, scientists had accumulated evidence of geological changes and species variation that countered this harmonious worldview. However, in the absence of a plausible theory for understanding these facts, they were most often read as peculiar exceptions to a divinely ordained rule. Charles Lyell, whose own geological research had done much to unsettle traditional views, noted in 1856, "belief in species as permanent, fixed, and invariable . . . is growing fainter [but] no very clear . . . substitute" had yet emerged to replace that view. Even before Charles Darwin had published his full argument for the theory of natural selection in 1859, scientists had already grown restless with scientific theories that were tied to religion and that denied some of their most recent research.[23]

While the practice of science in the nineteenth century turned away from religion, so too did the practice of religion grow increasingly distant from science. From the time of the eighteenth-century Great Awakening, evangelical religion had defied the demands of orthodoxy by emphasizing personal religious experience, a trend with seeds in the Protestant Reformation and special force in the New World where organized churches struggled to keep religious adherents.[24] With the Second Great Awakening, evangelical religion of the heart became the dominant strain in early- to mid-nineteenth-century American religion. Social trends toward the privatization of personal life and the feminization of the home led to a close association of religious belief with sentimentality.[25] While not overtly antagonistic to science, the emerging religious forms of the early to middle nineteenth century had little interest in science. Aside from quietly assuming its support of religious truths, most religious believers did not pay science much heed.

While the average believer became increasingly swayed by private feelings and religious sentiments, church leaders and intellectuals were more eager to find connections to science. Even the movement toward "higher criticism" of the Bible was originally motivated by a desire to prove Jesus's divinity; ironically, however, examination of the scriptures as historical documents and as literary texts would eventually become the standard methodology for critics of religious belief.[26] Religious leaders nervously observed the growing authority of empiricism, remembered the specter of the Enlightenment's antireligious science, and felt compelled to understand it and reconcile its insights with traditional religion. Scholars at Princeton or New Haven, for example, were more likely than the average evangelical believer to link their religious beliefs to the promises of harmony that science offered.[27] Their expectation of certainty in the congruence of religion and science was an old phenomenon in Western culture, but with a subtle new twist. The confidence that religious believers had felt for their faith before the nineteenth, and especially before the eighteenth, century came from deep, unquestioned assumptions about God's existence and governance of the world; it was not something they had felt compelled to justify. Now, when fundamental questions and doubts arose, believers were more anxious to find explicit confirmation of the harmony of science and religion. The eagerness and anxiety of their search reflects the importance of demonstrating what their ancestors had accepted as implicit.[28]

By the early nineteenth century, reasons to doubt religion were strong enough that religious leaders no longer felt comfortable relying on the power of assumptions to maintain faith. During the early to middle nineteenth century, religious leaders of many stripes sought out scientific investigations to reinforce or even prove religious truth. Henry James was among the most fervent in his desire to find scientific justification for religion, but, in doing so, he was demonstrating the same quest for religious certainty that was appearing in other parts of the culture. In fact, his zeal coincided with the millennial spirit of revival movements, the emergence of new religions, and the aggressions of manifest destiny. Meanwhile, professional trends and the growth of scientific knowledge in areas that had once been the province of religion raised fundamental questions about God, and these tendencies made the task of proving religious truth seem palpably urgent. These scientific and intellectual trends emerged even as evangelical, sentimental, and privatizing religious impulses left little need for science. In short, as the practice of religion and of science moved toward divorce, leading intellectuals and institutions, including the elder Henry James and most supporters of the Lawrence Scientific School where William James studied in the 1860s, strove mightily to keep them closely united.

Attempts to Heal the Breach

The continuing presence of naturalistic theories, such as the nebular hypothesis, in the thinking of even a minority of American scientists in the early nineteenth century was a constant reminder of the ominous potential of the growing split between scientific investigators and religious believers. Moreover, the growing complexity of science invited the rise of its popularizers, who, along with nonscientific intellectuals, were particularly interested in finding harmony with religion. Such efforts were not new, but as of the 1830s the self-conscious distinction between professional and popular scientific work began to emerge with some animosity between the two camps. When the elder Henry James wrote to Joseph Henry in the 1840s wondering about the broader implications of his scientific research, he grew confused and frustrated when the professional scientist had few specific and satisfactory answers for the religious science watcher. By the middle of the nineteenth century, popularizers of scientific work eagerly professed the harmony of science and religion, with steadily declining support from the practice of scientists.

Patrons of science were also anxious to see that their money supported a brand of science that would be both popular and sympathetic to religion. The Lowell Institute, a permanent lecture series in Boston, which William James frequently attended during his years of scientific education and at which he delivered two separate lecture series later in life, supported these mainstream goals. The intellectual agenda of the lectures matched the institute's social position, which placed it comfortably within a circle of private philanthropic organizations that flourished in the early nineteenth century under the direction of Boston's intellectually liberal but socially conservative merchant elite.[29] John Lowell, Jr., heir to the Lowell textile manufacturing fortune, conceived the institute in the 1830s at a time when it was still possible to have an intellectual institution that would be both professional and popular. With his premature death in 1836 Lowell's will provided generous salaries to attract world-class scientists and intellectuals to speak in a series of lectures. John Amory Lowell, who served as first trustee of the institute, took a keen interest in the family's support of science because, like many members of the educated elite before the age of intensive professionalization, Lowell was an avid amateur scientist. He kept a large plant collection and a botanical library, and he had considered becoming a naturalist until business at the Lowell mills and other concerns attracted most of his attention.[30]

The lectures, delivered without admission fees in eight- to twelve-week "courses," became truly popular, attracting large mostly middle-class audiences. Beginning with the first lectures in 1839 the Lowell Institute bridged not only the popular and the professional but also the religious and the scientific. The will that founded the institute stipulated that the lectures should be on the latest scientific topics but also insisted that one course each year must be devoted to "the historical and internal evidences of Christianity." With these words, John Lowell, Jr., expressed his generation's hope not only to find harmony between religion and science but also to do so with a self-conscious eagerness to maintain certainty in religious belief. Furthermore, when Lowell specified, "I wish all disputed points of faith and ceremony to be avoided," he was not only voting against controversy but also forbidding any scientific inquiry that would stray from his firm religious belief. A sympathetic Boston chronicler of the Lowell Institute's history frankly reported that "the selection of lectures and lecturers is made from a broad and comprehensive knowledge of the safe thought . . . of the time."[31] The scientific lectures may have been safe in themselves, especially when nestled in with courses explicitly devoted to the support of orthodox Christianity, but the very professional rigor of the lecturers contributed to the gradual dissolution of science's ties to religion in the institute's offerings.

The Lowell Institute was not unique. Large numbers of natural history societies, agricultural societies, lyceums, observatories, and organizations like the Smithsonian Institution, opened their doors between the 1830s and the 1850s. They were organized for the "increase and diffusion" of scientific knowledge, as the Smithsonian charter declared. These new organizations helped cope with the growth of scientific knowledge by fostering its dissemination and practical use.[32] In addition, the increasing demand for scientific training and its growing complexity also encouraged the opening of schools devoted to scientific education.

Mathematics and natural philosophy had been a part of the classical curriculum in schools and academies since ancient times. The new schools in the nineteenth century approached science differently than had previous educational organizations because of their practical professional orientation and their separate institutional status. From the 1820s the establishment of separate scientific schools, often organizationally adjunct to colleges, reflected science's growing authority and its slightly challenging relationship to traditional higher education. Motivation to found these scientific schools came from industrialists eager for technically trained workers, from occasional government funds, and from philanthropists captivated by the progressive promise of science. The first such American school was Rensselaer Institute, founded in 1824 in Troy, New York. In 1846 Yale College set up the Sheffield Scientific School, named for its largest benefactor, railroad and cotton industrialist Joseph E. Sheffield, with virtually no formal connection to the college. The Sheffield School offered professional training, but its science continued to operate with a view to supporting religious belief. Yale's most prominent scientist of the 1840s to 1860s, James Dwight Dana, typified the growing but still submerged tensions in scientific investigations: he conducted his research without reference to religion, but he still declared that nature was God's work. Within a few decades this institutional trend became extremely popular, with seventy colleges establishing affiliated scientific schools by 1873.[33]

The Sheffield School vied for national prominence with Harvard's Lawrence Scientific School, which had a similar relationship to its college. Textile magnate Abbott Lawrence donated $50,000 for the start of a new school that would be named in his honor in 1847. The school where the elder Henry James urged his son to study science had some of the same ambivalences about science and its relation to religion with which the culture as a whole was struggling. For instance, Lawrence was a good friend of the Lowells and shared many of their values. John Amory Lowell, who was trustee of the Lowell Institute at this time, helped persuade Lawrence to make the grant that established the school. He was also instrumental in hiring Louis Agassiz to teach there, having both invited the famous Swiss zoologist and geologist to give a course of lectures at the institute and participated in the negotiations to have him relocate permanently to the United States in 1848. Agassiz's approach to science was ideally suited to the dominant values of the time, and he dazzled Lowell, Lawrence, and almost everyone else who attended his lectures. In the words of one of the later deans of the school, Agassiz "stole the show" in the school's first years.[34] It took more than his Swiss accent and charm to win over their hearts. He was a rigorous and knowledgeable professional, yet he was also overtly and deeply religious, often making dramatic declaration of the way his scientific work reinforced his pious religious beliefs. Agassiz became a popular sensation both at the school and in the community at large; within a year of Agassiz's appointment at the scientific school, Abbott Lawrence donated funds to support his work, without any specification of duties, because he was "convinced that he [Agassiz] cannot live without being of essential service."[35]

Ironically, that essential service was gradually undermining the harmony of science and religion that Agassiz represented to Lawrence and countless others. Agassiz and his fellow teachers, including botanist Asa Gray, anatomist Jeffries Wyman, and chemist Charles Eliot, pioneered methods of teaching that within a generation would reorient higher education toward greater professionalism and secularism.[36] In the 1840s and 1850s, the Lawrence Scientific School put a premium on research in the appointment and promotion of faculty, introduced some elective qualities to the curriculum, and demanded that students engage in research rather than learning only from textbooks. None of these practices was inherently antireligious, especially when espoused by the frankly pious Louis Agassiz, but none of them presupposed religion or confirmed belief through the practice of science.

In 1869, when Eliot became the president of Harvard University, his scientific school experience served as his model.[37] By the early twentieth century Harvard no longer needed a separate scientific school because so many of its innovations had been incorporated into the university. The Lawrence Scientific School was disbanded in 1906 and most of its teachers and facilities merged with the university's graduate and undergraduate programs. Shortly thereafter, one former student reported that "instead of the university absorbing the School, the School has absorbed the University: for now the methods that were introduced in the School are used throughout the University."[38] From the perspective of the mid-nineteenth century, however, the scientific school was radically new in its approaches to science and education. The leadership of Louis Agassiz helped to assure its patrons and its public that the bold new scientific researches would remain wedded to religious belief.

In the late 1850s, when Henry James laid plans for his eldest son to attend the Lawrence Scientific School, he could have been attracted by the religious science of Louis Agassiz and the pious support of civic leaders. However, he could not have comprehended the professional work of the scientists, much less its religious and cultural implications. Darwin's theory assumed many of the recent professional trends in science through its purely naturalistic argument, its conspicuous neglect of connections to religion, and its novel use of theoretical explanations. With Darwinism, the long-standing break in the harmony between science and religion became dramatically manifest, and the fissure between religious belief and professional science, which Agassiz's flamboyant personality had held together so well, became an open chasm.

Darwinian Explanations: Naturalism and Probabilities

In 1861, when William James decided to abandon a career in painting, he inadvertently walked into a crucible: enrolling in the Lawrence Scientific School at Harvard, he joined a community that was just beginning to assimilate Charles Darwin. With some of the most influential intellectual and scientific leaders in the country, Cambridge, Massachusetts, was at the front line of a worldwide controversy. Here, as elsewhere, Darwin's theories generated bitter and fundamental disagreement. Often, antagonists on both sides of the debate eagerly exploited their differences and obscured the essential issues with talk of "warfare" between science and religion, or with attempts to gain professionally from the disagreements.[39] Because Darwin's book represented the culmination of naturalistic trends in the natural sciences and presented a novel approach to scientific explanation involving probabilities and hypotheses, it offered a fundamental challenge to thinkers like Henry James who believed that scientific advance could support religious truths.[40] The elder James's convictions found some support in his son's new circle in Cambridge, but within only a few years the Darwinian outlook would gain nearly universal support, especially among the young. The rise to prominence of Darwin's theories in the 1860s and 1870s is not a tale of scientific triumph over the unscientific, but a story of the increasing persuasiveness of new scientific methods that looked only to nature for their theories and that replaced expectations of certainty and proof with persuasive and authoritative, yet probabilistic, explanations.

Charles Darwin was a reclusive Englishman who maintained rigorous though unsensational goals for his science, but his ideas struck a nerve, especially within religious and scientific circles.[41] Along with most anti-Darwinists, Henry James dismissed *The Origin of Species* flippantly at first, saying, "I am not a chimpanzee ... in origin as Mr. Darwin would argue."[42] The book would disturb opponents even more profoundly because, in addition to its naturalistic explanations and unorthodox methods, it was also compellingly accessible. Others had made a case for naturalism and evolution,[43] but never before had those arguments been turned into a best-seller. The book is more than a scientific classic; it is a rhetorical masterwork. In striking contrast to other scientific classics, such as Isaac Newton's *Principia*, Darwin's book is eminently readable for specialist and nonspecialist alike.[44]

What is more, the work is overwhelmingly persuasive. It is no wonder that John Tyndall, a leading British supporter of evolutionism, noted that in the book, Darwin "moves over the subject with the passionless strength of a glacier; and the grinding of the rocks is not always without a counterpart in the logical pulverisation of the objector."[45]

Despite generations of Darwinian lore, the warfare of science and religion that the great English naturalist supposedly ignited actually entailed growing differences between traditional views of both religion and science, and newer approaches to each field. The best indications of this are the objections of leading contemporary scientists who disagreed with Darwin and accused him of practicing poor science. Darwin's work disturbed not only many religious believers who objected to its naturalistic, godless content, but also many others including scientists who disagreed with its method of explanation.[46]

Although Darwin tried to adhere to contemporary inductive standards in his analysis of the emergence of species, his data was too remote, his causal agent too chance filled and his theory too conjectural to provide proof.[47] His was not the first scientific theory to gain validity without demonstrable and predictive proof, but his theory of species development was the first major scientific theory to rely centrally on probabilistic thinking, even if Darwin himself viewed the theory as a proposition with a critical mass of inductive verifications and an argument posed to encourage the gathering of further factual support. However, many of his supporters advocated his theory in different terms, proclaiming Darwinism as a proven deterministic theory; for example, the German scientist Ludwig Boltzmann flatly equated Darwinism with "the mechanical view of Nature."[48]

Darwin's tone was never so bold and his method was never so certain. He argued for the transmutation of species through the accumulation of marginally adaptive traits, and he presented natural selection as a theory to be judged not as true or false, but rather according to its degree of plausibility. So, instead of proving his theory, he argued for it on the basis of one coherent and persuasive scenario after another. Although his method was radical, he did not emphasize it; his approach and the very logic of his materials involved probabilistic thinking, but without the use of statistics and without, it seems, the author's full intention to embrace this method. Instead, as his avid defender Thomas Henry Huxley said, the *Origin* is "a mass of facts," which on first reading do not have "an obvious logical bond"; however, "due attention will, without doubt, discover this bond, but it is often hard to find."[49] By drawing on an abundance of facts, Darwin implicitly and subtly asked his reader to follow his engaging and forceful—even if novel and unproven—interpretation of those facts.

In the first chapter of *The Origin of Species* Darwin presents the widely acknowledged facts of variation among domesticated animals and plants that breeders and farmers have developed. In the second chapter he calls upon his huge and wide-ranging experience of the natural world in order to describe variation in nature. In the third chapter he draws an analogy between the farmers' action on domestic breeds and the natural appearance of variation in the wild in order to suggest that struggle for survival within nature has served as a means for the preservation of favorable variations. He points out that just as farmers and breeders carefully select the strongest horses, the hardiest wheat, the largest dogs, and so forth, from their stock to produce improved varieties of the species, so nature impersonally selects the hardiest of each species for survival. Although breeders have never actually produced a new species of animal or plant, Darwin suggests by analogy that selection is likewise the source of change in nature from one species to another. The agent in nature's case is not the caring selective breeder, however, but the law of natural selection. Only after these first three chapters, which are filled with an abundance of diverse facts, but which persuade by analogy rather than by proof, does Darwin introduce the theory of natural selection as his explanation for the facts he has presented.[50] Later chapters enhance the persuasiveness of the book by anticipating potential objections to the theory of natural selection and by coordinating its ideas with the facts of established natural sciences.

Darwin was aware that his theory lacked proof and certainty. To compensate for that inevitable lack, he attempted to demonstrate his theory with an abundance of examples from the natural world. He drew on his vast knowledge of zoology, botany, embryology, morphology, geology, and geography to present fact after fact that supported his theory. In the introduction to *The Origin of Species* Darwin emphasizes, as if by apology to contemporary scientific standards, that he came to his conclusions about the origin of species only after "patiently accumulating and reflecting on all sorts of facts which could possibly have any bearing on it." Nevertheless, he was fully aware that he could be accused of rash speculation. In his own defense, he could only state, "I have not been hasty in coming to a decision."[51]

Because Darwin offered persuasion without proof, he was in effect asking his readers to accept his ideas despite their uncertainty. By marshaling so many facts, he pushed his explanation as close to the received wisdom as his topic would allow.[52] Darwin did, in fact, do what he could with the traditional inductive method: he not only filled his argument with facts that pointed to his interpretations, but also inscribed his book with the mottoes of two leading theorists of the inductive scientific method, Francis Bacon and William Whewell. But facts, no matter the quantity, were no substitute for proof, as many critics in Darwin's own day quickly pointed out.[53] His theory of evolution was indeed a clever hypothesis, they admitted, but without proof it was mere speculation, a clever suggestion, Darwin's guess.

Darwin struggled with his relation to the inductive method. For example, a few days after the *Origin* appeared, he lamented that his book was "grievously hypothetical, and [contained] large parts by no means worthy of being called induction." A few months later he wrote, "I have always looked at this doctrine of Nat. Selection as an hypothesis, which if it explains several large classes of facts would deserve to be ranked as a theory deserving acceptance." Elsewhere, he explained, "The line of argument often pursued throughout my theory is to establish a point as a probability by induction and to apply it as hypotheses to other parts and see whether it will solve them."[54] Facts alone would not construct the theory, but probable hypotheses could build up the theory of natural selection by linking many facts together into a plausible explanation of species development.

Darwin himself recognized that he was building a hypothesis on the basis of probability rather than proof. He explained that because processes of evolution are unobservable, "the change of species cannot be directly proved." Instead, Darwin offered another basis for his science: "The doctrine must sink or swim according as it groups and explains phenomena. It is really curious how few judge it in this way, which is clearly the right way."[55] From his personal retreat at Down, Darwin witnessed debates on his theory which pitted opponents, such as Agassiz, Britain's leading anatomist Richard Owen, and Harvard philosopher Francis Bowen, who called natural selection uncertain science, against proponents, such as Boltzmann, the popular generalizer of evolutionary theory Herbert Spencer, and his American disciple John Fiske, who claimed Darwin had established certain proofs. For example, Bowen charged that "the direct evidence fails altogether, and we are left exclusively to the guidance of conjecture and analogy." By contrast, Fiske claimed that by the 1870s Darwinism was "verified" because "such cumulative evidence has already been brought forward in sufficient quantity to amount to satisfactory demonstration."[56] While the reclusive scientist sided with the latter group, he never fully adopted their spirit of certainty about his own theory.

Darwin's theory lacked proof in at least two ways: first, the emergence of a new species had never been observed and therefore this possibility was, strictly speaking, conjectural; and second, the agent of variation within a particular organism was unknown, and therefore not only without proof but also, according to contemporary scientific understanding, random. Both issues involved indeterminate data, and his theory provided not proof but some highly probable explanations about the development of new species. His theory, then, assumed the existence of chance variations and used probabilities to explain their operation in species development. The power of his book came from its ability to integrate abundant facts into a theory that could explain their connection. Public pronouncement of his insights involved a degree of daring because his theory was formulated through a new approach to science, one based on plausible explanations rather than proof.

Darwin's method, including his use of evidence and explanation, sparked immediate debate in William James's Cambridge, just as it has left generations of readers puzzled about the truth or plausibility of the theory of natural selection. Despite the wealth of evidence for the theory, none of it constitutes conclusive proof of its assertions. Students of scientific method have debated the relation of Darwin's approach to twentieth-century standards of scientific inquiry. His departure from pure induction indicates a similarity to the hypothetico-deductive method as a way to assert scientific truths. While he clearly could not "foresee" or "anticipate" later practices, his theory is an important stage in the development of a method that demands an invention of a plausible, explanatory hypothesis as a guide to research in the facts, which in turn serve to test the hypothesis. Yet even his use of a rudimentary hypothetico-deductive method falters because his arguments for natural selection rely more firmly on analogy leading to plausible explanation.[57]

Questions concerning evidence and proof in Darwin's method also appear in the evolution of his work with the theory itself. As a recent flowering of scholarship has made clear, Darwin formulated at least an initial sketch of his theory in 1837, soon after his five-year voyage around the world as ship naturalist on board the *Beagle*. Privately, he wrote outlines, notes, and essays on his "species theory,"[58] but the reclusive Darwin kept them from public view and from all but a few trusted friends for two decades. During the 1840s and 1850s, Darwin worked diligently to accumulate evidence in support of his thesis. Spurred by fear of losing priority to Alfred Russel Wallace, a younger scientist who independently developed the theory of natural selection in the 1850s, Darwin began to write his ideas for public consumption in 1858. By then he had gathered a large mountain of facts that pointed to—even if they did not prove—the operation of natural selection. Even at that point he called the nearly five-hundred-page *Origin* "an abstract" of the larger, more detailed and scientifically technical treatise he had already been writing.[59] The great delay, therefore, suited both the temper of the times and the cautious scientist himself.[60]

The uncertainty in Darwin's theory was at the heart of his methodological challenge in his own time, and it disturbed religious and scientific thinkers alike. Henry James was not alone in his distaste for a scientific theory that demanded adherence through plausibility rather than certainty. In the context of the earlier generation's commitment to certainty, Darwin's theory of natural selection was both religious and scientific heresy. The nature of his scientific questions and the answers that he proposed challenged the conventional goals of both religious belief and scientific theory. Leaving religion completely out of his theory, Darwin provided a disturbingly plausible scenario for the transformation of species over eons without the active guidance of divine Providence; in addition, he demonstrated his theory not through a process of enlisting evidence for proof but rather with an extremely powerful explanation, which, if accepted, could provide a highly probable arrangement of the facts. In that shift from certain proof to plausible explanation Darwin started an intellectual earthquake.

Darwin's account of the origin of species was also disturbing to religious believers because it seemed to deny morality. The means for species change, Darwin argued, was the "struggle for life," the amoral and sometimes ruthless way living things survive and reproduce by controlling limited resources and adapting to gain a dominant position in their environment. He drew directly from Thomas Malthus's theory that the geometric growth of the human population would always far surpass any possibility of its gaining enough food and resources to maintain itself.[61] In fact, Darwin himself said that his theory of struggle is "the doctrine of Malthus, applied to the whole animal and vegetable kingdom." Some variations will better adapt the organism to the environment, and the animal or plant with that superior modification "will have a better chance of surviving, and thus be *naturally selected*."[62] Natural selection, Darwin argued, was a constant and pervasive force operating within every species for adaptation to the environment and thus for survival.[63] Because of their struggle for adaptation, some species survived and produced their hardy descendants while others became increasingly rare or even extinct. Darwin's theory of natural selection, with its ruthless, constant, and ubiquitous struggles for survival, implied that God had created a world without mercy or morality.[64] Furthermore, given the slowness of the natural process of variation, the theory eliminated the place for God's immediate interest in the world, even if it did not necessarily rule out divine creation in the misty past. The divine in Darwin's nature is almost irrelevant, certainly not caring, and perhaps nonexistent.

The question of purpose in nature was another source of disagreement between Darwin and the prevalent scientific theories of his day. Where the religiously inspired scientists and thinkers like Henry James saw the certainty and purposefulness of divine contrivance, Darwin postulated the impersonal operation of naturalistic patterns. As Darwin himself said: "There seems to be no more design in the variability of organic beings and in the action of natural selection, than in the course with which the wind blows." While he was distancing himself from religious readings of nature, he also avoided pictures of nature as random chaos; instead, the probabilistic law of natural selection could explain patterns even though it could not predict particulars. Incorporating uncertainty into his science, Darwin could declare that "everything in nature" is at once chance filled and "the result of fixed laws."[65] Thus Darwin presented not only a purely physical, naturalistic explanation, but also one positing the operation of uncertainty and chance in the sequence of events that most religious and scientific thinkers believed to be divinely ordained or spiritually ordered. When asked to believe that species evolve from chance variations, many critics agreed with British philosopher William Herschel's dismissal of the theory of natural selection as the "law of higgeldy-piggeldy."[66] Most critics did not notice that Darwin followed his claim of chance in nature with less brazen assertions about lawful order, which organizes the chance events into long-term patterns according to probabilistic rules, although Darwin himself rarely used these terms.

Darwin's theory of natural selection also delivered a fundamental challenge to the traditional notion of "species." Until Darwin's publication, the conventional scientific wisdom was that species never change. This conviction united a broad spectrum of religious and scientific thinkers who believed that God had created, either by indirect design or by direct formation, each species as it currently exists. Species, therefore, represented the divine intention for the natural world.[67] Darwin denied these assumptions in asserting that species evolve. By beginning his argument with variation under domestication, Darwin pointed to the easily recognizable variability of domestic breeds. From those facts, he demanded no great leaps of reasoning in asserting that species in nature vary in the same way; after all, no two members of a species are exactly alike. Darwin's ideas imply that all living things are in steady flux. The apparent constancy of species in nature is a function not only of the actual similarity within species due to the constant pressure of adaptation to the environment but also of the relatively short span of time during which we view them. From the perspective of millions of generations, species change constantly. Darwin premised his theory of species variability on the assumption that life has been on earth for millions of years, far longer than many then current beliefs about the age of the earth.[68]

In the history of an animal group, Darwin argues, the species is not an essence but part of a process of change. In fact, he says, "I look at the term species, as one arbitrarily given for the sake of convenience to a set of individuals closely resembling each other." The "species" that are observed in nature are not essentially different from the varieties developed by breeders. In both cases "these differences blend into each other in an insensible series," with varieties representing incipient species.[69] Preferring to think of a species as the most common and dominant elements along a spectrum of varieties within a group, Darwin inaugurated what would in the twentieth century be called "population thinking."[70] This outlook underscores the probabilistic elements of Darwin's theory, with the term "species" having its most distinct meaning not in individuals but in whole breeding populations, which are abundant with slight variations. Because most variations in a population are small, they crowd around the average we call a "species," but some creatures vary by greater amounts and strain our use of the term. According to Darwin, "These individual differences are highly important for us, as they afford materials for natural selection to accumulate, in the same manner as man can accumulate in any given direction individual differences in his domesticated productions."[71] Within a species, certain varieties will be better suited to the environment than other varieties, and those which are better adapted will have a higher probability of survival; after many generations, that new variety will dominate the species. Darwin's theory was therefore built not only on the uncertainties of natural variations but also on the statistical probability of the way those variations operate in nature.[72]

Varieties of Settlements between Science and Religion

When Henry James eagerly encouraged William to enter the Lawrence Scientific School in 1861, neither father nor son realized what controversies they were about to enter. Sharing the common views of science and religion in the generation before Darwin, Henry James expected that his son's scientific education would provide the intellectual means for understanding his brand of religious truth and achieving the serene spiritual certainty that he himself enjoyed. The elder James could not foresee that the recent advent of Darwin's ideas of species evolution would fundamentally challenge attempts to find religious truths through science, especially in the eyes of young students of science like William James. Wherever they were read, Darwin's ideas quickly spurred controversy.[73] Nowhere were the differences generated by Darwinism more intense than in the intellectual communities of Harvard and Cambridge where William James studied and circulated in the 1860s.

The controversy over the scientific legitimacy of Darwinism often found cultural expression in alternative ways of regarding the relation of religion to the new science.[74] Those who opposed Darwinism, especially those who adhered to orthodoxies of scientific method and religious belief, maintained that the theory of natural selection was flatly wrong for its uncertain and irreligious science and its lack of religious content.[75] The supporters of Darwin interpreted the new science of natural selection in dramatically different ways. Perhaps recalling the satisfying harmony between religion and earlier scientific theories, many sought to find compromises between religious belief and Darwinism. These compromises either accommodated religion to the new sciences or adapted science to satisfy traditional religious belief. While their advocates bore many similarities, these outlooks made philosophically opposite arguments: the former, often called religious modernists, proposed a liberal project to make religion relevant to modern times and flexible enough to adapt to any new scientific theory;[76] conversely, the latter, sometimes dubbed cosmic or progressive evolutionists, sought conformity of science to a quasi-mystical religion based on the insights of recent scientific knowledge.[77] More theologically radical, the advocates of New Thought also called for changes in religion to suit the new science, but, unlike the modernists, they actually broke with established churches in seeking out the spiritual meaning of science, often in the same tradition as Emanuel Swedenborg.[78] Still others, both believers and nonbelievers, accepted the new science without rearranging their religious ideas; for them, Darwin's naturalistic analyses of species change inspired a satisfactory divorce of religious faith from scientific investigation. According to this school of thought, science became not antagonistic to religion or even adapted to it, but rather wholly separate from the practices of natural investigation.[79]

Another influence of Darwin derived ironically from those who associated his theory with factual proof. Heady with the decline of certainty in religion, many of the new generation posited an alternative certainty in science. The sheer quantity of factual material and the strictly naturalistic subject matter in Darwin's book encouraged many secular thinkers to find in the *Origin* a motive for promoting science as a religion, while their secularity took the form of either atheism or agnostic uncertainty and unconcern for religion. In short, because of their enthusiasm for science, they felt no need for traditional religion and often openly scorned it.[80]

When William James embarked on his scientific education in 1861, he faced not only a wealth of new scientific material to learn but also an array of cultural choices about Darwinism and science in general. The choices ranged on a spectrum from the religious anti-Darwinism of his father to scientific antireligion, with various forms of accommodation of religion and science in between. During his decade of scientific education, he often expressed the issues in terms of opposition between scientific secularity and religious faith, even though he would ultimately become more comfortable with some form of compromise between the two fields.

James briefly flirted with a secular scientific outlook after encountering the work of bold advocates for the certainty of science, such as the British philosopher Herbert Spencer and German popularizer Ludwig Büchner. They made explicit the irreligious and atheistic implications of the natural science that had been lurking beneath the practice of science since the Enlightenment. James remembered that he had "read this book ([Spencer's] *First Principles*) as a youth when it was still appearing in numbers, and was carried away with enthusiasm by the intellectual perspective which it seemed to offer."[81] In a private notebook entry from September 10, 1863, James took extensive notes on Büchner's book *Kraft und Stoff* (1855) (*Force and Matter*), but the entry quickly became an exposition of his own thoughts as he wrestled with the truths of science and religion.[82] He began by summarizing Büchner's bluntly materialistic theme: "Force & Matter are inseparable. It is impossible to think of a pure force antecedent to matter creating matter; or, of a force existing independently after the creation of matter; or of a force springing into existence creating matter & then merging itself in the matter. Therefore, matter can never have been created & is eternal."

Characteristically, James quickly confronted the religious implications of this science: "We should not attempt to go farther back than the physical universe." He then heaped scorn on attempts to reconcile science and religion, deriding theism as "a kind of Asylum for facts wh[ich] we cannot otherwise explain." By contrast, science offers an escape from these dogmas, because with "natural, material laws, . . . we see every year a little farther into the misty unknown. . . . So that old Asylum is slowly and surely being emptied."[83] Just as his father had hoped, James was smitten by the allure of science, but the son found in his science an alternative naturalistic certainty from his education outside the household. Within a few years, he would grow disillusioned with scientism, but he remained uncomfortable with a return to religious certainty.

By the late 1860s, while young James struggled with his own individuation process, the bold contrast of absolutist science and dogmatic religion framed the depressing choices of his personal crisis.

In his youth James formulated his ideas without the nuance and sensitivity to complexity that age would bring. Besides, Darwinism presented a forceful intellectual challenge: all those in James's generation who were energized by its insights were tempted to think in bold strokes. In addition, for a decade and more after the publication of the *Origin*, most nonscientific religious and cultural leaders paid little attention to Darwin's ideas. They tended to dismiss the theory of natural selection as a poor form of uncertain and speculative science premised on a malicious brand of materialism. This extremist reaction tempted young students of science like James to cling to the opposite pole of the debate. In the 1860s the more sophisticated variety of cultural responses to Darwinism that would dominate the intellectual landscape of the late nineteenth century—and in which William James would become a key voice—was only beginning to take shape; meanwhile, public discourse on Darwinism revolved around a more simplified language that expressed deep feelings for and against Darwinism.[84]

James could not brush off Darwin's ideas so easily. He felt the weight of these issues and controversies as he pursued his vocational choice to become a scientist. Caught between the spiritual science of his father and the most enthusiastic proponents of scientific naturalism, he struggled to find his own way. His early education with his father had at least etched in him a permanent interest in religion, even if he could not abide by the elder James's particular beliefs; yet the seeming certainty and confidence of science also held a lure that briefly tempted him in the 1860s. Sorting through the Darwinian debates firsthand, he personally searched through the forms of accommodations that would become institutionalized in his lifetime. Yet there was something missing from most of the voices for reconciliation: in their eager attempts at compromise, they abandoned the comforting assurance that comes with philosophical certainty. The extremist positions of religious anti-Darwinism and Darwinistic antireligion could at least provide that certainty, even if James could not accept them on other grounds. At the beginning of his scientific education, such philosophical concerns already loomed large.

During the first decade of his adulthood, James set out on a quest for a philosophical outlook that could provide the assurance and coherence that, he had come to believe, only certainty can give. His search took many turns; it led him through a wealth of learning and through the darkest of despairs, and it also produced some big surprises. The major shock of Darwin for James turned out to be the great biologist's method and its implications for science and religion. Because the theory of natural selection was a plausible explanation rather than a proof of the origin of species, James began to doubt the need to expect certainty in either his science or his religion. Here, after all, was a major scientific theory that could not be proved but was persuading a whole generation of scientists. The uncertainty of science was such a radical concept that few regarded Darwinism in such terms, and James himself did not comprehend the implications of the methods of natural selection for years. Such a major step away from the demand for certainty could not come to him suddenly or easily. Darwin's approaches provided a signpost, but William James in the 1860s still had much learning and struggling to do in his journey toward adopting beliefs without certainty.

William James, self-portrait in pencil, ca. 1860s (courtesy of the Houghton Library, Harvard University, and Alexander R. James)

William James, ca. 1866 (courtesy of the Houghton Library, Harvard University, and Alexander R. James)

to us. The radiance of Harry's visit has not faded yet & I come upon gleams of it 3 or 4 times a day in my farings to and fro, but it has never a bit diminished the lustre of far off shining Newport all silver and blue & this heavenly group below

(all being more or less failures, especially the two outside ones). The more so as the above mentioned Harry could in no wise satisfy my cravings to know of the family and friends as he

James family portrait, pen and ink drawing by William James, ca. 1860s
(courtesy of the Houghton Library, Harvard University, and Alexander R. James)

Drawing by William James, ca. 1860 (courtesy of the Houghton Library, Harvard University, and Alexander R. James)

William James of Albany, ca. 1810, artist unknown (courtesy of the Houghton Library, Harvard University, and Alexander R. James)

Henry James, Sr., portrait from his youth (courtesy of the Houghton Library, Harvard University, and Alexander R. James)

Henry James, Sr., and Henry James, Jr., portrait by Mathew Brady, ca. 1855 (courtesy of the Houghton Library, Harvard University, and Alexander R. James)

Mary James, ca. 1850s (courtesy of the Houghton Library, Harvard University)

The Museum of Comparative Zoology, viewed from Divinity Avenue, as it appeared from 1859 to 1872 (courtesy of the Harvard University Archives)

Charles Darwin, ca. 1850s (courtesy of the Archives of the Library of the Gray Herbarium, Harvard University)

Louis Agassiz, late in life, portrait by A. Tonrel, Boston (courtesy of Hunt Institute for Botanical Documentation, Carnegie Mellon University)

Asa Gray, 1865 (courtesy of the Archives of the Library of the Gray Herbarium, Harvard University)

Jeffries Wyman (from *Popular Science Monthly* 6 [January 1875]; photograph by Christine A. Carlson)

Charles Sanders Peirce, from the Harvard Class Album of 1859
(courtesy of the Houghton Library, Harvard University)

Charles Sanders Peirce, 1875 (courtesy of the Houghton Library, Harvard University)

Chauncey Wright, from the Harvard Class Album of 1852
(courtesy of the Harvard University Archives)

CHAPTER 5

Darwinian Debates

I have just finished your Japan memoir, and I must thank you for the extreme interest with which I have read it. It seems to me a most curious case of distribution; and how very well you argue, and put the case from analogy on the high probability of single centres of creation. That great man Agassiz, when he comes to reason, seems to me as great in taking a wrong view as he is great in observing and classifying.

CHARLES DARWIN TO ASA GRAY, 1860

For William James, the Lawrence Scientific School at Harvard University was a natural choice. The elder Henry James had often mentioned his interest in moving to Boston or Cambridge because of its intellectual culture, especially the idealism of many thinkers associated with Harvard. Under his father's wing, young James had been developing an aptitude for science, but at the Lawrence Scientific School he received his first intensive education in both its professional practice and its philosophical implications. Here he circulated with some of the most prominent scientific thinkers and practitioners as they shaped the nation's opinions on the evolving relationship between science and religion. Like any good student, James did not follow instructions exactly; however, his teachers did establish the general framework of his education as they themselves debated scientific theories and their cultural consequences. Also like a good student, James came to embrace certain aspects of his education even as he reshaped and rejected others. His classes, his teachers, and their books provided James a stage on which to enact his interests in science and to muse about its implications. His years of scientific study in Cambridge marked his introduction to the swirling intellectual currents that would sweep his mind far away from the idealistic and religious certainties of his father's household.

Louis Agassiz: Popular Science and Resistance to Darwinism

The controversy over Darwin's recently published *Origin of Species* (1859) dominated the scientific community in Cambridge, Massachusetts, as William James entered Harvard's Lawrence Scientific School in September 1861. Although the theory of natural selection immediately gained some strong advocates on the faculty and in the community, Darwin's ideas did not earn unanimous approval in the early 1860s. The most commanding scientific presence at the school and in the whole United States at that time was the staunch anti-Darwinian and eloquent spokesman for the immutability of species, Louis Agassiz. The popular scientist based his position on an impressive combination of encyclopedic knowledge of natural history and an idealistic scientific system that found God's plan in every single fact of nature.

When father and son contemplated William's attendance at the Lawrence Scientific School, Agassiz's presence at the school reassured Henry James that his son's education in science would continue to confirm his education in religion. It did not hurt that the school, for all its bold claims to professional science, still stipulated that students "are expected statedly to attend religious worship, at such place as their parents or guardians may direct."[1] The unorthodox elder James may have chafed at the churchly and moralistic overtones of this requirement, but at least it assumed a religious orientation among practicing scientists, and it delivered the mandate with an air of tolerance and free choice. Moreover, with Henry James, Jr., enrolled in Harvard Law School and younger brothers Wilkinson and Robertson attending Franklin Sanborn's school in neighboring Concord, the dedicated father would be in closer contact with his Boston friends, especially Ralph Waldo Emerson and other members of the Saturday Club.

The Saturday Club, a gentlemen's cultural and intellectual club, met at three o'clock in the afternoon on the last Saturday of each month for a multiple-course dinner and conversation. The club grew from the earlier Town and Country Club and was founded in 1855 almost simultaneously with the Atlantic Club, which had virtually identical membership and which led to the founding of the *Atlantic Monthly*. In this exclusively wealthy, white, and male preserve, Boston's intellectual and civic leaders planned many of the region's cultural events and discussed their intellectual commitments. The membership drew from the most influential figures of the Boston area's literary, academic, political, and business culture and included many who would influence William James in the next few years: William Morris Hunt, Louis Agassiz, Charles Eliot, Jeffries Wyman, Oliver Wendell Holmes, Sr., who taught James science and medicine in the 1860s, and Benjamin Peirce, father of Charles Sanders Peirce, who was one of William's closest intellectual friends from his time at the Lawrence Scientific School until the end of his life.

These clubs and others were popular among intellectual elites in the middle of the nineteenth century. They tended to view themselves as daring and radical, although the members rarely challenged fundamental social or intellectual assumptions. The clubs were, however, important agents in the transmission of ideas: theories and outlooks first broached in discussion would then appear in classrooms, books, magazine articles, and speeches thanks to the influential positions of the members. Popular poet and frequent club member C. P. Cranch captures the dual role of the clubs as both dynamic conduits of new ideas and fundamentally conservative social institutions:

> How notions were started, how idols were shattered,
> . . . lists of names . . . would kindle a flame, and others would fan it.
> And how, as we homeward directed our faces,
> The universe still rested firm on its basis.[2]

Although Henry James was not elected to the club until 1863, he was friendly with the founders even in the years before 1855. His wealth as well as his intellect, forceful character, and idealistic leanings gave him access to the members of this elite club, indicating once again how William of Albany helped to shape a lifetime of cultural contacts for the James family. For example, Samuel Gray Ward, a future member of the club, was also Henry James's banker. In 1849 Emerson wrote a letter to Ward that included the gregarious and eccentric philosopher Henry James on a list of "men I should seek" for the future club. Emerson went on to praise James as "an expansive, expanding companion [who] would remove to Boston to attend a good club a single night."[3] The incentive of proximity to his children and fellow club members finally induced the elder James to move his household to Boston in 1864 and become a regular participant in the Saturday Club.

Louis Agassiz was one of the founding members of this distinguished Boston club of savants and scientists. It is doubtful that Henry James would have known much about the Lawrence school or its faculty if he had not known Agassiz through the Saturday Club. As in most of his activities, Agassiz dominated much of the club's affairs. In fact, the club was often called by outsiders "Agassiz's Club." And within the club, as Samuel Ward said with typical reverence, "Agassiz always sat at the head of the table by native right of his huge good-fellowship and intense enjoyment of the scene, his plasticity of mind and sympathy."[4] In his scientific work as in his conversations, Agassiz never inhibited his enthusiasm, which in turn fostered his reputation as a man of natural genius, especially among those with transcendentalist leanings. Oliver Wendell Holmes, Sr., described him as "robust, sanguine, animated, full of talk, boy-like in his laughter." The genial scientist emanated such warmth and enthusiasm that one friend remarked, "One has less need of an overcoat in passing Agassiz's house than by any other in Cambridge." Although he was clearly a world renowned scientist, Agassiz was most comfortable among general intellectuals and social elites. The Saturday Club was one of a number of intellectual groups and salons in the Boston area that he frequented.[5] Moreover, he found close friends and hearty supporters among the leading families of Boston; he sealed his place in Boston society when in 1850 he engaged to marry Elizabeth Carey, the daughter of a wealthy merchant.[6]

A major reason for Agassiz's popularity was the religious basis of his science, which appealed to the idealistic and genteel philosophy of his Boston area friends; in addition, his approach seemed a bulwark against the naturalistic science that was gaining increasing prestige in the middle of the nineteenth century. Fellow idealist Ralph Waldo Emerson said of Agassiz: "He made anatomy popular *by the aid of an idea.*" The Swiss naturalist seemed to fulfill Emerson's hope for science; in his essay, "Nature," Emerson declared: "I cannot greatly honor minuteness in details, so long as there is no hint to explain the relation between things and thoughts; no ray upon the *metaphysics* of conchology, of botany, of the arts, to show the relation of the forms of flowers, shells, [and] animals, to the mind, and build science upon ideas."[7] Agassiz's "idea" was the nonnaturalistic and spiritual one that all of natural history is organized according to divine plan.

Agassiz would often give lectures or perform scientific demonstrations for the club and in his classes. One former student remembers an impressive scene: "I have seen him stand before his class holding in his hand the claw of a crustacean. In his earnestness it seemed to be for him the centre of the creation, and he made us all share his belief. Indeed, he convinced us. . . . He felt the sublimity of what he was contemplating, and we glowed with him from the contagion of his fervour."[8] Agassiz's spiritual inspiration for even the simplest forms of nature enthused his nonscientific intellectual friends, most of whom, like Henry James, firmly believed in the religious qualities of investigations into nature and hoped for confirming evidence. Able and eager to identify almost every living creature and expound on its structure and place in nature, Agassiz also knit together his abundant command of facts with the conviction that "an intellectual unity hold[s] together all the various forms of life as parts of one Creative Conception."[9]

The legendary vigor and enthusiasm of Agassiz were the natural by-products of a life of uninterrupted success, from his birth in Motier, Switzerland, in 1807 to the early 1860s, the peak of his career, when William James met him.[10] For most members of the generation before Darwin, Agassiz was the premier scientist. From his earliest years he maintained a selfless devotion to the study of natural history, a trait that lent an air of heroism to his work and operated like a magnet on students and patrons alike. Everywhere he went as a young man, Agassiz impressed his peers and his professors as a mature and highly motivated student who was destined for success. He studied zoology at the Académie de Lausanne and, after two years, went to the medical school at the Universität Zürich. During Agassiz's studies there, one professor of zoology gave him a key to his private library so he could pursue his education in natural history. Even more remarkably, a wealthy gentleman was so impressed with the charismatic young man after meeting him by chance that he offered to adopt him and assume all costs of his education. The offer was declined, but it was the first of many offers of patronage that seemed to appear magically in support of Agassiz's many ambitious schemes.

From Zurich, Agassiz went to Heidelberg where he studied the works of Goethe, Lorenz Oken, and others of the German *Naturphilosophie* school, an outlook that strongly shaped his idealism, especially his view of the essentialist nature of species.[11] Agassiz defined species as immutable ideal types, each the result of a thought by the creator. The famous German scientist Alexander von Humboldt began to sponsor many of Agassiz's activities because he was convinced that the impressive young Swiss would make major contributions to the study of natural history.[12] Agassiz went to Paris to study with Georges Cuvier shortly before the great French naturalist's death in 1832. Agassiz became wholly convinced of Cuvier's theories, and he based his own ideas about the nature of species on his mentor's analysis of the structure of animals and their organization into four fundamentally distinct groups or "plans."[13] He regarded the organized classification of living things as the product not of human invention but of human finding; the proper classifications are "in truth but translations, into human language, of the thoughts of the Creator."[14] Agassiz exalted Cuvier's work as the key to understanding nature. He even maintained that, since Cuvier had discovered the essential plans of the natural world, his own work was "to investigate, not to discover."[15] Agassiz did not need a passion for overturning old theories (a vice he perceived in Darwin's work) to fire his appetite for investigating nature. The influence of Cuvier, coupled with Agassiz's conviction of the rightness of his views as they were continually reinforced from enthusiastic supporters in Europe and America, laid the groundwork for Agassiz's resistance to Darwin.

The career of Louis Agassiz was meteoric, even from his youth. He published his first book, *Brazilian Fishes*, at the age of twenty-two; and he was appointed professor of natural history at Neuchâtel at the age of twenty-five. In succeeding years, he began what was in effect a "scientific factory" at Neuchâtel with a staff of artists, clerks, engravers, and printers able to put together and publish his many books. In the 1830s and 1840s he reached the peak of his productivity, and he produced his most brilliant insight into the natural world. In 1837 he shocked the scientific world with his theory of the work of glaciers on geological formation and animal and plant life. By closely examining present-day geologic formations, Agassiz noticed that many of the earth's surfaces, even "the sides of mountains, [are] furrowed, scratched, and polished in exactly the same manner as the surfaces over which the glaciers pass at present."[16] From this fact he inferred that in prehistoric times the earth was covered with ice which etched out the essential contours of our present world. In fact, a major motive of his 1865–66 trip to Brazil, which William James joined as a student investigator, was to prove that the ice age was a universal and not a local phenomenon. If he could show evidence of glacial action even in tropical regions, then his theory positing extinctions from glaciers followed by special divine creation would gain standing against Darwin's theory of species development. By the 1860s glacial action versus natural selection was only the latest version of a decades-long contest between catastrophists and uniformitarians.[17]

Agassiz's glacial theory, which gave credence to theories of catastrophism and fixity of species, made him world famous. In a typical example of the Swiss scientist's influence, British scientist Edward Forbes joked to Agassiz in 1841, "You have made all the geologists glacier-mad here, and they are turning Great Britain into an ice house."[18] Agassiz called glaciers "God's great plough," and he believed that they were the agents of divinely inspired catastrophes that periodically interrupted the course of natural history.[19] He boldly asserted that their destructive action explained the extinction of species that are now known only through fossil remains. Accordingly, ancient animals and plants are not the ancestors of present-day life, but the separate and immutable creation of divine power, retaining the original "idea" and exact location of their first creation.[20] God's special creation of particular species periodically fills in gaps in nature created by glacial action and extinction. Agassiz even denied the possibility of variation within species; when others identified varieties or subspecies of recognized species, Agassiz, keeping firm to his outlook, regarded their findings as evidence for wholly separate species. Species never change, and they remain in their "centers of creation," Agassiz announced in unison with religious and scientific orthodoxy, and God acts directly on nature. At the peak of his career in the 1840s, Louis Agassiz was widely respected in popular and professional circles as a great and universal naturalist. Intellectuals such as the elder Henry James cheered his discoveries as evidence of scientific support for religious truth. Before he reached forty years of age, he had achieved his life goal to become "the first naturalist of his time."[21] His reputation was built on his great knowledge, his talent for communicating to the public, and his idealistic philosophy, all of which facilitated a harmonious reconciliation of science with religion.

Having accomplished so much so young, Agassiz was ready for new fields of conquest when the Lowell Institute invited him in the fall of 1846 to give three sets of twelve lectures. The offer was effectively for a few years' worth of work, and the generous pay of the Lowell Institute was three times his salary at Neuchâtel.[22] The extended stay also allowed enough time for Agassiz to become familiar with America and for institute organizer John Amory Lowell and others in Boston to get to know the august Swiss naturalist. The lectures bore shades of technical studies, but also of popular appeal: "The Plan of Creation as Shown in the Animal Kingdom," "Ichthyology," and "Comparative Embryology." They were not inherently crowd-pleasing topics, but Agassiz's style, personality, and religious fervor made the difference. His lectures inspired such great enthusiasm that Lowell, fellow industrialist Abbott Lawrence, and officials of Harvard University collaborated in efforts to keep him in Boston. When in 1848 he accepted an offer to stay as a professor of zoology and geology at the newly created Lawrence Scientific School, it was a position that was created expressly for him.

Agassiz strode onto the stage of American science as quickly as he had mastered the European scene. His life and work in Europe had begun to stagnate because his incessant toil had alienated his ailing wife and his publishing enterprise had recently disbanded due to personality conflicts and shortages of money. But perhaps his strongest motive for moving to America was the lure of the young republic; its newness and vigor appealed to his temperament, and its unexplored territory provided an open field "so full of promise to me." One point of promise was the thought of extending the application of his glacier theory. In fact, he looked for the evidence immediately, on first arriving in Boston: "I sprang on shore and started at a brisk pace for the heights above the landing.... I was met by the familiar signs, the polished surfaces, the furrows and scratches, the line engravings of the glacier ... and I became convinced ... that here also this great agent had been at work."[23] A student of his noted that he came to the United States "in a spirit of adventure and of curiosity; but he *staid* because he loved a country where new things could be built up." As he worked energetically to build up the practice of science in this country, his colleagues both in and out of the profession regarded him as an inspired hero, a slice of European excellence who would be a leaven to American science.[24] Although he had been accepted instantly in Boston society, Agassiz retained his Swiss citizenship for the first fifteen years after his emigration, until in 1861, to show his sympathy with the Union cause in the Civil War, Agassiz took out naturalization papers—an action that further endeared him to his circle of friends. Agassiz had become an instant success in his adopted homeland, as Americans opened their hearts and their coffers. The energetic student of nature responded with countless projects that found financial support as if by the sort of miraculous intervention that he believed lay at the origin of species.[25]

Campus activities were never enough for this scientist with the spirit of an empire builder. In addition to his college classes, Agassiz lectured to numerous popular audiences around the country. He also embarked on an exploration of the Florida reefs on a steamer provided by the Coastal Survey, established professional scientific networks and organizations, and, as a tribute to his new homeland, embarked on a massive multivolume study of American natural history whose large, beautiful folios he entitled *Contributions to the Natural History of the United States*. Because the lavish project would be expensive, he sought subscriptions throughout the world. He estimated a need for 500 subscribers but received 2,500.[26] He found himself supported for life when Abbott Lawrence died in 1854, leaving a provision for the exalted scientist in his will. The philanthropist intended "to show my estimate of the value of Mr. Agassiz's services to the cause of science and my high appreciation of the importance of his influence in every direction in which it has been extended."[27]

Having almost never experienced failure, Agassiz embarked in the late 1850s on one of his most ambitious projects: fund-raising for a large museum of natural history. Within six months he had raised over two hundred and twenty thousand dollars, an unprecedented and astronomical sum for scientific support in this era, especially considering the recent recession of 1857 and the general sense of insecurity that would soon be realized in the Civil War. In the spring of 1861, after just two years of work, the Museum of Comparative Zoology was completed. Exhibiting specimens from around the world, the museum was a citadel of Agassiz's approach to natural history. The omnivorous naturalist expected his institution, with its exhaustive collection of animal specimens, to represent the final strivings for scientific knowledge.[28]

The high public profile that Agassiz maintained from his first arrival in Boston revealed his twin talents for mobilizing people and for communicating his enthusiasm effectively. Yet the public forum was not the only place where he shone. He was also an inspirational teacher with a capacity for distilling his communication skills into his close relationships with his students. This was as true of his conventional classrooms and lectures as it was of his innovations in women's education and the teaching of children, which included the founding with his wife of a school for girls and a coeducational summer school designed to enrich the teaching of science in secondary schools. For all of his broad ambitions, Agassiz never regarded teaching as a chore; in fact, his students universally reported how comfortable he was in the art of instruction. As one student put it, "Teaching was as natural to him as breathing to others."[29] His most important innovation in the classroom was his use of primary materials. Instead of lecturing, Agassiz preferred to give his students specimens or to take them into the field. Many of his former students report that their first assignment was simply to look at a single fish for a few days, observing it in minute detail. Each time the students brought an abundant and "complete" reading of the fish, Agassiz would insist that more could be found; and the students invariably amazed themselves with the new things they would see.[30] Although his theories lost credibility in the generation that came to maturity with the growing authority of Darwinism, students of the great zoologist consistently praised him as a masterful teacher whose enthusiasm and skills left a lasting impact on their careers.[31]

Countless numbers of his peers and students credit him with revolutionizing American scientific education. Although he opposed Agassiz's position on evolution, the publicist Edward Youmans declared, "He denounced our wordy and bookish education as baseless and unreal, and demanded such a change in our system of instruction as shall bring the pupils face to face with nature herself."[32] Furthermore, this learning through experience carried a rigor that would deeply influence American education in general. Former student David Starr Jordan said that "in an important sense the Museum of Comparative Zoology was the first American university. . . . It was here that graduate instruction in science in America began."[33]

In addition to his work in Cambridge at Harvard, Agassiz became a national leader in scientific organizations. He collaborated with Alexander Bache, superintendent of the United States Coast Survey, and Joseph Henry, the first Secretary of the Smithsonian Institution, to encourage the professionalization of science in the United States. Their work included establishment of the American Association for the Advancement of Science and efforts to found a national university.[34] In addition, Agassiz appeared before the U.S. Congress and successfully pleaded, through his "commingled powers of conviction and persuasion," for remission of the tax on alcohol used for scientific purposes. His fellow teachers at the scientific school, in a resolution drafted upon his death in 1873, remained quiet on his Darwinian debates but praised his organizational skill, his zeal for accumulating specimens for the Museum of Comparative Zoology, and his gifted teaching, which would let his "spirit [live on] . . . into a large body of young men"; most important, they wrote, "he possessed in a wonderful degree the power of awakening popular enthusiasm and enlisting public sympathy."[35] Much of his enthusiasm in the classroom and in his institutional organizing came from his confidence that every honest observer of nature would come to the same idealistic conclusions that guided his investigations. This turned out to be more true of people in his own generation than of William James and his peers.

If in the early 1860s Louis Agassiz was famous and successful, he was ill prepared to meet the shock of Darwin and interpret the new theory of species development through natural selection. He was virtually a celebrity with the patronage and friendship of elites and a wide popularity in the public at large; tickets to his lectures were even sold on street corners by newsboys shouting "Professor Agassiz's lecture!" However, his idealistic renderings of mundane natural facts not only made science accessible, but also compromised recent research. For example, the British geologist Charles Lyell offered backhanded praise to Agassiz after one of his lectures: "It was so delightful, . . . [I] could not help all the time wishing it was true."[36]

Despite his popularity—or perhaps because of it—Agassiz had been losing touch with the most recent developments of science ever since his revolutionary development of the glacial theory. His tendency to identify new specimens as new species had increased his reputation early in his career as he claimed to widen human knowledge of the range of species in the animal world. This outlook also coincided with the early-nineteenth-century Baconian drive to identify new natural facts. But later in his career this tendency began to appear absurd as he became inundated with new species. One fellow scientist even joked, "[I] dread he will take me for a new species."[37] Just as the elder Henry James remained committed to his idealistic philosophy, Agassiz seized on his beliefs in species immutability and glacial action as irrefutably true, and he perceived his life task to be fleshing out the truths of these insights. The religious idealism and titanic confidence that served him so well in public often prevented his learning from the scientific community.

Agassiz took an instant dislike to Darwinism and gave many lectures against natural selection, including "Methods of Study in Natural History," a series of Lowell Institute lectures begun in September 1861, which William James attended during his first months at Harvard.[38] These lectures offered an overview of the field interpreted according to Agassiz's "methods by which scientific truth has been reached," methods that were based on his commitment to abundant fact gathering and his idealistic picture of divine Providence. According to his inductive approach, "practice always preceded theory."[39] In a thinly veiled criticism of Darwin, he chided "philosopher-naturalists" who develop theories for their abstract neatness without consulting nature. Agassiz identified himself with the "classifiers and pioneer-naturalists" who "observe without prejudice everything" in nature that they can examine. As he said elsewhere in unison with mid-nineteenth-century scientific orthodoxy, theories should not be founded on hypotheses, but on close observation of nature and comparison of facts.[40] Agassiz never paused to reflect on the philosophical difficulties of the inductive approach and its impossibility of demonstration with certainty; instead, he anxiously awaited "the removal of all doubts" in his scientific investigations.[41] For all of his commitment to induction, Agassiz ironically insisted that science is not merely the massing of facts. The abundant evidence from nature, such as the countless specimens he was stockpiling in the zoological museum, needed to be "fertilized by thought." Because "facts are the words of God," he declared that we need to "recognize the thought that binds them together as a consistent whole."[42] Agassiz found reasons on both inductive and idealistic grounds to object to Darwin's development theory.

The major agenda of the lectures, "Methods of Study in Natural History," was an "earnest protest against the transmutation theory." An irony in this was that much of his abundant research and discovery of a wide variety of new species contributed data in support of development theories.[43] Still, even without mentioning Darwin by name in these lectures, Agassiz made clear his opposition to the theory of natural selection for three reasons. Methodologically, Agassiz argued, the theory was mere speculation, "a phantom" of Darwin's imagination. Although Agassiz recognized the innovation inherent in Darwin's new method, ultimately he sided with more traditional approaches and clung to his own idealism. In addition, echoing the arguments of religious and scientific opponents of Darwin, Agassiz claimed that "this theory is opposed to the processes of Nature, . . . it is contradicted by the facts" of natural history. Finally, because of his spiritual and idealistic orientation, Agassiz also objected to the godless naturalism of Darwin's theory: "I confess that there seems to be a repulsive poverty in this material explanation, that is contradicted by the intellectual grandeur of the universe."[44]

When *The Origin of Species* was first published, Agassiz did not take Darwin's ideas seriously, regarding them as mere folly and their appeal as a passing fad.[45] In part this was due to his social position and his drift away from the mainstream of scientific investigation. Agassiz had allowed his image of himself and of his science to be shaped by the adulations of those who looked to him for confirmation of religious views of nature. These "appreciative laymen" were his literary and social friends, not his fellow scientists. Within a few years, the overwhelming support that Darwinism gained in the scientific community forced Agassiz to pay it serious heed.[46] After scrutinizing Darwin's work, he felt no increased sympathy for the theory of natural selection, and he amassed more and more formidable critiques. Most important, he focused on Darwin's analogy between natural selection and domestic breeding. He argued that while domestic breeds do produce an abundance of variation, they never alter the species, whose boundaries remain absolutely fixed and unaffected by all attempts at alteration. Moreover, the relics of even the oldest nations show no variation of living types; and, drawing on his exploration of the Florida reefs, he noted that "every species . . . that lives upon the present Reef is found in the more ancient ones."[47] Most damning of all to the Darwinian argument, especially in the days before genetics had developed answers to these objections, Agassiz noted that variations always return to the norm that defines the species type. Each individual has its own particular traits, but "no egg was ever known to swerve from the pattern of the parent animal that gave it birth."[48]

Agassiz also took issue with Darwin's work on theoretical grounds. Even if the objections he raised about domestic breeds could be answered, he pointed out that with natural selection, science will have gained no new knowledge but only a fine new theory with hypotheses about nature but no proof. He recognized Darwin's radically new, probabilistic method but dismissed it as poor science. The differences between Agassiz and Darwin represent sharply polarized views of science and of the nature of knowledge. In a striking display of what Thomas Kuhn and other twentieth-century philosophers of science call contrasting and incommensurable paradigms, Agassiz and Darwin used methods and expressed worldviews that rested on starkly different grand theories of nature: evolution through natural selection versus catastrophe through glacial action and God's special creation.[49] Beneath his orthodox tirades against godless naturalism and hypothetical speculation in science, Agassiz's attack on Darwinism was in a very important sense a defense of his own most important theoretical contribution to natural history.

Although Agassiz did not initially take Darwin's ideas seriously, he did not shirk his responsibility as America's most respected scientist to address the challenge of Darwinism. He met William Barton Rogers, a scientist at the Massachusetts Institute of Technology who had become convinced of the plausibility of Darwin's views, for debate at the Boston Society of Natural History in 1860. Nearly every observer agreed that Rogers was far more convincing; Agassiz simply derided this "ingenious but fanciful theory," while the less idealistic, more professional scientist used the anti-Darwinian's own facts and propositions to fit into an evolutionary pattern of explanation.[50] In the coming years, as the evidence and the scientific evaluations turned in Darwin's favor, Agassiz's arguments for creative design without the action of physical forces became discredited, especially when Darwinists found demonstrable physical causes to explain most of Agassiz's cherished principles. By 1862 even almost all of his own students began to rebel against him, in part because his ways of handling the museum struck many as autocratic, but also because he had lost standing in the wake of Darwin's impact.[51] Moreover, in 1864 his legendary titanic energy began to give out as he suffered from ill health.

Agassiz's enthusiasm and talent for communicating to the public once again proved his salvation. In 1864–65, he gave a series of Lowell Institute lectures on glacial action in South America. A wealthy businessman, Nathaniel Thayer, who was himself anxious to prove Darwin wrong, heard Agassiz's passing comment that an investigation of the Amazon River basin would provide ample proof of glacial action and abundant evidence against natural selection. Thayer volunteered funds to sponsor Agassiz on a trip to Brazil, and the promise of such a project rejuvenated the aging scientist. Agassiz was in his element organizing a large expedition, gaining public recognition and support, crusading against a godless theory, and directing investigation of nature according to a style of science that expected certainty from the facts of nature. The elder Holmes even wrote a poem about his venture. "A Farewell to Agassiz" includes the prayer: "Heaven keep him well and hearty, / Both him and all his party!" and he hoped that "when, with loud Te Deum, / He returns to his Museum," he would bring cartloads of specimen, "For all the world to look at!" Agassiz was sure he would disprove Darwin's scientific heresy.[52]

The Thayer Expedition was the work of a scientific elder statesman. He received enthusiastic support in the United States and in Brazil, where Emperor Dom Pedro II welcomed him as an honored guest and gave his investigations every possible help. He did perform valuable investigating in lands and waters that had received little previous scientific investigation, but the trip did not meet its much publicized promise. His work there was widely honored, and his team did some important exploring, but it was not on the cutting edge of science.

When Agassiz planned this trip in 1865, William James was reaching doubts about his scientific education. The young man, uncertain about his own future, seized on the chance to volunteer with the expedition, and his father heartily endorsed the idea.[53] On the trip to Brazil, William James worked with Agassiz at a time when the great scientist was scrambling to find support for the spiritual life of nature. The young scientist gained great respect for his teacher's character and his capacity for work, but he remained unconvinced of his scientific beliefs. James adopted an evolutionary outlook, as did most of his generation and every single one of Agassiz's other students, including his own son Alexander. Although he continued to be revered by intellectuals and admired by students as a great teacher, Louis Agassiz died in 1873 without ever embracing the theory of species development through natural selection. Even when dead, however, Louis Agassiz was not gone. His colossal energy lived on vicariously in his students: he educated and deeply influenced so many who would become prominent scientists in the next generation that his idealistic views became an important ingredient in the evolutionary views of the turn of the century.

Asa Gray: Secular Science and the Plausibility of Darwinism

When Darwin's ideas first became live topics of debate in 1860, the prominent botanist Asa Gray was Agassiz's major opponent on the Harvard faculty. Their disagreement over Darwin split the school, just as it was to divide the James family on the issue of science's relation to religious truths. At the scientific school Darwinism drew a line between two ways of approaching science. Agassiz stood for the older generation of science in harmony with religion, while Gray worked comfortably with naturalistic science, picturing the divine as distant enough from the created world that the practice of science could remain neutral on religious issues. Asa Gray was born a Presbyterian, and he maintained his ancestral faith all his life; he never thought of Darwinism or any science as a challenge to his religious beliefs because to his mind they were largely unrelated issues. Like William James, Gray was sympathetic to religious belief, but not because of its relation to the latest developments of science. Unlike Agassiz and others of the generation before Darwin—including the elder Henry James—both Asa Gray and William James kept their religion and their science in separate spheres. Gray's practice of science in separation from religion was a first step on young James's path away from spiritual science and certainty in religious belief. James would have to look elsewhere for the radical second step that Gray only hinted at: the conclusion that scientific theory and religious belief are parallel in their mutual uncertainty.

Much of the difference between Agassiz and Gray can be accounted for by their different backgrounds and temperaments. Asa Gray was born in 1810 in Sauquoit, a small town in upstate New York. His family was respectably middle class but not very wealthy. Like Agassiz and countless other men of science from middling circumstances in the nineteenth century, Gray went to medical school. He received his medical degree in 1830 from the College of Physicians and Surgeons of the Western District, the medical school associated with Fairfield Academy, where Gray had begun his higher education. While at Fairfield, Gray developed an interest in botany which soon became his keen delight, his avocation, and his ambition. His outstanding plant collections impressed Dr. John Torrey, one of America's leading botanists. Torrey was a pioneer in gathering specimens from the little-studied American landscape, and, working in the decades from 1820 to 1850, he retained the orthodox belief that collections of scientific data readily point to the designing hand of God in the natural world.[54] Torrey's mentorship and his own commitment to the Presbyterian Church helped Gray maintain his religious faith throughout his years of scientific investigation.

Agassiz achieved meteoric success because he was always perceived as a star in his field. Gray's approach was quieter and less flamboyant. He became America's leading botanist through steady, solid achievement. If Agassiz fulfilled the public's ideal image of a scientist, Gray was the premier scientist's scientist. Gray tried the practice of medicine, but soon most of his attention turned to botany. In 1832, when Agassiz was working with Cuvier, Gray taught in a high school in Utica, New York, and then at Hamilton College. Teaching left him some time for his research, which culminated in the well-received textbook *Elements of Botany*. In the early 1830s he started on *The Flora of North America*, a collaborative work with Torrey, who continued to encourage and support Gray's concentrated but nonremunerative botanical interests.[55] In 1836 he became the librarian of the New York Lyceum of Natural History and two years later was hired by the newly established University of Michigan, where he conducted research and gathered equipment and books for their scientific departments. In recognition of Gray's specialized expertise in the field of botany, Harvard University appointed him to the Fisher Professorship of Natural History in 1842. Gray spent the rest of his career at Harvard where he taught classes until the 1870s, directed the Botanical Garden, and took charge of a worldwide collection of plant specimens which became the basis of the herbarium that was named in his honor. While Agassiz was gaining a reputation as a universal naturalist, Gray established his reputation in botany alone. Gray had little of Agassiz's public charisma or political fund-raising ability,[56] nor did he take much interest in Boston's elite society. Late in his life, after Agassiz had died, Gray was invited to join the Saturday Club; by 1874, with Darwinism widely accepted, Gray's religiously based evolutionism was more attractive to Agassiz's old constituency than it had been at any time while the old hero had crusaded against the "transmutation theory."[57]

During the decades from 1830 to 1860, Gray gradually built up an unimpeachable reputation through diligent research and prolific writing. He showed great promise even early in his career, as Torrey noticed when he observed that Gray felt impelled "to make a noise in the world—and he will be continually publishing."[58] Gray's wife described him as "usually on a half run . . . [with] motions [so] quick . . . that he seemed always ready for a spring." In fact, Gray was so involved with his work and became such an authority in his field that he grew "fond of arguing" his scientific positions, but, given his modest temper, he was "no partisan" in his readiness for the give-and-take of discussion.[59] His biographer, A. Hunter Dupree, noted that he had "a way of showing immediately the deep enthusiasm which motivated him."[60] He did, however, show little patience for beginners. Feeling a sense of mission about his work, Gray asked students who were not yet ready to produce professional work to imagine "if you were in the position that I am, with a short life and a long task before you." With his earnest goals, he could grow angry with those who stood in the way of "progress," regarding inferior research as "cart loads of rubbish in [his] path" which took "weeks in digging" through "before [he] could proceed."[61] The botanist's reactions were typical of scientific professionals and specialists from the middle of the nineteenth century. Whereas Agassiz thrived on communicating the fruits of his research to students and those outside the field, Gray often chafed under this task.

Despite his occasional impatience, Gray was generally a thorough and dedicated teacher, one whose great genius was for professional training and close attention to the development of botanical knowledge and skills. One former student called him "the great warm-hearted teacher" who showed such drive and care in the field that either the students would turn away, or the unrivaled botanist would win "the pupil to himself and botany forever." Moreover, he showed "disregard of his own time when a duty to a student was apparent," provided the young person responded to his attention.[62] Whereas Agassiz appealed to a wide audience because of his willingness to connect his work with general, even cosmic questions, Gray confined his attention to his professional specialty. This difference also affected their speaking styles. Gray was awkward before a general audience, but when addressing a group of professionals, he could deliver some of "the best scientific lectures" of any of his American peers.[63] And yet, while his lectern manner could not match Agassiz's charismatic style, Gray did reach a wide popular audience through his writing. Within his specialty, he had an ability to write for a range of readers, from the most serious scientific colleague to the small child curious about plants.[64] Like William James, Asa Gray lived in a time of professional transition toward the separation of the specialist and the popularizer; even as James in the 1870s and 1880s would encourage professional rigor in psychology and as Gray led the movement within botany toward its professionalization, each also served as his own best popularizer.[65]

From the time of his earliest publications, Gray was instrumental in shifting the field of American botany from the collection of plant specimens to systematic scientific study. The traditional approaches suited the orthodox Linnaean system of classification, the uncharted, frontier character of the new republic, and the Baconian approaches that dominated American science before 1860. Gray gained respect for his close and careful attention to facts, but he was also a leader in the trend toward the use of the "natural system," which involved the grouping and analysis of plants according to their structures and their relationship with other species. This combination of wide-ranging knowledge and interpretive innovations catapulted him to undisputed leadership of the study of botany in the United States by the late 1840s. His scientific peers declared him "without rival" and indicated that "the systematic botany of our country owes nearly everything to Dr. Gray."[66]

Gray's prominence in his specialty made him not only a leader in botany but also an authority on science in general. This gradually emerging social role became most important in the 1860s when Darwinism made science a publicly controversial topic. The public was not aware that even before his explicit adoption of Darwinian perspectives, Gray's own rigorous fact gathering was leading him to interpretations that suggested species development through natural selection years before Darwin published on the topic. His most important observation came in 1840 when he noticed, while reviewing a book on Japanese plants, that they bore a striking resemblance to those in the eastern United States which he had been studying intensively for years. He wrote an essay about the parallels in 1846.[67] Remarkably, almost forty genera of plants could be found in both of these two far-flung locations, but not in between. Conventional wisdom, most forcefully articulated by Louis Agassiz, answered the puzzle by maintaining the separate and special creation of each species in each location. Gray was doubtful, and Charles Darwin found in his observations some possible support for his emerging theory of species development. He wrote to Gray in 1856 urging him to explore the topic further, and the American scientist responded eagerly.[68] While presenting papers at the Cambridge Scientific Club and the American Academy of Arts and Sciences in the winter of 1858–59, Gray used some of Agassiz's own theories against him. The botanist argued that during prehistoric times, similar plant species inhabited the territory from eastern Asia to eastern North America, but, during the succeeding ice age, glaciers cut through this vast region, killing many plants that could not adapt to the climate changes and therefore breaking up the contiguous spread of species. Evidence of remarkable similarity between plant species in North Carolina and Japan did not suggest the intervention of special divine creation, Gray maintained, but only the natural operation of geological processes and the steady adaptation of species to their environment.[69]

Soon after initiating correspondence with Gray, Darwin found the botanist's research so valuable that in 1857 the cautious theorist of natural selection let Gray into the small circle of colleagues to whom he confided his ideas of species development. Implicitly admitting the nontraditional probabilistic element of his theorizing, and also simply hoping to generate facts in its support, Darwin urged him to study the statistics of species distribution and the boundaries between varieties and species.[70] The correspondence helped to focus Gray's research and galvanize issues with which he had been concerned for years; along with Darwin, Gray progressed toward probabilistic interpretations. He traced variations within species and defined the word in less certain, more changeable terms than advocates of the permanent fixity of species would allow; both scientists were groping toward a definition of species as the statistical average within a range of variations among a group of animals or plants. In "The Statistics of the Flora of the Northern United States," Gray compiled long charts to present probability patterns in the distribution of plants.[71] By the late 1850s Gray peppered his writings with references to facts and ideas that strongly supported and reinforced Darwin's theory of natural selection. In 1855 he noted that "generally well-marked forms in nature are connected by certain occasional individuals of intermediate character." In 1856 he admitted the difficulty of drawing boundaries around species, thus indicating their variability and the "personal equation" in each scientist's determination. In 1860 he maintained that the cultivation of animals and plants pointed to "the essential variability of species" and, in keeping with Darwin's analogy between domestic and natural selection, "the same cause operat[es] in free as in controlled nature."[72] Darwin appreciated Gray's support, and he respected the botanist's work so much that in the same year he said, "No one other person understands me so thoroughly as Asa Gray. If ever I doubt what I mean myself, I think I shall ask him!"[73]

While Agassiz was active on the public stage advocating positions antagonistic to evolutionary science, Gray worked within scientific circles assembling evidence that chipped away at orthodox views of species fixity. Beyond his popular botany texts, he gained little general attention until Darwin's *Origin* projected the species question and America's botanical expert on species change into public prominence. Whereas his professional expertise had actually obscured his work from public view, now it became a valuable point of authority in dealing with a vexing popular question. Gray's response was at once sensitive to religion and unyielding in his commitment to the scientific method. Even before reading the *Origin*, Gray noted that Darwin's researches lay "within the domain of cause and effect" and that they were sure to "bear a prominent part in future investigations into the distribution and probable origin of species." Gray had so internalized both a humble approach to scientific research and the uncertainties sown into his statistical investigations that he expressed even his growing commitment to Darwinism in probabilistic terms. By contrast, Agassiz presented his "theory of separate and local creation" as an "ideal" with such unquestioned certainty that his approach "would remove the whole question out of the field of inductive science."[74] Like young William James, Gray found Agassiz's prodigious work impressive but his idealistic certainties ultimately unscientific.

Although he remained committed to Darwinism, Gray persistently defended natural selection on the basis of its congruence with scientific research "rather than as a speculation." He maintained, with veiled reference to his criticism of Robert Chambers's evolutionary theories in the 1840s, that "Philosophizers on evolution have not been rare; but Darwin was not one of them. He was a scientific investigator."[75] Gray regarded professional expertise as crucial to scientific theorizing, and while Darwin surely met the test, interlopers in science often failed. For example, Gray criticized John Ruskin's commentary on flowers because, in the name of aesthetics, it "parade[s]" a "want of sufficient knowledge . . . as a recommendation."[76] Speaking for a growing core of scientific professionals, he warned those outside of science to show respect for the experts. By the 1860s, with the increasing prestige of Darwinism, Gray and his peers could be assured of the public's growing deference to their authority—and they would be greeted with alarm by idealistic critics of naturalistic science such as the elder Henry James.

For Gray, the authority behind Darwin's theory, and therefore the power in any good scientific theory, lay not with its capacity to prove and its assemblage of data, but with its probabilistic methods and its ability to explain facts. Even after he read *The Origin of Species* and became an avid supporter of its theories, Gray maintained that natural selection had not yet been demonstrated, and he looked at his own research as "slender . . . thread[s]," which together with other bits of evidence "bind us firmly to the doctrine of the derivation of species."[77] He did not think that he and Darwin had been reading a theory artificially into nature as many critics charged, but rather that the facts of nature had forced observations about species derivation upon the naturalists. In fact, Gray maintained that "he had never accepted the Darwinian theory of the origin of species as anything more than a legitimate hypothesis."[78] Darwin's theory may not have been proven or even provable, but it did offer "plausibility, and even no small probability." In the history of species, with its immense spans of time and minutely subtle changes, "proofs, in the proper sense of the term, are not to be had. We are beyond the region of demonstration, and have only probabilities to consider." Gray did not find this a reason to despair, nor did he follow Agassiz's method of putting into God's hands that which we can not understand; instead, he supported natural selection because it served "to connect and harmonize [facts] into one probable and consistent whole." Gray believed in Darwinism because of his scientific passion to explain the unknown, and he regarded this probabilistic explanation as the best, most persuasive theory available on the question of species change.[79]

Despite Gray's enthusiastic public and professional support for Darwinism, he recognized its limits. The theory of natural selection presented a highly probable picture of patterns of change, without saying, to any great extent, *how* species change. This searching question represented a serious technical gap in nineteenth-century science: neither Darwin nor any other recognized scientist could provide a mechanism for variation. Although Gregor Mendel made his genetic researches during the years of initial Darwinian controversy, his theories went undiscovered and unlinked to the Darwinian system until the development of the science of genetics in the twentieth century. Gray, like most naturalists of his time, observed from the sidelines this mystery of regular inheritance of traits with occasional, random variation. He recognized Darwin's lack of explanation on this issue, but he could not fault him, because, he noted, "Why offspring should be like parent is more than any one can explain," and yet he added that in cases significant for Darwin's theory, some animals and plants emerge with "striking difference ... in a notable degree."[80]

Gray maintained a more thorough criticism of Darwin's position on the forces that motivate the operation of natural selection in nature. Gray, along with most scientists of his generation, found the analogy between selection of domestic breeds and selection in nature a brilliantly persuasive argument, but it left a glaring implication unaddressed: domestic selection has the farmer or breeder to direct the course of change, but nature has no equivalent, except the impersonal struggle to adapt to the environment. While Darwin was satisfied to give this much directing force to undirected nature, the American botanist believed that this outlook involved "too much personification" of nature. That nature could itself take on the purposeful direction that species development seemed to involve struck Gray as "too fanciful."[81] Darwin was content to keep his account of species development wholly naturalistic, referring only to forces in nature to explain the operations of nature. Gray agreed that natural forces, such as natural selection, explain how nature operates, but to understand what animates those forces, Gray argued that "something more than natural selection is requisite to account for the orderly production and succession of species."[82]

Gray's disagreement with Darwin on this point paralleled differences among supporters of probabilistic explanations for generations to come: some pointed to the connection between probabilities and chance-filled uncertainty, while others emphasized lawful patterns in the midst of chance. In the next few decades, William James would take up the argument for chance and uncertainty, while his friend and intellectual sparring partner Charles Sanders Peirce would become an advocate for the emergence of orderly probabilistic laws in a chance-filled universe. From his first encounter with the theory of natural selection, Gray disagreed sharply with Darwin's assumption that variations in nature emerge by chance and that evolution follows no certain direction. He asked, "How, then, can we suppose Chance to be the author of a system in which everything is as regular as clockwork?"[83] Gray looked for another author of the probabilistic laws of natural selection: there must be a "Divinity that shapes these ends" and that animates and directs the process of species development. In fact, Gray argued, using some of Darwin's own ways of thinking against him, "If . . . [Darwin] means a series of events which succeed each other irrespective of a continued directing intelligence, . . . then he has . . . accumulated improbabilities beyond belief."[84]

Gray admired Darwin's naturalistic approach but rejected the atheistic uses that many scientists were making of Darwinian theory. "Natural Selection," Gray asserted in a favorite motto, was "not inconsistent with Natural Theology." Gray interpreted Darwin's idea of chance variations as examples of uncertainty in nature's secondary causes, but he believed that they still ultimately depend on an absolutely certain first cause, namely God's providential design. Darwin's theory "leaves the doctrines of final causes . . . and special design just where they were." Gray explained his concurrent belief in God and naturalistic science with a vivid image: "Natural selection is not the wind which propels the vessel, but the rudder which . . . shapes the course."[85]

As a Christian Darwinist, Gray still believed in God as the origin of life, even if Darwin could explain the origin of species. This position usually placed Gray in between antagonists in the Darwin debate. For example, he tried to placate Harvard philosopher Francis Bowen, who regarded Darwinism as unscientific and irreligious, saying, "No thoughtful theistic philosopher, and least of all, Professor Bowen, could be justified in charging that a theory of the diversification of species through variation and natural selection was incompatible with final causes or purpose." Similarly, in a vigorous exchange of letters, Gray took on British scientist George Romanes for his casual dismissal of design arguments from the probabilities of Darwinism. He called Romanes an "anti-theologian" who "discards the factor of intelligence" and "assumes that everything natural is physical." Steering between religious and secular science, Gray argued that the emergence of a new species involves the same combination of physical secondary cause and ultimate divine power as does the birth of a child to human parents. In each case, worldly creatures are the instruments of divine action: "God . . . can make all things make themselves."[86]

Despite his close association with Darwin, Gray maintained a belief in the design arguments of William Paley, but with some modifications. Gray challenged his atheistic critics to ask, "What is to hinder Mr. Darwin from giving Paley's argument a further *a-fortiori* extension?"[87] In his classic proof for the existence of God, the English church leader and natural theologian observed the manifestly intricate designs of the natural world and concluded that "there cannot be design without a designer; contrivance without a contriver."[88] But whereas Paley thought of the universe on the model of a machine, Gray viewed it as an organism.[89] This vitalism was not derived from idealism or transcendentalism; rather it allowed him to view natural selection as a system animated by "beneficent variations" that were part of the grand divine design. Gray also retained Paley's argument about God's original creative role and his implication that natural laws are the means of continued divine action: "The whole system of Nature . . . received at its first formation the impress of the will of its Author, [who] fore[saw] the varied yet necessary laws of its action throughout the whole of its existence."[90] To Gray, evolution was only the most recently discovered of all the natural laws that God had implemented at creation. Divine action in the world, he argued, was not restricted to extravagant miracles.

Many Christian apologists of Darwinism, such as James Woodrow and George Frederick Wright, adopted Gray's ideas because they sought to keep their religion separate from or above specific scientific practice; they argued that Darwin's theory, or any scientific theory, could not discredit religion, because God created all natural processes, whose workings science would gradually uncover. In short, as Woodrow put it tersely, evolution was simply "God's plan of creation."[91] From Gray's point of view, Darwin had denied the immanence of God in the daily workings of nature, not the designing role of the Creator at the beginning of time. Darwinism neither denied atheism nor required it; rather it merely permitted a theistic view of nature. God's distant role in nature left theology beyond the reach of empirical investigation and science unaffected by religion.

While many of his contemporaries, including Agassiz and the elder Henry James, disliked this separation of the two realms and the lack of definite scientific support for religious belief, Asa Gray felt no difficulty in keeping his scientific investigations and his Christian faith in nearly separate spheres. In fact, the working scientist argued that religion is irrelevant to the practice of science, which in turn should be neutral on issues of religious belief. "Since natural selection deals only with secondary or natural causes," Gray explained, "the scientific terms of a theory of derivation of species—no less than of a theory of dynamics—must needs be the same to the theist as to the atheist." Yet Gray realized that Darwinism would be condemned as atheistic. Although he found this argument untenable, he admitted that "the theory in itself is perfectly compatible with an atheistic view of the universe [which is also] equally true of physical theories generally."[92] Gray was tolerant of religious beliefs different from his own and, in fact, relished the diversity of perspectives that would be generated by his neutral position on the relation between science and religion.

On the separation of religion from science, Gray was strongly influenced by Chauncey Wright, who was also a close friend of young William James. Wright advocated the philosophical position of "the neutrality of science" while Gray actually practiced it. The two complemented each other: Wright was a younger man with a theoretical interest in the methodology of science, while Gray was an established and knowledgeable scientist attempting to assimilate a new scientific theory. Although their personal views on religion differed greatly, Wright influenced Gray's formulation of his doctrine of the neutrality of science, while Gray served Wright as his model of the scientific, empirical investigator. They maintained different religious ideas with equal neutrality: Gray was an orthodox Presbyterian, while Wright was an agnostic humanist.[93] Especially through his friendship with Wright, William James as a young student of science at Harvard became a junior spectator of the great conflict between Gray and Agassiz. Despite his father's intentions, William James gravitated toward the neutrality of science as a starting point for his resolution of the conflict he perceived between religion and naturalistic science.

In the Harvard of the 1860s, Agassiz and Gray set the tone for scientific debate over the scientific merits and moral implications of Darwinism—and with their many publications and wide prominence, they were important national leaders as well. While the two great Harvard scientists held center stage and the theory of natural selection was the central drama, William James remained mostly in the audience, but he was an active spectator. While the titans clashed, James had more personal contact with his teachers: in chemistry, Charles Eliot; in anatomy, Jeffries Wyman; and in medicine, Oliver Wendell Holmes, Sr. He watched the Darwinian debates with keen interest, he weighed the merits of each side, and he began the process of formulating his own interpretations of the issues.

Charles Eliot, Jeffries Wyman, and Oliver Wendell Holmes, Sr.: Professional Science and Empirical Method

When William James took up his studies at the Lawrence Scientific School in September of 1861, he signed on as a student of the chemist Charles W. Eliot. Eliot is now better known as an educator than as a chemist because in 1869, at the tender age of thirty-five, he became Harvard's president and served as the university's astute and entrepreneurial leader for forty years and as a national advocate for the social purpose and utility of higher education for the rest of his long life. In the early 1860s, however, Eliot was a young chemist filled with enthusiasm for the ability of science to displace less rigorous forms of thinking. For example, in reviewing a work by John Herschel, he was relieved that it was "free from the flippant semi-religious sentimentalism which mars so many of the popular books on such subjects."[94] Perhaps because of his youth, his scientific interests, and his professional ambitions, Eliot was quickly persuaded by the theory of natural selection and readily used naturalistic perspectives in his work, but he was not a major participant in the great theoretical debates. Eliot was a more practically oriented thinker, and where he saw intellectual debate, his mind turned to the institutional implications of those controversies.

During the 1862–63 academic year, he served as acting dean of the Lawrence School, and in faculty debates he consistently sided with Gray on policy questions and on plans to revise the structure of the school to reflect changes in the professionalization of science.[95] To Eliot, the new sciences represented a new form of social authority, which he felt very comfortable wielding. For example, in 1865, while he was still teaching, he turned down a chance for a much higher paying job at the Lowell cotton mills. Within a few years, when he became president, he would apply his business skills and the science and administrative goals he learned at the scientific school to transform Harvard as a whole. He guided the university's metamorphosis from a small college to a major university and research institution.[96] One of his most important accomplishments was elevating the sciences to a crucial place in the university curriculum.

These institutional changes well suited the president whose first professional commitment was to the laboratory study and teaching of chemistry; the changes also reflected the growing importance of the sciences in turn-of-the-century America. As the citadel of research and the seat of learning, universities were on the cutting edge of the growing authority of science. Eliot's leading role in the maturation both of universities and of scientific power and prestige began with his own training and teaching in his professional specialty. He dedicated himself to the study of inorganic materials from his first years of undergraduate study at Harvard, which he entered at age fifteen in 1849. He resolved to become a man of science despite the taunts of his peers who invariably asked, "What *are* you studying chemistry for?"[97] This was a natural if impertinent question because until the middle of the nineteenth century, the study of science was largely an affair of amateurs who explored science in addition to their regular line of work, or who were independently wealthy and worked full-time on science.[98] Eliot was among a young generation who trained to become professional scientists and make science their careers.

This professionalization in the field encouraged its intellectual removal from its earlier position in harmony with religion. Eliot had no zeal for his own religious beliefs; as he once said, "I did not find in the Unitarian faith inspiration and strength. I was born into it, and brought up in it; . . . I am emphatically a birthright Unitarian." Eliot did not pay much attention to these abstractions. His public declarations, especially once he became university president, made nods to the traditional perspective, as he declared: "The man who daily labors in . . . the temple built by God . . . must sometimes lift his thought to Him who dwelleth therein." But most of the time, however, he acted with scientific purpose "to extend the boundaries of knowledge and to win new power over nature." Although Gray had a greater commitment to religion, Eliot shared with the botanist a specialized professional training and an eagerness to approach science in neutral separation from their religious beliefs.[99]

As teachers, Agassiz and Gray were older, more august and distant figures than Eliot. And, in their relationship to James, fellow students Chauncey Wright and Charles Peirce functioned more as philosophers of science who dedicated their efforts to sophisticated epistemologies of scientific knowledge and the nature of scientific theories. By contrast, James knew Eliot exclusively as a working scientist. In 1866 Eliot and Frank H. Storer[100] coauthored a textbook entitled *A Manual of Inorganic Chemistry, arranged to facilitate the Experimental Demonstration of the Facts and Principles of the Science*. The text includes thirty-five chapters analyzing the chemical properties of elements and compounds, along with instructions for student experimentation and demonstration of the facts and principles presented. An appendix on "chemical manipulation" explains the equipment and techniques to the student experimenter. The text was suited to classes like the ones James took with Eliot in 1861–62, and the teacher based his writing on this and other classroom experiences. These classes first introduced James into the world of professional science through Eliot's empirical, skeptical, nonreflective, and rigorous approach to science.

James found chemistry and Eliot's approach singularly unappealing. Eliot remembers James in his classes: "James was a very interesting and agreeable pupil, but was not wholly devoted to the study of Chemistry. . . . His excursions into other sciences and realms of thought were not infrequent; his mind was excursive, and he liked experimenting, particularly novel experimenting. . . . I received a distinct impression that he possessed unusual mental powers, remarkable spirituality, and a great personal charm."[101] James found the rigorous study of a basic science boring and frustrating because it conflicted with his philosophical inquisitiveness and the personal and religious sensibilities that he had acquired from his education by his father.

Eliot did not inspire James to become a chemist, but he did leave the younger man with an image of the intellectual character of a new generation of scientists. Eliot was not a person to reflect on the philosophical assumptions of his work, but his zeal for scrupulous laboratory work did ground his scientific thought in an implicit naturalism. In his text, he cautions his students that

> generalizations from observed facts, so long as they are uncertain and incomplete, are called hypotheses and theories; when tolerably complete and reasonably certain they are called laws. The attention of the student should be constantly directed to the keen discrimination between *facts* and the *speculation* founded upon those facts—between the actual evidence of our trained senses, brought intelligently to bear upon chemical phenomena, and the reasonings and abstract conclusions based upon this evidence—between, in short, that which we may know, and that which we may believe.[102]

To James, Eliot was a living example of the approach to science that sought to confirm truth and knowledge through empirical research.

James's chemistry teacher may even have contributed to his temporary attraction to the scientific quest for certainty exhibited in the work of Herbert Spencer and Ludwig Büchner; but at least these scientific popularizers grappled with large, cosmic, even religious issues, if only to reject, as James said during his materialistic phase in the early 1860s, "the notion of a supernatural finger interposing in Nature."[103] By contrast, Eliot was a technical scientist and an unreflective materialist, and so James soon became uneasy in Eliot's classrooms.

In addition to his disagreements with his teacher on the approach to science, James experienced a dislike for him on personal grounds. James held on to these negative feelings for his chemistry teacher even when he was appointed university president; he groused that Eliot's "great personal defects, tactlessness, meddlesomeness, and disposition to cherish petty grudges seem pretty universally acknowledged; but his ideas seem good and his economic powers first-rate."[104] Already in his youth, James was beginning to associate the imperialism of materialistic science with the personal aggressiveness and arrogance he saw in Eliot. Through this period, James was drawn to scientific perspectives but repelled by scientific practice, and even his sharp critique of religion shows the persistence of his interest in issues of belief, which Eliot's bluntly confident certainty in science could not satisfy.

In September 1863, after three semesters of chemistry with Eliot and one semester off, James shifted to the study of comparative anatomy with Jeffries Wyman. Wyman was himself a graduate of Harvard College in 1833 and of its medical school in 1837. He worked the following few years as a demonstrator in anatomy at Harvard, and then as curator of the Lowell Institute. After spending the year 1841 studying in Europe, he taught anatomy and physiology at Hampton-Sidney College in Richmond, Virginia, from 1843 to 1847. From 1843 he was a fellow of the American Academy of Arts and Sciences. In 1847, upon the retirement of the incumbent Hersey Professor at Harvard University, the appointment was split between Oliver Wendell Holmes, Sr., at the Medical School and Wyman at the college, where he taught zoology. Wyman also taught in the Medical School and the Scientific School, and Agassiz chose him to join the faculty of the Museum of Comparative Zoology. He retired from teaching in 1866, when he became curator of the Peabody Museum of archeology and ethnology.[105] It was in Agassiz's museum that James took Wyman's anatomy course in the fall of 1863. Just two weeks after the start of classes, James wrote his sister: "I have a filial feeling toward Wyman already."[106]

James admired Wyman greatly as a teacher; he spoke of him as a model scientist because of his high quality research, his reputation as a leading anatomist, and his unaggressive manner. Gray reported, "He was one of the best lecturers I ever heard, although, and partly because, he was most unpretending. You never thought of the speaker, . . . only of what he was simply telling and showing you."[107] Wyman's disposition was modest and dedicated: if Agassiz was the public hero of Harvard science, Wyman was its private saint. Ironically, James looked up to him because of the "unmagisterial manner" of his "complete and simple devotion to objective truth." Surrounded by scientific giants, the young student of science turned to Wyman for the more basic task of learning science without advocacy or controversy.[108]

Wyman was as devoted to empirical investigation as Eliot, but he leavened his fact gathering with intense intellectual curiosity. By the time James met him, Wyman had completely internalized and come to embody the emerging scientific ideals of "acute observation and wonder," which he readily expressed not only in his teaching, but also in touching letters to his young son.[109] The poet James Russell Lowell even wrote a sonnet about the nobility of Wyman's unassuming, humble, and "self-denying" approach to science: "He wisely taught, because more wise to learn; / He toiled for Science, not to draw men's gaze." Even more than Gray, Wyman gained his reputation from his scientific research addressed to his fellow scientists. Except for a few Lowell Institute lectures, he wrote only short, intensively specialized monographs reporting his research in anatomy and anthropology. He made little effort to popularize his science, but instead wrote for his fellow experts. Like increasing numbers of his peers who gained prestige through their profession without much attention to the public, Wyman was, as Lowell said, "safe from the Many, honored by the Few."[110]

Wyman was president of the Boston Society of Natural History from 1856 to 1870, and he wrote over 100 articles and notes, mostly in the pages of the Boston Society's proceedings. Gray called him "the ablest anatomist this country has yet produced"; Holmes reported that his reputation was so great that "his word would be accepted on a miracle"; and Agassiz pointed to his work as evidence of the progress of American science.[111] Gray went on to say that Wyman had the "happy faculty of clear, terse, and closely relevant exposition." His entries invariably reported careful investigation using rigorous research methods on highly focused topics, and he rarely speculated or generalized from his particular findings. Shaped in part by the Baconian resistance to speculation, which dominated American science through his early and middle career, and in part by his own modesty, Wyman believed that science lived in its mundane experiments and findings; he worked closely on the differential growth of mold in eggs, on the structure of bee cells, on the differences in the human cranium, and countless other specific areas of research. He was himself religious, but he made no effort to reconcile his scientific research with his beliefs. In addition, his topics had little public appeal, and his writing had little drama or charisma, but Wyman believed that this kind of research lay at the heart of science. Moreover, as he was fond of saying, "no single experiment . . . is worth anything"; but with enough honest investigation, real truths of the natural world would readily emerge.[112]

Wyman maintained this view of science even when the debates over Darwinism threw scientific questions into the public arena. He was generally too modest and reticent to get involved in public debates. He did not avoid the controversy; he was simply cautious in passing judgment and ill prepared to express his views with dramatic force or in broadly accessible language. For example, Wyman presented quiet, systematic evidence challenging Agassiz's controversial theory of the separate creation of races. Theoretically, polygenesis, the idea that each race of human beings is actually a separate species, well suited Agassiz's general proposition about the separate creation and specific localization of species as manifestations of distinct ideas in the mind of the creator. Politically, the august naturalist's endorsement of this racist view of human origins was a boon to Josiah Nott and other proslavery advocates, who welcomed scientific reasons for regarding African peoples as subhuman and therefore fit only for subordination and bondage. In this ideologically charged context, Wyman stuck to his empirical scientific investigations. He studied the crania of different races, concluding that "while there is a difference between the human races . . . , it is quite small when compared with the difference between the human races and the apes; . . . [and] the Negro does not make the nearest approach to the latter."[113]

Wyman also avoided the limelight of public debate in the controversy over Darwinism. Just one month after the publication of *The Origin of Species*, a group of scientists and other intellectuals, including Gray, gathered in Wyman's own workroom to discuss Darwin's radical ideas. In the next few years, when Gray, Agassiz, and other prominent scientists leaped to defend or attack Darwinism in reviews, essays, and debates, Wyman took no overt stand. His nonidealistic experimentalism suggested a kinship with Darwinism, but his Baconian hesitancy about speculation indicated a source of disagreement with the theory of natural selection. His research and teaching did not show immediate partisanship for or against the new theory, but his work was animated with a restless curiosity to discover the merits of Darwinism. This is the Jeffries Wyman that William James met in the early 1860s: a calm, inquiring mind in the midst of a storm of vigorous and angry debate. As James was anxious to learn science but was still under the sway of his father's philosophy, Wyman was an appealing presence; and because James had always shown a temperamental taste for seeing both sides of controversial issues— a trait sometimes bordering on indecisiveness—the mediating Wyman became an important intellectual role model, and one in sharp contrast with his impassioned father.

James was not the only one to recognize the merits of Wyman's mediating and inquiring position. Gray said of Wyman, "He was not one of those persons who quickly make up their minds, and announce their opinions, with a confidence inversely proportionate to their knowledge. He could consider long, and hold his judgment in suspense." The ardent defender of natural selection even wrote in a letter to Darwin that Wyman was "the person best prepared to criticize your book of anyone in America," because the meticulous scientist was "as cautious as possible."[114] These words of praise served as an introduction, and soon Darwin made ample use of Wyman's careful research and vast knowledge to test his theory of natural selection. Wyman regarded the theory as an important question for research to answer, and he gradually uncovered relevant information. To the Boston Society of Natural History he reported the remains of a species of horse "somewhat smaller than the horses of the present time"—thus suggesting structural development. Wyman also "gave an account of some irregularities noticeable in the cells of the hive bee." While critics of evolution "have attempted to show that the cells are mathematically exact in their construction," Wyman "found that all the kinds of cells varied." [115]

As Darwin came to value his careful observations, Wyman joined the reclusive British scientist's worldwide pool of sources of information to which he eagerly turned for facts in support of his theory. As part of this process, Wyman sent Darwin his observations on the varying marks on the face of a species of wasp; Darwin wrote back, "I particularly value such cases of variation. . . . Those who believe in [special] creation, will have to say this mark in the animal was thus created." [116] Darwin also gave prominent credit to Wyman's research on beehives. He quotes the American in the fourth edition of *The Origin of Species* (1866): "I hear from Prof. Wyman, who has made numerous careful measurements, that the accuracy of the workmanship of the bee has been greatly exaggerated; so much so, that, as he adds, whatever the typical form of the cell may be, it is rarely, if ever, realised." Wyman's research accorded well with Darwin's ideas that living things adapted for usefulness and that nature is full of change and small variation, rather than that God created the natural world in complete and unchanging perfection. Darwin wrote to Wyman, "This variability of size agrees well with the view which we both I think take of all instincts." [117] Darwin gingerly suggests Wyman's alliance, but wisely speaks of him not as an advocate but as a fellow research scientist, looking at the evidence and drawing tentative conclusions based on a plausible theory, not a proven conviction.

Gray observed that in Wyman's study of bee cells he came to agree with Darwin not at the beginning of his research, but only at the end. The botanist admired Wyman's close attention to facts and his Baconian way of keeping theories out of his investigations until the facts could tell their own stories. Even as his research was leading him to agree with Darwin's theory, Wyman was still no vigorous partisan. He disagreed with Agassiz, but he always had kind and respectful words for him: "Say what we will as to his views [on natural selection]," Wyman noted, "right or wrong, there is no mistake about it, Agassiz was head and shoulders above us." [118] The modest scientist once mused about Agassiz combining forces with Darwin in cooperation rather than in competition: "If Agassiz had brought his vast stores of knowledge in zoology, embryology, and palaeontology, his genius for morphology, and all his quickness of apprehension and fertility in illustration, to the elucidation and support of the doctrine of the progressive development of species, science in our day would have gained much."[119] Much like William James, Wyman had great respect for Agassiz's research and his knowledge, even if not for his idealistic philosophy.

Like many American scientists in the 1860s, as Wyman's research persuaded him of the merits of Darwinism, he came to doubt Agassiz's ideas more and more. Science according to the two major scientific theorists presented a stark choice, as Wyman recognized even in 1859 when he first read the *Origin*. From his workroom, he spoke cautiously, but he framed the issues without blinking: "If Darwin is right, Agassiz is wrong."[120] Unlike most of his peers, however, Wyman did not rush to extreme denunciation or endorsement. Instead, as Gray noted of his position on Darwin and Agassiz, "He states the case between the two general views with perfect impartiality, and the bent of his own mind is barely discernible." It was Wyman's practical approach to science that swayed his mind on the central scientific question of his day: while he could not find absolute certainty in either position, he knew which theory furthered research better. As Gray continued, "In due time he satisfied himself as to which of them was the more probable, or, in any case, the more fertile hypothesis."[121]

By November of 1863, when young James was beginning his studies with him, Wyman wrote to a colleague, Yale University scientist James Dwight Dana, criticizing Agassiz's theory of special creation as one that did not fit in well with the latest research: "Agassiz is often inconsistent with himself in the application of his principles, and his own students cannot make them work."[122] That same year, in a review of the British antievolutionist, Richard Owen, Wyman took his stand: "The practical study of the history of the earth and the changes which it has undergone, of the development of individual animals and plants points in one direction, viz.: to the process of differentiation."[123] Steady research and plausible explanations had persuaded even the cautious Wyman that, in all probability, species evolve through the operation of natural selection. Like Gray before him and James after him, Wyman accepted Darwinism not with the certainty of proof, but as a probable and plausible theory. Because his position was based on his experimental work, his Darwinism is representative of the way the practice of science evolved toward the theory of natural selection.

Wyman's stance on religion may have offered further appeal to the young James, who was sympathetic to religion because of his background but who also could not fully convince himself of religious truth, especially as he saw it promoted and practiced by his father or other vigorous believers. Wyman's colleagues thought of him as a "theist," "a devout man," and "an habitual and reverent attendant upon Christian worship and ministrations." But his friend Charles Eliot Norton knew a deeper, less public side of Wyman's religion. Norton noted that "he was a convinced theist in his earlier life, but in these late years he seemed to me to hold the question of the existence of a God as an open question." Wyman identified the reason why the question was open: "Darwin and his theories." On this subject, Norton observed, "For a moment he lost his usual calmness and with a voice full of emotion he said,— 'This struggle for existence is an awful spectacle,—not one perfect form on earth, every individual from crystal up to man, imperfect, warped, stunted in the fight.'" Wyman went on "to speak of the change that modern science had wrought in religious opinion, and of the fact that questions were now in dispute which we had been brought up to consider out of the reach of discussion."[124] Like William James's father, Wyman was of a generation that found it difficult to believe in either religion or scientific theories without certainty or proof. Exposure to Darwin in the early 1860s had been a training in a new approach to science and religion and in a new form of theory and belief formation for Wyman, young James, and the whole scientific community in Cambridge.

In 1865 James himself withdrew from the debates in Cambridge by traveling with Agassiz to Brazil where, his father hoped, he would "undergo the Professor's personal 'fascination.'" Henry James, Sr., had even more reasons to think the trip would encourage his son's development of a spiritual approach to science. Alonzo Potter, who was the Episcopal bishop of Pennsylvania and a friend of the elder James, accompanied the scientists on his way around South America to California. Potter told young William that he had "read 'Substance and Shadder,'" as James mockingly called his father's recent book, and "though disagreeing with the doctrine, [he] admires the ability displayed and the very fine style." Even on the Atlantic Ocean, James could not escape the Darwinian controversies. For example, Potter "preached a sermon particularly to us 'savans,'" which included one doctrine the father could agree with: he "told us we must try to imitate the simple child-like devotion to truth of our great leader [Agassiz]. We must give up our pet theories of transmutation." James was not persuaded, and even while working with Agassiz he said of him, "his *charlatanerie* is almost as great as his solid worth. . . . He wishes to be too omniscient." Graciously, he added a phrase that was a pale shadow of his father's hopes: "But his personal fascination is very remarkable."[125]

By the time he returned from Brazil in 1866, William James had decided to apply his study of anatomy and physiology to the practical field of medicine. He would still have some contact with Wyman, and his father could not have been more pleased that Oliver Wendell Holmes, Sr., would be his major professor. By the late 1860s Holmes was not only a prominent medical researcher and lecturer but also the well-known alter ego author of the witty and urbane "Breakfast-Table" books and a sought-after poet and speaker at lyceums. Moreover, he had been a member of the Saturday Club since 1857.[126]

The elder Holmes and Henry James did not share the same scientific opinions, but they held each other in mutual admiration and respect. Holmes praised James's vigorous writing style, comparing its vividness to Rembrandt's painting. Upon James's death in 1882, he remembered, "I greatly valued the friendship of Mr. Henry James. There was a sincerity and strong manhood joined to that deep power of reflection which was most attractive to all who were not afraid of his searching intelligence and outspoken honesty." For his part, James paid less attention to the particular features of Holmes's beliefs than to his energy and his breadth of interests outside science; "Holmes," he said in gushing praise, "you are intellectually the most alive man I know." Alice James remembered her father coming home from the Saturday Club exclaiming that "the Doctor . . . was worth all the men in the Club put together."[127] Although William James had already expressed sharp disagreements with his father, his choice for medical training kept the son safely within his father's circle.

If the elder James had examined Holmes's views more thoroughly, he would have found some things to dislike. The literary doctor was passionate for science, especially for the liberating social improvement that would come with medical advancement. So he dedicated his career to upholding "the starry flag of science" in the face of the "obstinate rebel ignorance." Because of his unusual combination of talents, Holmes could serve as a conduit of new, potentially threatening scientific ideas to the literary elite and to the public without compromising his professional credentials. One of Holmes's medical teachers, James Jackson, Sr., wrote to his own son, who was himself a medical student, that James Jackson, Jr., should not be fooled by Holmes's literary talents and witty poems: "Do not mind his apparent frivolity and you will soon find that he is intelligent and well informed. *He has the true zeal.*"[128]

Holmes developed his commitment to science despite his minister father's Calvinism. Abiel Holmes was dismissed by his congregation in a doctrinal squabble, and this experience seared into the son a disgust for the harshness of Calvinism and a conviction of the need for science to offer liberation from irrational dogma. His observations on child rearing resonated with the elder

James's: once a child has been raised with a belief in a stern Calvinist God, "he may . . . overcome these early impressions . . . in after years, but the wretches and strains which his victory has cost him leave him a cripple as compared with a child trained in sound and reasonable beliefs."[129]

Holmes conducted his career of liberation from Calvinism on two fronts: he mocked it in his literary creations, and he taught medical knowledge. Shortly after receiving his medical degree from Harvard in 1836, Holmes produced some pathbreaking clinical research. He investigated the causes of malaria, and, most influentially, he discovered that puerperal fever, which was killing many women and children after childbirth, was actually caught by contagion from the attending physicians. Although he shocked doctors who refused to believe that they themselves could be the cause of such ills, his work was a milestone in the study of the transmission of diseases.[130]

Despite his enthusiasm for medical improvements, Holmes was coy in assessing the general impact of science on religion and philosophy. In an address delivered shortly after William James studied with him, Holmes injected some medical insights into the timely and controversial topic of "Mechanism in Thought and Action." In order to stake out a territory between materialists and spiritualists, he began by pointing out that "the brain must be fed or it cannot work." Referring to the food chain and its ultimate source in energy from the sun, Holmes noted that even the mind's production of literature depends on a materialistic fuel: "Apollo [the god of both literature and the sun] becomes as important in the world of letters as ever." While examining the relation between the material and the spiritual, he invoked the name of Swedenborg as the empirical mystic "whose whole secret I will not pretend to have fully opened, though I have tried with the key of a thinker whom I love and honor," meaning, in all probability, the elder Henry James. Holmes does not show an extensive familiarity with Swedenborg, but he does indicate sympathy for the route out of pure scientific naturalism. In this spirit he mocked Thomas Henry Huxley, whom he regarded as a crude materialist, for "throw[ing] quite as much responsibility on protoplasm as it will bear." Despite his medical training and scientific commitments, Holmes declared, "I reject, therefore, the mechanical doctrine which makes me the slave of outside influences."[131]

He was much more circumspect about Darwinism and barely mentioned the theory of natural selection. He recognized that new theories would upset old beliefs, but he never grew troubled by this.[132] In fact, he reacted with whimsical amazement when other members of his generation crusaded against Darwinism. For example, in 1873 he charged that "Agassiz will not listen to the Darwinian theory" because he "is no longer young." He compared Agassiz to the protagonist in a patronizing and lurid story about "an old Feejee man" who hoped to end his life by having "his brains . . . beaten out . . . by his son." Similarly, Holmes noted with dark humor, "our sons beat out our brains in the same way. They do not walk in our ruts of thought or begin exactly where we left off, but they have a new standpoint of their own." In another context he expressed the same generational theory without dismay: "The old man says, 'Son, I have swallowed and digested the wisdom of the past.' The young man says, 'Sire, I proceed to swallow and digest thee with all thou knowest.'" Holmes even flippantly asked the elder James at one Saturday Club meeting "if he did not find that his sons despised him." The idealistic James scorned the thought, saying he was "not oppressed in that way." To this Holmes responded calmly, "It is only natural that they should, for they stand upon our shoulders."[133] When William James, Oliver Wendell Holmes, Jr., and their friends joined to discuss the impact of the new sciences on philosophy and religion, the elder James could not be so complacent or sympathetic, but the elder Holmes validated their youthful urge to chart new intellectual territory without breaking from their parents' values completely. Holmes understood the double meaning of standing on parents' shoulders: the children both stepped on previous outlooks and built upon them.

William James respected his medical teacher, but for all of Holmes's recognition of generational differences and zeal for science, James found him somewhat resistant to the contributions research science could make to medical practice. The young medical student noticed "a decided impatience with the mass of so-called science which is intruding and encroaching upon medical education in an ever-increasing degree." In his *Introductory Lecture*, Holmes groused that "the amount of baggage which a doctor is now expected to carry in his head is growing too great"; besides, "it must be granted that by far the greater part of the matter recorded in physiological treatises has as yet found no application." Moreover, he continued, "We must not expect too much from 'science' as distinguished from common experience." James called Holmes's train of arguments "absurd," and he held out more hope for the long-term benefits of science, even if "at first sight [they appear as the] most barren and merely curious speculations." Challenging the arguments of his own teacher, James admitted to the confusions of "this period of chaos and transition," but this brash youth preferred further speculations on science and its implications to reliance on traditional clinical practice.[134]

James wrote this critique of Holmes from Germany where he was studying physiological psychology. For all his learning, his career path was still unclear. Even as he engaged in deeper and deeper reflections, on paper and in conversations with his peers, he was deciding to complete his medical degree. He had hopes of having a vocation to fall back on, even though he was developing more theoretical interests. For all his scientific studies in the 1860s, he actually barely met the minimum requirement of three years of medical instruction "with which one can go up for examination [in order to graduate]."[135] He felt unprepared for the examination and even lacked much enthusiasm for the subject of medicine since he had discovered his more scientific and speculative interests.

James had little reason to worry. Before the 1870s, medical education lacked stiff requirements or extensive testing. Harvard was no exception: the candidate for the degree faced nine questioners for ten minutes each in an oral exam, and only five positive votes were required for passing. By tradition, teachers hesitated to fail candidates for fear of losing students, because medical schools were still proprietary institutions with intertwining social and family relations.[136] James counted on this, confiding to his brother, "Dr. Holmes will veto my being plucked no matter how bad my examination may be." True to his prediction, Holmes asked him one tough question, which James answered correctly; then his genial interlocutor said "If you know *that*, you know everything; now tell me about your family and the news at home." James himself found the exam "trifling enough," but being able "to write myself M.D." did not relieve him from his larger intellectual questions about the relation between science and religion.[137]

James's scientific education in the 1860s exposed him to a wide range of facts and theories. And while he learned much aside from Darwinism, the theory of natural selection was at the center of his educational experience. Agassiz believed this naturalistic science and probabilistic style of theorizing to be wholly repulsive; Gray embraced it as a new way to advance science without damaging religion; Eliot thought it the foundation for a new standard of professional scientific authority; Holmes mused on modern scientific changes without worrying much about theory. Wyman's views came closest to James's own: like his beloved teacher, the young science student would investigate and listen to the different positions, and endorse Darwinism without adopting an extreme naturalism. Also like Wyman, James realized that evolutionary theory suggested the uncertainties of religious belief. Charles Eliot Norton observed about Wyman, "His whole talk left upon me strongly the conviction that he held the question of theism,—as he held so many,—open."[138] For James, as for many of the younger generation, this openness would eventually be less shocking.

While James was still a young adult only recently graduated from his father's tutelage, however, Darwin's ideas and their reception at Harvard were full of an initial shock and confusion. Entering this theater of controversy in the 1860s, young William James not only learned science and its methods, he also saw played out vigorously and persuasively a variety of responses to the scientific, methodological, and religious questions raised by Darwinism. He learned much from each of his teachers; they served as models, even if not as partners, in his quest to decide his own outlook. Later in life, he remembered his desultory movement across the sciences and his gravitation toward more theoretical interests: "I originally studied medicine in order to be a physiologist, but I drifted into psychology and philosophy by a sort of fatality."[139] During his years of reading, thinking, and reflecting with anxious uneasiness about the science and religion of his background and education, he turned to his peers for more intimate discussion of the questions about truth and uncertainty that his scientific instructors had raised.

PART III

The Scientific
Persuasion

When James embarked on his formal scientific education in the 1860s, he also entered into a new circle of neighbors and colleagues. In Cambridge he joined a group of young intellectuals who felt themselves "the very topmost cream of Boston society," as he blithely described them, with an itch to "discuss the very tallest and broadest questions" generated by the scientific, religious, and philosophical theories of their day.[1] Of this Cambridge circle, Chauncey Wright, who computed mathematical statistics at the *Nautical Almanac*, and Charles Sanders Peirce, who graduated from the Lawrence Scientific School in 1863, were the recognized intellectual leaders, and they had the greatest impact on James as he assimilated his scientific education and weighed its implications for his religious thinking.

Toward the end of his life, Peirce remembered, "In the sixties I started a little club called the Metaphysical Club. It seldom if ever had more than half a dozen present."[2] The actual existence of an organized club remains an open question, for Peirce was the only one to mention it by name, and even this was only in retrospect.[3] It is clear, however, that there was at least an ongoing discussion group whose membership, however loosely organized, included some of the most prominent young intellectuals in Cambridge. Many of these young men had ties with each other that predated and transcended the "Metaphysical Club" itself and that may have contributed to both its formation and its informality. For example, Peirce "made the acquaintance of Chauncey Wright . . . about 1857," Wright was close to the James family at least as early as 1864, James and Peirce were both at the Lawrence Scientific School as of 1861 and James mentions him familiarly in a notebook of 1862, and all the members wrote letters to each other and about each others' work and visited frequently.[4]

In addition to Peirce, Wright, and James, the membership also included three future lawyers, Nicholas St. John Green, John B. Warner, and Oliver Wendell Holmes, Jr. Green, who later became an instructor at Harvard Law School and a dean at Boston University Law School before his premature death, was especially interested in Jeremy Bentham's utilitarianism and Alexander Bain's theory of belief as "that upon which a man is prepared to act." These ideas were important in the development of James's and Peirce's philosophy of pragmatism in later years; in fact, Peirce noted that "from this definition, pragmatism is scarce more than a corollary."[5] Warner was an occasional participant in discussions. He received his law degree from Harvard in 1873, practiced law until his death in 1923, and never wrote for publication except for assisting Holmes in editing James Kent's *Commentaries on American Law*. Holmes became the most famous member of the group. His father taught William James at Harvard Medical School. The younger Holmes went to Harvard Law School, fought in the Civil War, wrote the landmark legal treatise *The Common Law*, and became a justice of the United States Supreme Court.

Two members of the group became important religious thinkers with scientific interests who dedicated themselves to the accommodation of Darwinism to Christianity. John Fiske wrote many works of popular science, most notably *Outlines of Cosmic Philosophy based on the Doctrine of Evolution* (1874), which is an idealistic view of progress in nature. Francis Ellingwood Abbot wrote the influential *Scientific Theism* (1885) and as a liberal Unitarian minister sought to salvage religious belief from scientific criticism by advocating agnosticism, philosophical realism, and vitalistic organicism.[6]

The club members held a number of traits in common. They were all young men in their twenties and thirties when they met in the 1860s. Each had recently graduated from Harvard and had close connections to the elite culture of the Boston area. But as the young scions and cohorts of intellectual families, they felt simultaneously the tug of traditional religious and moral values and the lure of radically new ideas, especially in science, such as Darwinism, naturalistic empiricism, and probabilistic thinking.

The Metaphysical Club offered companionship for the intellectually inquisitive; even more important, it was a testing ground for assessing the members' theoretical commitments and personal convictions. C. Wright Mills called these young men pioneers of the "relatively free intelligentsia" of the twentieth century who gave rise to the "new intellectual style" of pragmatism, which involved applying scientific methods to philosophical and social questions.[7] Of course, the perspective on the future was less clear from within the club; the members leaned on each other in debating the relation of science to religion, and especially the fate of certainty in each field. While much of William James's course work exposed him to practices of science far removed from his father's outlooks, the crucible of discussions with his peers forced him to question the assumption that scientific investigation can or should confirm religious belief. In fact, spurred by study of Darwin's methods and discussion of them with his friends, James wondered if he could find certainty in either field, and he pondered what belief itself would be like without the assurances of certainty.

As an intellectual and social group, the Metaphysical Club was not unique among cultural elites in nineteenth-century America, especially in New England. The Saturday Club of their parents' and teachers' generation and the Transcendentalist Club of the 1830s were only two of the more famous clubs that dotted the cultural landscape in their social circles.[8] Like members of other clubs, James's circle belonged to a class that relished radical ideas in the life of the mind and sometimes in politics, but who maintained traditional social and moral values. Peirce admitted bluntly: "Uncompromising radical though I be upon some questions, inhabiting all my life in an atmosphere of science, . . . I . . . confess . . . [a] conservative sentimentalism . . . [which] recommends itself to my mind as eminently sane and wholesome." They rarely questioned their inherited social structure, they revered Harvard, they fervently believed in the importance of morality, and while most of them opposed slavery, they often sneered at the mores of ethnic minorities and the working class. Peirce made clear that his sentimentality included a patronizing attitude toward nonwhites and the poor, which he did not hide: "Among inferior races, there is less individuality than in the higher race. Among laboring men there is less true individuality."[9] Despite this haughty elitism, the Metaphysical Club avoided conformity to their culture, in style and in ideas. The organization of their group was self-consciously informal, and they were willing, as Peirce remembered, "to admit any new member from whose membership the Club will profit." And he added facetiously that in the club's "Constitution," there was "no sergeant-at-arms or other official, and no by-laws."[10]

Strict formalities were not the only rules of tradition that the Metaphysical Club shunned. They courted ideas that threatened mid-nineteenth-century scientific, religious, and philosophical orthodoxy. Before these firm beliefs had been established, radicals in the eighteenth century had posited science and human reason as adequate substitutes for the ancient "superstitions" surrounding religion and God.[11] By the early nineteenth century philosophical thinkers were eager to reinvigorate the legitimacy and authority of religion and claim its absolute truth with all the fervor sustained by their genuine fear of Enlightenment doubters. The different schools of thought that competed in the first six decades of the nineteenth century had generated their own disagreements, but implicitly, each group could agree with certainty that scientific investigation would inevitably conform harmoniously with religious belief. It had become an unquestioned assumption that even survived the massive transition in American philosophical orientation from Scottish realism to German idealism over this period.[12] By contrast, the members of the Metaphysical Club came to intellectual maturity in the 1850s and 1860s, when science was rapidly increasing in sophistication. They readily identified with the social position and moral values of their culture, and they imbibed many of their Scottish- and German-inspired philosophies, but they could not agree with their precursors' assumptions about science and religion.

Because of the tension between their position in a privileged class and their membership in a bold new generation, the Metaphysical Club held fast to some aspects of tradition even as they challenged and reshaped it. Their traditional values—especially their fear of a world without them—prevented the club members from rejecting the religious goals of previous generations. Instead, they simply observed that in their day, new developments in science could no longer be piously declared in harmony with religious belief. They took a middle ground between the religious and moral ideals of traditionalists and the rising authority of science, especially as popularized by positivism, that was used by many of their contemporaries as a means to justify an antireligious and materialistic philosophy of life. For example, Peirce declared in 1863 that "materialism fails on the side of incompleteness. Idealism always presents a systematic totality, but it must always have some vagueness and thus lead to error." In place of either pole, he longed for "a far greater faith than ever before."[13] The young members of the Metaphysical Club anxiously wanted to retain traditional religious and especially moral values, but they felt they could only be salvaged by careful attention to new scientific developments and wholesale reconstruction of the relation between science and religion. The central issue of their inquiries was certainty. They saw that neither scientific theory nor religious faith could generate conventional forms of certainty, and they searchingly asked whether there could be any other basis for belief and action. They answered, in varying degrees and with different applications to religion, that scientific method approaches certainty and provides a modern model for belief and basis for action.

The most important new scientific theory that the club members contended with was Charles Darwin's newly published theory of species development through natural selection. Historian Philip Wiener states bluntly that their most urgent question was "how to proceed through the tangle of ideas about evolution." Wright was the first to read *The Origin of Species*, and he served as an enthusiastic conduit of Darwinian ideas to the rest of the group. They were all deeply influenced by Darwinism, and as Peirce noted, "Wright, James, and I were men of science, rather scrutinizing the doctrines of the metaphysicians on their scientific side than regarding them as very momentous spiritually." Mills noted slyly that the pragmatic philosophy that would emerge from the Metaphysical Club had its origin in "intellectual pieties for scientific practice."[14] James's stance in the club, along with his years of scientific education and teaching in the 1860s and 1870s, indicates definitively that this speculative thinker who became famous for his philosophical and religious thought commenced his career as a scientist, identified himself as a scientist, and began his theoretical inquiries in an atmosphere in which science pervaded all intellectual thought and discussion.

Just as the conventional wisdom on Darwin has until recently evaluated natural selection as a science claiming empirical, materialistic certainties and vanquishing obscurantist religious faith, so traditional accounts of the Metaphysical Club's assimilation of Darwinism have portrayed the members as harbingers of positivist antireligious science. Wiener argued that they viewed Darwinism in "the tradition of secularized science"; C. Wright Mills declared that his purpose in studying the club was "to catch the larger secular and professionalizing movement of intellectual affairs." Bruce Kuklick brought recognition of the members' hope of finding a way to reconcile science and religion, but he presented their religious and moral hopes in *contrast* with the amoral views of "Darwinian materialists" who "den[ied] core religious beliefs."[15]

These works predate the recent revolution in Darwin studies, which demonstrates the scientific unorthodoxy of Darwin's probabilistic methods and attributes the materialistic claims of scientific certainty to Darwin's popularizers rather than to Darwin's science itself. This insight suggests that the Metaphysical Club members sought to find metaphysical and moral truths not *despite* their interest in Darwinism and other sciences but rather *through* scientific inquiry. Darwin's plausible but unprovable theory of natural selection, with its probabilistic method of explanation, became a focal point for reconstruction of the place of certainty in science and religion. Wright and Peirce, in different degrees, retained greater respect for the methods of science than James would allow, but in the 1860s and 1870s these three scientists believed in the validity of scientific methods if properly understood, and, specifically, they regarded Darwin's method as their philosophical starting point.

CHAPTER 6

Chauncey Wright and the Aim of Pure Science

The glory of the nineteenth century has been its science. . . . It was my inestimable privilege to have felt as a boy the warmth of the steadily burning enthusiasm of the scientific generation of Darwin, most of the leaders of which at home I knew intimately, and some very well in almost every country of Europe.

CHARLES SANDERS PEIRCE, 1901

Chauncey Wright has had a wraithlike presence in the history of the Metaphysical Club and of pragmatism. He clearly influenced a host of major figures during their young adulthood, including Charles Peirce, Charles Eliot Norton, William James, and his brother Henry; but, because he died too young to become influential in his own right, and because he never held a significant institutional position, he easily slips out of conventional categories. He came closer to living "the life of the mind" and treating "philosophy as a conversation" than most thinkers evaluated with those labels. He was a mathematical prodigy, he read deeply in nineteenth-century philosophy and science, and he loved to discuss for hours on end. Not fitting well into professional occupations or intellectual traditions, he pushed at their boundaries, always using science as his prod. His admiring comment about John Stuart Mill says as much about him as it does about the British philosopher: "He weighed his arguments as dispassionately as if his aim had been pure science."[1] His scientific enthusiasm helped to keep the attention of those around him on Darwinism as he evaluated its methodological innovations, searched for scientific verification of natural selection, and maintained a safe haven for morality separate from the rigors of his own scientific zeal.

Eccentric Insider

Chauncey Wright was born in Northampton, Massachusetts, in 1830 to a Unitarian family of "old New England stock,"[2] as his peers liked to say when describing one of their own. His father was a successful but not very wealthy grocer and deputy sheriff, and some of his other relatives were farmers. The family proudly traced its ancestry in Massachusetts to 1630 and in Northampton to the town's founding in 1654. Wright was raised according to the precepts of his family's liberal faith and was especially influenced by its emphasis on morality and distaste for formality. One of his earliest memories is of his reaction to a teacher who tried to introduce the custom of kneeling at morning prayers: "This I obstinately refused to do," Wright recalled, "or at least obstinately did not do."[3] He enjoyed this memory because it pointed to his radical nonconformity.

In school, especially at Select High School, an experimental institution for promising students, Wright showed an early and strong aptitude for the sciences, especially mathematics. Because his family took little notice of his academic performance, Chauncey left school and began to work for his father, driving an ice cart around town and working in the family store. He surely was not very happy, for as his minister Rufus Ellis recalled, he looked "out of place behind the counter." His intellectual promise, however, did attract the attention of Ann Lyman, a wealthy citizen, "a strong power in the community," and the widow of Judge Joseph Lyman. After her personal letter to Harvard president Edward Everett, his months of preparatory study at Williston Seminary and with Rev. Ellis, and a Harvard College entrance test at which the examiners, with "discerning spirit," overlooked his thin preparation in the classics, Chauncey Wright was admitted to Harvard.[4] These connections with cultural elites not only plucked him from the provinces but also helped to shape his values while ushering him into the Cambridge and Harvard society that would become his world from 1848 until his premature death in 1875. He liked to say that his favorite place to live was simply the "most familiar"; and so, he rarely left town, even for short trips, but when he did, he returned "to Cambridge . . . like a clod to its native earth."[5]

Wright adapted to the culture of the intellectual elites of his new home town with the zeal of a convert. He was a good but not an excellent student, graduating twenty-seventh in a class of eighty-eight. He rarely concentrated on required work, but he read widely even if not very thoroughly. His classmate E. W. Gurney even remembered that he was "utterly averse to reading"; instead, he browsed books for "stimulus and direction to his own thoughts."[6] Another classmate remembered that his "college studies were of wholly secondary importance," but in mathematics, "he would occasionally exhibit an original method of arriving at the same result with [mathematics] Professor [Benjamin] Peirce."[7] His great talent was in mathematics and theoretical physics, and his great passion was discussion. These would remain his twin interests, as he readily acknowledged later in life; when asked, "What is your favorite occupation?" he answered, "Mathematical problems"; but he responded to "what is your favorite amusement?" with recognition of his avocation, "metaphysics."[8]

In his conversations, he amazed his friends with the extent of his memory and understanding—and with his endurance, since he eagerly discussed late into the night. Although shy on first acquaintance, he was well liked on campus and widely respected for his intellectual abilities and social comradeship. He even earned a designation as "the homeliest man" in his class, testimony as much to his chumminess and ease in conversation as to his having "little knowledge, care, and taste in dress" and his being "large in person, . . . without grace, and slow and heavy in movement." Among the young and intellectually inquisitive social elite at Harvard, he was the perfect companion. Their loyalty to him, however, sometimes reflected class differences. Classmate James Bradley Thayer remembers that "his coming was always welcome . . . like the coming of a familiar member of one's family,—nay, rather like that of some pet animal."[9] Wright would probably not have objected to the phrase; he never used the patronage of his "social betters" to improve his social standing. Instead, he remained financially poor but culturally enriched by close—even if at times patronizing—relations with the elite of Cambridge and Harvard.

After graduating from Harvard in 1852, Wright continued to circulate in the same social and intellectual circles to which he had grown accustomed at Harvard, discussing broad theoretical issues and practicing mathematics and physics for both work and pleasure. Although his intellectual intensity set the tone for his social life, his social circles helped to perpetuate his eccentricities: "Exempt from public haunt," as he liked to quote from Shakespeare's *As You Like It*, he lived alone, he never married, and he never worked regular hours. He did, however, become almost a surrogate member of many families. For example, Harvard scholar and *North American Review* editor Charles Eliot Norton reported that Wright was "a frequent visitor at my house," one who became "an easy and familiar friend with all members of the household."[10]

Wright had long conversations and an active correspondence with Norton's daughters Grace, Jane, and Sara; in addition, he "shared in the common domestic interests," which even involved taking care of the children for long stretches. Wright could be a helpful companion and an entertaining guest, and he was particularly fond of children. He would play with them for hours with games, juggling, and even magic tricks. Wright often mingled his childlike intellectual enthusiasms with his fondness for children, as shown by an exchange of letters he had with Sara Norton about a "little animal-plant [insect-eating plant]" she had sent him. He said he had "read about them in Mr. Darwin's book," and provided simple lively explanations of the way they catch flies. He then launched into a gentle and charming description well suited to his audience's interests: "Don't you wish you were a *Drosera rotundifolia*,—such a fine name to have too,—to which a fly is as welcome as a letter, or more so? They only feel, probably, if they feel at all, just as you do when you get nearly or quite asleep, and a fly lights on your nose; only with your arms you would brush it away, instead of folding it in them so fondly as the Drosera seems to do." Almost like a child in his own passions for intellectual issues and discussion, Wright lived his personal life in an "unsexed condition . . . happily domesticated with my friends." In this time of sharply defined gender roles, Wright's eccentric taste for nurturing and playing with children made him seem "almost feminine" to his friends.[11]

Wright's idiosyncrasies never repelled him from his social circle; his political and social views helped to reinforce his sense of belonging because they so readily coincided with those of his Cambridge friends. He enthused over "our Revolutionary politics," in contrast to the "political creeds in Europe," and he hoped Louis Napoleon would "republicanize Europe." The only kinds of "radical change" he supported were those that came through "our very organization." Wright fretted over "the disturbances [of] the socialistic element," but he was, along with most of his social peers, more liberal on the slavery question and women's rights. At a time when even most antislavery people were antiblack, he lived in the house of Mary Walker, "an escaped fugitive slave"; he even quietly did "a little 'contraband' business" by mail in search of Walker's family in North Carolina. Furthermore, he not only supported women's attendance at Harvard lectures, but also wondered why "no woman has been appointed lecturer." Like the traditional elites he socialized with, he worried about massive accumulations of capital, declaring, "I think that the privileges of wealth might and should be curtailed." Yet also like them, he felt that money and social status brought a social obligation—and they permitted the intellectual pursuits he really treasured. Although he was never himself wealthy, he maintained that "wealth and leisure are indispensible requisites to the philosopher's and scholar's pursuits." Like Thoreau, Wright had another kind of wealth: he reduced his needs—and he relied on the support and patronage of his well-to-do friends.[12]

Immediately after graduating from Harvard College, Wright began working as a computer for the *Nautical Almanac*, work that ideally suited him because of his mathematical and scientific talents and because he so disliked routine. Even as a child he jokingly deified "Spontaneity" who kept him from doing things for which he had no inclination.[13] Because of this temperamental trait, Wright especially appreciated a major fringe benefit of his computational employment: it gave him plenty of time for his own intellectual work. The job was simple for him, especially after he invented new, more expeditious ways of computing that allowed him to do this piecemeal work in very little time. In fact, he would generally do all the year's work during the last three months in a "regular machine-like way," thus leaving the rest of his year free for his true vocation as Socratic sage and village philosopher of Cambridge.[14] His colleague at the *Almanac* from 1857, future astronomer and scientific popularizer Simon Newcomb, reports that philosophical questions were daily subjects of discussion.[15] The job provided him with a modest income, enough to answer his simple wants, and the leisure to participate in intellectual discussions such as those he had with Peirce and James in the 1860s and 1870s.

Chauncey Wright's participation in the Metaphysical Club was a natural outgrowth of his social position in Cambridge. Club society became his informal postgraduate training. Shortly after his graduation, he formed with his classmates the "Septem," a club where he read papers that would appear in the *Atlantic Monthly* and the *North American Review*.[16] Charles Eliot Norton had first met Wright in 1857 at "a little club of men of various interests." Wright was also a member of the Shakespeare Club where, one member reported with Victorian flourish, "he excelled us all."[17] He was elected to the American Academy of Arts and Sciences in 1860 and became its recording secretary from 1863 to 1870. By the 1860s he had gained a reputation as an intellectual authority while retaining his youthful enthusiasm for ideas and discussion. He eagerly challenged his friends in debate and grew confident and jaunty in his conversation style, which his friends described as his "serio-comic manner."[18] His former classmate E. L. Gurney marveled, "How like in mental habit was the young fellow of two-and-twenty to the man of two-and-forty." Part of what continually spurred his enthusiasm was his proximity to Harvard, which "furnished an unfailing supply . . . of . . . younger and more thirsty souls."[19]

For all of his analytical skill and powers in conversation, Wright was a poor teacher and lecturer. He had so impressed his friends in conversation that he was twice asked to lecture at Harvard, in 1870 on psychology and in 1874–75 on mathematical physics. The dean of the college, his old friend Gurney, said bluntly that the lectures "were not very successful" because he was too intellectually rigorous: "his heavy artillery was mostly over [the students'] heads." By contrast, when he was not trying to be rigorous, but instead drawing on his domestic sympathies for women and children, he was a better teacher. He taught successfully for a few years at Louis and Elizabeth Agassiz's school for women, and during his care for friends' children he would carefully and patiently explain complicated issues and natural facts. These differences are not only evidence of his separation of professional science from the sentimental and moral realm, but also of his excelling in small groups with face-to-face communication. This, of course, was his perennial attraction to the intense discussions at the clubs.[20]

The Metaphysical Club brought Wright together with an unusually promising crop of young, eager philosophical seekers while he was at the peak of his intellectual powers and energies and provided the type of setting he most enjoyed. Chauncey Wright was the senior member of the group and its intellectual leader, as Peirce noted with grudging modesty: "Wright was the strongest member and probably I was next."[21] Peirce also praised Wright's powers of disputation: "I was about to call him our corypheus; but he will better be described as our boxing-master whom we—I particularly—used to face to be severely pummeled."[22] Wright's empiricism was particularly bracing for his peers; his sharp mind and keen commitment to scientific facts served as a counterbalance to Peirce's idealism and James's religious interests.

The period of his involvement in the Metaphysical Club was also a time of fundamental philosophical questioning and change for Wright. Earlier in his career, Wright's ideas had stayed within the orbit of dominant nineteenth-century philosophies with their orthodox views of science and religion. For instance, he was a devotee of the philosophy of William Hamilton, who sought a compromise between Scottish realism and Neo-Kantian idealism. But his mathematical talents and close observations of the sciences had kept him in closer touch with the professionalization of science than most of his peers. Then, during the early to middle 1860s, about the time he met Peirce and James, Wright's thinking went through a fundamental shift as he became wholly convinced by the empiricism of John Stuart Mill's critical *Examination of the Philosophy of Sir William Hamilton* and the evolutionary naturalism of Charles Darwin. When asked who his "favorite prose authors" were, Wright gave these two names without hesitation.[23] Like Mill, Wright based his outlook on an admiration for science and on the continual need to test theories by the facts of experiential evidence. In 1865 he began the project that would occupy him for the next ten years and fill most of his published work: investigations to demonstrate the truth of Darwin's theory of natural selection.

The Neutrality of Science and Religion

Following Mill, Wright believed that empirical facts serve as the only standard of legitimate knowledge in all spheres of human experience. He defied the nineteenth-century consensus in denying that religious truth can be known with certainty or even known at all. He held that in religion, whose supernatural truths are beyond factual evidence, beliefs cannot be called knowledge but rather some form of emotion, mystical insight, or intuition about nature's orderly design or ideal correspondence with the divine. Attempts to find certainty in these religious ways of thinking "scarcely rise in dignity above the rank of superstition."[24] Because empirical evidence yields no indication of the truth or falsity of God or an afterlife, the only legitimate perspective on these issues is a frank human ignorance. Wright approached religion as an agnostic and labeled his own view of scientific knowledge "positivism."[25]

On the issue of the relation of science to religion, Wright advocated the neutrality of science, which became his most important contribution to philosophy. Showing clear descent from Kant, Wright believed that science and religion can thrive in their own "proper province[s]," each with its own methods, purposes, and goals.[26] This bold methodological statement defied the restless nineteenth-century attempts to find scientific confirmation of religious truth. Wright asserted that science could not and should not be made to harmonize with religion because science is a completely separate venture whose investigations are irrelevant to religion. Furthermore, religion has no significance for science because it introduces preconceived assumptions into the objectivity of empirical investigation. Wright articulated the working approach of such scientists as Asa Gray and Jeffries Wyman toward large religious questions.[27] Even for those who personally believed in religious ideas, Wright's methodology divorced those concerns from the proper province of scientific investigation.

Wright found philosophical justification for his neutrality in the exclusively naturalistic basis of certain scientific arguments, especially Darwin's theory of natural selection. Wright was not himself a practicing scientist, but he was an adept mathematician and a keen observer of the sciences, especially their methodologies. He was pleased to observe that the "experimental philosophy" lay at the base of the construction of "the sciences into a true philosophy of nature." He asserted that the natural sciences are "based on the induction, or, if you please, the *a priori* presumption, that physical causation is universal, that the constitution of nature is written in its actual manifestations, and needs only to be deciphered by experimental and inductive research; that it is not a latent invisible writing, to be brought out by the magic of mental anticipation or metaphysical meditation."[28] To the young William James, Wright's position was boldly scornful not only of his father's spiritual readings of nature, but also of Louis Agassiz and a whole generation of scientific thinkers who assumed that the natural world could readily confirm religious truths. In short, Wright's perspective suggested to the young student of science a radically new and frankly naturalistic way of looking at the world.

Although Wright was a great admirer of scientific investigation, he did not consider the theories of scientists a direct mirror of nature, much less "elements and constituents of the objects" of reality. Instead, Wright conceived of scientific theories as "the eyes with which nature is seen." Theories were means to the end of increased knowledge, not ends in themselves. Herbert Spencer is Wright's prime example of the abuse of the scientific method. Spencer's rash assumption that scientific theories are "ultimate truths" was to Wright a violation of the spirit of scientific neutrality because it made theory into dogma.[29]

Wright noted that because of their common support of evolutionary theory, "the names of Darwin and Spencer are closely associated," but he argued that "no two names are more widely separated by essential differences of method."[30] While Darwin collected abundant natural facts and offered plausible hypotheses based only on those facts, Spencer proposed grand generalizations on the basis of a few facts and a great philosophical enthusiasm for the ideas of science. Spencer's method, Wright argued, would be "correct only on the supposition that the materials of truth have all been collected and that the research of science is no longer for the enlargement of our experience or for the informing of the mind." Until this scientific millennium arrives, scientific theories will serve as our tools for the acquisition of piecemeal but not absolute knowledge. Scientific theories, Wright maintained, "are such working ideas,—finders, not merely summaries of truth."[31]

Wright's view of the nature of scientific theories deeply influenced Peirce and James, especially for its potential to establish a middle position on science and religion and as the groundwork for their pragmatism. Because "scientific investigations" are always "incomplete," Wright maintained, they cannot satisfy "that hunger . . . for assurance" that characterizes "the dogmatists of both sides": the scientific enthusiasts such as Spencer who regard science with certainty and the religiously orthodox who looked to scientific investigation to confirm their faith.[32] Spencer was a popularizer of science, but, whereas his predecessors had generally communicated science to the public to make it seem more religious than professional practice suggested, he was one of the first to go in the other direction: he presented science as antireligious and as a kind of substitute religion with nearly unlimited powers of problem solving. To the public, Spencer's ideas may have been irresistible, but to Wright, they were simply a pretentious misuse of scientific concepts. Spencer's approach treated science as a finished product and ignored the centrality of ongoing inquiry.

Wright did not hesitate to regard scientific knowledge as a marked improvement over religious explanations or human ignorance of natural phenomena. But he felt that when things formerly "ultimate and inexplicable" become subject to scientific understanding, they are not known with certainty as scientific enthusiasts eagerly claim; instead, science can only claim that, at best, its "explanations are probable and legitimate."[33] The theory of natural selection provided Wright with a good case in point: although it did not explain the origin of species with "demonstrative adequacy," it offered a "highly probable truth."[34] Despite his enthusiasm for Darwin's theory, he did not consider it any more than probably true. This formulation did not mean that he doubted the truth of Darwinism; on the contrary, he regarded it as a sound—and in fact the best—hypothesis dealing with species development. His probabilistic wording is an indication of his innovative way of thinking about the truths of science.

Probabilities and Certainty

Wright's mathematical training made him sensitive to probabilistic thinking, and he noticed Darwin's use of it not only as a justification for the adequacy of natural selection as a whole but also as a crucial element in the theory's structure. Wright ridiculed those, such as Louis Agassiz, who tended to limit the very "word 'species'" to the ideas of a "*fixed* species" because, he added flippantly, they seem "to assume . . . that unless a species . . . is tied to something it will run away."[35] By contrast, in anticipation of twentieth-century "population thinking" and in close relation to Peirce's view of Darwinism, Wright regarded species as "rough averages" filled with slight variations that are produced chaotically by nature. The "variable characters" within the species "are really close approximations to the characters of the best general adaptation."[36] Wright recognized the operation of chance in the production of varieties and the role of probabilities in the process of natural selection and species formation: "Some individuals are better fitted than others, and have, on the average, an advantage."[37] Species do not emerge wholesale, but gradually, with the increased probability of well-adapted varieties surviving the rigors of nature, and thus shifting the species' "average" in well-adapted directions.

Wright's probabilistic reading of scientific theories, especially natural selection, suggests that he believed they could not yield certainty. His critiques of Spencer's cosmic assurance seem to confirm this reading. Moreover, he rejected the idea that science—and even less any other form of human inquiry—can produce real knowledge. This theme left a major impact on members of the Metaphysical Club, as Oliver Wendell Holmes, Jr., testified. Remembering his early intellectual formation, he reported: "Chauncey Wright, a nearly forgotten philosopher of real merit, taught me when young that I must not say *necessary* about the universe, that we don't know whether anything is necessary or not. So I describe myself as a bet-abilitarian, I believe that we can *bet* on the behavior of the universe in its contact with us." Holmes was not one to pursue philosophical nuance, but he did glean this practical insight—well suited to legal inferences—from the probabilistic implications of Wright's thought.[38]

But Wright could not rest easy with the uncertainties of probabilistic thinking. He included verification in his scientific methodology, an important contribution to the effective certainty of scientific knowledge. He accordingly proclaimed that science has achieved a "standard of certitude . . . in its interpretations of natural phenomena."[39] Wright supported the growing professionalization of scientific research that relied on naturalistic assumptions and put aside metaphysical and religious issues. Before adopting these approaches, Wright maintained, humanity had produced little scientific knowledge. However, with the exclusive focus on material facts and the use of verification, Wright declared, scientists built up concrete knowledge of the natural world, thus showing the superior value of modern inductive research. Scientific knowledge would be possible if scientists bracketed off unanswerable supernatural questions and trusted to the usefulness of verification in assembling knowledge. Wright justified the authority of empirical facts on the grounds that "mankind are nearly unanimous about the testimony and trustworthiness of their senses," while by contrast, "all other kinds of authority . . . settle nothing [and are] liable to . . . uncertainty."[40] In keeping with his metaphysically neutral methodology of science, Wright urged that both skeptical qualms about the certainty of sensory perceptions and pious hopes of confirming religious truths be put aside to achieve genuine gains in scientific knowledge.

Despite his faith in empiricism, Wright observed that knowledge from the senses and from experimentation is not always readily obvious. Although he claimed, along with most of his contemporaries, that astronomy is full of mathematical precision, the life and social sciences give the impression of not operating by natural law because their subject matter is causally complex, irregular, and apparently chance filled. Yet this evidence of seeming uncertainty, Wright asserted, applies only on the microscopic level of particulars. Physical causation is still discernible on the macroscopic level. He equated the laws of biology, such as natural selection, to the economic laws of supply and demand or the meteorological laws of weather prediction: none can predict the behavior of individuals or particulars, but they do define general trends.[41]

Wright described this pattern of general certainties becoming clear from the clouds of particular uncertainties with the metaphor of "cosmic weather." In a parallel way he explained the role of accident in Darwin's theory of natural selection through minute chance variations over millions of years: "In referring any effect to 'accident,' he [Darwin] only means that its causes are like particular phases of the weather, or like innumerable phenomena in the concrete course of nature generally, which are quite beyond the power of finite minds to anticipate or to account for in detail, though none the less really determinate or due to regular causes."[42] There is no need to introduce chance or mystery into the universe, or to invoke supernatural explanations for natural phenomena: "To speak . . . of an event as *strictly accidental* is not equivalent to regarding it as undetermined."[43] Naturalistic explanations are sufficient because, Wright asserted, "the accidental causes of science are only 'accidental' relative to the intelligence of a man."[44]

Wright's belief in causation rather than accident introduces a quest for certainty that moved him beyond the view that scientific theories are no more than probably true. While his friend Peirce's treatment of probabilities would lead to a philosophy in which scientific truth could emerge only after long inquiry, Wright disagreed at least in emphasis and declared that even in his own day "the results of modern science . . . establish . . . a great body of undisputed truths [with] questions settled beyond debate."[45] Wright did not believe in waiting for truth to surface, because he felt that human prejudices would always be waiting to keep it submerged. An irony in his reasoning is that he felt that truth would require the strains of passion to gain it a hearing. Of all the sciences that he studied, none seemed a more important truth than Darwinism, and he bent the full force of his mind and the full vigor of his own passions in arguing for the logical truth and the factual certainty of natural selection.

Despite the unprovable nature of Darwin's theory and its hypothetical leaps to provide plausible explanations, Wright viewed Darwin's work as "the refinement of modern English Baconism." He completed his tendency to blend probable truth and truth from empirical demonstration by flatly equating the two: he asserted that Darwinism "is evident or probable on experimental grounds" and he contrasted those forms of effective certainty with nonscientific thinking, which "baffles all approaches of experimental inquiry."[46] Darwin himself did use an abundance of factual evidence to strengthen his argument and appeal more convincingly to scientists schooled in Baconian empiricism, but he realized that his theory ultimately would not fit into a Baconian framework because it could not be proven. Embracing the Baconian method and its contemporary exponent John Stuart Mill, Wright never fully came to terms with the hypothetical quality of Darwin's science.

Convert to Darwinism

Although Charles Sanders Peirce likewise hoped that science could provide truth in the long run, he was baffled by his friend's extreme confidence in empiricism and natural selection, and he criticized Wright for "tak[ing] up with the doctrine of Mill, to which . . . he was trying to weld the really incongruous ideas of Darwin."[47] While both discussion partners recognized natural selection's probabilistic elements, Wright sought to prove the theory with factual evidence. Most of Wright's writing is a defense of natural selection or an exposition of its wide applicability and general truth. In research conducted with Jeffries Wyman, he observed that honey bee cells do not have perfect symmetry, implying their "unreflective and unforeseeing economy" of construction rather than their rational design or "any reference to supersensible properties." Similarly, in a direct challenge to design theorists, he called the eye "a bungled work compared to that of the mechanical optician."[48] Like natural selection's need for hundreds of millions of years to work its impact, his cosmic weather thesis included the proposition that the universe follows physical laws without prior purpose for indefinitely long stretches. This chronology contrasted with the nebular hypothesis, which found support in Lord Kelvin's theory of the relatively short age of the earth based on its projected rate of cooling since formation.[49] Wright's article on phyllotaxis (the science of the arrangement of leaves on plant stems) countered idealistic treatments of that science. In it, Wright demonstrated that leaf arrangements are naturally adapted to maximize exposure to sunlight and moisture.[50] His "Evolution of Self-Consciousness," which was inspired by a personal request from Darwin himself, shows connections between animal and human intelligence and proposes that even human consciousness is a product of natural selection and evolution.[51]

By the early 1870s, like many scientists, Wright was looking at much of his research as a matter of getting "my head full of 'facts for Darwin,'" and he took up a lively if somewhat deferential correspondence with the British scientist, eagerly sending his scientific hero copies of his work. Darwin was gracious and supportive in reply and even reprinted his essay on leaf arrangements as a pamphlet for distribution to fellow scientists in England, among whom, Darwin noted, "it will do our cause good service."[52] According to Wright, such empirical investigations verified Darwin's theory with facts that transcended probability and uncertainty. These are the theories of science—and the enthusiasm for the authority of science—that Wright discussed in the 1860s and 1870s while James was deciding how to assimilate Darwinism.

Why was Wright so anxious to look at natural selection as a certainty, even after acknowledging its probabilism? One reason was that his commitment to empirical fact gathering and verification emphasized the material level of existence; as William James said, for Wright, "the mere actuality of phenomena will suffice to describe them."[53] This trait encouraged him to downplay the uncertain side of near-certain probabilities. Instead, he boasted that the "man of science . . . is moved by a true faith . . . and he prizes his facts genuinely."[54] Eager to support his "true faith" in science, he viewed Darwinism as a surrogate religion. Soon after reading "that new book on 'The Origin of Species,'—Darwin's," Wright confided to a friend, "I have become a convert. . . . I believe that this development theory is a true account of nature."[55] The theory of natural selection served him as a replacement for previous theological explanations of nature, yet, ironically, he embarked on a quest for certainty in science that was similar to the goals of the religious orthodoxy he opposed. With full and brash faith in science, Wright was pleased that Darwin did not rely on design arguments or idealistic systems, but rather "that exquisite atheism 'the nature of things.' "[56] Wright was especially eager to believe in Darwinism as if it were a sort of religion of nature because its implications reinforced his own view of religion.

In his passion for science, Wright grew impatient and angry with the propositions of traditional religion. He regarded orthodox belief as "superstitious faith in another life"; he was aghast that anyone could accept "that the world was made in six days"; he did not see "any essential mystery in the nature of things"; and he suspected theological leaders, such as Princeton's James McCosh, of wanting to keep church members "faithful through ignorance." Although he maintained a personal scorn for such brands of religion, he most disliked them when those "religious prejudices" became "serious obstacles to the progress of scientific researches."[57] Firmly believing in the neutrality of science and religion, he maintained that religious concerns were irrelevant to science. Despite the apparent equity of his methodological neutrality, Wright did not treat religion and science as equal partners. He clearly preferred science as a superior form of human thinking. The scientific method, Wright claimed, is the only route to true knowledge: "The modern development of science... [has] accumulat[ed]... a body of certified knowledge... independently of other philosophical motives." He even called the distinction between the "religious and [the] secular" the difference between "the effete and the effective." By comparison with scientific methods, the beliefs and ideas of religion can produce no knowledge, but only bland and uninstructive tautologies. "Starting from religious conclusions and interpreting nature in accordance with them, the theologian discovers 'law' and 'design' as symbols, and his proofs amount to pious circles."[58] Religious ideas, Wright claimed, are better left in their separate spheres. Wright's animus for traditional religion was actually similar to the unorthodox Henry James's disgust for religious convention. But as William James increasingly noticed, Wright differed from the earlier generation first by divorcing science and religion, and then by claiming great authority not for spiritual truth but for the scientific method.

Religion's Moral Remnant

Despite Wright's rigorous separation of the methodology of science from religious claims, he was not antagonistic to religious belief if kept in its proper place. He was agnostic in his strict separation of religion from scientific knowledge. When sometime Metaphysical Club member Francis Abbot asked what his beliefs were concerning the existence of a God and the immortality of the soul, Wright replied: "The verdict of 'not proven' is the kind of judgment I have formed on these matters." In fact, Wright maintained his scientific posture of neutrality even in religion, adding, "Atheism is speculatively as unfounded as theism." Part of Wright's position of neutrality may have come from a lack of curiosity: he had no particular interest in God, an afterlife, or cosmic truths, and his letters are sprinkled with ruggedly agnostic comments. Continuing with Abbot, he wrote, "I have no desire to wake into a strange, unknown future life, and I can discover no valid reasons for any confidence in such a waking."[59] He could stay friendly with religious people, but he agreed to disagree with them. The Congregational minister Peter Lesley noted in allegorical language that while he himself "preferred to keep house in the Old Jerusalem," Wright's "tendencies were all towards that New City which men are building on the fens of Mattershire." In response to a question from Grace Norton about the purpose of life, Wright responded, "All the ends of life are, I am persuaded, within the sphere of life." When she replied, "For what [purpose]?" he brashly answered, "Why, for nothing, to be sure! Quite gratuitously."[60]

The lack of purpose in Wright's scheme also left William James uncomfortable. In the 1870s he reeled in amazement that his friend could ask profound philosophical questions yet readily ignore basic human hopes: "Never in a human head was contemplation more separated from desire." Two decades later James's reaction would flower into the famous antiagnostic manifesto, "The Will to Believe" (1895), which, as is less well known, closely matches Wright's agnosticism in theory and intellectual approach, even as it differs in its practical conclusions and emotional tone. For both Wright and James, religion cannot be known with certainty; in direct anticipation of the younger philosopher, Wright declared, "Faith . . . is incapable of proof. The test of true faith is emotional and moral, not intellectual." The differences between Wright and James emerge in the way in which they segregated religion from scientific inquiry. James builds a case for the right to believe without certainty; by contrast, Wright mustered little enthusiasm for wondering about the spiritual order of the universe, because religion, except for its moral remnant, was not a "living . . . forced or . . . momentous" emotional issue for him, to use James's words from "The Will to Believe."[61]

Wright found James's religious interests alien to his own temperamental indifference and charmingly naive. When James was twenty-two, a few years into his scientific education but still under the heavy influence of his father's spirituality, Wright said, "We found the infant full of promise and all the foundations of greatness, as seen with the eye of faith and sympathy with parental aspirations." Wright retained this comical condescension even when James was in his thirties. Hearing James trying to articulate his nascent theory of the "duty to believe," Wright observed wryly that "one remains a boy longer in philosophy than in any other direction." The Metaphysical Club boxing master did not give up on James but did promise that "by laboring with him I shall get him into better shape by and by." Despite these tough-minded claims, Wright actually agreed with James to "allow . . . that unproved beliefs, unfounded in evidence, were not only allowable, but were sometimes even *fit, becoming, or appropriate* to . . . types of character which are deserving of approval, or even of honor."[62] Unfortunately, Wright died within months of this pledge and left James with a haunting memory of empirical, naturalistic checks on his religious impulses and with hints about the applications of agnosticism.

Despite his coolness to ultimate truths and his religious agnosticism, Wright was actually very much interested in religion—of the proper kind, as he would quickly point out. He made a distinction between traditional religious forms and the religious spirit. He criticized the kind of religion that was prominent in his day, for its assertion of harmony between science and religion disgusted Wright as "the dogmatism which would presumptuously interpret as science what is only manifest to faith, or would require of faith that it shall justify itself by proofs." Despite these sharp words, Wright was a mild agnostic—he was less aggressive than the notorious Thomas Henry Huxley or William Clifford—for he objected to religion only if it violated the neutrality of science. "He admitted the entire rightfulness of the claim of Faith," his friend E. W. Gurney noted, "provided she did it in her own name." This attitude might actually benefit religion by freeing it from the orthodox demand that religious belief gain support from science. He would agree with Edward Youmans, editor of *Popular Science Monthly*, who argued that religion "has no enemies so dangerous as those who insist upon staking its truth upon any conditions or results into which it is the legitimate business of science to inquire."[63]

Wright's old minister Rufus Ellis disagreed with his religious positions but proudly pointed out that "he destroyed no man's" religion and "no child's faith."[64] Apparently, however, prolonged discussion with Wright could have a dissolving effect on religious faith. Charles Eliot Norton said that "to argue with him was a moral no less than an intellectual discipline." He had good reason to know; a minister friend of Norton referred to Wright as "the one who led Charles Norton astray."[65] But Wright did acknowledge religion's right to prevail in its own realm. Just as he bridged the conventionally separate gender spheres of working world and religious home by circulating comfortably with women and children, he assumed a kind of intellectual separate sphere for religious values. He even wrote a whimsical "Philosophy of Mother Goose" in which he distinguished "make-believe" from the claims of "most audacious Mrs. Science." The very fantasies of childhood were presented as the basis for banishing unverifiable beliefs in adulthood: "Tell them impossible stories, that the limits of the possible may be known."[66] Wright's charming embrace of childhood fantasy set the stage for his dismissal of most traditional religious beliefs as pure fantasy.

Wright's sense of the religious spirit properly neutralized on scientific questions, was a humanistic faith not unlike the unitarianism of his boyhood. He believed in God, but he simply did not think his belief was relevant to scientific practice. His recognition of "the mysterious Power of the universe" was most likely to emerge at times when he was acknowledging the probabilistic limits of scientific knowledge.[67] The true religious spirit, he maintained, had nothing to do with the traditions of the human past or a spiritualized life after death; true religion exists in the human present, as action based on principled and disinterested human benevolence. A person with this religious spirit does not act from fear of punishment or hope of reward, but rather out of duty for the good of mankind. Wright praised both the ancient "Stoic doctrine that virtue is its own reward" and modern utilitarianism as practical "affirmation[s] of the same essential principle."[68]

Despite the unorthodoxy of Wright's neutrality method, his views of morality were very orthodox and consistent with those of his social circle, including the earlier generation whose scientific and religious ideas he had so flatly rejected. He criticized the intellectual structures and assumptions his predecessors had enlisted to support morality, but he agreed with their goals. He even hoped that "moral idealism" would become "the religion of our times." Like his Unitarian ancestors and intellectual companions, he posited "the character of Jesus" as his model, not spiritually, but for his "moral greatness." Wright's humanistic and moralistic religion gave him the optimism to hope for the world's improvement, especially with the aid of science. He hoped that dedication to "the future material well-being of mankind" would become "the monument of our age." From the perspective of this kind of moral engagement, "life . . . is neither good nor evil, but the theatre of possible goods and evils."[69]

Although Wright's practical ambitions were confined to discussions and his promise was cut short by his death in 1875, this Metaphysical Club boxing master effectively coached, during their formative years, an influential group of intellectuals in the direction of his moral and scientific enthusiasms. His importance is evident in the fact that in the 1860s and early 1870s he vigorously articulated the theoretical bases of values that would animate progressive thinking at the turn of the century.[70] According to Wright, humanity needs no transcendental truths to help in the moral fight. Even before he met Wright, young William James came to very similar positions on morality and the quasi-religious thrill of selfless, purposeful human effort, but he was wary when Wright linked morality with scientific authority.

Wright's religious beliefs complemented his argument for scientific neutrality. While traditional religions were subject to disproof by any scientific discovery, his humanistic "religious spirit" was beyond objective testing. Religion that seeks a harmony with science creates a distortion of both: scientific facts are forced into the metaphysical abstractions of faith, and the religious spirit is demeaned with irrelevant facts. Wright never challenged the moral position or value of traditional religion, only its claims to transcendent truth. He therefore described his philosophy as one that "denies nothing of orthodoxy except its confidence, but it discriminates between the desirableness of a belief and the evidence thereof. Faith is in this philosophy what it was with St. Paul, a sentiment, not a faculty of knowledge."[71] While traditional religion subordinated science to the certainty of faith, Wright subordinated faith to the relative certainty of science. He clung to his own faith in the effective certainty of science despite his own theories of scientific verification and probability. William James learned from his friend Wright to reject the certainties of traditional religion and to regard science in probabilistic terms, but James never accepted the claim that science offered alternative certainties. By considering the uncertainties of both fields, he extended Wright's ideas further than Wright himself could imagine.

Wright's insistence on the relative certainty of scientific theories despite the apparent role of accidental causation in natural selection bears a peculiar resemblance to design theory, which is based on the presupposition of teleology in nature, and which, he argued, artificially identifies neutral phenomena as either causes or effects according to the dictates of religious theory.[72] Wright wrote forcefully against natural theology and its justification of God's existence through evidences of design in nature: its argument was to him a cardinal case of non-neutral science. Despite Wright's criticism of natural theology, he exhibited a similar faith in design—not a religiously inspired design, but a scientific design.

The path of empirical naturalism led Wright to reject religious design, but his enthusiasm for the scientific method and experimental verification enforced his commitment to one fundamental tenet of the old design argument:

the universe is fundamentally ordered, not accidental. We may not yet know its design and it may seem accidental, but scientific inquiry allows us to understand its order. Even though Wright maintained a public and self-conscious position against design, his critique of accident and his faith in empirical fact and scientific verification illustrate his ironic kinship to pre-Darwinian thinking. Wright's ideas are particularly important as they contrast with William James, who listened attentively to the older and more confident Wright. But since the younger man had a less definite commitment to religious or scientific design in nature, his reading of Darwin led to the more modern notion that chance characterizes all attempts to read the deepest workings of the universe. Despite Wright's faith in science, his interpretation of Darwin served James as a vehicle for his eventual rejection of epistemological certainty.

Wright's view of events in nature that have no manifest cause gave him an important transitional status in the Darwinian debate. Despite his claims to the contrary, Wright was, in a sense, only half an agnostic. In classic agnostic fashion, he doubted religious claims to truth, but he never raised questions about his own assumptions that scientific explanations can yield only virtual certainty. By clinging to this scientific belief and proclaiming the ultimate tractability of nature, Wright revealed that he only partially understood the implications of Darwin. The theory of natural selection implied a universal natural causation, but as an explanation, not a proof. It acknowledged a fundamental uncertainty and fallibility in the scientific knowledge of nature, a notion that Wright could never accept. Even while he admired Wright's moralism, young James was both impressed with and repulsed by the religious agnosticism and tough-minded science of his elder colleague. But where Wright was comfortable keeping religion separate from science without attempting to find harmony between them, he recognized that James "wants to reconcile . . . views that are in conflict in his mind." The younger man's task of trying to find a "mediating way of thinking," as he would describe his philosophical goals later in life, was made all the more difficult by his respect for Wright's empiricism.[73]

As stated by James's colleague from his later years in the philosophy department at Harvard, George Herbert Palmer: "For a time James found in Wright's hard empiricism a welcome escape from the idealism which had oppressed him,"[74] but in addition, he also recognized the probabilistic nature of scientific theories, which Wright analyzed but often would not emphasize. Because of his bold confidence in science, Wright's discussions with Peirce and James were frankly liberating even if not wholly convincing. Charles Peirce pursued the same paths as Wright, but he explored the probabilistic character of scientific method and the role of uncertainty in belief more thoroughly and with a tantalizingly ambiguous confidence in science. Although he was also guided by a distinct scientific persuasion, Peirce would become an even more crucial influence in James's assimilation of Darwinism.

CHAPTER 7

Charles Sanders Peirce and the Elusive Certainty of Science

Science must have universal laws in order to be useful. At the same time, a universal law would imply a perfection of knowledge to which we cannot attain.

CHARLES SANDERS PEIRCE, 1861

Charles Sanders Peirce was born into the society that adopted Chauncey Wright. In 1864, at the age of twenty-five, he wrote a brief family history, which included descriptions of his ancestor Thomas Peirce, who was "the man who brought our family to these shores," his wife Elizabeth, and their admission to the church in 1634. Typical of Peirce's systematic intellectual style, he proceeded to list their descendants, numbered 1 through 207.[1] The New England pride and precise logical methods of his intellectual circle had already become integral parts of his identity. He was the second son of Harvard professor Benjamin Peirce, who was one of America's foremost mathematicians and a pillar of Boston intellectual society. Young Peirce's background was only a first step toward his becoming an enthusiastic member of the scientific community. He earned his scientific standing because he was superbly gifted in science, mathematics, and logical thinking, and his childhood talent bloomed into pioneering work in these fields and into a genuine enthusiasm for their capacity to gather truth. Yet his eagerness always carried a shadow of doubt: from his early years he maintained, sometimes reluctantly, but always with great logical sophistication, that the certainty of scientific and logical truths would remain ever elusive.

Dutiful Genius

Ironically, although he imbibed so many of the values of his cultural circle, Peirce never found a permanent professional place for himself.[2] In the family of upper-crust New England intellectuals, he was always the brilliant but eccentric relation. The precocious Charles Peirce attended Harvard at a younger age than the average student, and he was already showing his characteristic difficulty in working with other people. He was not a very good student, graduating in 1859 with a class rank of seventy-one out of ninety-one. He very much liked being a student, however, just as he would continue to have a large appetite for learning all his life. While still in school, he said, "If a fairy were to take up a Harvard undergraduate and put him down the road to Happiness, I believe . . . she would not stir him an inch." Despite these glowing words, Peirce was not complacent, and true to his Puritan ancestors, he sometimes slipped into self-castigation, laced whimsically with symbols from his mathematical study, as when he noted, "I = the college student . . . am lazy and sleepy."[3] These introspections spurred him to even greater intellectual labors, although his work was often outside course requirements. Through family background and commitment to his own education, Peirce felt part of and proud of the Harvard intellectual community.

Peirce identified with his intellectual community in his social and political views as well. In the early 1850s he proudly praised his fellow "Yankees" for "being ever on the alert." And although he would come to scorn the crass and greedy world of big business, he paraphrased a Reformation maxim into a motto for nineteenth-century enterprisers: "Every Man the Maker of his own Fortune."[4] Also like many of his social peers, Peirce feared the large accumulations of wealth that came with economic expansion; for example, he noted the "barbarizing influence of . . . the discovery of . . . gold" in California. Clearly displaying his social priorities, he was particularly miffed that "the day laborer in gold . . . is paid . . . ten times as much as the scholar." Like Chauncey Wright and most of their Boston-area friends, for whom the legacy of the American Revolution still burned bright, Peirce defined his politics in contrast with British monarchism and aristocracy. He said of the British, "They are ruled almost solely by a class of people educated to govern, which certainly is contrary to our republican notions of the conditions of a good government." But like most of his peers, his taste for republican forms of government was moderate in character, especially in his fear of radicals. The young college student praised the American system of justified revolution followed by orderly representative democracy, but unfortunately, he noted scoldingly, such is not "the common course of Revolutionaries. They begin with noble aspirations, [but] they end in reckless violence."⁵

Peirce's moral and social views also closely coincided with those of his family and community. Although by the middle of the nineteenth century religious revivals had swept the country in periodic torrents, Peirce and most of his intellectual peers found them more the products of a "weak and excitable temperament" than genuine manifestations of the religious spirit. "A man of nerve," Peirce countered, "be he ever so religious . . . will not be carried into the vortex." Peirce also criticized some aspects of his own cultural tradition. It was not uncommon for New Englanders of his time and class to dismiss the Puritanism of their forebears for the harshness of its religious doctrines and moral codes. While at Harvard, Peirce constructed a fanciful description of the vices of Puritanism suitable to a Nathaniel Hawthorne short story, but with a satirical twist.

> After the book has been opened on Judgement Day, and God is judging [the] man with five talents & [the] man with 2, [the] sorcerer, harlot, murderer, [and] Malthusian, the Puritan's turn will come. He will step forward and humbly confess his sins and shortcomings—his want of zeal, his want of patience, his cowardice; and then he will take from his breast a paper labelled "A Valid Excuse for Hard-Heartedness." And Christ will take it, for he never refuses to receive petitions; but someone in that august presence when he sees the Puritan's excuse will burst out laughing.⁶

Just as Christ the merciful was his religious model, humanitarianism was his moral goal. In particular, his own religious and moral values were derived from the socially dutiful reformism of his culture. He passionately felt the need to contribute to the community, declaring, "Use! Use! Everything has a use, and a man, too, was meant for use." As a college student he identified with other "young men" who as adults "shall no longer belong to themselves, but to their country or to science." Like William James he would not risk his life for his country in the Civil War, but unlike his friend, he had pro-Southern and antiabolitionist sympathies. The two did, however, feel a similar intensity for scientific work. Because of his personal and cultural drives, he insisted that "such men should regard every thought and every act of every minute of their lives as alike sacred to their future ideas." There is even a millennialist overtone to his conviction that "the happiness of the Christian . . . consists in . . . giving his infinitesimal aid to God . . . doing his mite in the work of the universe." Peirce was an earnest young man who felt driven to contribute to "the creation of a new universe." For the rest of his life he showed a passion for the importance of his work and an uncanny capacity for prodigious amounts of work, as his youthful claim amply suggests: "What is hell but an endless *ennui*?"[7] Feeling comfortable with the political, moral, and social views of his surrounding culture, Peirce reserved his bold innovations for his work in science and logic.

Peirce's strictly logical mind and his brash confidence in science, along with his tendency to work in defiance of conventional channels and his inheritance of his father's painful facial neuralgia, all contributed to his irascible temperament. In 1861 William James recorded a perceptive first impression, which captured many of Peirce's positive and negative traits: "There is the son of Prof. Peirce, whom I suspect to be a very 'smart' fellow with a great deal of character, pretty independent and violent though." At first, the two were not attracted to one another. They had very different personalities, and James persistently found Peirce frankly a "queer being." James warmed more to his senior colleague's ideas than to him personally. As early as 1862 James quoted Peirce's philosophy in his personal notebooks, even though for the next few years he would emerge from their conversations "without getting a great deal out of him."[8]

The friendship of Peirce and James did grow and last their whole lives, but it was built on intellectual grounds, with James showing strong respect for Peirce's ideas. At first his admiration for Peirce bordered on deference, especially for the latter's talents in science and logic, but after their youth, they became peers, respectful of each other's views—if often annoyed by them. When James was thirty-three, he described him as "thorny and spinous" to his brother, when Peirce and the young Henry James were both in Paris; despite this, William still recommended that his brother take the effort to get to know him and even offered tips on how to do so: "Grasp firmly, contradict, push hard, make fun of him, and he is as pleasant as anyone; but be overawed by his sententious manner and his paradoxical and obscure statements—wait upon them, as it were, for light to dawn—and you will never get a feeling of ease with him." He went on to admit that "for years" he had waited a bit too respectfully on Peirce's views, but thereafter, he said, "I changed my course and treated him more or less chaffingly." After that teasing comment, he concluded, "I confess I like him very much in spite of all his peculiarities, for he is a man of genius, and there's always something in that to compel one's sympathy." James's descriptions are a measure of how much he learned from Peirce, but also of how he quietly tended the disagreements that helped him to shape his own outlooks.[9]

Young Henry James did not even get that far with Peirce. He scoffed that he "has too little social talent, too little art of making himself agreeable." He tried to accommodate the scientific philosopher in doing what he could to "give him society," but they were just too different. So the very unscientific Henry James used his keen observation of human nature to reassure his brother about the awkward Peirce: "Though we get on very well, our sympathy is economical rather than intellectual."[10]

Peirce's personality helps explain why he never held a permanent academic position. The effects of Peirce's medical problems were exaggerated by his haughty sense of self-worth, his inability to cope with the details of life, and even his left-handedness. The problems reinforced each other until gradually—and surprisingly considering his birth in the very center of high intellectual culture—he became an outcast: poor, with few friends, and with few outlets for his brilliant writings.[11] He was opinionated and often rude in public, and he openly flaunted Victorian proprieties with his divorce from his first wife, the Boston reformer Harriet Melusina Fay;[12] he remained happily married, however, to Juliette Froissy until the end of his life. Except for his marriages and his long life, he was similar to Wright in many ways: he was self-consciously part of elite Boston intellectual culture and he worked hard to maintain a place for traditional values within the new scientific context; he relished radically new ideas but not disruptive social arrangements, thinking it "certainly not desirable . . . to live without living in [a] settled manner";[13] and he was as intellectual as Wright and as interested in discussion but more aggressive in his omnivorous reading, his abundant writing, and his scientific research.

Thanks to his father's connections and to the friendship of William James, Peirce had intermittent work at the United States Coast and Geodetic Survey between 1859 and 1891, taught for five years at Johns Hopkins University, and gave occasional lectures at Harvard University and the Lowell Institute. He spent much of his time alone—a trend that accelerated with age—working on his scientific and philosophic projects and often living on the charity of friends, including William James.[14] His writing is marked by a similar inaccessibility. Lacing self-reflection with humility, he himself said, "One of the most extreme and most lamentable of my incapacities is my incapacity for linguistic expression." Except for one scientific monograph published in 1878, Peirce published no books, although he started many, and he composed a virtually uncountable number of notes and essays, mostly unpublished, from youth to old age. Almost always brilliant, with an occasional striking and dramatic flourish, Peirce's essays are densely reasoned, often technical, and difficult throughout. He internalized and epitomized the professional approach to scholarship with his technical vocabulary, his scant attempts to draw readers into his outlooks, and his working assumption that his only audience would be those who already *"want to find out"* about the complex philosophical problems he worked at so urgently. After reading one of his articles in 1869, William James acknowledged that his ideas were "very acute and original" but added that "they are so crabbedly expressed that one can hardly get their exact sense." Peirce himself realized their difference, pointing out that by comparison with his friend, "I am a mere table of contents, so abstract, a very snarl of twine."[15] In striking contrast to James's genius as a teacher, Peirce was primarily a learner. His papers generally read like those of a scientist presenting results to peers with little attempt to appeal to a wider, more popular audience.

The difficulty of his writings, along with their scattered, piecemeal quality, contributed both to their limited recognition in his lifetime and to a wide range of commentary since his death. While the modern evaluations have been diverse, Peirce's reputation has grown to the point where he is now widely regarded as one of the premier philosophers of the modern world. But it is difficult to pinpoint the gist of his message: at times, he seems to anticipate logical positivism, and at other times he reads like a religious idealist. He himself in 1859 admitted to an eclectic "List of Horrid Things I am: Realist, Materialist, Transcendentalist, Idealist."[16] Until the 1970s, the abundant diversity of his writings contributed to a consensus that Peirce was hopelessly inconsistent, a point of view that the unsystematic organization of his *Collected Papers* further enhanced.[17] As the publication of his comprehensive, chronological *Writings* has begun, with the first volume appearing in 1982, the search for a unified system has become less important than the work of understanding and highlighting his extensive contributions, and central themes have begun to emerge in recent scholarship, especially in sign theory and the epistemology of long-term inquiry. Peirce's writings are admittedly fragmentary and never watertight, but he did sustain an intense desire to systematize philosophy, even if he strayed from the task; moreover, his insights have enormous ongoing philosophical and theoretical importance in mathematics, semiotics, the philosophy of science, the pragmatic theory of meaning, philosophical realism, and religious studies.[18]

Looking at Peirce through James's eyes focuses attention on some of the most culturally significant aspects of Peirce's philosophy. Although contemporary commentators have been tracing out ever more sophisticated paths of Peircean thought, William James's contact with him was less technical and more in terms of the general and cultural implications of his logical inquests. Peirce made brilliant contributions to modern philosophy in writings that most of his contemporaries—unfortunately and certainly to their loss—could not understand. Like the general audience, James also did not fully understand his friend's logical philosophy, but he did assimilate and apply his ideas. James paid careful and respectful attention to his discussions, lectures, and essays, but he grew impatient with his senior colleague's commitment to science and his relentlessly mathematical and logical emphases. He did not reject them; he simply listened selectively, often critically, and usually creatively.

Later in life James would often have a direct influence on Peirce's philosophy,[19] but in his young adulthood he was more often the student, and he especially learned from Peirce in three ways. First, Peirce in the 1860s and 1870s served as a paradoxical presence who was simultaneously enthusiastic in his commitment to science, yet firmly and idealistically religious. Second, he developed innovative insights on probabilities and hypothesis formation that laid the groundwork for his reinterpretations of the methods and implications of Darwinism and other scientific theories. Finally, he discussed in draft form and then wrote an essay series, "Illustrations of the Logic of Science," whose overview of scientific reasoning suggested that belief could be achieved gradually through inquiry and held in degrees rather than maintained in sharp contrast with uncertainty. In each of these segments of his early intellectual labor, Peirce served as a pacesetter for William James's assimilation of his scientific education. The younger student of science did not always agree with Peirce's positions or even fully understand the technical features of his arguments, but through these years James noticed a persistent theme in his friend's work: despite Peirce's profound confidence in the methods and results of science, he remained ambivalent about the certainty of scientific inquiry.

Commitment to Science

Although his performance as an undergraduate gave little indication of his great promise, Charles Peirce excelled at the Lawrence Scientific School; he graduated summa cum laude in chemistry in 1863, while James was still in attendance.[20] Even before his professional scientific training, his personal drive, genius for mathematics and science, and appetite for questions of logic and methodology had already appeared with full force. Moreover, much of his learning occurred outside the classroom, which was very much in character for a person who would live his whole life without fitting into established social structures. Remembering his intellectually intense upbringing, Peirce said of himself that he was "brought up in an atmosphere of exact science."[21] One of the chemistry books he used at the Lawrence School was a German text that had been translated by his aunt and uncle.[22] His father taught his precocious son mathematics, and his aunt and uncle prompted him "from the age of six" to do experimental laboratory work. Young Peirce did not need much encouraging in scientific or logical study. As a child, he took a keen delight in logically complex games and puzzles.[23] When his older brother brought home a logic book from college in 1851, the twelve-year-old Peirce lay down with it on the floor, became immediately engrossed, and read it cover to cover in a few days. By his early thirties, his interests had become so firm that he lamented, "I was sacrificing all hopes of success in life by devoting myself to logic . . . but . . . my bent of mind was so strong in that direction that it would be a very hard struggle to give up logic."[24]

In the spirit of emerging professionalism, Peirce identified primarily with the field of his training, although in this period before the solidification of specialization, he worked not only in chemistry but also very extensively in logic, mathematics, and physics.[25] Late in his life, Peirce admitted, "I am saturated, through and through, with the spirit of the physical sciences." Peirce frankly stated that because he was "trained from boyhood in physics [and] mostly associated with physicists," he "fully share[d] their prejudices," adding with typical open-mindedness, "whether legitimate or illegitimate." In addition to his honest recognition of the limits of his field, Peirce's acknowledgment of scientific "prejudices" shows the familiar joshing of a member of the professional club.[26]

From childhood Peirce felt "a disposition . . . to think of everything just as everything is thought of in the laboratory." His interest in philosophy, especially his attention to logic, grew out of his scientific work; in fact, he even noted that "laboratory life" led to his "becoming interested in methods of thinking." The type of philosophy he most liked to read and write was the "thought that recalled the ways of thinking of the laboratory"; all else seemed "loosely reasoned and determined by accidental prepossessions." He regarded logic as the chief philosophic lesson of scientific inquiry and dismissed philosophers "who have not thoroughly studied logic" because they "are so apt to confound questions of words and questions of fact." Ironically, although he would become most famous for his philosophical speculation, Peirce was keen to point out, "My attitude was always that of a dweller in a laboratory . . . and not that of philosophers."[27]

Peirce's distinction between philosophy and science signals a keynote for his lifelong confidence in scientific inquiry and disgust for unexamined, dogmatic certainties: while he felt "eager only to learn what I did not yet know," he criticized philosophers "whose ruling impulse is to teach what they hold to be infallibly true."[28] Peirce's interest in science was actually philosophical: his knowledge of a broad range of sciences and his enthusiasm for the truth-gathering possibilities of scientific inquiry encouraged his close examination of scientific method. In 1893 he described his philosophic outlook with its emphasis on science: "For the last thirty years, the study which has constantly been before my mind has been upon the nature, strength, and history of methods in scientific thought."[29] A few years later, he said, "the word *science* [means] . . . not knowledge, but the devoted, well-considered life-pursuit of knowledge." As he explained, it is "devotion to the truth that the man is not yet able to see but is striving to obtain." Significantly, he called the label a "misnomer" because " 'science' ought . . . to be called philosophy."[30] While he often spoke negatively of metaphysical philosophy, his antagonism was mostly directed at the method of assuming certainty before inquiry. Peirce's contributions to the philosophy of science were animated by his devotion to science and his enthusiasm for its capacity to discover truth.

Peirce's preference for scientific reasoning sometimes led to dyspeptic critiques of other forms of thinking. Even before he reached the age of twenty-one, he firmly maintained that "there are two sorts of opinions—the opinion which is the result of investigation conducted with scientific accuracy and the popular opinion." He proceeded to criticize novels for "addressing the imagination and feelings and not the cool judgment." For example, his family's notorious antiabolitionist position emerged as he called the contemporary best-seller *Uncle Tom's Cabin* "only an exhortation to abolish slavery," not a valid logical argument. He charged that the "false representations" of fiction make the reader "warm with the story," while "forcing an argument" without thorough and careful inquiry.[31]

As is clear in his critique of *Uncle Tom's Cabin*, Peirce often sprinkled his logic with his ideology despite his contention that "the scientific man . . . scrutinize[s] closely and narrowly and with the entire exclusion of the passions and emotional sensibilities." For instance, while giving a Lowell Lecture on "The Logic of Science" in 1866, he used an example from contemporary political debate to illustrate a logical problem: "All careful reasoners know what dangers lie in such syllogisms as these: The Negro is a man and Every man should vote therefore the Negro should vote." He was quick to backpedal from the political implications of his statement by adding, "Observe, I do not criticize the conclusion. That may be very very true."[32] He intended his logic to demonstrate the dangers of flawed reasoning in public affairs; in doing so, he showed his conservative political leanings.

Peirce's chief quarrel with novels was when their arguments conflicted with those of science. When novels were taken on their own terms, as "good incentives to action," his scientific combativeness turned to genuine approval. To return to his example—and to point again to his New England reformist sensibilities—Peirce did believe that Harriet Beecher Stowe's novel served a moral purpose by "incit[ing] us to good deeds." With a strong hint of both professional and aristocratic condescension, he declared, "The opinion thus obtained [in Stowe's novel] is not perhaps so certain as the scientific opinion," but for the average person, "it is more achievable." Peirce's combination of admiration for the power of novels to persuade and disgust for their perceived lack of rigor is matched by a comment in *Putnam's Magazine* written in the same era as Peirce's notes: an anonymous contributor wrote sarcastically, "Do you wish to instruct, to convince, to please? Write a novel! Have you a system of religion or politics or manners to inculcate? Write a novel!"[33] Scientific and logical conceptions not only dominated Peirce's thinking but also shaped the way he defined himself and judged the world around him, and novels purporting to be arguments, or anything else that did not meet his scientific standards, received his stern criticism. His passion for logic alienated him from his culture and from conventional forms of thinking. His sense of self-worth and of the importance of his work prevented him from compromising with ideas that were not logical or rigorous.

Beyond his work, Peirce's confidence in science cropped up in reflective and sometimes amusing ways. As if to underscore his own conceptual rigor, Peirce often used scientific and logical terms with mock seriousness. For example, in 1859 he remembered attending Miss Ware's School as a child; while there, he "fell violently in love with another Miss W whom for distinction's sake I will designate Miss W'." He then added a tongue-in-cheek melodrama about his first scientific interest: "hopelessly in love, [I] sought to drown my care by taking up the subject of chemistry." While his commitment to mathematics and science loomed large even in humor, it also colored his more serious moments. When Peirce was twenty, he composed a brief prayer that showed that even his religious sensibility had a scientific accent. Earnestly declaring his religious and moral commitments, he could find no higher form of expression than to equate them with the assumptions and objects of scientific inquiry. He solemnly beseeched: "I pray thee O Father, to regard my innate ideas as objectively valid. I would like to live as purely in accordance with thy laws as inert matter does with nature's."[34] The phrase sounds comically ironic or even impious when compared to the lyrical strains of most implorings of divine support and favor, but his words had no such implications in his mind. Peirce had great passion for logical thinking, and his interest in mathematics and science was so intense that it animated all his thinking and his outlook on the world.

A Greater Religious Faith

Unlike that of many positivists of his day, Peirce's scientific orientation did not make him antagonistic or indifferent to religion, as his hundreds of references to religion amply attest.[35] For all of Peirce's scientific and mathematical thinking, he never endorsed the antireligious enthusiasms of materialistic or deterministic promoters of science. He vigorously scorned "the palpable falsity of that mechanical philosophy of the universe" even before 1887 when he composed this phrase.[36] Yet with his enthusiasm for science, Peirce could sympathize with the intellectual critics of religion, who ranged in his day from the moderate and moralistic agnostics Chauncey Wright and Leslie Stephen to the fiercely anticlerical positivists John Draper and Auguste Comte.[37] Peirce himself regarded science as a challenge to religion, but not in all its forms. He endorsed what historian David Hollinger has called the "tonic destruction" of traditional religious beliefs.[38] He characterized the enduring religious impulse at its best as "a deep recognition of a something in the circumambient All." Although this powerful source generates the blossoming of any particular religious belief, no one expression of it can be the final truth: "Like a plucked flower, its destiny is to wilt and fade [as] some new creed treads it down." Peirce hoped that "when . . . skepticism and materialism have done their perfect work, we shall have a far greater faith than ever before."[39] So he welcomed scientific critics of religion, and he himself excoriated unquestioning dogmatism, especially intolerant forms of belief that set roadblocks to inquiry. But after the criticisms performed their task of tonic destruction on parts of religion, Peirce maintained a hearty endorsement of the truth and majesty of the religious spirit.[40]

Peirce's brand of religion could not be erased by scientific skepticism, because—at least in the present stage of human awareness—the two fields use distinct forms of inquiry and belief. The type of religion that Peirce supported was the kind he regarded as "not a belief, but a life." Such orienting truths cannot be demonstrated but must be accepted on faith. Science cannot shake faith once it is assumed, just as science cannot create faith by proving its legitimacy. Like Asa Gray, Peirce separated his science and his religion, noting as early as the 1850s that "reasoning should not disturb either a Theist's or Atheist's belief."[41] Peirce's background and cultural setting predisposed him to a theist's belief, which he maintained with an idealistic, almost romantic devotion, and which was unscathed by his scientific interests. As a young man, he readily thought of solitude as "walking with God," and he believed that if a person honestly looks at nature with its "sublimity and beauty . . . his spirit gradually rises to the idea of God." Peirce's own scientific enthusiasm did not suppress his religious beliefs.[42] In fact, they reinforced each other because of his hope of finding spiritual elements in nature and his religious devotion to truth igniting his passion for science. By the end of his life, Peirce's scientific and religious interests merged in his cosmological quest for ultimate truths behind and within empirical facts.[43] He came to believe that scientific inquiry would ultimately produce insights fully compatible with religious belief. Indeed, toward the end of his life, Peirce expanded his religious evolutionism into an association of God with the evolutionary growth of regularity and reasonableness in the universe and a belief in the similarity between religious belief and the insights of scientific inference.[44]

Although Peirce's exuberance for science flowed readily from his background and from his aptitude for rigorous logical thinking, his philosophical and religious interests were a still deeper well of his scientific commitment. From his youth Peirce maintained an idealistic religious faith, and by 1871 he proudly "declare[d] for realism," which he labeled an "objective idealism." These two labels suggest a tension which lies at the root of his ambiguity over certainty. He maintained both logical and transcendental interests, so that he regarded his empirical scientific work as part of a religious frame, motivated by an almost mystical purpose. Peirce himself called his philosophy "ideal-realism," which he defined as a belief in the unambiguous reality of ideal truth, unmitigated by subjective factors.[45]

Peirce's ideal-realism was religious in character and was similar to his father's, except that while Benjamin Peirce's outlook was shaped by his unitarianism, Charles's, especially by the end of his life, was mystical and even Swedenborgian in his interest in the physical immanence of the real. The younger Peirce admitted that through his family and his proximity to Concord transcendentalism in his youth, he may have contracted "some benignant form of the disease," but he had modified its influence "by mathematical conceptions and by training in physical investigations." Later in his youth, the elder Henry James taught him about Swedenborg; although Peirce never formally or dogmatically adopted these beliefs, the Swede's empirical mysticism reinforced his ideal-realism. Peirce's long-term scientific and religious hopes ran parallel to the Swedenborgian theory of correspondences, which includes the belief that the physical world is ultimately a manifestation of spiritual truths.⁴⁶

Just as Peirce's social circle helped to shape his cultural values, so his father influenced his approach to science and religion. Benjamin Peirce nurtured his son's scientific and logical talents, and Charles Peirce explicitly adopted his father's quest to find supernatural truths in the natural world. But while the elder Peirce's unitarianism and natural theology left a large impression on his son, Charles could not adopt the particulars of his father's faith. The young man became an Episcopalian as a young adult and remained a communicant until the end of his life. At first he was baptized into the church because his wife was a member, but he stayed even after his divorce because of his attraction to its traditionalism and because its trinitarianism coincided with the triads of his own thought. Despite this adherence, his dislike of the theologies and rituals of established religions kept him from being a very orthodox church member, and so his deepest religious commitment was to his scientific metaphysics.⁴⁷

Benjamin Peirce was part of the same intellectual culture as the elder Henry James, and he shared many of the same beliefs in the harmony of science and religion. Like William James, Charles Peirce inherited a set of values that included a hope to reconcile science and religion, but, especially in light of new scientific developments, he could not accept the previous generation's methods for doing so.⁴⁸ During his senior year at Harvard College he attended one of his father's lectures, and he astutely noted a central premise of the way idealists in his father's generation brought religion and science together. Professor Peirce virtually identified the two, declaring that science's "fixed laws are not incompatible with the spiritual origin of force." The august elder Peirce, who by common reckoning in Cambridge and on the Harvard campus had "a touch of the prophet in his make-up," was famous for interrupting his lectures with exclamations about the religious implications of his mathematical and scientific subjects. Once, when giving a class lecture on astronomy, he turned to the subject of force and noted that it must have a source in will; therefore, he blurted out to his students, "Gentlemen, there must be a GOD!"⁴⁹

By contrast, young Peirce maintained an attitude of fallibilistic uncertainty about his religious beliefs. As in his treatment of science, so in his religion he punctuated declarations of conviction with reservations about the certainty of the methods and subjects of faith. In the midst of his scientific education in the early 1860s, Peirce was not shy about declaring his confidence in faith and even its potential power to reveal the ideal truths that lay at the heart of his philosophical realism: faith is "that part of the mind which is in communication with the eternal verities." Yet in his early years, while he admired firm convictions, he hesitated to invest complete confidence in the certainty of faith, noting that for religion, "faith is the test of truth," but in "the search for divine truth . . . the highest truths cannot be proved."[50] Peirce was frankly ambiguous about the certainty of religious truths.

Despite his religious uncertainty and although he excoriated scientific theories held with unquestioned belief, he tolerated such beliefs for the morals that religion inspired: "To adhere to a proposition in an absolutely definitive manner, in matters of right and wrong," Peirce stated, "we sometimes cannot and ought not to avoid."[51] Yet when he turned to specific religious subjects he withdrew his feelings of certainty. Try as we might to think about and imagine the divine, Peirce observed, an accurate "human representation of God" is not to be found; "we cannot assume," he explained, that "human reason . . . is infallible" on this elusive topic. Peirce's religious doubts were even more explicit about the very existence of God. For all of his confidence in faith, his theism was "strictly hypothetical." Yet such strict uncertainty did not prevent his idealistic declaration: "No thing exists but God." And despite his theoretical ambivalence, he more admired Michelangelo, whose art gives witness that it was "impossible for him not to believe" in the divine, than Kant, whose grounding of religion in morality indicated a soul who "believes in God because he *ought to*, not because he *must*."[52]

Charles Peirce's religious thinking displayed many goals of the previous generation, but recent scientific developments forced him to seek different means to those ends. Moreover, despite his conviction about the long term resemblance of religion and science, he recognized, in disagreement with his father, that in the near term they involve fundamentally different approaches and beliefs. By freeing his religion from connection to specific scientific findings, Peirce relinquished his expectation that scientific knowledge can confirm religious truth with certainty. Peirce moved away from the early-nineteenth-century assumptions about the harmony of science and religion by rethinking the nature of science. Turning the tables on the previous generation's expectation that religion can gain the authority of certainty from science, his ambiguity about scientific certainty actually allowed him to find elements of faith in science; he noted as early as 1860 that "faith is not peculiar to or more needed in one province of thought than in another. For every premiss we require faith."[53] While the process of inquiry would lead to scientific and religious certainty in the indefinite future, in the meantime, such confidence in either field could not be warranted.

A Science of Realism in the Long Run

Peirce's early and persistent confidence in science stemmed from his belief that objectively real truths could best be ascertained by scientific inquiry. Realism was a central feature in his view of the beginning and the end of scientific research. "An impulse to penetrate into the reason of things" was the fundamental motive for starting an investigation, and he declared that the genuine work of science is the eventual discovery of "solid truth, or reality."[54] The idealism of Peirce's religious outlook frequently emerged in paeans to science, which, he declared, "does not consist so much in knowing . . . as it does in diligent inquiry into truth for truth's sake" motivated by a desire to know the truth. He was confident that such understanding could be achieved because "the eternal forms that mathematics and philosophy and the other sciences make us acquainted with, will by slow percolation gradually reach the very core of one's being, . . . because they are ideal and eternal verities."[55] The zeal of idealism lay just beneath the surface of Peirce's interest in science, and it eventually transformed his science into a religious quest.

Peirce unintentionally identified another major motivation for his belief in realism when he declared, "We must begin with all the prejudices which we actually have. . . . We do not doubt in our hearts."[56] He did not intend, in this context, a negative connotation for the word "prejudices," as he suggests that his realism began with the indubitability of religious faith that was in his heart, his background, and his culture. Once he established realism as a centerpiece of his philosophy, it became a prime motive for his scientific commitment and a major point of disagreement with William James, who did not maintain such confidence in the truth of realism.

While other forms of human endeavor were tainted by baser goals, Peirce enthusiastically proclaimed that the "single animating purpose [of science] is to find out the real truth."[57] Peirce had no doubt that the practice of science could and did in fact achieve this goal, as he confidently declared "a man must be downright crazy to deny that science has made many true discoveries."[58] The reason he could feel so sure about science was that it decided issues without reference to subjective viewpoints and biases. Just as "real things do not depend on my thought, but have an existence distinct from being perceived by me," so in the same way, science discovered truth "quite independent of how you, or I, or any number of men think."[59] When Peirce defined science as devotion to truth, he meant this as "diligent inquiry into truth for truth's sake, without any sort of ax to grind, . . . but from an impulse to penetrate into the reason of things."[60] There was no irony in his frequent quotation of William Cullen Bryant's militant personification of noble truth: "Truth crushed to earth shall rise again / The eternal years of God are hers / While error . . . writhes in pain / And dies amidst her worshippers."[61] While James was tentatively testing his vocational and intellectual commitment to science, Peirce had found in science a happy match between his personal interests and his philosophical and religious beliefs.

Although Peirce was confident in the methods of science, he did not declare its results with absolute finality. Instead, he maintained an ambiguous posture toward the certainty of scientific investigation: after many of his effusions over its possibilities, he almost invariably enumerated reasons to doubt the proposition. He admitted that his view of the certainty of scientific knowledge was "a very snarl of twine." The certainty of science was alluring to Peirce, but ever elusive—yet, "by conscientiously pursuing the methods of science," he maintained, the investigator "may erect a foundation upon which his successors may climb higher." That foundation earned its solidity because the scientist "recognizes that a phenomenon is of no use to him unless both it and its conditions can be subjected to exact analysis."[62] In the meantime, his confidence in the certainty of scientific results was full of qualifications. Although the philosophical realist believed that we can know things as they truly are, he also pointed out that "we can never be absolutely certain of doing so in any special case." He even enjoyed making a sly reference to backhanded praise he once received: "The praise . . . was meant for blame. . . . [A] critic said of me that I did not seem to be *absolutely sure of my own conclusions*."[63]

Through decades of philosophical inquiry, Peirce consistently provided a reason for the elusiveness of scientific certainty, which he recorded in a notebook written after 1909: "Now I say (and did say in 1868) that . . . knowledge is never perfect." Even our human reason and the tools of science are fallible human instruments which can only "approach to certainty." Of course, some kinds of inquiry are better than others, and true to his training and his talent, Peirce declared that a "practical certainty is attainable in mathematics alone of all branches of purely human knowledge."[64] In science, Peirce defined proof in a way that did not require its common sense association with certainty: "Proof does not consist in giving . . . super possible certainty to that which nobody ever did or ever will doubt, but in removing doubts which do, or at least might at some time, arise." He even claimed that "any truth more perfect ... [and] any reality more absolute" than his humble declarations about the limits of certainty "is a fiction of metaphysics."[65] Peirce's amendments to his philosophical realism and the checks to his confidence in scientific inquiry were no mere afterthoughts but were an accurate record of his view of scientific understanding as it could be achieved by fallible human beings at any one time in the long process of inquiry.

Peirce's confidence in science and religion sprang from deep—but never from complacent—conviction. He would not allow their uncertainties to check his broad idealistic belief in realism, whose truth required the constant attention and effort of genuine inquiry. Part of this impulse sprang from the intellectual humility which he rarely displayed publicly, but which he already felt as a college student: "I merely consider myself as so ignorant as to be obliged to inquire."[66] This temperamental trait coalesced into a pillar of his philosophical orientation: the emphasis on long-term rather than present truth. From his youth, he believed that both his own reasoning capacities and the enterprise of human reason in general must always be poised for further growth. To keep directed toward the goal of realistic understanding, Peirce urged that "our little function in the operation of creation [was in] giving a hand toward rendering the world more reasonable, ... it is 'up to us' to do so."[67] This takes time. So, while he was cautious about attaining certainty in the near term, the future, especially the indefinitely long future of ongoing inquiry, presented a different picture.

Peirce's tone of confidence returned as he held out hope for the achievement of long-term scientific certainty. Some of Peirce's most substantial enthusiasms for science emerged from citations of reasons to believe the eventual truth-gathering capacity of scientific inquiry. The process of verification, continued over a long time, not only judges a hypothesis but also allows for its constant revision in new lights. This scientific use of the process of induction, the enlistment and testing of innumerable examples of a scientific theory, has a "constant tendency ... to correct itself." This tendency is at the heart of Peirce's claim to scientific certainty—or at least its near certainty: induction "will in the long run yield the truth, or an indefinite approximation to the truth, in regard to every question."[68] Peirce was not, of course, the first to notice the self-correcting capacity of induction in scientific inquiry, but he was the first to argue for it in a systematic way.[69] William James, in the informality of his study and during the searching time of his youth, was privy to this pioneering work, and while he admired his friend's abilities and his great confidence in science, he also noticed that it was built on ambiguities that Peirce himself recognized and struggled with.

One possible source of Peirce's fascination with long-term thinking was the theory of evolution with its connotations of progress over long durations. Even if Darwinism was not an immediate source of Peirce's thinking, the scientific philosopher did interpret evolutionary thinking on his own terms. Like Christian Darwinists, he did not believe that evolution challenged religion, but he did maintain that, in the indefinite long term, evolution would ultimately support belief in God. Meanwhile, he fiercely objected to materialistic readings of species evolution and especially to the greed and arrogance of social Darwinism. He distinguished its "Gospel of Greed" from the "Gospel of Christ" by noting that the Darwin-inspired social outlook ruthlessly proclaims, "Every individual for himself, and the Devil take the hindmost!" while "Jesus, in his sermon on the Mount, expressed a different opinion." In opposition to social Darwinism, he developed a philosophy of "agapism" as another feature of his idealistic long-term vision; according to the "agapistic theory of evolution," cooperation and the power of love will eventually triumph over competition.[70]

Young Peirce generally agreed with his father's motto: there is "one God and science is the knowledge of Him," but he believed that such truths will only become apparent in the long run; meanwhile, he regarded such uses of science for religious purposes as too simple and too certain. He criticized those who thought religion could be proved beyond "an internal impulse" or who were "over anxious about the details of evidence of religion."[71] Beyond such present idealistic or empirical proof, Peirce held his long-term religious belief with as much conviction as he felt for long-term scientific truth; in fact, they were one and the same conviction: continued inquiry would eventually produce both religious and scientific truth. By following a different path, Peirce actually returned to a position on science and religion similar to that of his father; in sum, he agreed about the convergence of science and religion but postponed their reconciliation to the long run. Where other scientific inquirers either doubted the existence of any relation between science and religion or blithely expected the facts from the different fields to reinforce each other, Peirce comfortably supported each branch of inquiry in separate spheres until the long term would bring their harmony. Thus he hoped to salvage the moral and religious traditions of his culture, not directly, but as a by-product of his belief in the merits of inquiry over long durations.

At least in part because of his intellectual inheritance from his father and his cultural milieu, Charles Peirce felt a longing for certainty in science and religion that his philosophical outlooks allowed him to approach but never reach. Peirce understood this ambivalence as part of the process of inquiry, and he pursued it in complex and nuanced lines of reasoning, but to James, appropriating it in less logical terms, this tension over the certainty of science prompted an uncharacteristically harsh appraisal of Peirce: "He is an original fellow, but with a capacity for arbitrariness that makes one mistrust him."[72] James's feelings about Peirce usually softened after such moments, but he continued to mistrust what he regarded as an arbitrary enthusiasm for science. Without intending it, this rigorous pacesetter for James's understanding of science became a role model for the younger man's more thorough embrace of uncertainty. Peirce's ambiguities opened a wedge in the edifice of scientific authority which James expanded into wholesale questioning of the possibility for finding certainty in any beliefs.

The Logic of Probabilities

One of Peirce's first inquiries into philosophies of uncertainty was his study of probability theory, begun in the 1850s and continued with great thoroughness from the 1860s. His first reflections had less to do with philosophical musings about uncertainty than with the mathematics of probability. He was fortunate to have a mind attuned to the logic of probabilistic mathematics and its scientific applications and to live at a time when probabilistic thinking gained dramatic new levels of influence. Peirce was himself an innovative contributor to the probabilistic revolution that spanned his lifetime.[73] Along with many of his peers in Europe and America, Peirce pioneered in the reconceptualization of scientific methods away from the belief in deterministic certainty and toward the expectation of probabilistic plausibility and statistical near certainty.

Toward the end of his life, Peirce drew on probabilities to suggest the ultimate harmony of science and religion through his boldly creative theory of primordial chance gradually giving way to increased regularity with probabilistic laws left in its wake.[74] But even before he formulated this philosophy of chance, or "tychism," and before his formal accounts of the role of probabilities in induction, he sprinkled his writings with references to probabilistic theory and its importance for scientific thinking and other philosophies. As early as 1859 he began to study "the chance of a thing" and "the degree of plausibility" of facts and propositions. In particular, he surmised that this way of thinking applied especially to knowledge that "is not determinate," in other words, to "that which we are not certain of." Moreover, he investigated the probabilities of error in scientific research and applied these ideas to a critique of certainty, maintaining that "the probability that a proposition . . .

is perfectly true is next to nothing." Instead, he sought to measure and understand the probability of a proposition as the "degree that it can be more or less" true.[75]

Peirce was not only on the cutting edge of the probabilistic revolution in scientific and logical thinking, he was also aware of its implications for other fields, especially philosophy, religion, and morality. He even suggested that the character of probabilistic thinking reveals connections to these nonscientific realms. Referring to the type of thinking that dominated science up to the nineteenth century, Peirce noted that "in demonstrative reasoning the conclusion follows from the existence of the objective facts laid down in the premises." While there is a claim to certainty in this process, probabilistic conclusions gain their confidence by reference to nonscientific factors, that is, the "various subjective circumstances" of the proposition. While it was not uncommon for scientists to banish such considerations from scientific thinking, Peirce argued with fidelity to both his modern scientific interests and the religious and moral values of his cultural milieu, "Good faith and honesty are essential to good logic in probable reasoning." Also, where "necessary reasoning" had traditionally provided the philosophical inquirer with a certainty of conclusion, in using "probabilistic reasoning," Peirce was, he said, "following a general maxim that will usually lead us to truth."[76]

Peirce goes even further in using probabilities to bridge science and religion. In the midst of notes on his 1878 essay, "The Doctrine of Chance," and surrounded by calculations dealing with the probabilities of chance occurrences, Peirce made a bold and radical claim: "I propose here, without going into the evidence of the doctrine, to [examine] a specimen of the manner in which it may be applied to religious questions."[77] He does not reveal in these notes how he would pursue this tantalizing suggestion, but in other unpublished notes he went into more detail. Clearly his studies did not diminish his commitment to traditional religious beliefs, but they did provide a new scientific vocabulary and logical structure for thinking about them. Peirce declared, "The existence of God . . . I should say was .93 a probability." While some religious believers might regard Peirce's statistical reasoning as irreverent, he continued coolly, noting that, by contrast, "no other dialectical conclusion [is] so high as .75, perhaps not more than .68." Just as probabilistic thinking turned scientific investigation away from expectations of certainty, so it also provided Peirce with the scientific means to account for the uncertainties and plausibilities of religious belief.[78]

Peirce devoted even more time to probabilities and related logical and methodological issues in his reflections on scientific theories, especially Darwinism. Rather than dwell on the technical uncertainty that probability theory implied, Peirce emphasized the practical near certainties that it provided. He held a strong commitment to the power of the scientific method to confirm beliefs, even if it could not secure certainty. In a revealing aside, Peirce defines precision as "a high degree of approximation only attainable by the thorough application of the most refined methods of science."[79] His version of scientific precision would posit not definite truths, but probable truths. Based on this thinking, Peirce urged belief, especially scientific belief, in all that is beyond reasonable doubt.[80]

Peirce gave mixed signals and contradictory reports about the role of uncertainty in science. His conflicting words indicate a tension between his probabilistic findings as an honest scientific investigator and his profound commitment to science as the premier way of knowing. At times he argued for the role of chance: "Try to verify any law of nature, and you will find that the more precise your observations, the more certain they will show irregular departures from the law. . . . Trace their causes back far enough and you will be forced to admit they are always due to arbitrary determination, or chance." Although he believed that "absolute [or] real chance"[81] lay at the heart of the natural world, he also declared that "the scientific man certainly looks upon a law, if it can really be a law, as a matter of fact as objective as fact can be." He even declared that the only way a "law differs from a fact" was if the scientist is "not quite sure that it *is* a law."[82]

One way in which Peirce did attempt to reconcile his simultaneous embracing of chance and his distaste for its uncertainties was to assert the centrality of unceasing inquiry in scientific investigation. Peirce was satisfied in thinking that the certainty of inquiry is only in the long run, but this answer was beyond most of his peers. Even as the practice of science veered away from the production of certainty, most observers of science still expected it to generate certainty, until the twentieth century when Peirce's insights took on a prophetic quality. Beginning at the end of the nineteenth century and accelerating in the twentieth century, scientists presented their theories in probabilistic and hypothetical terms, on a path of self-correcting inquiry. William James's emerging view of science also differed from Peirce's, but unlike most of their peers, James regarded even the indefinite future as an uncertainty, and he continued to puzzle over science's relation to certainty.

The Probability of Darwinism

Because Peirce felt uneasy about the place of probabilities in science, he held out hope that the scientific method could establish standards of certainty. His interpretation of Darwin's theory of natural selection in probabilistic terms was, in large part, a point of criticism, even as it provided James with a powerful suggestion about the uncertainty of theory, scientific or religious. This probabilistic perspective on Darwinism was a rare insight at the time. Most scientific enthusiasts of Darwin, including Chauncey Wright, saw the theory of natural selection as an example of empirical, scientific theorizing that would provide genuine and certain knowledge of the natural world. As Philip Wiener says: "Wright saw, in the detailed manner in which Darwin had discovered and demonstrated his theory of natural selection, a vindication of [John Stuart] Mill's nonmetaphysical, piecemeal, pluralistic logic."[83] But Peirce realized that Darwin's ideas differed sharply from the empirical nominalism of Mill and Wright. He felt that the probabilistic uncertainty of evolution theory would destroy the mechanistic arguments of the empiricists. According to Peirce, Darwin's theories are probabilistic in two ways. First, the means of selection are chance variations; this randomness, Peirce noticed, is the source of all change in nature, and therefore the uncertainty of chance lies at the heart of evolution. Second, the theory of the origin of species by means of natural selection is beyond proof. The emergence of a new species has never been observed. Therefore, Darwin's theory is probable because it explains many of the facts of nature, but it is neither provable nor certain.

Peirce's view of Darwin grew out of an idea of the probabilistic nature of theories that was similar to Wright's but more consistent. Peirce did not expect to find causation underlying nature's seemingly accidental movements, at least not all at once. Instead, Peirce believed that variations and uncertainty are an important component of the universe along with its more orderly parts, and that not only does our knowledge become more certain in the long run, so too does the universe itself: "An element of pure chance survives and will remain until the world becomes an absolutely perfect, rational, symmetrical system."[84] Peirce paired this theory of "tychism" with the theory of "synechism," the proposition that the universe is increasing in continuity and regularity through formation of habits. Peirce's agapistic theory of evolution involved the universe's transit from a tychistic basis to a synechistic one; chance repetition "would have started the germ of a generalizing tendency."[85]

Despite his different focus from the content of Darwinism, Peirce's understanding of probabilities equipped him to recognize a fundamental logical quality of Darwin's ideas: their plausibility despite their unprovability. Reflecting in 1893 on his first contact with the natural selection hypothesis in the 1860s, he had the highest praise for the persuasiveness of Darwin's argument, which he found "without dispute one of the most ingenious and pretty ever devised, . . . with a wealth of knowledge, a strength of logic, a charm of rhetoric, and above all with a certain magnetic genuineness that was almost irresistible." But with his desire for scientific knowledge, Peirce was not fully satisfied, and he noted that Darwinism "did not appear at first, at all near to being proved; and to a sober mind its case looks less hopeful now than it did twenty years ago." During the years between Darwin's lifetime and the rise of the neo-Darwinian synthesis of Darwinism and the genetic science begun by Gregor Mendel, Peirce was not alone in doubting the truth of Darwinism, but he was more aware of the methodological questions behind the proof of natural selection than were most scientists.[86]

Chauncey Wright treated the abundance of facts in Darwin's book as confirmation of his belief in empirical proof. To Peirce, the importance of Darwin's theory of natural selection was not in its factual provability but in its probability. Peirce was one of the first observers of Darwin's work to recognize its probabilistic elements. Shortly after being introduced to the new theory of species development, he flatly stated that "the Darwinian controversy is, in large part, a question of logic. Mr. Darwin proposed to apply the statistical method to biology." With a philosopher's eye for patterns among the sciences, he added that "the same thing has been done in a widely different branch of science, the theory of gases." Peirce clearly explained the importance of probabilities for aggregates of phenomena:

> Though unable to say what the movements of any particular molecule of gas would be . . . [James Clerk] Maxwell [was] yet able, eight years before the publication of Darwin's immortal work, by the application of the doctrine of probabilities, to predict that in the long run such and such a proportion of the molecules would, under given circumstances, acquire such and such velocities; that there would take place, every second, such and such a relative number of collisions, etc.; and from these propositions [he was] able to deduce certain properties of gases.

Extending the application of his insight, he noted that "in like manner, Darwin, while unable to say what the operation of variation and natural selection in any individual cases will be, demonstrates that in the long run they will, or would adapt animals to their circumstances."[87]

Toward the end of his life, Peirce was even more explicit about Darwin's methodological innovativeness: "In biology, that tremendous upheaval caused in 1860 by Darwin's theory of fortuitous variations was but the consequence of a theorem in probabilities."[88] Peirce explained by expressing the argument for natural selection in probabilistic language: species exist as "very many similar things . . . subject to very many slight fortuitous variations, as much in one direction as in the opposite." The variations in one direction are bound to suit the environment less favorably than those in the other direction. Therefore, while the former variations are gradually "eliminate[d] from nature, . . . the result must in the long run, be to produce a change of the average characters of the class of things in the latter direction." Therefore, while the former variations are gradually eliminated from nature, "in the long run the average number of such parts in members of the [well adapted] class must gradually increase according to the quantitative law which is determined by the principles of the doctrine of chances."[89]

Peirce noticed that Darwin was at least as important for his method as for the content of his biology. Most significantly, Darwinism exemplified the successful use of the probabilistic method in science. Where his ambivalence about the place of certainty in science had at one time led him to lament the theory's lack of proof, his satisfaction with probabilistic near certainties could make that same trait a virtue: "Anyone who is old enough, as I am, to have been acquainted with the spirit and habits of science before 1860, must admit that in this case, at any rate, the work of elevating the character of science that has been achieved by a simple principle of probability has been truly stupendous." While discussing Darwinism, Peirce pointed to even broader implications of his methodological insights. He asserted that "the Science of Probabilities . . . has raised every other science to which it has been applied to a distinctly higher plane . . . and there will be great triumphs for it when the science has reached the stage at which it can be applied more thoroughly."[90] Here Peirce forecasts the wide use of probabilities in the twentieth century; the philosopher Ian Hacking even says that this scientific method became like a "Victorian valet, ready to be the loyal servant of the natural, biological and social sciences."[91] While the lure of scientific certainty still attracted him, to Peirce, the role of probabilities in Darwinism and other theories set new standards for conducting science as explanation rather than proof.

The clearest indication of the power of Darwin over the minds of his generation was the way many of them saw his ideas as prime examples of their own methods. Wright, James, and Peirce were no exceptions. Wright believed that Darwin fulfilled the standards of empiricism. James gradually came to believe in the uncertainty of inquiry that it implied. Peirce saw the probabilistic nature of Darwin's ideas in light of his own view of the nature of theories. This was a major concern of his work: How do we form hypotheses to explain the nature of things? When certainty is so elusive, how can we gain genuine knowledge of the world? For Peirce, natural selection was an example of a hypothesis that does not give certainty to our knowledge of nature, but does provide intelligent, plausible explanations. In the 1870s, inspired by the example of Darwinism and by his own practice of science, Peirce took up these theoretical questions directly in discussions and writings that would culminate in his "Illustrations of the Logic of Science" series.

Scientific Work and Scientific Reflections

While the fertile paradoxes of Peirce's early observations on science and religion and on the plausibility of the Darwinian hypotheses provided a rich context for James's speculations, Peirce's analysis of the philosophy of science offered specific theoretical arguments for the young student of science and other Metaphysical Club members to discuss and argue. Ironically, however, in galvanizing the group's long-standing methodological concepts of science, Peirce not only offered a logic of science but also opened up reflection and discussion about the authority of scientific truths and the certainty of beliefs in general. Peirce's innovative ideas carried implications beyond his intentions. He did not set out to initiate broad questioning of science, but instead to create a rigorous logic of science. While his interest in science and his commitment to logical thinking attracted him to questions about how inquiry establishes belief and how beliefs attain certainty, they also drew him to the conclusion that science is the surest path of human inquiry. True to Peirce's careful thinking, his conclusions about science were hard won through much rigorous investigation and cautious judgment, of which he left ample evidence in his lectures and notes.

Peirce's working life during his years of logical reconstruction was dominated by scientific research. His father worked closely with the Coast Survey, the most important scientific agency of the federal government, and became its superintendent in 1867. Through his father, Peirce began working for the survey immediately after graduating from Harvard in 1859. His employment there, which continued intermittently for over three decades, included a number of scientific trips to Europe and throughout the United States, where he performed gravity measurements that earned him an international reputation. He also worked at the Harvard Observatory from 1869 to 1872, did research on solar eclipses and pendulum movements, represented the United States at two International Geodetic Association meetings, and was elected to both the American Academy of Arts and Sciences and the National Academy of Sciences. One of Peirce's biographers, Max Fisch, notes of the 1870s that "there was no more scientific . . . period of Peirce's life."[92] Much of his writing during his young adulthood reflects what his résumé would declare: Peirce was a working scientist. His reading, lecturing, and discussion of philosophy and especially of logic tended to reflect on the nature and methods of science as he was practicing it every day.

By the early 1870s Peirce had been working in the logic of science for years. It was a field at the intersection of his idealistic religious and philosophical interests and his scientific work, and he delivered two sets of lectures on "The Logic of Science" in the mid-1860s at Harvard University and at the Lowell Institute. For all of his privileged background as the son of Benjamin Peirce, these were significant accomplishments for a precocious young man in his middle twenties. The logically rigorous scientific philosopher often even expressed sympathy for his audience. "I fear I have wearied you in these lectures," he apologized, "by dwelling so much upon merely logical forms" and their elusive complexity and technical sophistication. He knew his work was not entertaining, but he regarded it as "full of great importance," adding flippantly, "to everyone who is to use his mind at all."[93] William James liked to use his mind in different ways, but active philosophic curiosity, genuine scientific interests, and friendship drew him to at least one of the Lowell lectures. Late on the night of November 14, 1866, he reported to his sister with frank recognition of his differences from the more logically rigorous scientific philosopher: "'Where have I been?' 'To C. S. Peirce's lecture, which I could not understand a word of, but rather enjoyed the sensation of listening to for an hour.'"[94] James learned more than his characteristic self-deprecation would allow, but he was accurately implying that whatever he learned from Peirce would not be on Peirce's terms.

Peirce delivered many of the earlier Harvard lectures while William James was with Louis Agassiz in Brazil, but he repeated some of this material in another set of lectures organized by new president Charles Eliot in the winter of 1869–70 to encourage serious scholarship. After attending one of Peirce's lectures, James was more complimentary: "It was delivered without notes, and was admirable in matter, manner and clearness of statement. . . . I never saw a man go into things so intensely and thoroughly." Astutely observing the philosophical heart beating beneath the scientific structures of Peirce's logic lectures, James noted, "He has recently been made assistant astronomer. . . . But I wish he could get a professorship of philosophy somewhere. That is his forte, and therein he is certainly *très fort*."[95] Peirce himself approached these lectures with the zeal of the passionate intellectual. Despite his own inclination to trust the results of scientific inquiry, he frankly asked what was the "degree and character of the certainty of scientific ratiocination."[96] Willing to put even his own commitments to the test of inquiry, Peirce characteristically did not emerge with a single definite answer, but instead proposed a nuanced series of responses to the place of certainty in the logic of science.

Even in his admiration for science, Peirce was careful to distance himself from positivistic enthusiasts for scientific certainty such as Auguste Comte. He chided "M. Compte" [*sic*] for his confidence in the "present perceptions of sense" and for his pride in the certainty that empirical verification can give to science. Despite its bold claims, Peirce argued, "positivism is only a particular species of metaphysics open to all the uncertainty of metaphysics." His chief quarrel with positivism was its impatience, for, after all, he would make similar claims for the long run. Meanwhile, in the inductive evaluation of scientific facts, he recognized the impossibility of "total . . . enumeration" of all relevant instances, so he admitted that the scientific investigator is "left utterly powerless to account for any certainty or even probability in the inference from induction." More certain responses to the results of inquiry may be appropriate in "the court-room where questions *must be decided* one way or the other," but they are inappropriate to science "where indefinite suspension of judgment is permissible." Despite this, Peirce readily sanctioned an effective certainty which slips into the practice of induction, because, he said, "we are led to believe what is easy to believe though it is entirely uncertain. . . . No one thinks of questioning a good induction."[97]

Despite these cautious turns to certainty in scientific investigation, Peirce offered some subtle qualifications: "If any proposition can be shown to be universal . . . and even if it be proved to be true . . . I do not thereby admit that it is certain." Such fine distinctions reflected Peirce's constant awareness of the fallibility of human inquiry. However, by pinning lack of certainty to human frailty, Peirce ironically reinforced his hope for certainty in scientific investigations. For example, in seeking to determine causes, Peirce did not abandon certainty in the face of human limitations, but instead proposed that "it was more rational to suppose that our inability to assign the causes of . . . phenomena . . . arose from our ignorance, than that they were phenomena which were uncaused."[98]

While causes and certainties could not be established through the process of inquiry itself, Peirce recognized a "transcendental principle" in scientific investigation, namely the "assumption . . . that the course of nature is uniform." This and other assumptions served as the "hypothes[es] with which we must start." Peirce added that throughout inquiry "we find ourselves taking certain points for granted which we cannot have observed." He does not treat this situation as a license for claiming psychological dimensions of logic or for proclaiming a role for will in belief—positions he would harshly criticize William James for in later years—but instead regarded it as a motive for reinforcing his commitment to logic: "We can thus take for granted only what is involved in logical forms. . . . Everything else admits of speculative doubt." Peirce declared that formal logical expressions "admit of absolutely certain answers," while more psychological logic is "little better than guess-work." Peirce hoped his work would "weed out" the latter and "reduce the whole" of logic and scientific method "to mathematical exactitude."[99]

While surrounded by a sea of uncertainty and clinging to the assurances of mathematical logic, Peirce indicated still another element of his "logical forms." In anticipation of his method of hypothesis formation that he called "abduction," he argued that in a scientific investigation "facts are not only brought together, but [also] seen in a new point of view." He went on to identify that elusive and unprovable but crucial "new mental Element" as "shrewdness," and he called it "the essence of genius." In the Lowell lectures, Darwin's method served as a chief example of this kind of uncertain but valid assumption: a scientist "observes the regularities of the animal kingdom now, and he knows from that how it was in some geological era—millions of ages ago." Peirce even argued that this form of shrewd assumption despite uncertainty is "essentially Inspiration" and indicates "the alliance of man with the divinity."[100] The manifest effectiveness of unproven but inspired assumptions embedded in humanity's logical powers reinforced his belief in God, and, in turn, his religious belief increased his enthusiasm for logic.

In Search of a Popular Scientific Method

By the late 1860s, after years of studying and practicing science and analyzing its logic, Peirce felt he had produced, particularly in his Harvard and Lowell lectures, an "exact and satisfactory" logic for "tracing out the forms of propositions and arguments" in science. "But," he added, "logic cannot stop here." It "is bound, by its very nature," Peirce boldly declared, "to push its research into the manner of reality itself," and he pledged to develop a logic of "how and what we think." Enthused by what he had learned of the logic of science, he wanted "to teach something of the art of investigating the truth" in general, beyond the rarified circles of scientists and logicians.[101] Peirce's goals were similar to those of Simon Newcomb, who had worked with Chauncey Wright in the Nautical Almanac Office in Cambridge and who became a prominent astronomer and economist by the late nineteenth century. In addition to his strictly scientific work, Newcomb also actively advocated the dissemination and widespread use of the scientific method.[102]

In the more general logic that Peirce began conceiving at least as early as 1868 and writing at least as early as 1872, he modeled his thinking on scientific reasoning but began to direct his attention to doubt, belief, and hypothesis formation in general. When he had finally gotten some of his ideas in print, he mused that "a book might be written to signalize all the most important of [the] guiding principles of reasoning."[103] Even while he was actively pursuing his scientific research, his conversations with fellow Metaphysical Club members gave him a chance to speculate more broadly and to test out some of his new ideas in logic. Peirce caused a stir within his circle of friends and discussion partners with his formulation of a scientific logic of belief formation in the early 1870s. Much like Ralph Waldo Emerson's reading of "Nature" at the Transcendentalist Club in the middle 1830s,[104] Peirce's logic papers were a thunderbolt that generalized and highlighted the implications of the perspectives on philosophy and scientific method the group had been grappling with for years. Peirce's logic gave a sharp intellectual identity to the discussion group. Peirce remembered that "it was there that the name and doctrine of pragmatism saw the light."[105] At its birth, pragmatism showed one of its major lines of descent in Peirce's philosophical reflections on science. After Peirce and the Metaphysical Club members had spent over a decade discussing the implications of science, his papers on logic assumed a scientific basis to philosophy and defined the belief structures of scientific inquiry.

Peirce spent most of his time in the 1860s and 1870s on scientific research, but, as he wrote to his mother in April of 1872, "On clear nights I observe with the photometer; on cloudy nights I write my book on logic." With a joking self-deprecation that reveals the duration and seriousness of his avocational commitment to his logic, he went on to say his was a book "which the world has been so long and so anxiously expecting."[106] In November, William James recorded, Peirce shared with the Metaphysical Club "an admirable introductory chapter to his book on logic the other day." The chapter dealt with "the Difference between Doubt and Belief" considered "according to . . . degree" of certainty.[107]

The whole world may not have been anxiously awaiting Peirce's application of scientific logic to belief in general and his insights about levels of uncertainty, but *North American Review* editor Thomas Sargeant Perry was. The very day after Peirce met the Metaphysical Club, Perry sent him a note: "I write to beg of you to let me have that paper you read the other night in Cambridge for the N.A.R., I'll pay you bountifully & I *must* have it. Be a good boy & send it." A few weeks later, Perry still gushed in enthusiasm for the essay, declaring "how welcome are the words written!" But he balked at Peirce's technical language and inaccessible style even as he noted the philosophical importance of his ideas: "[Your] views . . . may not be of general interest but to the particular mind they will be of inestimable value." For the more general audience of the *Review*, Perry urged that Peirce "cull some logical flowerets, such as seem sweetest, and send them to me."[108] Such suggestions did not sit well with Peirce because he preferred to influence the general public by educating them in logic rather than by simplifying his philosophy.

Peirce courted a higher destiny than such simplified versions of his logical theory would allow, and so he did not send a shorter piece to Perry. Instead, he kept working on his "logic book" and discussing it at the Metaphysical Club, where "it was much admired"; portions of "the ms. went around to different members who wished to go over it more closely than they could in hearing it read."[109] The club with its fortunate and fruitful combination of members, who were similar enough to work together but different enough to stimulate and challenge each other, enthusiastically debated Peirce's ideas. Lest the "winged words" of these exchanges be lost, Peirce said he "drew up a little paper expressing some of the opinions that I have been urging all along."[110] This and other papers that Peirce presented to the Club or simply recorded in unpublished draft form became the basis of a six-part series, "Illustrations of the Logic of Science," which was little known in its own time but later became famous because of its genesis status in the history of pragmatism and was widely anthologized in the twentieth century as Peirce's most important contribution to philosophy. With publication of the new chronological edition of Peirce's works and extensive research on his early philosophical orientation, it is now increasingly clear that the essay series is important especially as a culmination, because it was part of Peirce's two-decade quest to understand how much certainty could be vested in scientific logic and belief in general.

Peirce never did publish his logic book, but the six essays he hoped would serve as a basis for the book were published in the 1877–78 issues of *Popular Science Monthly*. The publisher, W. H. Appleton, an admirer of Herbert Spencer and a scientific enthusiast, first suggested publication in 1875, when he discussed with Peirce his "studies of the nature of the cogency of scientific reasoning." A brief encounter with Peirce and familiarity with his scientific work led Appleton to view the young scientist as an intellectual ally for his work of publicizing scientific approaches to social and intellectual problems. When the publisher and his editor saw the essays in 1877, however, they were less enthusiastic because of the "metaphysical character" of Peirce's writings, but the essays went to print anyway, complete with the philosophical scientist's equally enthusiastic but often ambivalent propositions about the truth-gathering possibilities of scientific inquiry.[111]

Part of Peirce's misunderstanding with his publishers stemmed from the varieties of audiences that his essays could address. His reputation, training, and current work suggested that his writing would be suited to a specialized audience of scientists and philosophers, but Peirce hoped to reach a broader range of readers. When revising the essays years later, Peirce considered broadening the wording of the title to "Studies in Meaning" or "Essays toward the Interpretation of our Thoughts."[112] But even the original title, "Illustrations of the Logic of Science," indicated his hope to communicate the general methodological fruits of his technical learning. Like an evangelist, he sought to spread the benefits of scientific reasoning to thinking in general.

Convinced of the merits of scientific reasoning, Peirce wanted to whip public discourse into better logical shape. The need was critical; he lamented that "few persons care to study logic," but he hoped that his logic, published in *Popular Science Monthly* without mathematical or technical apparatus, could attract a wider reading. Most people are satisfied, he observed, that they are "proficient in the art of reasoning already" because they keep their logical formulations safely confined to their own biases and tastes. But living in society requires the art of logic to provide the legitimation of beliefs that go beyond the limits of "one's own ratiocination."[113] In applying logic to thinking in general, Peirce wrote these essays as an inquiry into the possibilities of establishing confident beliefs in the face of uncertainty. The title of the essay series left little doubt that he regarded science as the best way to gain knowledge, and thus as the model for the establishment and legitimation of beliefs in general, but he presented his case only after surveying the nature of inquiry and the variety of ways in which people come to claims of knowledge and belief.

Thought Fixed by Science

The argument in the first essay, "The Fixation of Belief," proceeds on two tracks; one concerns inquiry leading to knowledge, another leading to belief.[114] At first, Peirce suggests that logic's main goal is to spur the acquisition of knowledge: "The object of reasoning is to find out, from the consideration of what we already know, something else which we do not know." This definition assumes the strong link between logic and science that Peirce had proposed a decade earlier in his "Logic of Science" lectures. The two reinforce each other in the increase of knowledge: "Each step in science has been a lesson in logic," Peirce declared, and logic provides the mental tools for scientific inquiry. This scientific phase of the art of reasoning includes a harmonious coincidence of knowledge and belief, with scientific knowledge as the basis for belief and things believed because of their ability to be known logically. If all people were as convinced as Peirce was of the virtues of scientific logic, "The Fixation of Belief" would have been shorter and blunter, or perhaps even unnecessary. But he hoped to reach a wider audience because he realized that not everyone was so impressed by science, and, unfortunately, forms of belief other than the scientific commanded wider attention—beliefs with slim links to knowledge. Peirce declared hopefully, "We are, doubtless, in the main logical animals," but added soberly, "we are not perfectly so."[115] Expanding the application of logic to thinking in general would involve trying to understand and cope with the ways people establish their beliefs, complete with the human errors in applying logic and with the avowedly nonscientific methods of those who spurn or ignore logic.

Peirce's popularizing goals forced him to philosophical generalizations about belief formation, which would eventually form the basis of pragmatism. This perspective reveals that, especially in the first essay, he was engaged in the sociology of knowledge, as his enterprise would be described in the twentieth century—although Peirce was more prescriptive in wanting to fix thought than most social scientists.[116] Examining belief in light of how it functions whether or not it is linked to knowledge, Peirce could gaze squarely at its structure: "That which determines us . . . to draw one inference rather than another, is some habit of mind," whether born of logic or some other motive force. "The feeling of believing," he said, "is a more or less sure indication of there being established in our nature some habit which will determine our actions."[117] These inclinations or tendencies to action, even without logical structure, are the basis for the beliefs that fill most people's heads.

Peirce's definition of belief in terms of habit and action was based on a new psychology whose most prominent spokesman, Alexander Bain, Peirce credited with laying the groundwork for pragmatism. In particular, he wrote that pragmatism is "scarcely more than a corollary" of Bain's declaration that "belief has no meaning, except in reference to our action." By emphasizing the terminus of belief in action rather than its source in human reason, Bain suggested that belief has more to do with willing than with thinking. By the middle of the nineteenth century, when the egalitarian features of mass culture meant that religious, political, and social leaders needed to inspire belief less with the serene light of reason than with nonrational forces, including, as Bain said, "superstitions, dreams, [and] vagaries," Peirce and the other members of the Metaphysical Club enthusiastically warmed to Bain's psychology of belief.[118]

While such suggestions were not uncommon among religious revivalists or in popular opinion, this was a radical proposition among academic philosophers because of its suggestion that beliefs resided beyond the realm of rational persuasion, in commitments that were not necessarily logical. However, Peirce's use of this train of thought on habit and belief was not ultimately very radical, because he still asserted the primacy of scientific logic despite the many habits that shape beliefs, and he hoped to persuade people to adopt the "scientific habit" in establishing their own beliefs. So, like his defense of traditional morality and religion, Peirce's "Fixation of Belief" is actually a rearguard action to keep from conceding belief to nonlogical, purely habitual acts. And despite his generosity to Bain, Peirce extended the analysis of nonrational sources of belief and added his own scientific model for belief formation as crucial corollaries that contributed to his own philosophy's distinct identity.

In setting up his argument, Peirce acknowledges that for the vast majority of "activity [that] moves along thoroughly-beaten paths," habitual beliefs form the unreflective and uninspiring but still essential "fly-wheel of society," as William James would later say in his *Principles of Psychology*. But when one is confronted with "an unfamiliar field," habitual beliefs are a less sure guide, and, Peirce adds with a Victorian flourish, even "the most masculine intellect will ofttimes lose his orientation."[119] Habits alone usually allow beliefs to be maintained, serene and unperturbed, on the model of the nineteenth-century nonemotional male ideal, but they are not always sufficient. Some situations bring confusion to beliefs and force reflection about where they come from and whether they should be endorsed. Peirce devotes the rest of the essay to laying bare the structure of belief formation and positing his claim to science's superiority. In a cultural world full of surprising challenges to traditional belief, Peirce's essay offers his projected audience of mostly middle-class men the logic of science as a tool to maintain their composure in uncertain intellectual or cultural territory.[120] But first he sets up his case with an overview of the nature and variety of belief formation.

Peirce observes that before beliefs can be established, inquiry begins with a measure of doubt. Revealing his admiration for knowledge, Peirce displays frank impatience with doubt, calling it "an uneasy and dissatisfied state from which we struggle to free ourselves," but he acknowledges that doubt has a purpose: "The irritation of doubt causes a struggle to attain a state of belief" and the resultant line of inquiry continues "until [doubt] is destroyed." The end of inquiry is doubt's opposite, belief, "a calm and satisfactory state which we do not wish to avoid." Significantly, Peirce contrasts belief with doubt rather than with nonbelief. In other words, he does not equate belief with absolute truth or certainty, but rather maps it on a continuum of decreasing uncertainty; as doubt recedes, belief emerges as a tentative truth, a provisional certainty. This view of belief reinforces his pragmatic emphasis on habit and action; by implication, when we cross the threshold from doubt to belief we become willing to take action according to a belief. Using extreme examples of beliefs hardened into the certainty of conviction, Peirce illustrates his point: "The Assassins, or followers of the Old Man of the Mountain, used to rush into death at his least command, because they believed that obedience to him would insure everlasting felicity." From this analogy to a belief with a drastic attendant action, Peirce declares, "So it is with every belief, according to its degree." Beliefs, ranging from positions that barely surpass doubt to firmly held convictions, "truly guide our actions." In the next essay in the series, Peirce admitted that his terms "doubt" and "belief" involved a borrowing from the language of "religious or other grave discussions," but in his analysis of methods of fixing beliefs, he uses these terms "to designate the starting of any question."[121] In his first essay popularizing the logic of science, Peirce is neither pious nor earnest, but instead he is explaining the ways people come to believe what they do.

Peirce's theory of belief, in its positing of various degrees of certainty and in its link with human action, differed dramatically from a wide range of perspectives in both the science and the religion of his day, which serenely assumed that belief can be based on a provable truth, a total assurance. Peirce asks his audience, including the young William James in discussions at the Metaphysical Club, to "put this fancy to rest." The belief itself, not its necessary truth or certainty, is the focus of attention, "for as soon as a firm belief is reached we are entirely satisfied, whether the belief be true or false." Peirce is not here enshrining self-deception, but rather acknowledging the importance of habits, which, especially when practiced by those untrained in scientific logic, can follow the undisciplined logic that allows us to "seek for a belief that we shall *think* to be true."[122] Peirce recognizes the plurality of human motives and maintains that in the context of most people's way of establishing beliefs, the certainty of any one individual's belief cannot be made universal.

In the rest of the essay, Peirce reviews the ways in which human beings ease their doubts and attain belief—or to use his terminology, the way they "fix" their beliefs. His four methods of fixing belief constitute a brilliant cultural application of philosophical ideas. The first method, using tenacity, involves stubborn holding to "a steady and immovable faith." Born of an urge to "cling spasmodically to ... views ... already take[n]," and motivated by a "vague dread of doubt," this method does "yield great peace of mind." Yet while this method may satisfy one person "hold[ing] steadfastly" to a set of beliefs, it has "the social impulse against it": "The man who adopts it will find that other men think differently from him ... and this will shake his confidence in his belief." Peirce then identifies the method of belief established by obedience to authority, which allows an institutional control of individual belief. Following authority satisfies the social impulse but works best when people are "kept ignorant" or even "terrified into silence." This has been an effective and common method of fixing beliefs for "the mass of mankind," but it keeps people as "intellectual slaves." Peirce had higher goals for popular belief, and the problems with the method of authority begin with recognition that it is a "mere accident" that the believers who follow an authority "believe as they do and not far differently," which "giv[es] rise to doubts in their minds."[123] Such doubts mean that the path to belief formation based on authority remains inconclusive and open to a surer method of fixing beliefs.

The methods of tenacity and authority are starkly habitual and require little intellectual inquiry. At this point in his essay, Peirce turned to the more "intellectual and respectable" methods of fixing beliefs. He credited Descartes with the metaphysical innovation of finding the "natural fountain of true principles ... in the human mind," rather than "looking to authority as the ultimate source of truth." Adopting positions "agreeable to reason" adds the strength and thoroughness of philosophical thinking to a belief, but Peirce argued that it runs into a more sophisticated version of the problem with tenacity: there is no criterion by which one person can convince another. In fact, he adds, the "pendulum" of philosophical authority has swung so widely among various positions, each held as the road to certain truth, that this a priori method also encounters problems similar to those of the method of authority. In sum, Peirce remained dissatisfied with the method of metaphysical reasoning, which "makes of inquiry something similar to the development of taste," because "the very essence of it is to think as one is inclined to think."[124] This third method can raise hopes for the establishment of firm and rational beliefs, but like the previous two, it leaves lingering doubts even among its adherents.

Peirce maintained that "a method should be found by which our beliefs may be determined by nothing human," be it willful tenacity, social authority, or changing philosophies, but instead "by some external permanency—by something upon which our thinking has no effect." As the beginning of the essay already suggested and the rest of his work amply testifies, Peirce believed that science provides such solid ground; it teaches that there are "real things" that "affect our senses according to regular laws," and "by taking advantage of the laws of perception, we can ascertain by reasoning how things really are." Peirce did not present science in stark opposition to the method of reason, but as its culmination. Science is, in effect, reason disciplined, and the method of science can lead any inquiry to the truth; as Peirce said, "Any man, if he have sufficient experience and he reason enough about it, will be led to the one true conclusion." Positing scientific logic as the superior method of fixing beliefs and the culmination of his inquiry into the topic, Peirce waxed romantic in admiration for science, maintaining that "a man's logical method should be loved and reverenced as his bride."[125] In his enthusiasm and even affection for science, Peirce came close to claiming absolute certainty for scientific investigations, but in his more sober moments, he maintained that they produced no more than very sound beliefs. James learned Peirce's ideas, but being neither as enthusiastic about science nor as disciplined in logic, he was more attuned to Peirce's ambiguity about science than to his conclusions about the need to fix beliefs scientifically.

How to Make Methods Scientific

In the second essay of his series, Peirce continued his efforts at popularization with—literally—a how-to guide to the methods of his logical and scientific researches. While "The Fixation of Belief" provides a conceptual map of Peirce's outlook on belief formation, "How to Make Our Ideas Clear" steers the reader through the newly charted terrain and points out some of the implications of viewing beliefs as mental habits. The theme of the first essay endures with still greater force: scientific logic is the way to make our ideas clear because it provides a clear sight of the real. Peering further down the spectrum from belief to doubt, Peirce discussed the way a belief held tenaciously becomes like a bad habit, a treasured but "vague shadow of an idea," which obstructs clear thinking. He also observed that when believers remain secure and unquestioning in the "stronghold" of the method of authority, "the idea of loyalty [has completely] replaced that of truth-seeking."[126] Beliefs held through both tenacity and authority create counterfeits of true inquiry which prevent clear thinking.

In an earlier essay, Peirce reserved his most extensive and harshest criticism for the scientific method's closest rival. Citing Descartes as his representative case, Peirce praised the method of reason as clearly an improvement over the dogmatic tendencies of the methods of tenacity and authority. However, he noted that inquiry based on metaphysical reasoning has an unfortunate appeal to "dilettanti" who become vexed at the notion that "questions upon which they delight . . . may ever get finally settled." As Peirce never tired of arguing, the point of inquiry is "the production of belief" with some degree of accuracy and confidence, and scientific inquiry can ensure more and better such beliefs.[127]

It is in Peirce's wranglings with the method of reasoning that he recorded what would become the most famous and influential passages of these essays and the idea that would earn him priority as the founder of pragmatism. Ever since the 1860s Peirce had had an ongoing quarrel with Descartes and the trends in modern philosophy that the early modern French philosopher helped to initiate. In particular, Peirce disagreed with two of Descartes's key philosophical moves: the critical stance that demands doubt of all which cannot be proved, and the confidence in mental intuition that gives us knowledge wholly free of doubt. Peirce took positions in direct opposition to Descartes: "We cannot begin with complete doubt. We must begin with all the prejudices which we actually have."[128] If he thought that in this sense Descartes was much too lacking in confidence, Peirce felt the French philosopher had granted intuition far too much certainty. Peirce maintained that intuition combined two faulty methods of fixing belief: as an internal authority, intuition was simply an intellectual's version of the stubborn method of tenacity, and reason's obedience to that authority limits the range of inquiry.

According to Descartes, reason did not have to look beyond itself to discover true beliefs, because "self-consciousness was to furnish us with our fundamental truths." This premise subjects the rationalist philosopher to the problem of not being able to see the "distinction between an idea *seeming* clear [within the confident bounds of one's self-consciousness] and really being so," because of his great confidence in the mind's ability to intuit with certainty. The upshot of this problem, as Peirce saw it, is that "since the time of Descartes, . . . philosophers have been less intent on finding out what the facts are, than on inquiring what belief is most in harmony with their system."[129] By contrast, scientific logic is guided more by a method which directs the process of inquiry than by an a priori philosophic system that forecasts its results.

There remained one nagging problem in Peirce's dismissal of metaphysical reason as a method of fixing beliefs: if reason could discern essences and truths beyond and behind the factual world, then despite its other problems, it could stake a plausible claim to legitimacy among the variety of ways of fixing beliefs. Peirce's own realism would seem to suggest a sympathy with this method of reason, but his earlier writings undercut this claim and prepared for the more famous pragmatic maxim, which would posit the scientific method as the more authentic method for discovering truth. His emphasis on the long term shows one way in which science cannot discover the real surely or immediately; his dialogue with the rationalists reveals another case.

Again opposing Descartes, Peirce argued that the mind's power of reasoning cannot "refer . . . immediately to its object." Peirce issued a cutting dismissal of this rationalist proposition by maintaining that our minds can never reach the essences of things, but only come to know them in mediated ways. In a pair of articles in the *Journal of Speculative Philosophy* of 1868, Peirce put this anti-immediatism tersely: "We have no power of thinking without signs," the physically sensed, mentally interpreted manifestations or outward effects which represent ideas or things.[130] William James read these essays with his usual combination of deep respectful interest and bafflement for Peirce's technical virtuosity. In early 1869 he wrote to a friend that he had just talked with Peirce about "a couple of articles in the St. Louis 'Journal of Speculative Philosophy' by him, which I have just read. They are exceedingly bold, subtle and incomprehensible, . . . but they nevertheless interest me strangely."[131]

In his 1878 "Illustrations" series Peirce assumes the importance of signs, and he completes his critique of the method of reason by summarily declaring that "our idea of anything *is* our idea of its sensible effects."[132] This maxim, and in fact Peirce's whole search for a general application of scientific logic, became the basis for the emphasis on action, usefulness, and practical effects in the pragmatism of Peirce, James, and others. The first statement of pragmatism, born in Peirce's fight with Descartes and articulated to demonstrate the poverty of the method of reason, once again shows Peirce's ambivalence about certainty. He was opposed to both Cartesian doubt and self-evident truth; he claimed our minds can really know the world (at least in the long run), but that such knowledge will always be mediated; and, ironically, while the first three methods of fixing beliefs fill their supporters with the most confidence, the method of science recognizes its limits in mediated knowing and fallible methods and yet offers the best program for fixing beliefs. Following Peirce's arguments, the field was now cleared of rationalist philosophizing: where ideas can form only around sensible effects, science is the most plausible method of fixing beliefs, because it deals explicitly with physically manifest signs. When compared to its closest rival, the method of reasoning, the method of science is focused correctly on effects, not essences, and it uses a method for open-minded inquiry rather than being tied to a preconceived system.

Peirce closes the second essay by returning to some initial concerns of the essay series. In belated recognition of his original mandate to popularize the logic of science, he realizes that the average reader "has been at . . . pains [in] wading through this paper," but adds firmly, "there is no royal road to logic." Despite his initial goal, Peirce could still be quarrelsome with his target audience, as he indicates with his dismissive aside, "In the matter of ideas the public prefer the cheap and nasty." He promises that the next paper will "return to the easily intelligible," but, incongruously, he identifies still more complicated material to cover. In laying the groundwork for the wide application of scientific logic, the first two essays surveyed the sources of belief and the ways of making ideas clear, and while they each argued that science is a superior method of establishing plausible and clear beliefs, neither "crossed the threshold of scientific logic."[133] As the essay series went further in trying to educate the public to more logical thinking, Peirce made ever fewer compromises in presenting his logic. So, even though the third essay begins a trend in the essay series toward analysis of more particulars of scientific reasoning, the last four essays have more technical issues and are therefore even less accessible than the first two essays. After the first two and justifiably most famous essays, Peirce lost the glow of his initial impulse to popularize his logic of science and wrote more as an expert asking his readers to follow his reasoning.

The Uses of Probabilistic Thinking

In "The Doctrine of Chances," Peirce returned to an issue that opened the first essay. While the bulk of "The Fixation of Belief" dealt with the path from inquiry to belief in general, its first few pages enunciated Peirce's conviction that scientific inquiry leads not just to beliefs but to knowledge. Similarly, the first few pages of the third essay offer a case study of a scientist formulating a knowledgeable belief. Significantly, he chooses an instance appropriate to the Darwinian debates that he and James had witnessed in the 1860s. "When a naturalist wishes to study a species," the inquirer does not begin with the prior suggestions of authorities or systems but instead "collects a considerable number of species more or less similar." Then the scientific reasoning begins: "Observ[ing] that they are not *precisely* alike . . . he builds up . . . a new general conception of the character in question." By inadvertently being "a logical engine," the scientist is coming up with both knowledge and belief about the species. The feature of logic used here is "the idea of continuity," which involves the development of "a notion of a species" or general category from a comprehension of the relations among many individuals which appear to the investigator to be distinguished from each other only "by insensible degrees." If we can regard such naturalists as "our teachers," their logic can be "a powerful aid to the formation of true and fruitful conceptions."[134]

Peirce's derivation of a logic from the work of scientists provided a forum for him to express various forms of ambivalence about the certainty of science. He admitted that the logic of continuity involves some use of fictions to generate knowledge, but his argument that such fictions have "great utility . . . in science" is a natural extension of his earlier propositions about the role of assumptions and faith in all knowledge, including the scientific. His more immediate purpose in this essay is to show that the naturalist's method implicitly involves quantification and probability. With the logic of continuity, the scientist looks at physical attributes as measurable variations around a norm. Peirce specified the connection by acknowledging parallels with leading figures in the probabilistic innovations of his time: an "example is that law of the distribution of errors which [Adolphe] Quetelet, [Francis] Galton, and others, have applied with so much success." This feature of scientific logic is particularly important, because "a science first begins to be exact when it is quantitatively treated." While many might regard this as a move toward greater certainty in science, Peirce actually thinks of it as ushering in a role for uncertainty in the form of probabilities, which he defines in its simplest terms as "the science of logic quantified." Without probabilistic thinking, "reality and fiction" are distinguished absolutely and without proportion—"the heaven-and-hell idea in the domain of thought." Probabilities allow the more moderate alternative of measuring "the proportion of cases in which . . . a mode of argument . . . carries truth with it."[135]

While Peirce's references to probabilities seem to be an introduction of uncertainty into statements that would otherwise have simpler and more definite declarations of truth or falsehood, he also pointed out that this does not constitute a kind of fuzzy claim to knowledge. "The general problem of probabilities is," Peirce declared in stiff defense of its link to factual knowledge, "from a given state of facts, to determine the numerical probability of a possible fact."[136] Probabilities can provide certainties, but with important qualifications: as Peirce had already realized at least as early as 1867, they provide answers only about groups and in the long run. So he declared it "unsound" to claim "that knowing a thing *to be* probable is not knowledge."[137]

Like Chauncey Wright's "cosmic weather," probabilities deal with the

The Elusive Certainty of Science   217

macroscopic and not the microscopic level. As Peirce explained, "An individual inference must be either true or false, and can show no effect of probability; and therefore, in reference to a single case considered in itself, probability can have no meaning." Likewise, in short stretches of time, the results of probabilistic thinking are uncertain. In the long run, however, where the number of instances sampled for probabilistic inquiry "is indefinitely great," it can determine truth about patterns of instances and trends with certainty. Peirce used these large-group and long-term qualities of probabilities to make the scientifically unorthodox but culturally sober point that his very scientific logic is rooted in "the social impulse": scientific inquiry can discover real truths, but not all at once, as "unlimited continuance of intellectual activity" is the "indispensible requirement . . . of logic."[138] In a revision of this essay three decades later, he added that the truths of probabilistic inquiry include "no syllogistic certainty, no 'mathematical' certainty" of the chances of individual events.[139] Peirce's probabilities not only add specifics to his goal of extending the logic of science to thinking in general, but also underscore his expectation of achieving truth in the long run and his ambivalence about the place of certainty in science.

In his fourth essay, "The Probability of Induction," Peirce connects his inquiries into belief formation and probabilities from earlier essays in the series. He once again takes on the role of the stern logic teacher, distinguishing proper and improper ways to use these terms. Following John Venn, whose work he had first learned in the 1860s, Peirce favors "the materialist view of the subject" according to which probabilities are "the proportion of times in which an occurrence of one kind is accompanied by an occurrence of another kind." By contrast, according to "the conceptualist view, . . . probability has often been regarded as being simply the degree of belief which ought to attach to a proposition."[140] While the materialist view has all the virtues of scientific inquiry, Peirce argues, the conceptualist view invites sloppy logic. More particularly, the materialist view involves the logic of induction in assessment of the chances or frequency patterns of large groups; the conceptualist view involves the logic of deduction in assessment of the plausibility of belief for individual instances.

Peirce's distinction is particularly significant in light of his place in the Metaphysical Club: while Wright could agree with his logically oriented colleague, James was inclined to favor the conceptualist orientation. There were many parts of Peirce's writings that would support James's leanings, such as Peirce's softening of the contrast between the materialist and the conceptualist viewpoints by noting that "it is incontestable that the chance of an event has an intimate connection with the degree of our belief in it." He linked the two views even further by adding, "When there is a very great chance, the feeling of belief ought to be very intense.... As the chance diminishes[,] the feeling of believing should diminish." While this much could coincide with James's views of belief formation, Peirce pursued a more rigorous logic about the limited truth-telling capacity of perceptions about individual events for the long run and concluded that "the conceptualist view, though answering well enough in some cases, is quite inadequate."[141]

In favoring the materialist view of probabilities and the inductive approach to the acquisition of knowledge, Peirce linked them to his ambivalence about the role of certainty in science. Despite his confidence in these tools of scientific logic, he added, "All human certainty consists merely in our knowing that the processes by which our knowledge has been derived are such as must generally have led to true conclusions." Incongruously, Peirce rested his confidence in induction and probability on the very methods he had criticized. Induction leans on deduction: "That the rule of induction will hold good in the long run may be deduced from the principle that reality is only the object of the final opinion to which sufficient investigation would lead." For all of his ambivalence about epistemological certainty, Peirce did not turn to metaphysical uncertainty; he maintained that reality itself is certain, even if the scientific logic for accessing it is excellent but fallible. Still, he had to take his confidence in it on faith, since the assurance that scientific inquiry gradually fixes belief is "one of the facts with which logic sets out."[142] His experience and extensive research led him to the conceptualist proposition that a high degree of belief ought to be attached to the arguments in this essay about the methods of induction and the materialist view of probability.

Between Certainty and Uncertainty

The cosmological title of and religious comments contained in the fifth essay, "The Order of Nature," suggest a return to the popularizing goals of the essay series, but in the body of the essay, Peirce continued his move toward more and more complex exposition of his logic of science. While the fourth essay ends with a word of faith that inquiry, if properly logical, will lead to knowledge of reality, "The Order of Nature" is dedicated to the source of Peirce's confidence in scientific inquiry. An orderly nature makes logical inquiry and its discovery of reality possible and plausible. While this argument suggests a connection to natural theology, Peirce actually scorned the attempt to prove the divine through order in nature because it arrogantly offers God only "circumspect homage," and then "only after having scrutinized his credentials." As his earlier thoughts on science and religion had already shown, Peirce preferred the idealism of outlooks that induce the believer to "recognize . . . his adorable God, and sink . . . upon his knees at once." Despite his intense technical sophistication, this idealism in the form of faith in logic and reverence for the orderliness of nature actually lies at the fountainhead of his analysis of scientific reasoning. He said that the discovery of "any general characteristic of the universe" and of "any law everywhere applicable and universally valid" would be a "singular assistance to us in all our future reasoning," and such order would deserve a place "at the head of the principles of logic."[143] Peirce clearly believed in a divine creator and an orderly universe, but in this essay his prime goal is not to announce a theology but to lay the cosmological ground for his scientific logic.

In exploring the logical implications of different conceptions of order in the universe, Peirce placed his outlook between certainty and uncertainty. It seemed to him that the universe is not "a pure throw of the dice" in which there could be "no laws" and "no general proposition"; on the other hand, "there does not seem to be any precise system in [the] arrangement" of the world either. While the question is metaphysically unanswerable, the choice between the two pictures of the world is crucial to scientific logic's reliability in gaining knowledge with confidence. Inductive inquiry, which gains knowledge through "a process of sampling," relies on the assumed orderliness of its sample to do its business, since the inquirer presumes that the randomly selected portion "has nearly the same frequency of occurrence" as the whole class of things under evaluation. The process of induction betrays Peirce's familiar ambivalence about certainty in scientific inquiry. He pointed out, "We have no right to assume . . . that [with] induction . . . we ever do discover the precise causes of things." But his confidence rebounded with the following assertion: "There are certain of our inductions which present an approach to universality so extraordinary that, even if we are to suppose that they are not strictly universal truths, we cannot possibly think that they have been reached merely by accident." Peirce clearly favored the latter view, which suggests that induction provides, if not certainty, then at least near certainty. He leaned his faith in induction on the orderliness of the human mind and the world it comes to investigate: "It seems incontestable . . . that the mind of man is strongly adapted to the comprehension of the world" and that "the only scientific presumption is, that the unknown parts of space and time are like the known parts."[144]

Peirce's discussion of the workings of induction at the heart of "The Order of Nature" shows that the essay is not a religious aside, but a frank testimony to the role of faith—in this case faith in an orderly nature, a faith that sustains induction. There is a faith-filled impulse behind his bold statement that "all science rolls upon presumption," but this concession did not lead him to think that scientific inquiry produces only suggestions or impressions; instead, he firmly maintained, induction produces "solid . . . human knowledge." Most important, even if scientific processes are misused or ignored, no one "can long arrest the triumphal car of truth." Peirce showed his faith in the acquisition of knowledge by maintaining that "the facts . . . will surely get found out." After steering this essay on induction's cosmological background toward the pulse of faith surging beneath scientific inquiry, Peirce ended the piece the way he began it, with references to religion. He defended religion for reasons that parallel his faith in induction and that hark back to his elite social standing. He warned that "to shake the general belief in the living God would be to shake the general morals." He went on to suggest that even those who disagree with parts of a church's principles should not dismiss the religion as a whole. Just as a less than certain faith in order sustains his confidence in the results of induction, so in religion: to reject either because not perfect "would be to estimate those errors as of more consequence than the truth."[145] Still ambivalent about certainty, Peirce embraces careful science and moral religion as near certainties.

The sixth essay, "Deduction, Induction, and Hypothesis," introduces to the essay series the third mode of logical inference, hypothesis formation, which complements Peirce's earlier references to induction and deduction. In fact, the last essay so readily follows earlier discussions that Peirce later considered changing its order to fit between "The Doctrine of Chances" and "The Probability of Induction."[146] This arrangement would have had the merit of introducing all three terms earlier in the series, but for the general goal of the essays—to clarify the logic of scientific inquiry—the order as written in the 1870s works well. There is a natural flow from the fifth essay's justification for induction based on the order in nature to the sixth essay's introduction of hypothesis as the next logical step after induction.

While induction remains closely tied to its justification through orderliness in Peirce's definition of it as "the inference of a rule," hypothesis, which is equivalent to what he would later and more famously call "abduction," is a less secure method; it involves inference "as a probability, or as a fair guess." Because hypothesis is based less on long strings of orderly facts than on surmises in a relatively disorderly situation, Peirce called it "a weak kind of argument," which "often inclines our judgment so slightly toward its conclusion that we cannot say that we believe the latter to be true." Despite its weakness, which means that it produces still less certainty than induction, hypothesis provides more explanation than induction. Using a biological example suitable to Darwinian investigation, Peirce illustrated this advantage with a problem that requires thinking beyond the enumeration of induction: "Fossils are found; say, remains like those of fishes, but far in the interior of the country." The hypothetical thinking comes when the investigator seeks "to explain the phenomenon" in supposing that "the sea once washed over this land."[147]

The two modes of inference are actually very similar in that both make judgments from samples, but where induction makes a "simple enumeration" in a long string, a hypothesis "only examine[s] a single line of characters"; it is therefore "a bolder and more perilous step." With recognition of the kind of criticism that greeted Darwin's natural selection hypothesis, Peirce acknowledged that "there is some justice in the contempt which clings to the word hypothesis." Bold hypothetical inferences provide far less than certain knowledge, as he noted dismissively: "To think that we can strike out of our own minds a true preconception of how Nature acts, is a vain fancy." But Peirce did not go to the other extreme as he retrieved reasons for confidence in the work of hypothesis, saying that the successful ones "are not pure guesses, but are guided by reasons." While the two modes of inference are similar in quality, they differ in degree. "Accordingly, when we stretch an induction quite beyond the limits of our observation, the inference partakes of the nature of hypothesis." The move to hypotheses shows Peirce's recognition of the limits of the human mind. Induction works well with "cases which are similar," which the investigator can observe, but there are many cases that leap beyond those familiar channels or even for which "it would be impossible for us to observe directly." These situations call for hypotheses that are not arbitrary declarations but that deserve merit as they "explain . . . some fact which we can and do observe." Hypotheses are not simply provisional conclusions or second-class inductions, because there are so many instances demanding this method that it gains its rightful place as a distinct mode of inquiry.[148] Peirce's humility about the capacity of human knowledge ran deep, but no deeper than his confidence in the capacity of hypothetical inference to come up with reasonable explanations.

Peirce closed his last essay of the "Illustrations" series with the ideas of belief and habit that opened the series. Linking the language of the essays, he stated that "induction infers a rule, . . . [and] the belief of a rule is a habit." Recurrent patterns are indications of nature's characteristics, and induction is our understanding of them. The scientific fixation of belief uses at least two different methods, induction or hypothesis, depending on the situation. In either case, as with Peirce's statements in "The Fixation of Belief," "knowledge can only be furthered by the real desire for it." Scientific inquiry involves approaching problems as open questions, with a "fair and unbiased" frame of mind. The investigator's use of induction and hypothesis avoids "the methods of obstinacy, of authority, and every mode of trying to reach a foregone conclusion," Peirce noted, reviewing his dismissal of the first three methods of fixing beliefs. At this end point in the essays, after explaining so much logic in so much detail, Peirce seemed to realize his limits as a popular communicator. Whereas a writer such as James would have clarified his points with metaphor and vivid application, Peirce coolly stated, "I shall leave the reader to find out by experience" the advantages of this logical counsel. In closing, he pointed out that there are many advantages to the scientific methods of reasoning but also admitted that his "reasoning [was] somewhat severe and complicated"; still, he added, "I can promise [the reader] that he will find his advantage in it, in various ways."[149] True to his unteacherly style, Peirce left unspoken his hope to persuade more people to seek true knowledge, to think clearly, and to adopt scientific habits in the formation of belief.

Peirce was not the only one distracted from his goal of popularizing scientific logic. His essays did not have wide popular appeal, although eventually they did gain fame among the emerging academic intellectuals of the late nineteenth century. Ironically, considering his scorn for the method of reasoning and for philosophizing, his greatest impact was among philosophers, but true to his goals, he did help to pull professional philosophy in more scientific directions.[150] Yet even among these movements that he helped to inaugurate, Peirce was not at home. His enthusiasm for science obscured notice of his equally strong feeling for religion and for the religious and idealistic sources of his scientific logic. While many philosophers read him as a rather stern logical taskmaster and patron of professional philosophy, James read Peirce in terms of his titanic tensions between science and religion, between certainty and uncertainty, between realism and fallibilism.

Because James knew Peirce as a young man and shared so many of the same experiences and issues, he understood the centrality of the conflict between science and religion in his philosophical quest. They both reflected philosophically in a context of simultaneous great respect for morality and religion and for the methods of science exemplified by Darwin. Within this setting, however, they differed: Peirce addressed the problems of science's relation to religion by increasing the sophistication of science and logic, while James remained unsatisfied with Peirce's solution, even though he did learn from it. The less logically oriented James was not as impressed by Peirce's technical sophistication as he was by the irreducible philosophical ambiguities to which his friend's thorough and honest logic kept returning. When Peirce said that "to admit as a theory is the same as to believe,"[151] he may not have intended the notion that scientific and religious epistemologies parallel each other in offering plausible and probable propositions about the nature of the world, but this is the view that James gleaned from his logic. Without his friend's commitment to logic and enthusiasm for science, James would face the ambiguities of his insights more squarely and eventually embrace uncertainty more thoroughly.

Peirce disapproved of James's extensions of his insights beyond science and logic. When Peirce read James's versions of "his bantling 'pragmatism,'" he decided to give his form of their philosophy the new name "'pragmaticism,'" which, he added in grudging recognition of his failures at popularizing his scientific outlooks, "is ugly enough to be safe from kidnappers."[152] In strictest terms, James misread Peirce, but it was a creative misreading that allowed for his development of a more popular and general philosophy. The younger philosopher would develop a host of theories that involved an embrace of uncertainty in the form of flexibility, practicality, openness, will, risk, freedom, and pluralism. He was much more attuned than his more logical colleague to addressing the growing suspicion among scientists, religious believers, science watchers, and religion watchers that their propositions could not provide the certainty that previous generations had cherished.

James's philosophy was a response to the proposed certainties that he saw all around him in the scientific and religious assumptions of his culture, in his father's ideas, in his teachers, and even to a certain extent in the scientific thought of Chauncey Wright and Charles Peirce. But James recognized outcroppings of uncertainty, and he even observed a profound inconsistency in his friends' scientific persuasion: they recognized the impossibility of certainty in human knowledge, and then they implied in various ways and in varying degrees that science provides certain knowledge. Peirce was more sophisticated than Wright, but his zeal for science kept bringing him to a similar point. With a friendship shaped by discussion and constructive disagreement, they each nurtured each other's thoughts. Wright held James's impulse to believe in check and served as his lifelong model of the scientific temper, but he died too young to feel the impress of James's insights in return. Peirce exposed James to the role of habit in belief formation, to the juxtaposition of certainty and uncertainty in probabilities, and to the ambiguities of scientific knowledge.

James valued these ideas but used the inconsistencies of Wright and Peirce as a wedge to introduce uncertainty into the domain of legitimate intellectual inquiry. While steering away from their formulations, he asked more general and tougher philosophical and cultural questions about the place of uncertainty in science and religion. Peirce unintentionally showed James the abyss of uncertainty but covered it with his confidence in science. Recklessly, from Peirce's point of view, James, still in his youth, tore back the cover of scientific logic and starkly faced the lack of certainty in our understanding of the world. Recognition was only the first step, because he realized even more acutely than his peers the psychological appeal of certainty. To maintain the moral commitments that his whole circle cherished, to avoid a slide into nihilism, and to reconstruct belief for a scientific audience, James would need to find the moral equivalent of certainty. He could not do this all at once. It would take over two decades of learning and assimilation of his scientific education before he could present outlooks freed of epistemological certainty as templates for coping with the soft underbelly of uncertainty beneath the brazen confidence of modern American culture.

CONCLUSION

William James and the Culture of Uncertainty

Philosophies of uncertainty cannot be acceptable; the general mind will fail to come to rest in their presence, and will seek for solutions of a more reassuring kind.

WILLIAM JAMES, 1880

Objective evidence and certitude are doubtless very fine ideals to play with, but where on this moonlit and dream-visited planet are they to be found? ... We must go on experiencing and thinking over our experience, for only thus can our opinions grow more true.

WILLIAM JAMES, 1895

What place can uncertainty have in a cultural and intellectual study of mid nineteenth-century America? Well-educated, middle-class descendants of Europeans were the ones with social power; uncertainty seems irrelevant to their condition. In particular, William James's early years spanned an era of Jacksonian go-ahead spirit, westward expansion, Civil War ferocity, and Gilded Age aggressiveness. By most accounts, the United States was full of certainty, even reckless confidence. Even the controversies of the time were debated and fought between advocates and adversaries harboring wholesale confidence in the truth of their positions. Scratch at the surface of a Northern reformer for abolition or women's rights, a Southern supporter of the peculiar institution, an evangelical minister, a writer or reader of popular novels, a teacher of philosophy, a student of science, or even a liberal Unitarian, radical transcendentalist, or a crusader for sanitary reform, and you will find anxiety about the pace of change, but little doubt about the truth of their beliefs. But scratch away the veneer of their particular convictions to look at their sense of place in the world, to examine the kind of perspectives that science and religion can give, and you'll find nagging doubts emerging in steady increase through the nineteenth century.

Most Americans had only fleeting glimpses of the culture of uncertainty, even if they had an uneasy premonition of feeling less at home in the modern world. Scientific theories and religious beliefs were becoming less and less reliable road markers toward confident assurance. William James is an extremely valuable figure in understanding these cultural trends for three main reasons. First, his early years span the period of the most intense change in ideas of uncertainty. Prophetically, he noticed trends while they were still in nebular form. Second, his own background and early life included close contact with some of the major figures and movements in the evolution of uncertainty. He experienced firsthand some of the major temptations, confusions, and traumas of declining certainty of his family, teachers, and peers. And third, as will become even more apparent in my planned second volume, he not only came to understand the intellectual and cultural place of uncertainty in science and religion, but also devised strategies to cope with it and its difficulties. James reached adulthood at a time when uncertainty was just beginning to seem apparent, but when there were as yet virtually no intellectual resources for dealing with it. From the raw material of his own life and education, he would construct his own prototype of ways to cope with uncertainty in science and religion.

Of the stage sets on which James performed his cultural work, his family was his first small and genial but intense arena. His father, the elder Henry James, directed the upbringing of the children with a degree and kind of freedom that was unorthodox for the middle of the nineteenth century but that would become more common among the middle class in the next century. The freedom of James's education, while often troubling and usually perplexing, would serve as a fund of familiarity with uncertainty from which he would draw when confronting scientific theories and religious beliefs that failed to offer complete assurance.

Leaving his family only gradually, James followed his father's advice to pursue science in order to find confirmation of the spirit. Instead, he found more uncertainty, and often in surprising ways. To begin with, the new scientific theories, most prominently Darwinism, presented a picture of the world that raised doubt about both the empirical proofs of natural theology and the ideal correspondences of his father's philosophy. In addition, the practice of science up to the 1860s had been veering away from fact gathering and proof and turning toward hypothetical constructions based on plausibility rather than certainty—trends that Darwinism underscored, exploited, and furthered. In particular, the new theory of species development through natural selection shocked supporters and antagonists alike not only for its frankly naturalistic assumptions and bluntly antisentimental morality but also for its implicitly probabilistic methodology. As William James and a few other science watchers noticed, the persuasive power of natural selection resided on a theoretical uncertainty—even if it was an enormously plausible proposition. Because James assimilated Darwinism in a probabilistic way, he turned toward uncertainty not in spite of Darwinism but because of it.

During James's scientific training at Harvard's Lawrence Scientific School, Louis Agassiz and Oliver Wendell Holmes, Sr., suggested links to the certainties of his father's spiritual science, but those assurances withered with James's further study. Agassiz's hopes to find divine presence in nature seemed increasingly unconnected with the facts of scientific research. And for all of Holmes's literary appeal to the likes of Henry James, Sr., he was as staunch an advocate for empirical and professional research as any of Harvard's aggressively scientific professors. Ultimately, William James found that he must reject the serene confidence of these teachers if he was to make sense of his own perceptions of the uncertainty inherent in knowledge.

Asa Gray confronted Agassiz's opposition to Darwin in the name of factual research and probabilistic methodology. He recognized the innovation in Darwin's approach to scientific theory formation on which the hypothesis of species development was built. Gray anticipated James in his recognition of the theoretical uncertainties in scientific theories as well as in his willingness to separate science and religion and his eagerness to cling to religion even in its separate sphere. James worked more closely with Charles Eliot and Jeffries Wyman, who served as examples of empirical scientific investigators. While his distaste for Eliot is indicative of his rejection of reductively antireligious scientism, his enthusiasm for Wyman shows his appetite for grounding theory in fact and for embracing science without the biases of extreme naturalism.

James made his closest inquiries into the theoretical foundations of science and religion in discussions with his peers. Chauncey Wright and Charles Peirce were frankly enthusiastic about science, but their zeal produced study that raised fundamental questions about the certainty even of scientific truths. Despite these suggestions, the avowedly positivistic Wright made few forays into the ways that generalizations on the nature of scientific thinking could reveal the growth of uncertainty. Instead, he devoted himself to advocating the truths of empirical science, confirming the truths of Darwinism, and separating his agnostic, moralistic, and humanitarian religion from scientific inquiry. Wright died too soon to flesh out—or to purge—the full contours of those parts of his thought which suggested that the agnostic's scalpel of uncertainty could also be applied to the intellectual methods of science itself. This legacy fell to William James, who would embrace the uncertainties of scientific inquiry.[1]

One of Charles Peirce's first audiences was James himself, who by the 1870s was in the early stages of his own theoretical reconstructions. Discussion with his more logical friend was a starting point for James's reflections, as he reveals in early notes that already show his hope for a wider application of Peirce's insights: "Peirce's def[inition] of doubt w[oul]d seem to cover all emotional dissatisfaction & disquiet."[2] In a little-known part of a famous essay, "The Sentiment of Rationality," James echoes Peirce's stages in "The Fixation of Belief" but finds simpler, more evocative language to express the same pattern of inquiry leading to conviction. James reveals his friend's influence in stating that "when the future ... is perfectly certain ... 'we do not mind it,' as we say," and we rest with ease in our beliefs or assumptions. Uncertainty, however, is uncomfortable; it disturbs and stimulates us to inquiry because "an uneasiness takes possession of the mind." James completes the Peircean parallel by stating that "novelty *per se* becomes a mental irritant, while custom *per se* is a mental sedative."[3] Peirce provided James with his best map to the emerging terrain of uncertainty, but Peirce's logical and scientific propositions were far from adequate solutions to James's search for ways to cope with uncertainty. While Peirce juggled the logical tensions between realism and fallibilism, James took these ambiguities as ample suggestions that scientific and religious inquiry could not produce certainty.

At this point in his education James realized the difficulty of achieving epistemological certainty, although he recognized its attractions and importance. He faced a dilemma because of his simultaneous recognition, first, that serious inquiry no longer assumes or generates certainty, and second, that "philosophies of uncertainty cannot be acceptable."[4] He sought a philosophy that answered the "craving for rationality," the desire to have an assuring view of one's position in the world. Feeling at home and confident of one's place in, and understanding of, the world are all human needs readily provided by certainty, but they seem to have no clear compatibility with uncertainty. This philosophical path would be difficult because it needed to steer between the

Scylla of the appetite for certainty and the Charybdis of the evidence for uncertainty. In a private notebook entry during the middle 1870s, James framed his goal: "Unless we find a way of conciliating the notion of truth and change, we must admit that there is no truth anywhere."[5] Toward the end of his scientific education James became committed to the vocation of philosophy in order to answer this theoretical dilemma and cultural paradox.

These broad questions animated James's popularly accessible philosophy, just as his position on the borders of scientific and religious inquiry framed his philosophical career. He began his education surprised by the elusiveness of religious understanding and of scientific knowledge, notably the implausibility of his father's religion and the probability of Darwin's science. By the end of his training and at the beginning of his professional career, he fully recognized the presence of uncertainty even if he could not yet fully accept it. As he expressed it in "The Sentiment of Rationality," uncertainty may have been all around him, but he would not go quietly into what seemed like the dark night of lost belief.

Even when James did accept uncertainty by the end of his career, he still could not agree with skeptics or relativists who dismissed the possibility of there being any ultimate truths. In 1895 he declared his position: "The postulate that there is truth, and that it is the destiny of our minds to attain it, we are deliberately resolving to make, though the sceptic will not make it." But he also parted company with "the absolutists," who "say that we not only can attain to knowing truth, but we can *know when* we have attained to knowing it." James took a position in between the relativists and the absolutists in maintaining that "although we may attain [truth], we cannot infallibly know when."[6] In other words, he chose to cling to metaphysical certainty but doubted the possibility of epistemological certainty. The fallibility of scientific and religious knowledge was a chief lesson of his education; finding a way, despite those limitations, to attain truth and its positive fruits was the challenge of his adulthood.

James devoted himself both personally and philosophically to the search for the benefits of certainty without an epistemology of certainty. Arthur Lovejoy wrote that James gave, in his works and in his own life, "full recognition to the reality of eternal truths." His colleague George Herbert Palmer remembered of James, "To the last he kept ample room in his empiric universe for spiritual forces." And so, he wrote, for James "an approachable God exists, reverence for whom is the beginning of wisdom." Palmer added that James "himself was a peculiarly devout man, and though living at a distance, liked to begin his day with the service at Appleton Chapel."[7] Much of James's mature work was devoted to finding the words to construct persuasive arguments out of the template of the hard-won beliefs of his own life.

Toward the end of his life when, as he said whimsically, "I'm just getting fit to live,"[8] he did more fully embrace the lack of firm assurances and proof in science and religion and formulate a philosophy for retrieving belief despite the inevitability of uncertainty. He became a widely persuasive essayist and speaker because his theoretical concerns paralleled the emerging cultural problem of uncertainty: he argued for a scientific psychology despite its provisionality, for a will to believe despite empirical doubt, for a science of religion despite the haziness of the human psyche, for the truth of pragmatic meaning despite the lack of absolutes, for the integrity and purposefulness of the universe despite its disparate plurality. These intellectual and cultural contributions grew from his own struggles with the science and religion of his day, as he matured from a youth confused by uncertainty, to a young adult recognizing yet fighting it, to a mature adult devising usable theories to cope with it. Heroism of battle he could not achieve in his youth in the Civil War; but he finally did construct a philosophical heroism as an adult.

Before he could advocate courage and risk taking in the face of uncertainty and well before he could formulate philosophies based more boldly on uncertainty, James needed to grow up. Surrounded by his father and a whole older generation that assumed scientific and religious certainty, by a culture whose religious and moral values he cherished, and by his peers who were zealous for the assurance of science, James was drawn into years of anxious searching and feelings of personal crisis. In the crucible of his young adulthood, he started to build up the possibilities for reaping the fruits of certainty in a world without certainty. This was still a very tall order for a young man uncertain of his own career, who was reading widely and taking up the professional study of science in the 1860s and 1870s. Before he could become a pioneer in constructing philosophies that cope with uncertainty, James was a student assimilating the layers of cultural and intellectual concerns that had built up his world through his twenties. During his years of education and early professional development, these scientific and religious ideas became points of inner debate as James struggled to formulate his own philosophy of life.

When he finally did establish his philosophy, which was full of recognition of the eclipse of certainty in science and religion, he did not need to reject religion or to defy science; he did not even need to overcome the legacy of his scientific education. On the contrary, he built on his years of learning science and studying its methodological workings. As he gradually understood the implications of his education, he found himself in new and treacherous territory. While he had come to understand the problems of uncertainty, it would be years before he could comprehend the possibilities for reconstructing belief despite uncertainty.

NOTES

Complete bibliographic information on the works cited below will be found in the bibliography. When I used a primary source that could also be found in a more accessible source, I have cited both, putting the primary source first and the more accessible source in square brackets []. All notes include author, title, and pages, with some exceptions: frequently cited sources are indicated with an abbreviation from the list below; and numbers following the entries on the *Collected Papers of Charles Sanders Peirce* (CPCP) refer to volume and to paragraph number.

Abbreviations

CPCP   Peirce, Charles Sanders. *Collected Papers of Charles Sanders Peirce*. 8 vols. Edited by Charles Hartshorne et al. Cambridge: Harvard University Press, 1931–58.

LCW   Wright, Chauncey. *The Letters of Chauncey Wright*. Edited by James Bradley Thayer. Cambridge: Press of J. Wilson and Son, 1878.

LR   James, Henry. *The Literary Remains of the Late Henry James*. Edited by William James. Boston: James R. Osgood, 1884.

LWJ   James, William. *The Letters of William James*. Edited by Henry James. Boston: Atlantic Monthly Press, 1920.

PD   Wright, Chauncey. *Philosophical Discussions*. Edited by Charles Eliot Norton. New York: Henry Holt, 1877.

TCWJ   Perry, Ralph Barton. *The Thought and Character of William James*. 2 vols. Boston: Little, Brown and Co., 1935.

WCP   Peirce, Charles Sanders. *Writings of Charles Sanders Peirce: A Chronological Edition*. 5 vols. to date. Edited by Max H. Fisch et al. Bloomington: Indiana University Press, 1982–92.

Preface

1. Most scholarship on William James has emphasized his psychology, philosophy, and religious thought. More specifically, he has been credited with providing a profound influence on the following disciplines: On the practice of psychology, see Browning, *Pluralism and Personality*; and Donnelly, ed., *Legacy of William James*. On non-Freudian psychotherapeutics, see Taylor, *William James on Exceptional Mental States*. On philosophical psychology, see Seigfried, *Chaos and Context*; and Myers, *William James*. On philosophical realism, see Ford, *William James's Philosophy*; and Roth, *British Empiricism and American Pragmatism*. On process philosophy, see Eisendrath, *Unifying Moments*; and Fontinell, *Self, God, and Immortality*. On phenomenology, see Wilshire, *William James's Phenomenology*; and Edie, *William James and Phenomenology*. On existentialism, see John K. Roth, *Freedom and Morality*;

Vanden Burdt, *Religious Philosophy of William James*; and O'Connell, *William James on the Courage to Believe*. On the scientific study of religion, see Levinson, *Science, Metaphysics, and the Chance of Salvation* and *Religious Investigations of William James*. On humanism, see Clebsch, *American Religious Thought*; and Dooley, *Pragmatism as Humanism*. On religious studies, see Bixler, *Religion in the Philosophy of William James*; Bradford, "Practical Theism and Pantheism"; Ruf, *Creation of Chaos*; Gavin, *William James and the Reinstatement of the Vague*; and Ramsey, *Submitting to Freedom*. On literary modernism, see Schwartz, *Matrix of Modernism*. James scholarship has even been connected to deconstruction theory: see Rorty, *Consequences of Pragmatism*. For a feminist study, see Seigfried, ed., "Feminism and Pragmatism." On folklore theory, see Mechling, ed., "William James and the Philosophical Foundations." In addition, of course, he had been important in the philosophies he himself identified. For studies on James and pragmatism, see Ayer, *Origins of Pragmatism*; John E. Smith, *Purpose and Thought*; Suckiel, *Pragmatic Philosophy of William James*; and Olin, *William James: "Pragmatism" in Focus*. On radical empiricism, see Wild, *Radical Empiricism of William James*; and McDermott, ed., *The Writings of William James*. Moreover, some works have integrated the various parts of his philosophy, including Flournoy, *Philosophy of William James*; Ralph Barton Perry, *Thought and Character of William James*; Corti, ed., *Philosophy of William James*; and Seigfried, *William James's Radical Reconstruction of Philosophy*.

2. A minority of James scholarship deals with the impact of his context on his thinking and of his work on the culture he lived in: Allen, *William James*; Conkin, *Puritans and Pragmatists*; Marcell, *Progress and Pragmatism*; Strout, "William James and the Twice-Born Sick Soul"; Fullinwider, "William James's Spiritual Crisis"; Gilbert, *Work without Salvation*; Madden and Madden, "Psychosomatic Illness of William James"; Anderson, "Why Did William James Abandon Art?" and "'The Worst Kind of Melancholy'"; Richards, *Darwin and the Emergence of Evolutionary Theories*; Schwehn, "Making the World"; Barzun, *Stroll with William James*; Bjork, *Compromised Scientist* and *William James*; Feinstein, *Becoming William James*; Hollinger, "The Problem of Pragmatism," "William James and the Culture of Inquiry," and "Justification by Verification"; Kloppenberg, *Uncertain Victory*; Cotkin, *William James, Public Philosopher*; Lentricchia, "Return of William James," "On the Ideologies of Poetic Modernism," and *Ariel and the Police*; Spears, "William James as Cultural Hero"; Halttunen, "'Through the Cracked and Fragmented Self'"; Posnock, *Trial of Curiosity*; Clive Bush, *Halfway to Revolution*; and Lewis, *The Jameses*.

3. The two-volume division of labor explains why there are only brief references to James's formulations in reaction to many of the issues discussed in this book: for example, his rethinking of scientific investigations during his trip with Agassiz to Brazil, his quarrel over nihilism with Chauncey Wright, his discovery of medicine as a practical version of his emerging realization of the uncertainties of science, his learning from German physiological psychology and British positivism, and his personal crisis about what to do in life and what philosophy to hold. These stories, which are weighted more toward James's response to his context, will continue, with more detail and depth, in Volume 2.

4. Peirce, "The Century's Great Men in Science" (1901), in Wiener, ed., *Charles S. Peirce*, pp. 267–68.

Introduction

1. Poe, "Purloined Letter," pp. 979, 980, 983, 975, and 990.
2. See Eco and Sebeok, eds., *Sign of Three*; and Ginzburg, "Clues."
3. See Scott, *Gender and the Politics of History*. Much recent historical writing has come to recognize the place of gender as a historical factor alongside and within other factors. For example, see Rosalind Rosenberg's examination of the crucial influence of gender in early-twentieth-century social science in *Beyond Separate Spheres* and Skocpol's argument about the importance of women's voluntary organizations in the formation of the ideas and policies of the American welfare state in *Protecting Soldiers and Mothers*.
4. See Crosby, *Columbian Exchange* and *Germs, Seeds, and Animals*. Verano and Ubelaker, eds., *Disease and Demography* adds the important qualification that the Americas were not a disease-free paradise. For a popularized overview of this topic, see Diamond, "Arrow of Disease."
5. William James, *Principles of Psychology*, chapter 4: "Habit," pp. 109–31, and chapter 19: "The Perception of 'Things,'" pp. 722–75.
6. My use of the term "certainty" in its cultural role parallels the more technical terms of philosophers. Tom Rockmore, in his introduction to Rockmore and Beth Singer, eds., *Antifoundationalism Old and New*, defines "foundationalism" as the position which "contend[s] that all knowledge claims . . . must rest on and be justified by an epistemology that guarantees certainty" (p. 5). While foundationalists use building metaphors about firm foundations, antifoundationalists make efforts "to validate knowledge claims without appealing to an absolute or ultimate basis known with certainty" (ibid., pp. 6 and 8).

Rockmore, in his introduction, and Joseph Margolis, in "The Limits of Metaphysics and the Limits of Certainty," in Rockmore and Singer, eds., *Antifoundationalism Old and New*, and Toulmin, in his introduction to Dewey, *Quest for Certainty*, point out that debate between foundationalism and antifoundationalism has had an ancient history. Foundationalism grew out of the ancient Greek rationalist tradition and received its modern expression in the work of René Descartes and the train of philosophy that followed in the wake of his quest for certainty and necessity, whether by rational or empirical means.

Along with other modern antifoundationalists, James and other pragmatists rejected foundationalism in favor of an epistemology that assumes an active inquiry and participation by the knower in the thing known. As Sandra Rosenthal, in "Pragmatism and the Reconstruction of Metaphysics: Toward a New Understanding of Foundations" (also in Rockmore and Singer), argues, the novelty of pragmatism is that it is neither foundational nor antifoundational, but instead undercuts the frameworks of each (pp. 165–66). Similarly Charlene Haddock Seigfried, in "Like Bridges without Peirs: Beyond the Foundationalist Metaphor" (Rockmore and Singer), points out that James "did not altogether escape the seduction of foundationalism" (p. 144). She argues that although he held out hope for establishing certainty, his critique of foundationalism was so thorough and effective, and his inquiries into the role of interests and lived experience in knowing were so radical, that he suggests an antifoundational direction for contemporary philosophy. Seigfried, in *William James's Radical Reconstruction of Philosophy*, both analyzes his "pathfinding" (p. 24) through the antifoundationalist possibilities and begins construction of an antifoundationalist philosophy, inspired by James's insights.

This work by philosophers is the theoretical backdrop to the historical analysis of the evolution away from certainty in science and religion of James and his circle.

7. See Bushman, *Refinement of America*; and Wyatt-Brown, *Southern Honor*. For a recent set of examples proposing an expanded attention to the role of culture as a historical force, see Fox and Lears, eds., *Power of Culture*.

8. Kant, *Religion within the Limits of Reason Alone* and *Critique of Practical Reason*. On Kant's religious philosophy, see Wood, *Kant's Moral Religion*; for a recent succinct summary of his epistemology, see Green, "Kant's Philosophy."

9. Geertz, *Interpretation of Cultures*, p. 112.

10. Tocqueville, in *Democracy in America*, observed a tension between the impossibility of every citizen achieving an understanding of complicated issues, because "if a man had to prove for himself all . . . truths, . . . he would never come to an end of it" (p. 434); he also noted the impulse of Americans to rely on "their own judgment as the most apparent and accessible test of truth" (p. 430): Americans wanted to sidestep authorities and make their own decisions, but that would become increasingly difficult with more things to know and more complicated religious and scientific questions; the net result was a steady increase in uncertainty. Tocqueville anticipated the rise of professionalism—and its simultaneous social confidence and theoretical uncertainty—as a response to this situation when he observed that "cleverer men" can discover truth that others should accept (p. 434); but even that elite realm is vulnerable, as he indicates: "Philosophers themselves are almost always surrounded by uncertainties" (p. 443).

11. Cashdollar, *Transformation of Theology*, pp. 146–50; but Cashdollar does not emphasize the potential uncertainties within positivism. His theme is the popularity of positivism and the way it undercut religion and forced it to reconstruct itself in positivistic terms.

12. See Haskell, ed., *Authority of Experts*. The contributors to this volume disagree on many issues, especially on the sources of experts' power and their ways of legitimating it and commanding deference, but the essays agree on the socially confident position of the professional. Further explorations of this line of inquiry include Furner, *Advocacy and Objectivity*, Haskell, *Emergence of Professional Social Science*, JoAnne Brown, "Professional Language," and *Definition of a Profession*, and Ross, *Origins of American Social Science*.

13. For example, in a broad-ranging cultural analysis of the alleged affair between Henry Ward Beecher and Elizabeth Tilton in the 1860s and 1870s, Fox observes that the trial brought such a contest of ideologies that it "may have helped prepare some

Americans to give up the objectivist faith that truth was 'out there' waiting to be discovered"; see "Intimacy on Trial: Cultural Meanings of the Beecher-Tilton Affair," in Fox and Lears, eds., *Power of Culture*, p. 127. On Dewey's participation in this trend, see *Quest for Certainty*; Stephen Toulmin introduction to this volume; and Westbrook, *John Dewey and American Democracy*.

14. Cotkin has used a parallel theme to organize many facets of culture in the late nineteenth century: his "reluctant modernists" were the intellectuals who embraced ideologies of change and reform, but with regret and an unwillingness to accept "chaos and disorder"; see his *Reluctant Modernism*, p. xiv.

15. See the overviews of Shalhope, "Toward a Republican Synthesis" and "Republicanism and Early American Historiography"; and Appleby, "Republicanism in Old and New Contexts"; and the critique by Rodgers, "Republicanism."

16. On the ancient background and on the seventeenth- and eighteenth-century origins of the probabilistic revolution, see David, *Games, Gods, and Gambling*; Hacking, *Emergence of Probabilities*; and Daston, *Classical Probability*. On the probabilistic revolution itself, see Krüger et al., eds., *Probabilistic Revolution*; Gigerenzer et al., eds., *Empire of Chance*; and Hacking, *Taming of Chance*. Also see Hacking, "Nineteenth-Century Cracks in the Concept of Determinism."

17. Daston, introduction to *Probabilistic Revolution*, 1:1.

18. Theodore Porter, *Rise of Statistical Thinking*, p. 150.

19. Hacking in *The Taming of Chance* puts the two sides this way: "There is a seeming paradox: the more the indeterminism, the more the control; if nature is at bottom irreducibly stochastic, this enhances our ability to interfere with and alter the course of nature" (p. 2). Also see Gleick, *Chaos*; Kellert, *In the Wake of Chaos*; and Field and Golubitsky, *Symmetry in Chaos*.

20. Shilts, *And the Band Played On*; and Fee and Fox, *AIDS*.

21. Religious flyer from Evangelism Explosion III International, P.O. Box 23820, Ft. Lauderdale, FL 33307. See Marsden, *Fundamentalism and American Culture*.

22. *Nova* episode, "In the Path of a Killer Volcano," aired on February 13, 1993. See Ronald Perry, Michael K. Lindell, and Marjorie Greene, "Threat Perception and Public Response"; and Saarinen and Sell, *Warning and Response*, especially "Interpreting Scientific Data," pp. 48–51.

23. In the last decade of his life, while defining pragmatism and defending it from critics, James himself showed clear recognition of chance in our understanding of the world—but without the probabilistic move to find certainty amid the uncertainty. He explained three major influences that had contributed to the formulation of pragmatism: first, the emphasis on the "incongruence of the forms of our thinking with the 'things' which the thinking nevertheless successfully handles"; second, "the doctrine of Evolution [which] weaned us from fixities in general, and [gave] us a world all plastic"; and third, "the enormous growth of the sciences in the past fifty years has reconciled us to the idea that 'Not quite true' is as near as we can ever get"; see review of F. C. S. Schiller, *Humanism: Philosophical Essays* (1904), in *Essays, Comments, and Reviews*, pp. 550–51. Levinson, in *Religious Investigations*, observes that by the end of his life, James came to recognize that "natural scientists [have] abandoned the

quest for certainty in favor of statistical analysis and the generation of probability statements" (p. 178). I explore James's connection to the probabilistic revolution in "From History of Science to Intellectual History."

24. See Hofstadter, *Social Darwinism in American Thought*, and Russett, *Darwin in America*. Bjork, in *William James*, assumes this view in his identification of Darwinism with "late nineteenth-century deterministic thinking" as he presents James struggling against such trends (p. 121).

25. Chadwick recognizes the definition of secularism as religious decline but prefers to think of it as a transforming of the religious impulse: "We keep running, suddenly and in unexpected by-ways, into the idea that secularism is a religious process, instead of an irreligion"; see *Secularization of the European Mind*, p. 156. Similarly, Lightman, in *Origins of Agnosticism*, discovers that the notoriously godless British agnostics of the nineteenth century were actually religious; and Cashdollar, in *Transformation of Theology*, shows that positivism both undercut theological claims and offered a passionate religion of humanity.

26. See Neuhaus, *Naked Public Square*; Berger, *Sacred Canopy*; Marty, *Modern Schism*; David Martin, *General Theory of Secularization*; and James R. Moore, *Post-Darwinian Controversies*.

27. Commager, *American Mind*, pp. 166–67; Carter, *Spiritual Crisis of the Gilded Age*; and Gary Scott Smith, *Seeds of Secularization*, p. 2.

28. Hutchison includes this charming anecdote in his preface to *Between the Times*, p. ix.

29. See Higham and Conkin, eds., *New Directions in American Intellectual History*. Proceeds from the book helped to spawn *Intellectual History Newsletter*, which has been published annually since 1979.

30. In addition to the work of Hollinger, Kloppenberg, and Turner cited below, a number of other historians have come to assume the growth of secularism in their study of related fields. For example, the main characters in Peter Dobkin Hall, *Organization of American Culture*, and Ross, *Origins of American Social Science*, are an influential group of highly educated Northeastern gentry who, while coming to maturity in the mid-nineteenth century, witnessed without sorrow the declining influence of orthodox religion on elite cultural institutions and came to believe that "natural science had the power to provide a total worldview" (Ross, p. 54). In addition, Cashdollar, in *Transformation of Theology*, uncovers the way Auguste Comte's positivist philosophy set the terms of debate in theological thought of the middle to late nineteenth century.

31. Hollinger, "Justification by Verification," p. 119.

32. Hollinger, "William James and the Culture of Inquiry," pp. 11 and 22.

33. See Rorty, *Consequences of Pragmatism* and *Contingency, Irony, and Solidarity*; Mitchell, ed., *Against Theory*; Poirier, *Poetry and Pragmatism*; and Gunn, *Thinking across the American Grain*.

34. Hollinger, "William James and the Culture of Inquiry," p. 3.

35. The quotation is adapted from William James's comment about initial psychological perception before the learning that makes experience coherent: "The baby,

assailed by eyes, ears, nose, skin, and entrails at once, feels it all as one great blooming, buzzing confusion," *Principles of Psychology*, p. 462.

36. Kloppenberg, *Uncertain Victory*, pp. 45, 35, 24, and 4.

37. In a similar vein, Febvre, examining the place of religion among the most radical freethinkers of sixteenth-century Europe, concludes that even for the few who contemplated unbelief, "it had retained the status of an unverifiable idea, vague and without force. How could it have been otherwise?" Febvre answers: because the culture was so "totally involved in Christianity" that there was "no material . . . for forming valid doubts or for supporting those doubts with proofs that, on the basis of experimentation, could have the force of real, veritable convictions"; see *Unbelief in the Sixteenth Century*, pp. 456 and 455.

38. Westfall, in *Science and Religion in Seventeenth-Century England*, points out that "with the growing prestige of science," Christians tended to adjust their beliefs "to conform to the conclusions of science" (p. 3). Buckley, in *Origins of Modern Atheism*, argues that religious apologists sought to become less devotional and more philosophical in an attempt to partake of the authority of science. These new religious approaches were part of a broader philosophical trend in Europe from the seventeenth through the nineteenth century, most especially in the tradition of John Locke, which James Hoopes calls "the consciousness concept." This label identifies an epistemological assurance and cultural confidence based on "the notion that the self enjoys complete knowledge of its thoughts"; see *Consciousness in New England*, p. 2. This trend in the religious and intellectual life also parallels changes in material culture toward increased demand for order and regularity; see Deetz, *In Small Things Forgotten*.

39. See Hovenkamp, *Science and Religion in America*, especially "Knowing and Believing," pp. 19–36, which depicts the eagerness of scientists and religious leaders seeking to unite these two ways of comprehending the world. Also see Bozeman, *Protestants in an Age of Science*; Cashdollar, *Transformation of Theology*; and Conser, *God and the Natural World*.

40. Wolf has made such a comparative study of the economic relations of *Europe and the People without History*.

41. Juan Nentuig quoted in Spicer, *Cycles of Conquest*, p. 322. Spicer points out that "dogmatism about the spiritual world was a difficult idea to get over to the Indians" (ibid.).

42. Jon Roberts argues similarly that theology encouraged the "transfer of cultural authority to science [and the] impoverishment of the religious vision of the world" in *Darwinism and the Divine*, p. xv. Cashdollar, in *Transformation of Theology*, emphasizes the shift of cultural authority to science that the popularization of positivism brought, but he does not blame theologians for trying to cope with these changes (pp. 446–48).

43. Turner, *Without God, without Creed*, pp. 30, 55, 73, 105, 50, and 144; and Orville Dewey quoted in Burnham, *How Superstition Won and Science Lost*, p. 145.

44. Turner does not refer to at least two groups who might serve as counterexamples to the trend in religion to imitate science in the quest for treating faith as certain knowledge: namely, Roman Catholics, especially those respecting mystery and

adhering to institutional pronouncements to beware of atheistic science; and the religion of African-American slaves who had little access to or concern for scientific ideas and much commitment to the nonrational emotional comforts of religion. See Dolan, *American Catholic Experience*, and Raboteau, *Slave Religion*. Investigation of these and other nonmainstream groups could produce evidence for the modern endurance of religious assumptions unassailable by epistemological inquiry. This in turn could suggest reasons for the limited cultural power of intellectuals with their epistemologies of uncertainty and their social claims to authority: marginal groups are doubly alienated from intellectual and professional elites; not only are they of a different class, but also they have different styles of thinking.

45. See Burnham, *How Superstition Won and Science Lost*.

46. I explore the certainties of popularized science, including the way they were framed in masculine terms, in "William James in Search of an Audience."

47. For a work with a parallel theme, namely the seeds of American modernism in the literature, popular culture, reform movements, and politics of the second third of the nineteenth century, see Lewis Perry, *Boats against the Current*.

48. The introspective James clearly used his own life as one source when stating that "in most of us, by the age of thirty, the character has set like plaster, and will never soften again. If the period between twenty and thirty is the critical one in the formation of intellectual and professional habits, the period below twenty is more important still for the fixing of personal habits" (*Principles of Psychology*, p. 126).

49. Dewey, "William James," pp. 95 and 96. Kloppenberg uses the phrase *via media* as a defining characteristic of late-nineteenth-century thought, in *Uncertain Victory*, pp. 15–63. Recent studies of James's religious thought have emphasized the deliberate open-endedness of his theorizing. Ruf, in *Creation of Chaos*, evaluates the way the eclectic and vivid style of *Principles of Psychology* and *Varieties of Religious Experience* is chaotic in constructive and stimulating ways. Gavin, in *William James and the Reinstatement of the Vague*, argues that James embraces vagueness in that "the text is never finished [and] . . . closure is always deferred" (p. 10). Ramsey, in *Submitting to Freedom*, depicts James by the end of his career relinquishing the assertive self in favor of a religious acceptance of forces beyond its control. While the themes of these works parallel my own evaluation of eroding certainty, none of them shows this trend developing from James's early years or emerging from his scientific education, and none sets it in relation to James's hopes for the fruits of certainty despite the erosion of certainty. By contrast, Seigfried, in *William James's Radical Reconstruction of Philosophy*, emphasizes James's moves toward epistemological uncertainty but recognizes that he did not fully give up hoping for the equivalent of certainty in the construction of belief.

50. On this difference, see the pointed commentary of Wells, *Pragmatism*; Carey, "Reshaping the Truth"; and Clive Bush, *Halfway to Revolution*. By contrast, Coon, in "Courtship with Anarchy," has found strong evidence of James's radical sympathies despite his mainstream social role, especially toward the end of his life.

51. See Beisner, *Twelve against Empire*, pp. 35–82; and Cotkin, *William James, Public Philosopher*, pp. 95–151.

52. By treating the ideas of James and his circle not as abstracted ideas, but as cul-

tural factors, I partake of the method that Livingston, in *Pragmatism*, describes of his own work: "To put it in a way that William James would appreciate, I had to write as if thoughts were things" (p. xv).

53. See Prucha, ed., *Americanizing the American Indians*; and Prucha, *American Indian Policy in Crisis*.

54. "Methods for Attaining Truth" (1898), CPCP, 5.583.

55. Kessler-Harris, "Cultural Locations," p. 311; also see R. Laurence Moore, who suggests the historical roots for this outlook in "Insiders and Outsiders," and who provides case studies for this outsider identification in American religious history in *Religious Outsiders*. Limerick argues that with this approach to multiculturalism, "you are set free of the intellectually crippling temptation to take white people's ways for granted"; she adds whimsically, "Considered from this anthropological distance, white people are really quite interesting"; see *Legacy of Conquest*, p. 221.

56. For a parallel argument on the emergence of social and political radicalism from an "adversary tradition" within elite culture, see John L. Thomas, *Alternative America*; in particular, this is a study of Henry George, Edward Bellamy, and Henry Demarest Lloyd.

57. See Mahowald, "A Majority Perspective"; Frankenberry, "Pragmatism, Truth, and Objectivity"; Seigfried, "Feminism and Pragmatism"; and Larry Miller, "William James." The prominent African-American intellectual W. E. B. Du Bois provides a personal example of James's openness. When he was a student at Harvard, he described James and Albert Bushnell Hart as his favorite teachers, and he added, "I was repeatedly a guest in the house of William James; he was my friend and guide to clear thinking"; see Du Bois, *Dusk at Dawn*, p. 38.

58. See Toulmin, *Human Understanding*; Rorty, *Consequences of Pragmatism*; Bernstein, *Beyond Objectivism and Relativism*; West, *American Evasion of Philosophy*; Diggins, *Promise of Pragmatism*; Hoopes, "Objectivity *and* Relativism Affirmed"; and Livingston, *Pragmatism*. This outlook is by no means universal, but it has become such a usable theory that it sometimes appears without direct identification: for example, Kessler-Harris concludes her essay "Cultural Locations" with suggestions for the evolution of multiculturalism from a study of particular groups to a method for "seeing relationally" and for "refus[ing] to acknowledge a stable meaning or precise unchanging definition of America" (p. 311)—these outlooks resonate with a distinct Jamesian tenor. For a history of classic pragmatism and an overview of its legacy in twentieth-century philosophy, see Thayer, *Meaning and Action*; and Murphy, *Pragmatism*.

59. See David D. Hall's observations about the elite "conservative revolutionaries" who came of age in the 1850s to 1870s, in "The Victorian Connection."

60. This line of inquiry bears some similarity to Steve Fuller, *Social Epistemology* and *Philosophy, Rhetoric*; Galison, "History, Philosophy"; Law and Williams, "Putting Facts Together"; and Danziger, *Constructing the Subject*. But where these historians and philosophers of science are concerned with how society and culture influence the production of knowledge—and emerge with competing conclusions about the influence of theorist on audience or of audience on theorist—my focus is on how society and culture appropriate knowledge once produced. For recent examples of works

written with this rare combination of scholarly concerns, see McDermott, *Culture of Experience* and *Streams of Experience*; and John E. Smith, *America's Philosophical Vision*. McDermott and Smith are philosophers who ask cultural questions, but historians have been more hesitant to look for the cultural role of philosophy.

Part I Introduction

1. Henry James, Jr., *A Small Boy and Others* (1913), in *Autobiography*, p. 4. In another example, Robertson remembered, "It was a beautiful and splendid childhood for any child to have had, and I remember it all now as full of indulgence and light and color and hardly a craving unsatisfied"; Robertson James to Alice Howe Gibbens James (William James's wife), February 24, 1898, TCWJ, 1:184–85.

2. William James to Alice James, London, July 29, 1889, TCWJ, 1:412.

Chapter 1

1. Henry James's actual date of birth was June 2, 1811. For biographical background, see Grattan, *Three Jameses*, pp. 22–106; Warren, *Elder Henry James*; TCWJ, 1:3–166; Feinstein, *Becoming William James*, pp. 37–100; and Lewis, *The Jameses*, pp. 37–70. The fireworks story is from his pseudonymous autobiography, "Immortal Life: Illustrated in a Brief Autobiographical Sketch of the Late Stephen Dewhurst, edited, with an Introduction, by Henry James." When he wrote it in the late 1870s at the urging of his family, he wrote himself in as the main character under a pseudonym. It remained unpublished until collected posthumously with other works in *Literary Remains*; it has most recently been published in the anthology edited by Matthiessen, *James Family*, pp. 17–38. In his introduction to the volume, William James noted that his father had no taste for "egoistic analysis," which explains why he used "an entirely fictitious personage" in place of himself, and why he left the fragment of autobiography incomplete (LR, p. 7). The sons William and Henry James regarded their father's autobiographical account as authentic and generally factual. Howard Feinstein offers important qualifications for reading Stephen Dewhurst as a direct stand-in for Henry James in his article "*Autobiography* of the Elder Henry James." Not finding striking differences between author James and his fictional persona, Feinstein points out that Dewhurst does not wholly represent James, but instead "had all the ideal qualities which the elder Henry aspired toward, after a lifetime of spiritual development" (p. 306). This "spiritual allegory" (p. 295) expresses James's personal and intellectual goals, including his religious aspirations, his philosophy of education, and his theories of child rearing.

2. On William of Albany, see Hastings, "William James of Albany"; Larrabee, "The Jameses"; Grattan, *Three Jameses*, pp. 2–20; Feinstein, *Becoming William James*, pp. 23–36; Croce, "Money and Morality"; and Lewis, *The Jameses*, pp. 3–32.

3. Henry James, Jr., *A Small Boy and Others*, p. 190 [Matthiessen, *James Family*, p. 5].

4. Recent research on Irish immigration in the eighteenth century indicates that James's attitudes toward the United States, republicanism, and business enterprise were

not at all uncommon; see Kerby A. Miller, *Emigrants and Exiles*. Also see Leyburn, *Scotch-Irish*; Dickson, *Ulster Migration to Colonial America*; Maldwyn A. Jones, "Ulster Migration"; and Doyle and Edwards, eds., *America and Ireland*.

5. Hastings, "William James of Albany," pp. 101–2; Grattan, *Three Jameses*, pp. 6–7.

6. Paige, "Hawley vs. James," *Cases Argued and Determined*, 5:337. The land was in Greenwich Village between Bethune and Troy (now West 12th) Streets from Greenwich Street to the Hudson River; also see Hastings, "William James of Albany," p. 102.

7. Munsell, *History of Albany*, 4:460. The phrase on social status, common in early-nineteenth-century America, is described in Leonard L. Richards, *"Gentlemen of Property and Standing,"* pp. 132–33. For discussion of the elites of Albany during the eighteenth and nineteenth centuries, see Kenney, *Gansevoorts of Albany* and Rowley, "Irish Aristocracy of Albany," pp. 275–84.

8. On the transformation of republicanism, see Berthoff, "Independence and Attachment"; Appleby, *Capitalism*; and Watts, *Republic Reborn*.

9. William James, transcript of speech delivered at the Erie Canal opening celebrations (1825), in Munsell, *History of Albany*, 4:463, 444, and 461. Also see Chase, *Syracuse and Its Environs*, 1:63.

10. Munsell, *Collections on the History of Albany*, 4:466, 460, 464, 443, 463, 444, 464, and 445. William of Albany was not alone in linking the Erie Canal to republican politics. In his study of the rituals and rhetoric of celebration surrounding the completion of the canal, John Seelye points out that to Americans of the 1820s, the Erie Canal was "a technological mechanism designed to carry out the geopolitical function of the Constitution—the great Republican machine—which was to assist in the spread of the Union while ensuring its stability"; see Seelye, " 'Rational Exultation,' " p. 263; on this theme in nineteenth-century America in general, see Kasson, *Civilizing the Machine*.

11. Munsell, *History of Albany*, 4:444; Grattan, *Three Jameses*, pp. 15–16.

12. Feinstein, *Becoming William James*, p. 28; this was typical in Ulster communities, and indeed in immigrant communities generally. E. R. R. Green, in "Ulster Emigrants' Letters," observes that "the immigrant group had many of the characteristics of an extended family and its members were under similar obligations to a new arrival as would have been expected by a relative at home" (p. 97). Hastings, in "William James of Albany," cites two nephews of William of Albany who "came to New York from Ireland; and under their uncle's patronage, became established finally as merchants" (p. 102).

13. *LR*, pp. 147–48 [Matthiessen, *James Family*, pp. 18–19].

14. *LR*, pp. 152–53 [Matthiessen, *James Family*, p. 21].

15. Grattan, *Three Jameses*, p. 14. On the Sabbatarian movement in another New York city, see Johnson, *Shopkeeper's Millennium*, pp. 83–94.

16. Gordon S. Wood, in *Creation of the American Republic*, provides a masterful statement of the nature of republicanism in the early American republic; see especially pp. 46–90. Wood argues that republicanism gave the American revolutionary war and the politics of the new nation a fiercely antiaristocratic character. Americans

saw themselves as more virtuous than their European counterparts because they were "a new people for a new world . . . where there were no hereditary distinctions . . . [and] where only sense, merit, and integrity commanded respect" (pp. 46–47). The new republic would lack hereditary privilege but not be devoid of all subordination: the public-spirited virtuous citizenry would "change the flow of authority . . . but . . . in no way . . . do away with the principle of authority itself" (p. 67). The partisans of republicanism were ambivalent about equality: virtue flourished best in a context of general equality, and the republican system would by common agreement "result in rough equality of station" (p. 72), yet, at least before the democratizing dynamics of the early nineteenth century, republicans urged subordination of the majority to the moral status and authority of community leaders. Wood's more recent book, *Radicalness of the American Revolution*, shows that the antiaristocratic impulse served as a gradual solvent on the lines of deference that republican leaders hoped to establish in the new nation.

17. *LR*, p. 149 [Matthiessen, *James Family*, p. 19]. Mary Kelley discusses the ambivalence that a later generation of prominent women felt about their public role in *Private Woman, Public Stage*.

18. *LR*, pp. 147–48 [Matthiessen, *James Family*, pp. 18–19].

19. *LR*, p. 174 [Matthiessen, *James Family*, p. 30].

20. Matthiessen, *James Family*, p. 34.

21. *LR*, pp. 158–60 and 171–72 [Matthiessen, *James Family*, pp. 23–24 and 29].

22. *LR*, p. 166 [Matthiessen, *James Family*, p. 27]. On James's distaste for moralism, see Ralph Barton Perry, "Religion versus Morality."

23. Albanese, in *Corresponding Motion*, analyzes the religious element of America's most prominent romantic movement, transcendentalism, and highlights the importance of a generational split; also see Ahlstrom, *Religious History of the American People*, pp. 583–614. Flower and Murphey, in *History of Philosophy in America*, especially pp. 397–514, provide a helpful overview of the German idealism that animated the romantic spirit of Henry James, the transcendentalists, and many other intellectuals and religious believers at this time.

24. *LR*, p. 191 [Matthiessen, *James Family*, p. 38]. Howard Feinstein, in *Becoming William James*, suggests that the artisans "had in fact been feeding the boy and his friends 'raw gin and brandy' morning and afternoon when they stopped by on their way to and from school from the time Henry was ten years old" (p. 47). W. J. Rorabaugh, in *Alcoholic Republic*, points out that drinking among children was very frequent in the early republic period.

25. Henry James, Sr., to Robertson James (no date), quoted in Strouse, *Alice James*, p. 11; and Feinstein, *Becoming William James*, p. 47.

26. See Hislop, *Eliphalet Nott*, pp. 73–150 and 209–33. There were many reforms of college education in this period; see Cremin, *American Education*, p. 272.

27. See Hislop, *Eliphalet Nott*, pp. 153–206 and 275–346; and Feinstein, *Becoming William James*, pp. 48–51, for descriptions of the finances of the college, including the use of a lottery and other more shady dealings that Nott engaged in to keep the college going.

28. Benjamin Rush quoted in Kaestle, *Pillars of the Republic*, p. 7.

29. Archibald McIntyre (William James's lawyer) to Henry James, Sr., November 12, 1829, Warren, *Elder Henry James*, p. 17; and Feinstein, *Becoming William James*, p. 52. Young James was not alone in his passion for fraternities and extracurricular campus life, which blossomed in the early nineteenth century; see Rudolph, *American College and University*, p. 149.

30. Henry James, Sr., to Isaac Jackson (tutor in mathematics at Union College and confidant of the young James), January 30, 1830, Warren, *Elder Henry James*, p. 18; also see Larrabee, "Flight of Henry James the First," pp. 774–75.

31. The will is reprinted with the legal opinions from the court cases that it generated in Paige, "Hawley vs. James" (1835), in *Cases Argued and Determined*; and Wendell, "Hawley vs. James" (1836), in *Cases Argued and Determined*.

32. Paige, *Cases Argued and Determined*, 5:324; and Wendell, *Cases Argued and Determined*, 16:64–65. The trustees were two of his business partners and his business-minded son, Augustus James. His first two wives had died years before: Elizabeth (Tillman) James died in 1797 and Mary Ann (Connolly) James in 1800; see Hastings, "William James of Albany," pp. 104–11.

33. Paige, *Cases Argued and Determined*, 4:116. Feinstein, in *Becoming William James*, mentions Catherine James's court success (p. 60). Lewis, in *The Jameses*, discusses the ways the will was unenforceable because of its moralistic wording (pp. 27–29).

34. Paige, *Cases Argued and Determined*, 5:323; and Wendell, *Cases Argued and Determined*, 16:62. The Reverend William James, a son of William of Albany by his first marriage, was also virtually disfranchised by the will as originally written. Although he was a Presbyterian minister, he had alienated his strict father because of his unorthodox religious ideas, and also apparently, for simply becoming a minister; Lewis, in *The Jameses*, points out that the elder James "liked having [ministers] over . . . after church on Sunday to sit . . . at his feet," but he held them in "secret contempt" (pp. 26–27).

35. Most historical accounts of the will and its effect on the son Henry James follow the same general but limited pattern: William of Albany's restrictive will withheld from the eccentric son all but a small portion of an inheritance. The young James challenged the will in court, won his case, and gained an inheritance that earned at least $10,000 annually. Upon hearing the news from court, Henry James whispered to himself, "leisured for life." See *LWJ*, 1:6; Grattan, *Three Jameses*, pp. 17–19; Warren, *Elder Henry James*, p. 21; *TCWJ*, 1:6; Matthiessen, *James Family*, p. 4; Edel, *Untried Years*, pp. 20–21; Allen, *William James*, p. 7; Myers, *William James*, p. 16, Lewis, *The Jameses*, pp. 26–32. Two recent works go into greater detail on the will and its place in the family dynamic: Feinstein's *Becoming William James* and my own "Money and Morality." They focus on different material and on different aspects of the situation. For Feinstein, the will is the center of a psychological family curse; beginning with Henry's rebellion and continuing through William's career indecision, the Jameses maintained an ambivalence over their proper vocation. My essay focuses on the political ideology of the will and the way in which the legal upshot of the case helped the family to join an American cultural elite which had difficulty finding a vocational role in democratic America. These interpretations overlap on the important

point that for the Jameses, wealth brought not only benefits, but also the launching of great indecision in search of suitable and respectable vocations.

36. See Charles Rosenberg, *Cholera Years*, especially pp. 43–46.

37. Scholarship on women's domestic sphere has emphasized the private home as caring asylum, separate from men's public world of competitive work. Some key texts include Welter, "Cult of True Womanhood"; and Cott, *Bonds of Womanhood*. Also see Ryan, *Cradle of the Middle Class*, on the way in which the movement of production out of the home set the stage for women's domesticity; Harvey Green, *The Light of the Home*, on the daily life of average middle-class white women; Sklar, *Catharine Beecher*, on the leadership of a woman advocating domesticity; and Fox-Genovese, *Within the Plantation Household*, which argues that the ideal of the home as asylum from the work world was more popular in the North, because Southern white women preferred to celebrate privilege rather than the more homey virtues of domesticity. Much recent scholarship, however, has pointed to the way "separate spheres" was more an ideological standard than a social practice. For example, Jensen, in *Loosening the Bonds*, argues that farm women were very connected to the public economy of work and wages; and Boydston, in *Home and Work*, explains that a "pastoralization of housework" hid the role of women as workers (pp. 142–63). This line of inquiry suggests that the James family division of labor was one of many variations on the theme of separate gender spheres.

38. Even though his religion was not orthodox, Henry James's experiences fit with broad cultural patterns. While women in conversion tended to turn away from dependence on others, men's conversion narratives show the urge to overcome an alienating self-sufficiency; see Juster, " 'In a Different Voice,' " p. 51.

39. *TCWJ*, 1:112. According to his spiritualized philosophy of marriage, men who enter into the discipline of loyalty are uplifted by women to a higher spiritual plane; see James, "Marriage," in Sargent, *Sketches and Reminiscences of the Radical Club*, pp. 208–44. Habegger, in *Henry James and the "Woman Business,"* connects James's conventional admiration for his wife with his antagonism for the women's movement (p. 50).

40. See Allen, *William James*, pp. 10–45; and Bjork, *William James*, pp. 1–63. Elaine Showalter points out styles of thinking and gender divisions of labor in the Alcott family which have a striking similarity to those in the James family: father Bronson directed the children's education, while mother Abigail May became the decision maker and daughter Louisa May the breadwinner. See Showalter, introduction to *Alternative Alcott*, pp. xii–xiv.

41. Scholarship on Mary James indicates the difficulties of finding information and developing interpretations about her; see, for example, Anderson, "In Search of Mary James." Some inferences can be drawn about how Mary James nurtured the children, especially in their early years and in providing for their physical needs, from Hoffert, *Private Matters*.

42. *LR*, p. 170 [Matthiessen, *James Family*, p. 28]. Strouse examines Henry James's struggle to move from his father's paternal view of God to his own maternal view of God in "Divine Maternity and a Calvinist God," in *Alice James*, pp. 3–21.

43. Henry James, Sr., to Charles Eliot Norton, May 1, 1865, Norton Papers.

44. William James to Alice Gibbens James, September 24, 1882, *LWJ*, 1:211; William James to Alice James, November 14, 1886, *LWJ*, 1:80; and Henry James, Jr., to E. L. Godkin, February 3, 1882, *TCWJ*, 1:111.

45. Anderson, in "In Search of Mary James," notes that the children, especially William, resented their mother because she was "fundamentally unempathetic and anxious" (p. 64). He cites William's jokes about his mother's appearance and her scolding him for draining the family resources. Anderson's point is that William felt that "his mother despised and ridiculed him" (p. 65) because of inconsistent care in the early years and that this relationship helped to cause his identity crisis and his "fragile self-structure" (p. 63). This analysis provides a valuable complement to the family's public position on Mary James: it probes the misty world of their personal feelings yet it does not acknowledge the family's partially reversed gender roles or the cultural "pattern of idealizing the mother" in the nineteenth century. On these cultural issues, Anderson simply states, "It was possible for individuals to break free of these pressures" (p. 65). By focusing his interpretation exclusively on personal factors, he provides an important part of the puzzle of Mary James's role in the family.

46. *LR*, pp. 159–60 [Matthiessen, *James Family*, p. 24].

47. Henry James, Jr., *A Small Boy and Others*, p. 216 [*TCWJ*, 1:150].

48. Henry James's views of child rearing, including his belief in childhood innocence and his emphasis on nurturing natural impulses, bear striking resemblance to the theories of childhood and of education in, for example, Alcott, *Infant Instruction*; Ralph Waldo Emerson, "Education," in *Early Lectures*; and Child, *Mother's Book*. Also see Strickland, "Transcendentalist Father"; and Elbert, "Model Children," in *Hunger for Home*. The novelist William Dean Howells had a similar experience: he was born in 1837 and he grew up in a Swedenborgian family; like the elder James, father William Cooper Howells, instilled his outlook through "force of affection"; see Olsen, *Dancing in Chains*.

49. *LR*, p. 154 [Matthiessen, *James Family*, p. 21].

50. *LR*, pp. 178 and 184. Significantly, James blithely looks forward to his children growing into "manhood," thus slighting the youngest child, his daughter Alice. This was in character for him and for most fathers of his generation. In *Alice James*, Strouse discusses the elder James's view of women and astutely comments that "to be a James and a girl, then, was a contradiction in terms" (p. xiii).

51. Henry James's mixed messages to William about his career choices hounded him through his twenties. This book explores the cultural and intellectual motives and implications of the father's plans for his son, especially his enthusiasm for science. Feinstein's *Becoming William James* offers helpful psychological explanations of the sources for the father's peculiar behavior: Henry James had an unresolved oedipal conflict and guilt over his prodigal relationship with William of Albany over his youthful defiance; these feelings hung over him and his children "like a family curse" (p. 252); the "labyrinth of contradictory paternal injunctions" (p. 93)—the ideal of freedom and the recoiling from any particular free choice—was Henry James's way of projecting his own anxieties on his son. The elder James's hopes for his son were a "parental tyranny ... shrouded in vague benevolence" (p. 115). Although there are also genuine differences between intellectual and cultural history and psychohistory,

these two particular interpretations are wholly complementary: this work begins with Henry's plans for his son portrayed in their intellectual and cultural contexts; Feinstein explains the personal sources of those plans.

52. Allen, *William James*, p. 64.

53. Henry James, Sr., to Ralph Waldo Emerson, March 26, [1861], *TCWJ*, 1:92.

54. Bjork argues that this is James's most characteristic and creative intellectual quality. In fact, he maintains that the "center of his vision" was in his genius for making connections across disciplinary boundaries by being "experimentally inclined [and] interested in an astonishing variety of phenomena" (*William James*, p. 32); Bjork adds, "he thought in terms of connection" (p. 264). But Bjork does not emphasize James's upbringing in the development of this intellectual trait; rather, he charges that "William's intellectual and emotional indebtedness to his father, the eccentric, one-legged mystic-philosopher, Henry James, Sr., has been considerably overplayed." Bjork is reacting to "Howard Feinstein's provocative Freudian" interpretation (p. xv) and, like most other commentators on James, overlooks the seeds of youthful intellectual development when he turns to reject the psychoanalytic interpretation of James's youth.

55. Henry James, Sr., *Nature of Evil Considered*, p. 99.

56. *LR*, p. 170 [*TCWJ*, 1:170; and Matthiessen, *James Family*, pp. 28–29].

57. Henry James, Jr., *Notes of a Son and Brother*, pp. 52 and 50–51 [*TCWJ*, 1:171]. Millicent Bell, in "Jamesian Being," argues that, according to this parental directive, "expressive selfhood was evil" (p. 120).

58. Henry James, Jr., *A Small Boy and Others*, pp. 232–35 [Matthiessen, *James Family*, pp. 82–83].

59. See Hatch, *Democratization of American Christianity*; Handy, *Christian America*, pp. 24–56; Ahlstrom, *Religious History of the American People*, pp. 385–509; Alice Felt Tyler, *Freedom's Ferment*; and Abzub, *Cosmos Crumbling*. The culmination of Jon Butler's *Awash in a Sea of Faith* is the chapter "Toward the Antebellum Spiritual Hothouse," in which he emphasizes the pluralism of beliefs, including many alternative religions, coexisting in marketplace competition. Levinson, in *Religious Investigations*, includes brief coverage of the antebellum period, especially from the point of view of religious phenomena that would figure in James's composition of the *Varieties of Religious Experience* (1902).

60. Henry James, Jr., *A Small Boy and Others*, pp. 232–35 [Matthiessen, *James Family*, p. 82].

61. Alice James, *Diary of Alice James*, p. 192 (December 31, 1890) [*TCWJ*, 1:170–71].

62. Allen, *William James*, p. 13.

63. Henry James, Sr., to Ralph Waldo Emerson, August 31, 1849, *TCWJ*, 1:59.

64. Henry James, Sr., to Isaac Jackson, January 30, 1830, Warren, *Elder Henry James*, p. 19. Bjork notes that the elder Henry James spoke only English (*William James*, p. 13).

65. William James to Charles Ritter, July 31, 1861, *TCWJ*, 1:194.

66. William James to Edgar B. Van Winkle, July 1, 1856, William James Papers.

67. *TCWJ*, 1:172.

68. Edward Waldo Emerson, *Early Years of the Saturday Club*, p. 328 [*LWJ*, 1:17–18].

69. Henry James, Jr., *A Small Boy and Others*, p. 204 [*TCWJ*, 1:173]. Edel, in *Untried Years*, points out how confident and aggressive William James was as a child (especially in contrast with the shy Henry).

70. Wilkinson to Henry James, Sr., [December 1859], *TCWJ*, 1:188. The sketch is reproduced in Feinstein, *Becoming William James*, p. 282. William's repeatedly affectionate words toward Alice have aroused disagreement among commentators over whether this is the language of displaced sexuality or the rhetoric of Victorian sentimentality. Feinstein interprets this scene as evidence of an "erotic tension between them [Alice and William]" (p. 283). Myers disagrees, arguing that William's relation to Alice was "more likely to be smart than sexy" (*William James*, p. 33).

71. Ralph Barton Perry and R. W. B. Lewis provide fuller descriptions of these schools; see *TCWJ*, 1:169–89; and Lewis, *The Jameses*, pp. 71–100. Also see Henry James, Jr., *A Small Boy and Others*, p. 271; Cornelia Kelley, *Early Development of Henry James*, pp. 18–21; and Bjork, *William James*, pp. 7–8.

72. Henry James, Sr., to Edmund and Mary Tweedy, [ca. Spring 1855], *TCWJ*, 1:181. Switzerland's reputation in children's education had grown especially from the work of Heinrich Pestalozzi (1746–1827), whose theories of childhood innocence and techniques of education through direct concrete observation closely coincided with Henry James's own views. See Pestalozzi's *Leonard and Gertrude* and *The Education of Man*. He commanded great influence among romantic era intellectuals; see Bronson Alcott, "Methods of Instruction"; Monroe, *Pestalozzian Movement in the United States*; Barlow, *Pestalozzi and American Education*; and Lee, *Joseph Neef*.

73. Ralph Waldo Emerson to Sir Arthur Helps (Clerk of the Privy Council and a writer interested in American culture), July 17, 1855, *TCWJ*, 1:82. This was one of many letters of introduction that Emerson gave to Henry James for presentation to friends of intellectual and cultural standing.

74. Henry James, Jr., *A Small Boy and Others*, p. 294 [*TCWJ*, 1:182].

75. Henry James, Jr., *A Small Boy and Others*, pp. 326–27 and 364 [*TCWJ*, 1:182–83].

76. William James to Charles Ritter (a Geneva academy classmate), July 31, 1860; the letter, touchingly addressed to "Dear Friend," is quoted in *TCWJ*, 1:193–94.

77. Henry James, Jr., *A Small Boy and Others*, p. 216 [*TCWJ*, 1:150].

78. Lears, *No Place of Grace*; Crunden, *Ministers of Reform*; and Kloppenberg, *Uncertain Victory* examine elites who grew up in the mid-nineteenth century and whose freedom in upbringing contributed to their cultural and philosophical impact.

79. Quoted in Grattan, *Three Jameses*, p. 89; and Matthiessen, *James Family*, p. 5.

80. Henry James, Sr., quoted in Henry James, Jr., *Notes of a Son and Brother*, p. 69.

81. Alice James, *Diary of Alice James*, p. 4.

82. Alice's vocational indecision was in some ways worse: while she did not have William's brief period of intense anxiety about the future, Alice James never did find a vocation, except, as she said with dark humor, her "glorious role" of being an invalid; see *Diary of Alice James*, p. 48; also see Strouse, *Alice James*, and Feinstein, *Becoming*

William James, pp. 251–97. Alice's failure, despite her talents, especially when compared with her brilliant brothers, has inspired modern feminists with questions about what she could have accomplished with more opportunity. See Yeazell, *Death and Letters*, and Sontag, "Scenes from a Play."

Chapter 2

1. Henry James, Sr., to Ralph Waldo Emerson, 1842, Matthiessen, *James Family*, p. 42.
2. Henry James, Sr., to Edmund Tweedy, July 18, [1860], *TCWJ*, 1:191.
3. *LR*, pp. 172 and 167 [Matthiessen, pp. 29 and 27].
4. Pelikan places antinomian arguments at the center of the Reformation, by describing it as a contest of "spirit versus structure"; moreover, with an attitude similar to that of Henry James, Martin Luther felt "captive in ecclesiastical structures that no longer served as channels of divine life and means of divine grace," and he sensed that "the spiritual power of the Christian gospel pressed to be released"; see *Spirit versus Structure*, p. 5. On the American scene, antinomianism has been associated most closely with an incident in early New England history: Anne Hutchinson challenged the authority of the Puritan church on the basis of direct spiritual communication with the divine. On this controversy and the antinomian tradition in American culture, see Winthrop, *Short Story*; Perry Miller, *New England Mind*; Stoever, *Faire and Easie Way to Heaven*; and Schrager, *Prophetic Woman*.
5. It is easy to see how James must have disliked his Princeton experience: his spiritual seeking readily clashed with the Christian orthodoxy that dominated the seminary. On the "Old School Presbyterianism," which flourished there to such a great extent that it took on the nationally recognized name "Princeton Theology," see Noll, ed., *The Princeton Theology*. During Henry James's years at the seminary, two of the staunchest defenders of Calvinist orthodoxy dominated the scene, Archibald Alexander and Charles Hodge. Despite his fundamental differences with their institutional orthodoxy, James actually supported their doctrine of human depravity and fallenness. For more on the religious outlooks, broad cultural influences, and controversies of the Princeton Theology, see Marsden, *Evangelical Mind*; and Hodge, *Way of Life*.
6. *LR*, p. 124; Warren, *Elder Henry James*, p. 23; and Lewis, *The Jameses*, pp. 37–41.
7. James's attraction to Sandemanianism produced his first known publication; he edited and wrote a preface to Sandeman's *Letters on Theron and Aspasio*.
8. Ralph Barton Perry, in *TCWJ*, notes James's attraction to Sandemanianism but asserts that he "was Calvinistic in his acceptance of the doctrine of justification by faith" (1:12). Frederic Young, in *Philosophy of Henry James*, concludes that "In Sandemanianism, James found antinomianism and anti-ecclesiastical views, which rested on the basic Sandemanian doctrines of the supremacy of the Gospel over the Law, . . . and the paramount importance of the Gospel as over the Church, respectively" (p. 61).
9. Warren, *Elder Henry James*, pp. 32–33; and Joseph Henry to Michael Faraday, October 9, 1838, *Papers of Joseph Henry*, 4:116. For more on Faraday's Sandemanianism and his humble piety, see Gladstone, *Michael Faraday*; Crowther, *Life and Discoveries of Michael Faraday*; and Cantor, *Michael Faraday*. Joseph Agassiz, in *Faraday*

as a Natural Philosopher, suggests that his religion may have contributed to his innovative scientific speculations—and his being "ostracized by the scientific community" (p. ix).

10. In his introductory essay to *LR*, William James suggests that all of his father's writings were elaborate expositions of "ideas that were being settled . . . between 1842 and 1850" (p. 26). A more recent student of Henry James's thought, Frederic Young, in *Philosophy of Henry James*, even more bluntly explained the reasons for James's single-minded repetitiveness: Henry James spent the last decades of his life "in a sustained literary effort to expound the ideas which he acquired during this pregnant period from 1846–1850" when he formulated "his basic stock of conceptions" (p. 165).

11. William James, introduction to *LR*, p. 9; and Thomas S. Perry quoted in Henry James, Jr., *Letters of Henry James*, 1:9.

12. William to Henry James, Jr., January 9, 1883, *TCWJ*, 1:165.

13. Henry James, Sr., to Ralph Waldo Emerson, March 1842, Warren, *Elder Henry James*, pp. 42–43.

14. Henry James, Jr., *A Small Boy and Others* [Henry James, Jr., *Autobiography*, p. 7; *TCWJ*, 1:39].

15. Henry James, Sr., incorporated these autobiographical memories into his book, *Society the Redeemed Form of Man* (pp. 44–45). William James excerpted these accounts of his father's spiritual awakening in his introduction to *LR* (p. 59), which is reprinted in Matthiessen, *James Family* (p. 59). For explorations of the psychological dimensions of the crisis, see King, *Iron of Melancholy*, and Habegger, *Henry James and the "Woman Business"*; King argues that "Henry James psychologized Calvinism" (p. 113), and Habegger speaks dismissively of "a regular outbreak of little green men" (p. 54), but he also has more serious analysis of "the shape" as an embodiment of James's noxious selfhood, especially his ambivalence about his maleness and his sexuality (pp. 40–41).

16. See Epstein, *Politics of Domesticity*, pp. 47–55; and Leverenz, *Manhood and the American Renaissance*.

17. *Society the Redeemed Form of Man*, p. 44 [*LR*, p. 58; Matthiessen, *James Family*, p. 160].

18. *Society the Redeemed Form of Man*, pp. 48–49 [*LR*, p. 63; Matthiessen, *James Family*, p. 162].

19. On the son's experience of spiritual terror, see *LWJ*, 1:145–47. For a comparison of the crises of father and son, see Feinstein, *Becoming William James*, especially pp. 241–45; and King, *Iron of Melancholy*, pp. 84–140. Both of these works emphasize the structure of the crises and their psychologically troubling features rather than their religious and cultural values.

20. *Society the Redeemed Form of Man*, pp. 47–48 [*LR*, p. 62; Matthiessen, *James Family*, p. 162].

21. Swedenborg wrote numerous books recounting his spiritual insights and visions, and Henry James read most of them. For a modern sampling of Swedenborg's work, see Swedenborg, *Theological Writings of Emanuel Swedenborg*.

22. *Society the Redeemed Form of Man*, pp. 49–50 [*LR*, p. 64; Matthiessen, *James Family*, p. 163]. The friend was a Mrs. Chichester, whom he met in England. Unfor-

tunately, he never did further identify her—although Mary James referred to her in 1846 as "our old friend"; quoted in Deck, "Vastation of Henry James, Sr.," p. 222. Although Swedenborg had few followers in Sweden, his writings, with their romantic suggestions of the spiritual life in nature, became extremely popular among the cultural elite of Britain and America in the nineteenth century. See Brock et al., eds., *Swedenborg and His Influence.*

23. Henry James, Jr., *Notes of a Son and Brother*, pp. 148–49. For more on the elder James's volumes of Swedenborg and their influence on his thought, see Deck, "Vastation of Henry James, Sr.," pp. 216–47.

24. *Society the Redeemed Form of Man*, p. 50 [*LR*, pp. 164–65; Matthiessen, *James Family*, p. 163]. Hoover argues that "there was nothing" in James's antinomianism and antiecclesiasticism "that would not have been developed from Swedenborg"; see Hoover, *Henry James, Sr.*, p. 46. This is an important part of Swedenborg's thought, but Hoover underemphasizes the Enlightenment seer's attempt to heal the Reformation split between Catholic justification by works and Protestant justification by faith with a blending of rational faith and a life of use; see Synnestvedt, ed., *Essential Swedenborg*.

25. Howells quoted in Norton, *Letters*, 2:379; Mary to Henry James, Jr., 1874, *TCWJ*, 1:105.

26. William James, introduction to *LR*, p. 16.

27. William to Henry James, Jr., January 9, 1883, *TCWJ*, 1:165.

28. See Daniels, *American Science*; Bruce, *Launching of Modern American Science*; and Conser, *God and the Natural World*.

29. See, for example, Charles Hodge, *Way of Life*.

30. The British church leader William Paley offered the classic and popular statement of natural theology, and the title of his major text serves as a summary of his argument: *Natural Theology, or, Evidences of the Existence and Attributes of the Deity, Collected from the Appearances of Nature*, p. 28. American proponents of natural theology also used Paley as an authority and pointed to the manifest design in nature as evidence of the harmony between science and religion; see Bozeman, *Protestants in an Age of Science* and Hovenkamp, *Science and Religion in America*.

31. Quoted in Stevenson, *Scholarly Means to Evangelical Ends*, p. 67.

32. Finney, *Revivals of Religion*, p. 218. Also see Bowden, *Church History*; and Hoopes, *Consciousness in New England*, pp. 120–23.

33. Thoreau's work in natural history carried him from expectations of harmony between science and religion to a frankly Darwinian perspective. In the early 1850s he became a corresponding member of the Boston Society of Natural History and an enthusiastic supporter of Louis Agassiz, who was the most prominent scientist supporting the spiritual link of nature to the divine: he even did extensive collecting for Agassiz while the scientist taught at the Lawrence Scientific School, and he avidly read *Principles of Zoology*, which the scientist coauthored with Augustus Gould. But like many of his scientific contemporaries, Thoreau began to find Agassiz's theories implausibly hopeful, especially after reading Darwin's *Origin of Species* (1859). On Thoreau's scientific evolution and his late natural history phase, see Thoreau, *Faith in a Seed*; Richardson, *Thoreau*, pp. 362–79; and Dean, "Thoreau and Horace Greeley."

34. Ralph Waldo Emerson, "Nature" (1836), in *Collected Works*, 1:18, 25, and 26.
35. See Kohlstedt, "Parlors, Primers, and Public Schooling."
36. Henry James, Sr., *Substance and Shadow*, p. 16.
37. Henry James, Sr., *Substance and Shadow*, p. 16, and "Faith and Science," p. 373; Henry James, Sr., to Ralph Waldo Emerson, undated letter of 1842, Warren, *Elder Henry James*, p. 45. James does not offer the last word on Emerson. Hallengren, in *Code of Concord*, discusses Emerson's turn to modern science in search of "new foundations" (p. 59).
38. Henry James, Sr., *Society the Redeemed Form of Man*, p. 51.
39. Henry James, Sr., *Secret of Swedenborg*, pp. 13–14.
40. Henry James, Sr., *Substance and Shadow*, p. 104. For more on Swedenborg's life and his remarkable journey from scientist to religious seer, especially from the point of view of his admirers, see George Bush, ed., *Memorabilia of Swedenborg*; William White, *Life of Emanuel Swedenborg*; Trobridge, *Swedenborg*; Spalding, *Introduction to Swedenborg's Religious Thought*; Jonsson, *Emanuel Swedenborg*; Van Dusen, *Presence of Other Worlds*.
41. For an account of the importance and meaning of correspondences to Swedenborg's thought written during James's own era, see Madeley, *Science of Correspondences Elucidated*; most important for James, Swedenborg had provided "a certain and universal rule of interpretation" to discover "an inward spiritual sense or meaning . . . within the letter of the Word of God" (pp. 13 and iv).
42. Henry James, Sr., "Scientific Statement," p. 53; *Christianity the Logic of Creation*, p. 193; *Substance and Shadow*, p. 268; "Faith and Science," p. 377; *Lectures and Miscellanies*, p. 61; and *Christianity the Logic of Creation*, p. 182n.
43. Henry James, Sr., *Substance and Shadow*, p. 289. Also see his "Dialogue between a Parent and Child," Henry James [Sr.] Papers.
44. See Matthiessen, *James Family*; and King, *Iron of Melancholy*, for further discussion on William James's thought as a secularized version of his father's outlook. On Henry James as a precursor of pragmatism, see Gunn, "Pragmatic Repossessions," in *Thinking across the American Grain*. Eugene Taylor finds an intellectual genealogy from Swedenborg to the elder Henry James to Charles Sanders Peirce to William James; see his "Swedenborgian and Transcendentalist Roots," "Peirce and Swedenborg," and "Peirce and James."
45. Henry James, Sr., *Substance and Shadow*, p. 105.
46. Lewis, *American Adam*, pp. 55–60. With the doctrine of the fortunate fall, James tapped an ancient Christian tradition; see Lovejoy, "Fortunate Fall." Lewis, in *The Jameses*, returns to this theme in his chapter on Henry James, Sr., "The Endangering Self" (pp. 37–70).
47. Emerson to Henry James, Sr., April 4, [1867], Emerson Papers; and Henry James, Sr., to Norton, June 6, [1867], Norton Papers. Habegger offers a psychological interpretation of James's personal and philosophical antagonism to selfishness, calling it self-loathing (*Henry James and the "Woman Business*," p. 40).
48. Henry James, Sr., *Nature of Evil Considered*, p. 143.
49. Henry James, Sr., *Substance and Shadow*, p. 249.
50. With millennialist hope, Fourier predicted that just as the "laws of physical mo-

tion" had been discovered by earlier scientists, his "calculus of harmony" offered the "laws of social motion," whose "invention will lead mankind to opulence, voluptuous life, and global unity"; quoted in Riasanovsky, *Teaching of Charles Fourier*, p. 7; also see Fourier, *Utopian Vision*; Jonathan Beecher, *Charles Fourier*; and Guarneri, *Utopian Alternative*.

51. Although Fourier did not see his thought as an agent for the spread of Swedenborgian spirituality, James and other romantic thinkers did. See, for example, Charles Julius Hempel, *True Organization of the New Church*; and Henry James's own "Fourier and Swedenborg," pp. 132, 140–41. For a modern discussion of this connection, see Gladish, *Swedenborg, Fourier*. Similarly, Romantic era thinkers linked Swedenborg to other reforms; see, for example, George Bush, *Mesmer and Swedenborg*; and best known of all, Ralph Waldo Emerson, "Swedenborg, or the Mystic" (1845), *Representative Men*, pp. 53–81. For an overview of the cultural context in which Swedenborgian and related ideas flourished, see Robert C. Fuller, *Americans and the Unconscious*.

52. Henry James, Sr., *Society the Redeemed Form of Man*. James's reform sentiments and his brash style of expression sometimes got him into trouble. For example, early in his career, he wrote a preface to a Fourierist book on love and marriage, Hennequin's *Love in the Phalanstery*, which suggested that monogamy was not the only legitimate form of marriage. This suited his vigorous antagonism for morality and convention, but it also produced a tension between his radical ideas and his social conservatism. He attempted to mediate the tension by emphasizing the spiritual lessons of marriage, especially the impact a woman could have on a man—this proposition not only conformed to nineteenth-century convention but also drew directly from his relation with his wife. Habegger presents a psychological reading of James's views, emphasizing his antagonism to women's rights, a devious obscurity of language, and an erotic longing for promiscuity; he concludes that, "evidently, Henry James, Sr., had a dream of what used to be called free love." Even without twentieth-century cynicism and its psychological perspective, James's position shocked mainstream observers; a critic in the *New York Observer* scowled that he "clothe[s] an essentially sensuous dogma in spiritual dress." See Habegger, *Henry James and the "Woman Business,"* pp. 31 and 34.

53. See Westfall, *Science and Religion in Seventeenth-Century England*; Dobbs, *Janus Faces of Genius*; Daniels, *American Science*; Bruce, *Launching of Modern American Science*; and Conser, *God and the Natural World*. While Gigerenzer et al., eds., in *Empire of Chance*, especially pp. 37–69, discuss secular theories—specifically probabilistic thinking—that contributed to the rise of modern social science, Robert C. Fuller, in *Americans and the Unconscious*, presents the religious context of that history.

54. Henry James, Sr., "Morality and the Perfect Life," a lecture delivered in New York in December 1849 and published in *Moralism and Christianity*, p. 126.

55. Quoted in Warren, *Elder Henry James*, p. 106.

56. Henry James, Sr., to Edmund Tweedy (his cousin), July 18, [1860], *TCWJ*, 1:192. Emerson had similar hopes and showed a surprising familiarity with the use of statistics to understand and improve society: he mentioned the statistical social scientist

Adolphe Quetelet in his essay "Fate" (1860) and he paraphrased one of his key probabilistic principles: In "the new science of Statistics, . . . it is a rule that the most casual and extraordinary events, if the basis of population is broad enough, become matter of fixed calculation"; see Emerson, *The Conduct of Life*, pp. 9 and 17. On Quetelet's statistical innovations, see Victor L. Hilts, "Statistics and Social Science," in Giere and Westfall, eds., *Foundations of Scientific Method*, pp. 206–33. Also see Hallengren, *Code of Concord*, pp. 117–253.

57. Henry James, Sr., *Church of Christ*, quoted in Warren, *Elder Henry James*, p. 122.

58. I discuss this theme in "Scientific Spiritualism."

59. This is the change that Gillespie describes as the shift, during the nineteenth century from the "creationist episteme" to the "positivist episteme," which facilitated the success of Darwinism; *Charles Darwin*.

60. Henry James, Sr., to Ralph Waldo Emerson, 1842, quoted in Matthiessen, *James Family*, p. 42.

61. On the life and work of Joseph Henry, see Coulson, *Joseph Henry*; Reingold, "Joseph Henry"; Reingold, "New York State Roots"; Molella and Reingold, "Theorists and Ingenious Mechanics"; Henry, *Scientist in American Life*; and Henry, *Papers of Joseph Henry*.

62. Henry James, Sr., to Joseph Henry, July 9, 1843, *TCWJ*, 1:16–17, and in Henry, *Papers of Joseph Henry*, 5:368.

63. Joseph Henry to Henry James, Sr., August 22, 1843, *Papers of Joseph Henry*, 5:387–88.

64. Henry James, Sr., to Joseph Henry, July 2, 1863, Incoming Correspondence, Office of the Secretary, Record Unit 26, Smithsonian Institution Archives, Joseph Henry Papers.

65. This is the phrase Henry James used to describe his feeling of the uselessness of all his thought previous to his crisis; *Society the Redeemed Form of Man*, p. 48.

Chapter 3

1. Most studies of James's vocational choices have been psychological interpretations. Habegger, in *Henry James and the "Woman Business,"* argues that, complementing his scientific goals for William, "the father wanted his second son, his namesake, to inherit his own sense of social life" (p. 27). Strout, in "William James and the Twice-Born Sick Soul," proposes that the elder James selected William "as the particular child who must justify the parent" (p. 207). James Anderson, in "Why Did William James Abandon Art?," explains why William was so dutiful toward his father: with his mother's lack of warmth, "his needs for love and care became predominantly focused on his father," and therefore, he "could not separate his own interests from his father's" (pp. 301 and 302). Feinstein, in *Becoming William James*, treats the father's insistence on ambiguity and the son's vocational indecision as a projection of the lingering anxieties over Henry's unresolved oedipal conflict with William of Albany. Bjork, in *William James*, interprets the variety of James's interests and talents as the unconscious formation of his genius for seeing connections across fields. Although

Bjork explicitly discounts the influence of the elder James on his son, he does admit that "he may have suggested that William balance scientific with spiritual arguments" (p. 47). But Bjork does not follow up on the suggestion. The following pages discuss William James's vocational questions in light of his father's child rearing philosophy and practices. No matter the ultimate motive for William James's approach to his vocation, some facts are clear: he came to scientific study haltingly, and often with consideration of and excursions into other fields, and his path both suited his tastes and followed his father's dictates—at least until father and son started disagreeing on the nature and purpose of science in the middle of the 1860s.

2. Edel, *Untried Years*, p. 128.

3. Henry James, Sr., to Catherine James, October 15, 1857, *TCWJ*, 1:184.

4. *LWJ*, 1:21. Henry James bought William another microscope in October 1861, when he was just starting his education at the Lawrence Scientific School; see Bjork, *William James*, p. 31.

5. Henry James, Jr., *Notes of a Son and Brother*, pp. 122–23 [*TCWJ*, 1:205–6].

6. Ibid. The younger brother regarded this fraternal difference with whimsy, as he recorded in a letter to their mutual friend, Thomas Sergeant Perry: "Your second letter quite put me to the blush. (If you examine my paper with Willie's microscope you will see that it reflects a faint ruby tinge.)" See Henry James, Jr., to Thomas Sergeant Perry, March 25, 1864, Harlow, *Thomas Sergeant Perry*.

7. William James to Edgar Van Winkle, March 1, 1858, William James Papers. Edgar Beach Van Winkle was a friend to William and his brother Henry James from when they had lived in New York City. Anderson, in "Why Did William James Abandon Art?," refers to parts of this letter and the letters of January 4, 1858, and November 12, 1858 (pp. 292–95). Grohskopf, in "'I'll Be a Farmer,'" discusses many of the Van Winkle letters.

8. William James to Edgar Van Winkle, March 1, 1858, William James Papers.

9. William James to Edgar Van Winkle, January 4, 1858, William James Papers.

10. William James to Edgar Van Winkle, May 26, 1858, and March 1, 1858, William James Papers.

11. William James to Edgar Van Winkle, March 1, 1858, William James Papers; these portions of this letter are also quoted in *TCWJ, Briefer Version*, pp. 52–53, and in Myers, *William James*, pp. 3–4.

12. William James to Edgar Van Winkle, January 4, 1858, March 1, 1858, and May 26, 1858, William James Papers.

13. *LWJ*, 1:20–21.

14. William James to Edgar Van Winkle, November 12, 1858, and December 1, 1859, William James Papers.

15. William James to Edgar Van Winkle, August 12, 1858, January 4, 1858, and May 26, 1858, William James Papers.

16. William James to Edgar Van Winkle, August 12, 1858, William James Papers.

17. William James to Edgar Van Winkle, September 18, [1858], William James Papers.

18. William James to Edgar Van Winkle, November 12, [18]58, William James Papers.

19. William James to Edgar Van Winkle, Dec[embe]r 1, 1859, November 12, [18]58, and August 12, 1858, William James Papers.

20. William James to Edgar Van Winkle, March 1, 1858, William James Papers; this passage of the letter is also quoted in *TCWJ, Briefer Version*, pp. 52–53, and Myers, *William James*, p. 4.

21. Notebook 1, p. 2, William James Papers.

22. William James, *Will to Believe*, p. 145.

23. Notebook 1, pp. 37–38, William James Papers.

24. On this theme in American culture, see Gilbert, *Work without Salvation*, especially pp. 180–96; Feinstein, *Becoming William James*; and Cotkin, *William James, Public Philosopher*, pp. 40–122. Also see the classic study of British Victorian elites in personal crisis: Houghton, *Victorian Frame of Mind*.

25. See Feinstein, *Becoming William James*, pp. 182–205, on William James's exaggeration of work-stopping illnesses. Similarly, Bjork argues that even when "caught in the grip of great spiritual depression, James was wonderfully creative" (*William James*, p. 69).

26. Notebook 1, p. 37, William James Papers.

27. Ibid., p. 61. The quotation is from Faraday's essay, "Observations on Mental Education"; actually, it is a close paraphrase, indicating either that James copied it to his notebook with free embellishments or that he found it so important that he put its lessons to memory. The very similar, but not exact phrase-for-phrase meaning of the two versions supports the latter interpretation. The young man seems to have taken the great scientist's words to heart. Faraday wrote: "to those who reflect upon the many hours and days devoted by a lover of sweet sounds to gain a moderate facility upon a mere mechanical instrument, it ought to bring a correcting blush of shame if they feel convicted of neglecting the beautiful living instrument wherein play all the powers of the mind"; quoted in Gladstone, *Michael Faraday*, p. 129.

28. Henry James, Jr., *A Small Boy and Others*, p. 345 [*TCWJ*, 1:183].

29. Henry James, Jr., *A Small Boy and Others*, p. 207. William James had seen an exhibit of Delacroix paintings in Paris in 1855. Feinstein and Bjork both show that the French painter, especially his "Lion Hunt," directly influenced William's sketches and his thinking in general. Feinstein, in *Becoming William James*, proposes that the romantic and violent painting expressed William's feelings for his father as he struggled "to extricate himself from his father's entangling mass of contradictory ideas" (p. 112); Bjork, in *William James*, suggests that the painting's "huge verbal puzzle in colors" inspired "young James's first original insight: that visual forms were initially indistinct and unorganized, and only later developed into what was supposed to be the real world" (p. 17).

30. Henry James, Sr., to Edmund Tweedy, July 24, [1860], *TCWJ*, 1:192.

31. See, for example, *Being and the Beautiful*; in particular, in his commentary on "Sophist," Seth Benardette notes that Plato scornfully "likens the painter's duplication of reality to the sophist's replacement of reality" (2:106).

32. Henry James, Sr., *Moralism and Christianity*, p. 63.

33. William to Henry James, Sr., August [24, 1860], *TCWJ*, 1:199. The elder James held a view of art that was strikingly similar to that of the Puritans, who believed that

"graven images" were a sacrilege. By contrast, painters of the Hudson River School, like many of the transcendentalists, believed that artistic images could serve as vehicles of spiritual truth; see Durand, "Letters on Landscape Painting"; and Cole, "Essay on American Scenery."

34. Henry James, Sr., "Scientific Statement," p. 62.

35. William James to Charles Ritter, July 31, 1860; and Henry James, Sr., to Edmund Tweedy, July 18, [1860], *TCWJ*, 1:193 and 191.

36. Henry James showed little regard for equality in the treatment of his children. Even as he changed his family plans to suit William's choices, he declared doubts about the potential of his younger children: "They are none of them cut out for intellectual labours" (Henry James, Sr., to Edmund Tweedy, July 18, [1860], *TCWJ*, 1:191). Similarly, in 1861 when all the boys eagerly rushed to enlist to fight in the Union army in the Civil War, James allowed his younger ones to do so but forbade William and Henry from fighting, presumably preserving them for a higher purpose. The elder James said: "Affectionate old papas like me are scudding all over the country to apprehend their patriotic offspring and restore them to the harmless embraces of their mamas.... I have had a firm grasp upon the coat tails of my Willy and Harry, who both vituperate me beyond measure because I won't let them go. Their coats are a very staunch material, or the tails must have been off two days ago, the scamps pull so hard" (Henry James, Sr., to an unknown correspondent, Edel, *Untried Years*, pp. 171–72). He set up no such restrictions on the two youngest sons, who served in the war and who were both wounded in action; see Maher's *Biography of Broken Fortunes*. On the scars left on William James from not fighting in the war, see Cotkin, *William James, Public Philosopher*, pp. 19–39; and on James's ability to translate that youthful lacking into creativity late in life, see Fredrickson, *Inner Civil War*, pp. 217–38.

37. Henry James, Sr., to Edmund Tweedy, July 18, [1860], *TCWJ*, 1:191.

38. Henry James, Jr., quoted in Danes, "William Morris Hunt," p. 147.

39. See Shannon, *Boston Days*.

40. See Edward Waldo Emerson, *Early Years of the Saturday Club*.

41. Byrd, "Artist-Teacher in America," p. 131.

42. *Late Landscapes of William Morris Hunt*, p. 5.

43. Hunt, *On Painting and Drawing*, pp. 102 and 122.

44. Frank D. Millet, "Mr. Hunt's Teaching," p. 190.

45. Ibid., pp. 189 and 191. Novak calls him the great Boston teacher (in 1862, he moved to Boston, where he took on even more students than he could in his small Newport studio); *American Painting*, p. 247.

46. La Farge quoted in Danes, "William Morris Hunt," p. 146.

47. Hunt quoted in *Late Landscapes of William Morris Hunt*, p. 21. Max J. Friedlander pointed out the central place of religion in Millet's work: "A peasant sowing is undoubtedly the subject for a *genre* picture. Jean-François Millet, from his idea of the sanctity of work on the land, raises it, however, into the sphere of the religious"; in Jean-François Millet, *On Art and Connoisseurship*, p. 108.

48. Frank D. Millet, "Mr. Hunt's Teaching," p. 190.

49. Bjork, in *Compromised Scientist*, argues that James's interest in art never left him, and that, in fact, his work in other fields was actually "his attempt to project

a lost Atlantis of art into other media, into psychology and philosophy" (p. 25). As evidence, Bjork points to later comments James made about his work; one of the more effective examples is James's remark in "The Stream of Thought" chapter of *Principles of Psychology*: "This chapter is like a painter's first charcoal sketch upon his canvas, in which no niceties appear" (1:220, quoted in Bjork, p. 30). Also Leary, "William James"; and Seigfried, "Poetic Invention and Scientific Observation" and *William James's Radical Reconstruction of Philosophy*, pp. 164–70, argue that James's artistic sensibility was crucial for the development of his psychology and philosophy. Lovejoy, in *Thirteen Pragmatisms*, makes a similar suggestion (p. 92).

50. La Farge quoted in Cortissoz, *John La Farge*, p. 117; William James to Charles Ritter, July 31, 1860, *TCWJ*, 1:193. Anderson, in "Why Did William James Abandon Art?," argues that he followed his father's wishes in pursuing science because he felt that "his father's well-being depended on him"; moreover, when he did finally abandon art, his loyalty overrode his great artistic leanings so strongly that "he had to try to persuade himself that he did not care for art by avoiding it altogether" (pp. 301 and 302). Lewis, in *The Jameses*, conjectures that William's phrase "bad artist" may have meant someone who practices the wretched field that his father disapproved of (p. 111).

Chapter 4

1. William J. Jones, *Christ in the Camp*, p. 319.
2. The shock of Darwinian science has many layers of significance. Traditional interpreters of the field viewed the advent of Darwinism as a signal of the triumph of science over religion. This was a common view until the early 1960s; see, for example, Himmelfarb, *Darwin and the Darwinian Revolution*. By contrast, Bowler, in *Non-Darwinian Revolution*, has even documented the way many scientists accepted Darwin's evolutionary premises but not his particular theories or worldview. Similarly, Dupree, in "Christianity and the Scientific Community," argues that Darwinism did not bring about a revolution in religious belief. This work of revision forces attention to what exactly was revolutionary in Darwinian science: his theories were not all-triumphant as earlier legends imply, but they were a highly influential and a crucial turning point in the practice of science away from expectations of certainty. Ghiselin, in *Triumph of the Darwinian Method*, and Hull, in *Darwin and His Critics*, redirected attention toward Darwin's radical innovations in scientific method. In *Politics of Evolution*, Desmond shows the boldness of Darwin's scientific propositions, even as he was wary of the radical associations of his ideas with disruptive generalizations about religion and science or with reform politics.
3. Leland, *Memoirs*, p. 158. Leland had attended Bronson Alcott's school and became editor of *Graham's Monthly* in 1856. Conser indirectly endorses this interpretation: in his argument about the importance of a pre-Darwinian harmony between science and religion, he says, "The Darwinian controversy was more the catalyst for the debate within American Christianity than it was its originator" (*God and the Natural World*, p. 7). Although Conser does not directly discuss the evolution of scientific trends away from each other, he does point out that "challenges . . . assail[ed] the

union of science and religion," and "an even more powerful challenge had emerged, a challenge . . . perceptive observers . . . summarized in just one word: *Darwin*" (p. 135).

4. See Watts, *Republic Reborn*, on the culture of the United States in the decades after the War of 1812; Daniels, *American Science*, on the place of science in this context; Charlotte Porter, *The Eagle's Nest*, for a case study of the scientists surrounding Philadelphia's Academy of Natural Sciences; Chandos Michael Brown, "Gloucester Sea Serpent," on some of the cultural tensions generated by scientific investigation; and Conser's study entitled *God and the Natural World*. Also see the documents in Reingold, ed., *Science in Nineteenth-Century America*.

5. Orville Dewey (1830) quoted in Burnham, *How Superstition Won and Science Lost*, p. 32n.

6. The British philosopher William Whewell was the first to use the term "scientist" in 1840, and it quickly displaced "natural philosopher" and "experimentalist" in general use; see Kohlstedt, *American Scientific Community*, p. xi; Kuritz, "Popularization of Science"; and Bruce, *Launching of Modern American Science*, p. 80.

7. See Sinclair, "Americans Abroad."

8. On the place of science in early- to mid-nineteenth-century colleges, see Axtell, "Death of the Liberal Arts College"; and Guralnick, *Science and the Ante-Bellum American College*, and "American Scientist in Higher Education," in Reingold, ed., *Sciences in the American Context*, pp. 99–141. On scientific and learned societies, see the essays in Oleson and Brown, eds., *Pursuit of Knowledge*, especially: A. Hunter Dupree, "National Pattern of American Learned Societies, 1769–1863" (pp. 21–32); James M. Hobbins, "Shaping a Provincial Learned Society" (pp. 117–50); and Walter Muir Whitehill, "Early Learned Societies in Boston" (pp. 151–73). The leading journal at first had the more general name *American Journal of Arts and Sciences* and its editor, Benjamin Silliman, while a greatly important organizer and teacher of science, was not himself a very original experimentalist; see Chandos Michael Brown, *Benjamin Silliman*. Similarly, Bates, in *Scientific Societies*, describes the proliferation of scientific societies as the work of amateurs with professional ambitions. For an account of other scientific journals, see Baatz, " 'Squinting at Silliman.' "

9. Flower and Murphey, *History of Philosophy in America*, pp. 397–516; Diehl, *Americans and German Scholarship*; Stevenson, *Scholarly Means to Evangelical Ends*; and Kuklick, *Churchmen and Philosophers*. Conser's *God and the Natural World* provides a case study of the influence on American theologians of specific German idealists, namely, the proponents of "mediating theology," including Friedrich Tholuck, Johann Neander, Carl Nitzsch, and Karl Ullmann, who set out to bridge both modern science and religion and the various Protestant confessions.

10. See Ducasse, "Francis Bacon's Philosophy of Science." Charlotte Porter, in *Eagle's Nest*, p. 87, points out that many admirers of Bacon were also interested in his scientific utopianism.

11. Daniels, *American Science*, p. 65; on Baconianism in American culture in the early to middle nineteenth century, especially in its relation to religious belief, see Bozeman, *Protestants in an Age of Science*, and Hovenkamp, *Science and Religion in America*.

12. On Scottish Common Sense philosophy in America, especially as an influence

on religion, see Ahlstrom, "Scottish Philosophy and American Theology"; Terence Martin, *Instructed Vision*; Meyer, *Instructed Conscience*; and Noll, "Common Sense Traditions."

13. Lewis R. Gibbes to Joseph Henry, March 13, 1844, Henry, *Papers of Joseph Henry*, 5:54–55.

14. Joseph Henry to Robert Hare, October 1843, Henry, *Papers of Joseph Henry*, 4:415; and Joseph Henry, notebook, August 19–21, 1837, ibid., 3:475–77. Hare was a professor of chemistry at the University of Pennsylvania and a prolific contributor to the *American Journal of Science* before becoming interested in a wide range of social issues and the spiritual meaning of science late in life when he published *Spirit Manifestations*. This work was an unorthodox version of the mainstream hope to reconcile science and religion; however, its spiritualism alienated him from the scientific community. Henry wrote his 1837 notebook while visiting David Brewster, a leading British scientist, who was a fellow of the Royal Society and who did most of his experimental work on optics and the properties of light. Brewster adamantly maintained that scientists did not use Bacon's method, even though nonscientists thought they did. Scientific innovation did not involve the avoidance of hypotheses, but rather the use of imagination and speculation; see notes to *Papers of Joseph Henry*, 3:475–76.

15. Daniels, *American Science*, especially pp. 102–17.

16. See Tyler, *Discourse on the Baconian Philosophy*. He was confident that Baconian science would harmonize with religion and retrieve science from its association with atheism; he said "the Baconian philosophy . . . has revived the study of natural theology after it had been abandoned . . . by the philosophers of the continent of Europe"; see Tyler, "Influence of the Baconian Philosophy," p. 504. Also see Daniels, *American Science*, pp. 69–83. The Swiss-born Louis Agassiz was a professor of zoology and geology at Harvard University, the astronomer Alexander Dallas Bache was the first president of the National Academy of Sciences and an agitator for greater national scientific leadership, and physicist Joseph Henry was the first Secretary of the Smithsonian Institution; see Bruce, *Launching of Modern American Science*, pp. 98 and 189; and Slotten, *Patronage, Practice*. Burkhardt, in *Spirit of System*, reveals that European science was simultaneously moving away from science as taxonomy (pp. 46–47).

17. Wayland, "Philosophy of Analogy"; also see Daniels, *American Science*, pp. 167–70, and Meyer, *Instructed Conscience*, pp. 43–50. Wayland, in turn, leaned on British antideist Joseph Butler, whose *Analogy of Reason* (1736) introduced analogical thinking to the Anglo-American world. Wayland freely admitted his debt to Butler in *Elements of Moral Science* (1835), p. 4.

18. See Numbers, *Creation by Natural Law*, especially pp. 58–64. Laplace proposed that the sun had once been the size of the solar system; then as it condensed it left behind rings of matter that gradually coalesced into the particular planets. See Laplace, *System of the World*, 2:363–65; Numbers, *Creation by Natural Law*, p. 9; and Roger Hahn, "Laplace and the Mechanistic Universe," in Lindberg and Numbers, eds., *God and Nature*, pp. 256–76. Laplace was not the only exponent of a nebular hypothesis, but his was the most detailed and persuasive. See Collier, *Cosmogonies of Our Fathers*, p. 283; and Numbers, *Creation by Natural Law*, p. 12. For an example

of the religious "domestication" of this radical and naturalistic Enlightenment theory, see Benjamin Peirce, "The Nebular Hypothesis" (1880), in Sargent, ed., *Sketches and Reminiscences*, who argued that "the wonderful uniformity of motion and position prove a great plan behind [the development of the solar system], and an intelligence to execute it" (p. 247). Laplace's theory was a particularly potent version of the broad threat of positivism, which in its most general form proposed a purely naturalistic causation and a thorough scoffing at religious claims. Although more influential in Europe than America, it contributed to the wariness about the antireligious potential of science; see Cashdollar, *Transformation of Theology*.

19. Conser, in *God and the Natural World*, points out that "the fact that the distinctive approaches of Scottish Common Sense and [German] romanticism could be utilized in the mutual effort to reconcile science and religion merely underscores the broad-based desire within antebellum American culture to see that end achieved" (p. 83). Conser, however, does not treat the trends in the practice of science that would lead to separation of science and religion even as the desire for their harmony remained strong.

20. Hitchcock, "Study of Natural History," p. 292; Dana, "Science and Scientific Schools," p. 364; and Thornwell, *Collected Writings*, 3:275–76. Also see Daniels, *American Science*, pp. 48–55; and Guralnick, "Geology and Religion before Darwin."

21. Kohlstedt, *American Scientific Community*, p. 114. Even Conser, who, in *God and the Natural World*, emphasizes the belief in scientific and religious harmony of American theologians, admits that their work was directed toward "mediating the controversies between science and religion" (p. 36).

22. [Chambers], *Vestiges of Creation*; see Ruse, *Darwinian Revolution*, pp. 127–30; and Pfeifer, "United States," p. 171.

23. Lyell quoted in Ruse, *Darwinian Revolution*, p. 202. The naturalist Thomas Say simply avoided variations; instead he noted only such characteristics "as will probably prove to be permanent, or nearly so, and characteristic of the species"; quoted in Charlotte Porter, *Eagle's Nest*, p. 61. Also see Bowler, "Scientific Attitudes to Darwinism," p. 670.

24. See Bushman, *From Puritan to Yankee*; and Jon Butler, *Awash in a Sea of Faith*.

25. See Douglas, *Feminization of American Culture*; and McDannell, *Christian Home in Victorian America*.

26. On biblical interpretation, see Frei, *Eclipse of Biblical Narrative*; Morgan, *Biblical Interpretation*; and Hurth, *In His Name*. Also see Hatch and Noll, eds., *The Bible in America*; and Gunn, ed., *Bible and American Arts and Letters*.

27. See Marsden, *Evangelical Mind*; Stevenson, *Scholarly Means to Evangelical Ends*; and Rabinowitz, *Spiritual Self in Everyday Life*.

28. See Buckley, *Origins of Modern Atheism*; Febvre, *Unbelief in the Sixteenth Century*; and James Turner, *Without God, without Creed*. Keith Thomas argues, by contrast, that religious unbelief and atheism were not uncommon in early modern Western societies. See *Religion and the Decline of Magic*. These were, however, exceptions that proved the rule: until the eighteenth century, religious doubt did not have enough social and intellectual authority to worry the orthodox. By the Enlightenment, and especially in the nineteenth century, the religiously orthodox felt defensively com-

pelled to show the truths of religion—and more avidly sought scientific demonstrations of religious certainty.

29. See Story, *Forging of an Aristocracy*; Peter Dobkin Hall, *Organization of American Culture*; and Farrell, *Elite Families*.

30. To Lowell and his peers, botany gave palpable expression to their sense of harmonious order and certainty in both their religious beliefs and their social status; see Thornton, *Cultivating Gentlemen*.

31. John Lowell, Jr., quoted in Weeks, *Lowells and Their Institute*, pp. 11 and 49; and Harriette Knight Smith, *History of the Lowell Institute*, p. 30. Also see Rossiter, "Benjamin Silliman and the Lowell Institute."

32. See Bates, *Scientific Societies*, pp. 28–84; Shapiro, "Western Academy of Natural Sciences," in Oleson and Brown, eds., *Pursuit of Knowledge*; Kohlstedt, "Nineteenth-Century Amateur Tradition"; Keeney, *Botanizers*; and Rivinus and Youssef, *Spencer Baird*. Mary Ann James, in *Elites in Conflict*, examines Albany's Dudley Observatory as a case study of the social and cultural conflicts generated by these new and uncharted professional entities.

33. See Chittenden, *Sheffield Scientific School*; Stevenson, *Scholarly Means to Evangelical Ends*, pp. 67–85; and Bruce, *Launching of American Science*, pp. 327–28.

34. Love, *Lawrence Scientific School*, p. i. Also see Rossiter, "Louis Agassiz."

35. Abbott Lawrence to the Treasurer of Harvard College, September 20, 1849, quoted in Faculty and Administrative Board Minutes, Lawrence Scientific School.

36. See Rudolph, *American College and University*; and Veysey, *Emergence of the American University*.

37. See Eliot, "New Education"; and Hawkins, *Between Harvard and America*. For a helpful social history reminder that these intellectual plans were neither put into practice immediately nor without continuity with earlier approaches, see McCaughey, "Transformation of American Academic Life."

38. Sharples, "Some Reminiscences," p. 539. Livingstone, in *Nathaniel Southgate Shaler*, points out that, because of Eliot's interest in applied science, he made several attempts to disband the Lawrence Scientific School before Shaler became dean in 1891.

39. Active, vocal, and prominent polemicists on both sides of the Atlantic popularized the notion of an age-old, irreconcilable set of differences between progressive science and reactionary religion, while championing the cause of professional science in institutions of higher learning. See, for example, Thomas Henry Huxley, *Man's Place in Nature*; Draper, *Religion and Science*; Andrew Dickson White, *Warfare of Science and Religion*. Frank M. Turner discusses the professional aspirations that lay behind these controversies in *Between Science and Religion*. James R. Moore offers an astute and well-researched corrective to the "warfare" model of religion's relation with science in *Post-Darwinian Controversies*.

40. Darwin's naturalism is a well-known and well-documented feature of his science. See, for example, Greene, *Darwin and the Modern World View*; Himmelfarb, *Darwin and the Darwinian Revolution*; and Carter, *Spiritual Crisis*. A newer theme in Darwin studies, which is central to the argument in this chapter, concerns the novelty of Darwin's method of explaining his theory through reference to probabilities rather than certainties: Himmelfarb notes this as a problem in the theory of natural selection

(p. 334); Ghiselin, in *Triumph of the Darwinian Method*, praises Darwin as a herald of the modern method of scientific explanation; Cannon, in *Science in Culture*, recognizes the innovation of Darwin's method in the context of the nineteenth century; and Hull, in *Darwin and His Critics*, demonstrates how Darwin's method directly challenged conventional philosophies of science. Even in the midst of his search for religion's compatibility with the new science, Moore, in *Post-Darwinian Controversies*, admits that Darwinism encouraged a crisis of belief among thoughtful people (see pp. 13–14) and that it involved a new approach to scientific explanation (pp. 194–96). Also see Young, "Historiographic and Ideological Contexts"; and Gillespie, *Charles Darwin*, on the important differences that remain when we clear the smoke from the polemical battles: two radically different worldviews or "epistemes" separated the religiously oriented traditional view of science and the new scientific approaches, which were neutral or hostile toward religion.

41. On the life of Charles Darwin and the impact of his ideas, see Himmelfarb, *Darwin and the Darwinian Revolution*; De Beer, *Charles Darwin*; Bowler, *Charles Darwin*; Bowlby, *Charles Darwin*; and James R. Moore and Adrian J. Desmond, *Darwin*.

42. Henry James, Sr., quoted in Habegger, *Henry James and the "Woman Business,"* p. 56.

43. In particular, Darwin's own grandfather, Erasmus Darwin, *Zoonomia*; Lamarck, *Zoological Philosophy*; and [Chambers], *Vestiges of Creation*. For a thorough history of theories of evolution in Western thought, see Bowler, *Evolution*.

44. For a discussion of the role of rhetoric and persuasive language in science, especially in Darwinism, see Campbell, "Scientific Discovery and Rhetorical Invention"; Gross, "Origin of Species" and *Rhetoric of Science*; and Bulhof, *Language of Science*. The parallel of Darwinism with Newton's work is more than a convenient historical reconstruction or a result of their being buried next to each other in Westminster Abbey as Britain's two greatest scientists. Michael Ruse points out that Darwin was self-conscious of the parallel and actively sought to imitate the genius of physics in method and scope with a grand biological theory. See *Darwinism Defended*, p. 49.

45. Tyndall, "Belfast Address," p. 316.

46. In *Darwin and His Critics*, Hull has gathered contemporary scientific responses to the theory of natural selection in essays by reputable European and American scientists who objected to Darwinism for scientific reasons; see especially the essays by Thomas Vernon Wollaston, François Jules Pictet, Adam Sedgwick, Richard Owen, William Hopkins, Henry Fawcett, Frederick Wollaston Hutton, Fleeming Jenkin, St. George Jackson Mivart, and Louis Agassiz. Agassiz was America's most prominent scientist, and he devoted almost all of his work after 1860 to discrediting Darwinism: see especially *Journey to Brazil* (with Elizabeth Agassiz), and *Geological Sketches*. Daniels has collected and edited American responses to Darwin in *Darwinism Comes to America*; see the essays that exhibit scientific objections to the theory of natural selection by prominent contemporary scientists, including William North Rice, D. R. Goodwin, and J. Lawrence Smith. Also see Roberts, *Darwinism and the Divine*, especially pp. 32–63. For scientific responses after Darwin's lifetime, see Bowler's account of the fall and rise of widespread support for Darwinian natural selection from the 1880s to the twentieth century in "Scientific Attitudes to Darwinism."

47. Ghiselin, in *Triumph of the Darwinian Method*, points out that "the very nature of organic processes demands a probabilistic manner of thinking" (p. 55). In *Darwin and His Critics*, especially pp. 16–36, Hull argues that *Origin* represents a revolutionary new approach to science, one which did not adhere to the demands of nineteenth-century philosophy of science for inductive fact gathering leading to proof. Explanation without proof in the argument is not a flaw, according to Hull, but a necessary element of his science and the key to the revolutionary character of Darwin's theory. By contrast, Ruse, in *Darwinian Revolution*, argues that contemporary philosophies of science motivated Darwin's investigation and represented his hopes for the nature of scientific inquiry. These interpretations deal with two sides of the same historical situation: Darwin earnestly tried to adhere to contemporary scientific methods, but his subject matter and the structure of his theory took him beyond them. Even Ruse acknowledges that species variation and adaptability simply could not fully fit his methodological goals and hopes (pp. 237–39).

48. Boltzmann, "Second Law of Thermodynamics," p. 15.

49. Thomas Henry Huxley, *Darwiniana*, p. 25. Darwin was ambivalent about statistics, even as his theories relied on the probabilistic thinking that emerges from statistical analysis. His sons claimed that he had a "nonstatistical" mind and "no liking for statistics"; however, Darwin himself claimed in a letter to Francis Galton, who was an accomplished investigator of the statistical processes of natural selection, that they shared "a common family weakness for statistics." See Theodore Porter, *Rise of Statistical Thinking*, pp. 134–35. One contemporary mathematician noticed the implicit probabilism in Darwin's theory, but argued that there was a greater "chance against . . . these transformations" being caused by natural selection; see Bennett, "Theory of Natural Selection," p. 31. On Darwin's implicit probabilism, see M. J. S. Hodge, "Law, Cause, Chance, Adaptation, and Species"; Schweber, "Aspects of Probabilistic Thought"; and Schweber, "Origin of the *Origin* Revisited."

50. Because Darwin uses the analogy with artificial selection so prominently in the *Origin*, but less so in his private writings, controversy has developed over its importance to the theory of natural selection. Herbert argues, in "Darwin, Malthus, and Selection," that the analogy is not crucial to his argument and that he only uses it as a way to explain the theory clearly. Robert J. Richards, in *Darwin and the Emergence of Evolutionary Theories*, points out that Darwin did not use the analogy with his initial formulation of the theory of natural selection. Ruse, in "Darwin and Artificial Selection," and Mayr, in "Darwin and Natural Selection," argue that references to artificial selection are scattered throughout Darwin's work on species development and that the analogy is a basic element of the theory of natural selection. Robert M. Young, in *Darwin's Metaphor*, analyzes the metaphorical language of Darwin's use of analogy in the theory of natural selection and maintains its crucial importance for Darwin's conceptual breakthrough. No matter its role in the evolution of Darwin's own thinking, its prominent place in the published, popular work has made the analogy with artificial selection an indispensable part of the explanation of the theory, one that seeks justification for the truth of the theory through plausible persuasiveness rather than proof.

51. Charles Darwin, *Origin of Species*, p. 1.

52. As Ruse points out in "Darwin's Debt to Philosophy," Herschel and Whewell were crucial to the formulation of Darwin's theory and represented his goals for good science. On the differences between the empiricist Herschel and the Kantian Whewell, see Ducasse, "John F. W. Herschel's Methods" and "William Whewell's Philosophy"; and Robert E. Butts, "Whewell's Logic of Induction," in Giere and Westfall, eds., *Foundations of Scientific Method*, pp. 53–85.

53. Hull, in *Darwin and His Critics*, emphasizes that Herschel and Whewell themselves challenged Darwin's theory as unscientific because of its differences with the standards of inductive proof. According to these epistemological premises, scientific investigations yield truth through the patient accumulation of facts. Once the mind is thoroughly grounded in the facts, generalizations could be formed only slowly and tentatively. The advocates of the inductive method, which predominated in the nineteenth century, believed that a thorough factual presentation constituted a certain proof. The advocates of induction scorned Darwin's theory as an example of excessive speculation even though their own philosophy possessed a serious problem: the "evolutionary theory," Hull argues, "did fail to meet the standards of proof established by these philosophers for the simple reason that no theory could possibly fulfill them" (p. 16); therefore, the *Origin* represents a revolutionary new approach to science.

While Britain was the locus of the philosophical debates Hull discusses, the Americans who maintained similar goals of religious certainty in their science employed a similar faith in induction. See Bozeman, *Protestants in an Age of Science*; Hovenkamp, *Science and Religion in America*; and Mark A. Noll, ed., *Princeton Theology*.

54. Darwin to Asa Gray, November 29, [1859], Charles Darwin, *More Letters*, 1:126; Darwin to J. D. Hooker, February 14, [1860], Charles Darwin, *Correspondence*, 8:84; and Darwin quoted in Hull, *Darwin and His Critics*, p. 13.

55. Darwin to J. D. Hooker, April 23, [1861], Charles Darwin, *Correspondence*, 9:99.

56. Francis Bowen, "Latest Form of the Development Theory," p. 98; and Fiske, "Darwinism Verified" (1877), in *Darwinism*, pp. 1 and 11.

57. On the modern hypothetico-deductive method, see Popper, *Logic of Scientific Discovery*; and Carl Hempel, *Philosophy of Natural Science*. In the nineteenth century John Herschel and William Whewell developed an early form of this modern method by allowing a place in induction for hypotheses; see Herschel, *Study of Natural Philosophy*; and Whewell, *History of the Inductive Sciences*; also see Hopkins, "Physical Theories." In *Triumph of the Darwinian Method*, Ghiselin argues enthusiastically that Darwin used this modern method in his willingness to speculate and form hypotheses, and in his insistence on verification of those hypotheses through experiential tests. Ruse, in "Charles Darwin's Theory of Evolution," counters that Darwin used argument by analogy, rather than the hypothetico-deductive method; especially given the state of biological knowledge, Darwin could not use deductive reasoning to develop or demonstrate natural selection. Clearly there is evidence for Darwin's use of both methods in his work; significantly, neither one provides conventional certainty or proof.

58. See Charles Darwin, "*H.M.S. Beagle*"; and Barrett et al., eds., *Charles Darwin's Notebooks*. His first mention of a transmutationist idea is in a notebook of 1836–

37 (Herbert, ed., "Red Notebook," *Darwin's Notebooks*, pp. 17–81). In the next few years, he developed his theory in a "sketch" written in 1842 and an essay written in 1844. On the way the sea voyage contributed to his maturation, see Sulloway, "Darwin's Early Intellectual Development."

59. Part of Darwin's massive but never completed work has been published as *Charles Darwin's Natural Selection: being the Second Part of his Big Species Book, written from 1856 to 1858*. While working on this treatise, although he was shocked to receive Wallace's paper on natural selection, Darwin cooperated with him in giving a pair of papers on the theory before the Linnaean Society of London on July 1, 1858; for a recent publication of the essays, see Darwin and Wallace, *Evolution by Natural Selection*. Two spare and scholarly essays, however, made virtually no impact on the professional or popular community compared to Darwin's thorough but accessible *Origin of Species*.

60. For analysis of why Darwin delayed, ranging from internal problems with the theory to Darwin's fear of religious persecution or association with radicalism, see Gruber, *Darwin on Man*; Gould, "Darwin's Delay"; Gale, *Evolution without Evidence*; Ospovat, *Development of Darwin's Theory*; Robert J. Richards, *Darwin and the Emergence of Evolutionary Theories of Mind and Behavior* and "Why Darwin Delayed"; and Desmond, *Politics of Evolution*.

61. See Malthus, *Principle of Population*. On Darwin's relation to Malthus, see Wallace, "Malthus's 'Principle of Population'"; Vorzimmer, "Darwin, Malthus"; Herbert, "Darwin, Malthus, and Selection"; Manier, *Young Darwin*; and Kohn, "Theories to Work By."

62. Darwin, *Origin of Species*, p. 5.

63. Recent research confirms that Darwin only gradually came to believe in natural selection as a constant and thorough force driving adaptation; see Ospovat, *Development of Darwin's Theory*; Robert J. Richards, *Darwin and the Emergence of Evolutionary Theories*; and Kohn, "Darwin's Principle of Divergence."

64. Darwin was concerned with this issue of the ruthlessness of nature as a personal religious question; and he did in fact gradually lose his Christian faith in a loving God. Without his sanction, however, others drew on his ideas to develop "Darwinian" religious, ethical, and social theories; see Hofstadter, *Social Darwinism in American Thought*; and Bannister, *Social Darwinism*.

65. Charles Darwin, "Autobiography," in Darwin and Huxley, *Autobiographies*, p. 51. Darwin's reference to chance and law is a good example of the way probabilistic thinking stemmed from a scientific belief that uncertainty could be subjected to law; see "Chance and Life," in Gigerenzer et al., eds., *Empire of Chance*.

66. Herschel quoted by Darwin, December 12, 1859, Charles Darwin, *Life and Letters*, 2:37.

67. Louis Agassiz was the most prominent and ardent spokesman for the immutability of species in Darwin's day. See Lurie, *Louis Agassiz*.

68. Darwin drew confidence for his belief in the earth's antiquity from Charles Lyell, who, in *Principles of Geology*, persuasively argued that current geological forces "explain the former changes in the earth's surface." Darwin extended that gradualist, evolutionary vision to changes in living things, which would also require millions of

years to take shape. After publication of the *Origin*, critics of natural selection drew strength from doubts about the age of the earth, which evolutionary theory required. Most important, British physicist Lord Kelvin demonstrated, to the satisfaction of many contemporaries, that according to the thermodynamics of the earth's rate of cooling, it could not be as old as the theory of natural selection demanded; see Burchfield, "Darwin," and *Lord Kelvin*; and Crosbie Smith and M. Norton Wise, *Energy and Empire*. Twentieth-century theories of the age of the earth helped to vindicate Darwin's theory.

69. Charles Darwin, *Origin of Species*, pp. 52 and 51.

70. On the twentieth-century view of population thinking, see Mayr, *Animal Species and Evolution*. On Darwin's use of population thinking, see Kottler, "Charles Darwin's Biological Species Concept." Beatty points out the difference between this nineteenth-century scientist and this twentieth-century science in his essays, "What's in a Word?" and "Speaking of Species."

71. Charles Darwin, *Origin of Species*, p. 45.

72. Merz, in *European Thought in the Nineteenth Century*, points out that use of the population approach to species, like James Clerk Maxwell's theory of gases, required an acceptance of scientific theories based on statistical explanation rather than on fixed law. Merz sees Darwinism as the beginning of a trend toward probabilistic and statistical thinking that would dominate late-nineteenth- and twentieth-century science. For a more recent statement of Darwin's innovative use of statistical thinking, see Hull, *Philosophy of Biology*. In "Natural Selection," M. J. S. Hodge analyzes natural selection as "a probabilistic contribution to causal science," p. 266; also see Hodge, "Darwin's General Biological Theorizing," in Bendall, *Evolution from Molecules to Men*.

73. For an overview of the impact of Darwin's ideas around the world, see Glick, ed., *Comparative Reception of Darwinism*.

74. The traditional view of religion and Darwinism in warfare has been relegated by recent scholarship to one response among many in the post-Darwinian world. See James Moore's stinging and definitive critique of the "military motif" in *Post-Darwinian Controversies*, pp. 1–121. Moore goes on to describe a variety of religious responses to Darwinism as does Wilkins in *Science and Religious Thought*. Wilkins's work is an application to the Darwinian controversy of Niebuhr's four categories of religion's relation to its culture in *Christ and Culture*.

With some adaptations, Moore and Wilkins discuss a pattern of four religious responses to Darwinism, and to their work a fifth and sixth can be added. Their helpful categories accurately describe, with two additions, the array of choices in the cultural world of William James as a student of science in the 1860s: (1) the "religion against Darwinism" of idealists and orthodox Christians who scorned Darwinism's challenge to traditional beliefs in the divine order of nature and in God's moral purpose; (2) the "religion of Darwinism" of religious modernists whose enthusiasm for Darwinism included an urge to adapt their religious vision to recent scientific discoveries; (3) the position of "religion and Darwinisticism in concert," which encouraged adaptations of scientific theory to reflect religious hopes for progressive spiritual development; and (4) the "religion above Darwinism" of both Christian believers and nonbelievers who kept their religion and science in strictly separate spheres. They do not mention two other groups, one of which advocated "Darwinism as religion," the secular anti-Christian enthusiasts for science who treated Darwinism as a substitute religion (this is the group that promoted the warfare of science and religion motif); the other group, "religion blended with Darwinism," encouraged an adaptation of religion to science similar to the thought in Moore's and Wilkins's second group, the religion of modernism, but who were more theologically radical (this group is more commonly labeled harmonial piety or New Thought).

For similar interpretations of responses to Darwin, see Frederick Gregory, "The Impact of Darwinian Evolution on Protestant Theology in the Nineteenth Century," in Lindberg and Numbers, *God and Nature*, pp. 369–90; and Cashdollar, *Transformation of Theology*, pp. 209–439.

75. For some American examples, see Burr, *Pater Mundi*, published in two volumes, *Modern Science Testifying to the Heavenly Father* and *Doctrine of Evolution*; Brownson, "Physical Basis of Life," "Cosmic Philosophy," and "Darwin's Descent of Man," in *Works*, pp. 365–79, 439–56, and 485–96; Charles Hodge, *What Is Darwinism?*; and Townsend, *Mosaic Record and Modern Science*.

76. See, for example, Frothingham, *Religion of Humanity*; Abbot, *Organic Scientific Philosophy*; the secular religious thought Persons describes in *Free Religion*; and the modernist liberal Protestantism Hutchison evaluates in *Modernist Impulse*.

77. See, for example, Drummond, *Natural Law*; Henry Ward Beecher, *Evolution and Religion*; McCosh, *Religious Aspects of Evolution*; Fiske, *Cosmic Philosophy*; Cooke, *Religion and Chemistry*; and LeConte, "Agassiz and Evolution." In its blend of idealism and evolution, this group showed as much influence from Agassiz as from Darwin.

78. Ahlstrom called the scientific position of New Thought "harmonial piety"; see *Religious History of the American People*, p. 1019. Also see Quimby, *Quimby Manuscripts*; Gottschalk, *Emergence of Christian Science*; Parker, *Mind Cure in New England*; Robert C. Fuller, *Alternative Medicine*; Albanese, *Nature Religion in America*; and William James's own discussion of mind cure and New Thought in *Varieties of Religious Experience*.

79. See, for example, Asa Gray, *Darwiniana*; Chauncey Wright, *Philosophical Discussions*; and George Frederick Wright, *Studies in Science and Religion*.

80. Examples of the antireligious response to Darwin tell a story of British influence on American culture. See, for example, Draper, *Religion and Science*; and Fleming's analysis of his exaltation of science to a religious sphere in *John William Draper*. Also see Frank Turner's argument that a new group of secular-minded scientists sought to unseat religion's control of the academy, in *Between Science and Religion*; and Youmans's publishing agenda in *Popular Science Monthly*, begun in 1872. For a study of twentieth-century versions of this tradition, see Midgley, *Evolution as a Religion*. Agnostics were a related group to these advocates of scientific naturalism; see Thomas Henry Huxley, *Science and Christian Tradition*; Clifford, *Lectures and Essays*; Spencer, *Illustrations of Universal Progress*. Lightman, in *Origins of Agnosticism*, points out that while the agnostics were generally perceived as antireligious and even materialistic, they actually sought to find a stronger basis for religion.

81. William James, "Herbert Spencer" (1904), *Essays in Philosophy*, p. 116. Ralph Barton Perry dates James's reading of Spencer to "between 1860 and 1862"; *TCWJ*, 1:474. Soon thereafter, James lost respect for Spencer, thanks largely to discussions with Chauncey Wright and Charles Sanders Peirce, and he came to regard the many works of the British popularizer of evolution as "a museum of blundering reason"; see "Herbert Spencer," p. 116.

82. See Büchner, *Force and Matter*; the book went through many English translations in the late nineteenth century, and there were even a few editions in the twentieth century. The first English edition (1864) came out at about the same time as James's interest in the book. James's Notebook 3, entitled "Reading Notes & Observations; Sketches," bMS Am 1092.9 (4497) in the William James Papers, begins on October 1, 1862. The Büchner entry, marked "Sept. 10th." without the year, must be from at least eleven months later. An entry in the Harvard University Charging Records confirms the year 1863 for James's notebook entry: on September 4, 1863, James charged out *Kraft und Stoff* from the school library; see Library Charging Lists, 1863-64, Harvard University Archives.

83. Notebook 3, pp. 52, 55, and 56, William James Papers. Levinson briefly discusses James's attraction to Spencer and Büchner, although he dates James's reading of Büchner to 1862; see *Religious Investigations*, pp. 6 and 27-29.

84. See Roberts, *Darwinism and the Divine*, especially pp. 3-87. James came to assume the facts and methods of Darwinian science. For example, he reviewed Darwin's *The Variation of Animals and Plants Under Domestication* (1868) in the *Atlantic Monthly* and the *North American Review*, both in *Essays, Comments, and Reviews*, pp. 229-39; in the 1878 lectures on "The Brain and the Mind," he stated, "Darwinism has made us understand so much about organic animal and vegetable forms" (*Manuscript Lectures*, p. 30); and in the 1907 *Pragmatism* lecture he spoke in passing of the need to "embrace the darwinian facts" (p. 57). In addition, James read most of Darwin's works, had many social contacts with the Darwin family, and incorporated Darwin's ideas into his psychology; see Priebe, "William James's Application of Darwinian Theory," pp. 46-56; Taylor, "William James on Darwin," pp. 8-11; Seigfried, "Extending the Darwinian Model"; Robert J. Richards, *Darwin and the Emergence of Evolutionary Theories*; Schull, "Selection"; and Woodward, "James's Evolutionary Epistemology."

Chapter 5

1. "Catalogue of the Officers and Students of Harvard," p. 75. The formal religious declaration was in place at least as early as 1855 and continued all through James's years of education in the 1860s; see Faculty Records (May 4, 1855), Lawrence Scientific School, and the catalogue for each year in Pusey Library, Harvard University Archives. Another Harvard scientist, Josiah Cooke, set a similar tone. He delivered his lectures "Religion and Chemistry; or, Proofs of God's Plan in the Atmosphere and Its Elements," at the Brooklyn Institute, and the Lowell Institute in 1861. His lectures were published with a different subtitle in 1864.

2. Edward Waldo Emerson, *Early Years of the Saturday Club*, p. 11. For an astute discussion of the role of maleness in Northern, white, antebellum literary culture

and the inspiration men drew in their self-confident intellectualism and elitism from the "men of force" of the business world, see Leverenz, *Manhood and the American Renaissance*; also see Carnes and Griffen, eds., *Meanings for Manhood*. Cranch's poem, "The Poetical Picnic," is quoted in Sargent, ed., *Sketches and Reminiscences*, p. 406. For discussion of nineteenth-century intellectual clubs, see Kuklick, "Amateur Philosophizing," *Rise of American Philosophy*, pp. 46–62. David Hall discusses the people in this social group as "conservative . . . revolutionar[ies]" in "The Victorian Connection," p. 94.

3. Edward Waldo Emerson, *Early Years of the Saturday Club*, p. 8.

4. Ibid., pp. 30 and 23.

5. Holmes quoted in Marcou, *Life, Letters, and Works*, 2:131; the anonymous friend is quoted in Weeks, *Lowells and Their Institute*, p. 53. See discussion of his attendance at Mrs. George Ticknor's literary salon in Marcou, 2:133.

6. Elizabeth Carey's mother provides a graphic example of the ease with which Agassiz was accepted by Boston elites. When she first saw Louis Agassiz in 1846, she said, "He is the first person I ever saw whom I would like Lizzie to marry"; quoted in Tharp, *Adventurous Alliance*, p. 6.

7. Edward Waldo Emerson, *Early Years of the Saturday Club*, p. 34; and Ralph Waldo Emerson, "Nature" (1836), in *Collected Works*, p. 40. Ian Bell, in "Divine Patterns," discusses the romantic idealism that Agassiz and his literary admirers had in common.

8. Edward Waldo Emerson, *Early Years of the Saturday Club*, p. 32. Because of Agassiz's wide lecturing, his "enchanting verve," and his ability to "infect . . . everyone with his zeal for nature," Brooks, in *Flowering of New England*, calls him "a sort of Johnny Appleseed of science" (pp. 447–48).

9. Agassiz, *Methods of Study*, p. 268.

10. See Lurie, *Louis Agassiz*.

11. Johann Wolfgang von Goethe (1749–1832), famous as a poet, dramatist, novelist, and philosopher, was also a devoted scientist. He was convinced that nature could be understood through the discovery of ideal forms or basic models of all its manifestations. Lorenz Oken (1779–1855) was a German biologist and philosopher who stimulated great interest among New England transcendentalists as a "poet in science," in Emerson's phrase. Oken maintained a pantheistic and vitalistic belief that divinity manifests itself in nature and that we can understand that spirit in nature through its correspondence with mathematical structures and metaphysical essences. See Lenoir, "Göttingen School," and Lurie, *Louis Agassiz*, pp. 23–28 and 51.

12. The aging German was a role model for the ambitious young scientist; Agassiz later said that the example of Humboldt showed him "how to work, what to do, what to avoid, how to live, how to distribute my time, what methods to pursue"; see Louis Agassiz, "Address."

13. Louis Agassiz, *Methods of Study*, especially pp. 7–13; and Lurie, *Louis Agassiz*, pp. 59–62.

14. Louis Agassiz, *Contributions to the Natural History*, p. 8.

15. Louis Agassiz and Elizabeth Agassiz, *Journey to Brazil*, p. 7; in a letter to Cuvier which he never sent, Agassiz said that he "revere[d]" his mentor "as a father . . . whose

works have been till now my only guide"; quoted in Tharp, *Adventurous Alliance*, p. 48.

16. Lurie, *Louis Agassiz*, pp. 108 and 94–104; and Louis Agassiz, *Geological Sketches*, p. 27.

17. Agassiz, *Geological Sketches*, p. 154; Louis Agassiz and Elizabeth Agassiz, *Journey to Brazil*, p. 399. Gillispie, in *Genesis and Geology*, observes that glacial theory "gave catastrophism a new lease on life" (p. 151). Rudwick, in *Meaning of Fossils*, points out that catastrophism and uniformitarianism are somewhat misleading names; Cuvier preferred the label "revolutions" to describe regular and natural events that produce sudden changes (p. 132). Similarly, it was the philosopher William Whewell who dubbed Charles Lyell's "steady-state" theory of geological changes without catastrophes the "uniformitarian" view (p. 188). See James R. Moore, "Geologists and Interpreters of Genesis in the Nineteenth Century," in Lindberg and Numbers, eds., *God and Nature*, pp. 322–50, for a critique of the dichotomy.

18. Edward Forbes to Louis Agassiz, [1841], Imbrie and Imbrie, *Ice Ages*, p. 41.

19. Louis Agassiz, *Geological Sketches*, p. 99; the image of God commanding glaciers to plow and transform the earth, a dramatic version of secondary causes doing the work of divine providence, was a favorite metaphor which he repeated often: ibid., pp. 6 and 162; Louis Agassiz and Elizabeth Agassiz, *Journey to Brazil*, pp. 100, 404, and 425.

20. The former student of Agassiz and president of Stanford University, David Starr Jordan, provides a good description of his theory of species creation: "The species was the thought-unit, the individual reproduction of the thought in the divine mind at the moment of the creation of the first one of the series which represent the species"; Jordan, "Agassiz at Penikese," p. 728. On the location and range of species, even after creation, see Louis Agassiz, *Methods of Study*, p. 100.

21. Marcou, *Life, Letters, and Works*, 1:x.

22. Agassiz's annual salary at Neuchâtel was $400; see Weeks, *Lowells and Their Institute*, p. 53.

23. Louis Agassiz, *Geological Sketches*, p. 77; and Agassiz quoted in Imbrie and Imbrie, *Ice Ages*, p. 45.

24. Lyman, "Recollections of Agassiz," p. 223; Bruce, *Launching of Modern American Science*, p. 54; and Lurie, *Louis Agassiz*, pp. 114–64.

25. Marcou, *Life, Letters, and Works*, 2:156. Agassiz's fund-raising ability figures prominently in Howard S. Miller's study of scientific patronage, *Dollars for Research*, especially pp. 67–70.

26. Teller, *Louis Agassiz*, p. 68.

27. Abbott Lawrence to Treasurer of Harvard College, September 20, 1849, Faculty and Administrative Board Minutes, Lawrence Scientific School.

28. See Lurie, *Louis Agassiz*, pp. 212–51; and Winsor, *Reading the Shape of Nature*, pp. 1–42. Agassiz was not alone in using museums to showcase anti-Darwinian principles; see Sheets-Pyenson's descriptions of Frederick McCoy in Melbourne, G. M. Dawson in Montreal, and Hermann Burmeister in Buenos Aires, in *Cathedrals of Science*.

29. Lurie, *Louis Agassiz*, pp. 200–201; and Marcou, *Life, Letters, and Works*, 2:211.

30. Shaler, "Chapters from an Autobiography," pp. 221–22.

31. In addition to Jordan and Marcou, also see, for example, George B. Emerson, "What We Owe to Louis Agassiz"; LeConte, "Agassiz and Evolution"; Lyman, "Recollections of Agassiz"; Shaler, "Chapters from an Autobiography"; Teller, *Louis Agassiz*; and Wilder, "What We Owe Agassiz." Agassiz also left a lasting impact on their scientific thinking: although his particular brand of idealistic science was discredited in his own day, it did gain a renewed reputation by the turn of the century. By then, although evolution was well established scientifically, Darwin's own theories were widely criticized, especially because they did not have the support of a theory of genetics, which would become important to neo-Darwinism in the twentieth century. In place of Darwinism, many scientists turned to an idealistic, teleological neo-Lamarckianism, which emphasized the inheritance of acquired traits. Agassiz's students were very prominent in this trend; see Winsor, *Reading the Shape of Nature*, p. 36; Livingstone, *Nathaniel Southgate Shaler*, pp. 55–117; and Bowler, *Eclipse of Darwinism*, pp. 118–40. Blum, in *Picturing Nature*, points out that major factors in Agassiz's continuing influence were the illustrations of his work, which, even when stripped of their antievolutionary theory, suggested the scientist's idealistic outlooks.

32. Youmans quoted in Wilder, "What We Owe Agassiz," p. 12.

33. Jordan, "Agassiz at Penikese," p. 722.

34. See Lurie, *Louis Agassiz*, pp. 180–88; Kohlstedt, *American Scientific Community*; Bruce, *Launching of Modern American Science*; and Slotten, *Patronage, Practice*. For an example of the work of this group in campaigning for science, see letters of Benjamin Peirce and Louis Agassiz to [Congressman] Charles Upham (1855), Benjamin Peirce et al., "Six Letters upon the Smithsonian Institution."

35. Wilder, "What We Owe Agassiz," p. 13; and [faculty resolution], December 16, 1873, Faculty and Administrative Board Minutes, Lawrence Scientific School.

36. Teller, *Louis Agassiz*, p. 67; and Lyell quoted in Darwin to Joseph Hooker, March 26, [1854], Charles Darwin, *Life and Letters*, 1:403.

37. Leopold von Bush quoted in Teller, *Louis Agassiz*, p. 106. Agassiz's tendency to split groups into species was typical of American naturalists before the 1850s and was a source of contention with Asa Gray even before the Darwinian debates; see Charlotte Porter, *Eagle's Nest*, pp. 78 and 121.

38. See Lurie, *Louis Agassiz*, pp. 252–302. The twelve lectures were also published serially in the *Atlantic Monthly* in 1862, and collected in book form in 1866 under the same title.

39. Louis Agassiz, *Methods of Study*, p. 31.

40. Marcou, *Life, Letters, and Works*, 2:112–14; Louis Agassiz, *Geological Sketches*, p. 39.

41. Louis Agassiz and Elizabeth Agassiz, *Journey to Brazil*, p. 427.

42. Louis Agassiz, *Methods of Study*, p. 202.

43. The infamous Robert Chambers had drawn on Agassiz's ideas in support of evolution; see Ruse, *Darwinian Revolution*, p. 97. Asa Gray reported slyly that "a

very clever friend" had been converted to the development theory by reading Agassiz's reaction to Darwinism; see Lurie, *Louis Agassiz*, p. 298.

44. Louis Agassiz, *Methods of Study*, pp. iii–iv.

45. His attitude coincides with a majority of religious thinkers in the 1860s; see Roberts, *Darwinism and the Divine*.

46. Lurie, *Louis Agassiz*, p. 211. On the swift conversion of scientists to Darwinism, see Fiske's descriptions in *Darwinism*, pp. 1–19; and Agassiz's own shocked response: "I regret that the young and ardent spirits of our day give themselves to speculation rather than to close and accurate investigation"; his choice of words once again emphasizes the methodological split. See Agassiz, "Evolution," p. 101.

47. Agassiz, *Methods of Study*, pp. 142 and 191.

48. Ibid., p. 29; also see Louis Agassiz and Elizabeth Agassiz, *Journey to Brazil*, p. 41. This particular objection is similar to that of Fleeming Jenkin, who, writing before awareness of genes as discrete units of mutations, challenged Darwinism because any single variation would be overwhelmed by the mainstream traits within the species; see Jenkin, "The Origin of Species" (1867), Hull, *Darwin and His Critics*, pp. 302–50.

49. Kuhn, *Structure of Scientific Revolutions*; Hull evaluates Darwinism in Kuhnian terms in *Darwin and His Critics*.

50. See the report of the debate of Louis Agassiz and William Barton Rogers in the *Proceedings of the Boston Society of Natural History* (1859–61), pp. 231–63; and Edward Pfeifer, "United States."

51. Marcou, *Life, Letters, and Works*, 2:100; and Bruce, *Launching of Modern American Science*, p. 292. Some students even organized a "Society for the Protection of American Naturalist against the Oppression of Foreign Professors," quoted in Lurie, *Louis Agassiz*, p. 314; and Winsor, *Reading the Shape of Nature*, p. 46.

52. See Lurie, *Louis Agassiz*, pp. 345–50; Winsor, *Reading the Shape of Nature*, pp. 66–80; and Holmes, "A Farewell to Agassiz," in *Early Science at Harvard*, p. 70.

53. See *TCWJ*, 1:217–26; Carleton Sprague Smith, "William James in Brazil"; Bjork argues in *William James* that the natural settings James encountered were of "lasting symbolic importance" (p. 67) in providing him with a fund of images for his later creative work in psychology and philosophy.

54. See Dupree, *Asa Gray*, pp. 1–73; and Andrew Denny Rodgers, *John Torrey*, especially p. 81.

55. Gray, *Elements of Botany*; and John Torrey and Gray, *Flora of North America*.

56. Gray was, however, quite successful in raising money for the Harvard Herbarium; see Gray, "Harvard University Herbarium."

57. Dupree, *Asa Gray*, pp. 221–22, 118, and 353; and Gray to Ralph Waldo Emerson, May 11, 1874, Emerson Papers.

58. John Torrey quoted in Andrew Denny Rodgers, *John Torrey*, p. 114.

59. Jane Loring Gray, in Gray, *Letters*, 1:323.

60. Dupree, *Asa Gray*, p. 111.

61. *Proceedings . . . In Memory of Dr. Asa Gray*, p. 70.

62. Ibid., pp. 62 and 63.

63. Gray to Torrey, March 1, 1844, Gray, *Letters*, 1:319.

64. Gray wrote serious scholarly works, including *Flora of North America*; and numerous articles and notices published in the *American Journal of Science* and other journals, many of which are collected in *Scientific Papers of Asa Gray*. Gray also wrote and published in numerous popular edition volumes for schools and for the interested layman, including *Elements of Botany*; *Botanical Text-Book*; *First Lessons in Botany*; *Botany for Young People*; *How Plants Grow*; and *Field, Forest, and Garden Botany*.

65. Burnham, in *How Superstition Won and Science Lost*, laments that while many nineteenth-century scientists engaged in works of popularization, "specialists in popularizing, especially journalists" took over that job in the twentieth century (pp. 31, 37, and 7). I explore James's cultural role between professionalism and popularizations in an unpublished essay, "William James in Search of an Audience."

66. *Proceedings . . . In Memory of Dr. Asa Gray*, pp. 58 and 60. On Gray's early rise to dominance of botanical study, see Dupree, *Asa Gray*, pp. 155–215. On the early-nineteenth-century debates about systems of classification, see Charlotte Porter, *Eagle's Nest*, pp. 31, 75–77.

67. Gray, review of *Flora Japonica* and "Flora of Japan."

68. Charles Darwin to Asa Gray, October 12, 1856, Charles Darwin, *More Letters*, 1:434.

69. See Dupree, *Asa Gray*, pp. 249–56. Gray's research on the flora of eastern Asia and eastern North America appears in much of his published work in the 1850s; see reports on the "Flora of the Northern United States." In addition, he made supporting observations about the similarity of Scandinavian plants and those in Alpine zones in his review of Joseph D. Hooker, "Outlines of the Distribution of Arctic Plants," *Scientific Papers of Asa Gray*, 1:123–30.

70. Dupree, *Asa Gray*, pp. 241–45; and Bruce, *Launching of Modern American Science*, p. 108.

71. Gray, "Flora of the Northern United States"; portions of this research appeared in many issues of the *American Journal of Science*.

72. Review of Hooker and Thomson, *Flora Indica*, *Scientific Papers of Asa Gray*, 1:65; "Flora of the Northern United States," p. 211; and Remarks on Darwin, p. 413.

73. Charles Darwin to Jeffries Wyman, October 3, [1860], Dupree, ed., "Charles Darwin to Jeffries Wyman," p. 107.

74. "The Flora of Japan," *Scientific Papers of Asa Gray*, 2:133 and 135.

75. Notice of Charles Darwin, *Scientific Papers of Asa Gray*, 2:432.

76. Review of John Ruskin, *Proserpina, Studies of Wayside Flowers*, *Scientific Papers of Asa Gray*, 1:202.

77. "Phytogamy," a review of Darwin, "Different Forms of Flowers on Plants of the Same Species," *Scientific Papers of Asa Gray*, 1:246.

78. Gray, Remarks on Darwin, p. 424.

79. Gray, *Darwiniana*, p. 86.

80. Ibid., p. 315. Also see Dupree, *Asa Gray*, pp. 268–79. On the merging of Darwinism and Mendelism in the "Neo-Darwinist synthesis" in twentieth-century biology, see Fisher, *Genetic Theory of Natural Selection*; Dobzhansky, *Genetics and the*

Origin of Species; Julian Huxley, *Evolution*; Provine, *Origins of Theoretical Population Genetics*; Mayr and Provine, *Evolutionary Synthesis*; and Bowler, *Mendelian Revolution*.

81. Gray quoted in Dupree, *Asa Gray*, p. 268.
82. "Variation and Distribution of Species," *Scientific Papers of Asa Gray*, 1:144.
83. Gray, *Darwiniana*, p. 298.
84. Ibid., pp. 49 and 48.
85. Ibid., pp. 72, 119, and 316; see also Dupree, *Asa Gray*, pp. 229 and 275.
86. Gray, Remarks on Darwin, p. 424; Gray, "Natural Selection," pp. 291 and 528; and Gray, *Darwiniana*, p. 232.
87. Gray, *Darwiniana*, p. 46.
88. Paley, *Natural Theology*, p. 14.
89. Dupree, *Asa Gray*, p. 138.
90. Gray, *Darwiniana*, p. 46.
91. Woodrow, "Evolution" (1884), in Blau, ed., *American Philosophical Addresses*, p. 513. Also see McGiffert, "Christian Darwinism"; and Livingstone, *Darwin's Forgotten Defenders*. Toward the end of his life, Wright rejected Darwinism and became a fundamentalist; see Numbers, "George Frederick Wright."
92. Gray, *Darwiniana*, pp. 119 and 44.
93. In some ways, Horace Bushnell anticipated the position of Gray and Wright on the neutrality of science and religion, and thus he serves as a partial exception to the early to middle nineteenth century advocacy of harmony between science and religion; his thought fits with the pre-Darwinian group, however, in his antagonism to species evolution, in his use of neutrality to protect religion from the extensions of science, and in his belief that the truths of religion are higher than those of science; see Bushnell, *Nature and the Supernatural*.
94. Eliot, "Popularizing Science," p. 34.
95. For example, on November 4, 1862, the faculty charged Eliot with the job of preparing "a complete statement of the plan of the School." On November 18, a discussion of the plan pitted Agassiz and Benjamin Peirce, "urging objection to the plan proposed," against Gray, Jeffries Wyman, and Eliot. The Lawrence faculty deferred to the president, who characteristically "said that he should consult Prof. Agassiz, and consider any plan he might suggest in connection with the other papers referred to him." See Faculty and Administrative Board Minutes, Lawrence Scientific School.
96. See Morrison, *Three Centuries of Harvard*, pp. 325–26. Eliot wrote a manifesto about his hopes for higher education in "New Education," pp. 203–20. Also see Morrison, *Development of Harvard University*; Henry James III, *Charles William Eliot*; and Hawkins, *Between Harvard and America*.
97. Henry James III, *Charles William Eliot*, 1:45.
98. See Kohlstedt, "Nineteenth-Century Amateur Tradition"; and Keeney, *Botanizers*.
99. Eliot quoted in Henry James III, *Charles William Eliot*, 1:34 and 64; Eliot, "Character of the Scientific Investigator" (1906), in Eliot, *Charles W. Eliot*. Eliot's scientific zeal was supported by many in the field of chemistry, which by 1860 was

already among the most naturalistic of the sciences; see Bozeman, *Protestants in an Age of Science*, p. 90.

100. Both graduates of Harvard, Storer and Eliot were teaching chemistry at the Massachusetts Institute of Technology at the time of publication.

101. Charles Eliot to Henry James, *LWJ*, 1:31–32.

102. Eliot and Storer, *Manual of Inorganic Chemistry*, p. 4.

103. [Notebook 3] September 10, 1863, pp. 55–56, in William James Papers.

104. William James to Henry Bowditch, May 22, 1869, *TCWJ*, 1:296.

105. Although there is no modern biography, there are a number of early biographical portraits of Wyman: Gray, "Address"; Holmes, "Professor Jeffries Wyman"; Packard, "Memoir of Jeffries Wyman"; Putnam, "Jeffries Wyman"; Wilder, "Sketch of Dr. Jeffries Wyman"; and Clark, "Jeffries Wyman."

106. William to Alice James, September 13, 1863, *LWJ*, 1:50; also see Allen, *William James*, p. 94.

107. Gray et al., "Jeffries Wyman," *Scientific Papers of Asa Gray*, 2:396.

108. William James, "Professor Jeffries Wyman," in *Essays, Comments, and Reviews*, p. 8.

109. Wyman, *Dear Jeffie*, p. v.

110. Lowell quoted in Love, *Lawrence Scientific School*, p. 8.

111. Gray quoted in Love, *Lawrence Scientific School*, p. 7; Holmes quoted in Edward Waldo Emerson, *Early Years of the Saturday Club*, p. 427; and Agassiz, as reported in Lurie, *Louis Agassiz*, p. 193.

112. Most of Wyman's papers and reports were published in the *Proceedings of the Boston Society of Natural History*: see, for example, "Development of Moulds in the Interior of Eggs," vol. 10 (May 18, 1864), p. 41; report on fossil bones, vol. 10 (March 15, 1865), p. 105; account of irregularities in bee hives, vol. 10 (November 15, 1865), pp. 234 and 278; reports on the skull shapes of Hawaiian Islanders and on the Caribbean customs, vol. 11 (December 5, 1866), pp. 70 and 100; report on Indian shell mounds at the St. John's River in Florida, vol. 11 (April 17, 1867), pp. 158–59; report on the similar method of obtaining fire in South Africa, the Pacific Islands, St. Domingo, and the Arctic, vol. 11 (July 3, 1867), p. 285; report on the measurements of human crania, vol. 11 (November 20, 1867), p. 322–23; "Observations on Crania," vol. 11 (April 15, 1868), pp. 440–62; and "On a Thread Worm Infesting the Brain of the Snake-Bird," vol. 12 (October 7, 1868), pp. 100–104. Packard, *Memoir of Jeffries Wyman*, has a list of his works. Gray's quotation of Wyman is in *Scientific Papers of Asa Gray*, 1:245; expressing a similar idea in different words, Wyman said: "The isolated study of anything in natural history is a fruitful source of error" (ibid., 2:394).

113. Even aside from its racism, another problem with the polygenesis argument, of course, is that separate species cannot produce fertile offspring. Nott in particular was avid in his attempts to show that children of mixed descent were actual hybrids, frail and destined to produce still weaker descendants. On polygenesis, see Stanton, *Leopard's Spots*; Fredrickson, *Black Image in the White Mind*; Gould, *Mismeasure of Man*; Horsman, *Race and Manifest Destiny*; McCardell, *Idea of a Southern Nation*; and Lurie, *Louis Agassiz*, pp. 256–66. Wyman, "Observations on Crania," p. 447.

114. Gray to Charles Darwin, January 23, 1860, Dupree, *Asa Gray*, pp. 292–93; and "Jeffries Wyman," *Scientific Papers of Asa Gray*, 2:398.

115. Wyman, *Proceedings of the Boston Society of Natural History*, vol. 10 (March 15, 1865), p. 105, and (November 15, 1865), p. 234; also see Wyman, "Notes on the Cells of the Bee."

116. Charles Darwin to Jeffries Wyman, February 3, [1861], in Dupree, ed., "Charles Darwin to Jeffries Wyman," p. 109.

117. Ibid.

118. Wyman quoted in Morrison, *Development of Harvard University*, p. 378n.

119. Wyman quoted in *Scientific Papers of Asa Gray*, 2:399.

120. Wyman quoted in Dupree, "Jeffries Wyman's Views on Evolution," p. 243.

121. Gray, "Jeffries Wyman," *Scientific Papers of Asa Gray*, 2:398.

122. Wyman quoted in Lurie, *Louis Agassiz*, p. 311.

123. Dupree, "Jeffries Wyman's Views on Evolution," p. 243.

124. Ibid., p. 245.

125. Henry James, Sr., to Charles Eliot Norton, September 1, 1865, Norton Papers; and William James to his parents, April 21–25, 1865, and May 3–10, 1865, *TCWJ*, 1:217 and 219.

126. See Tilton, *Amiable Autocrat*; and Gibian, "Oliver Wendell Holmes."

127. Oliver Wendell Holmes, Sr., to Henry James, Sr., April 27, 1881, and to James R. Osgood, December 17, 1884, *TCWJ*, 1:127 and 117; Henry James, Sr., quoted in Small, *Oliver Wendell Holmes*, p. 100; and Alice James, December 14, [1889], *Diary*, p. 68. Brooks, in *Flowering of New England*, has a similar description of the James-Holmes friendship (p. 358).

128. Holmes, *Border Lines of Knowledge*, p. 8; and James Jackson, Sr., to James Jackson, Jr., March 29, 1833, *Memoir of James Jackson*, p. 346.

129. Morse, *Life and Letters of Oliver Wendell Holmes*, 1:39–40.

130. Holmes's best-known satire on Calvinism is his poem "The Deacon's Masterpiece; or, the Wonderful 'One-Hoss Shay,' A Logical Story"; in *Poetical Works*, 2:131–35. On his medical research, see his essays "Facts and Traditions Respecting the Existence of Indigenous Intermittent Fever in New England," "On the Nature and Treatment of Neuralgia," and "On the Utility and Importance of Direct Exploration in Medical Practice" in Holmes, *Boylston Prize Dissertations*; a brief abstract of the third essay appeared as "Contagiousness of Puerperal Fever."

131. Holmes, "Mechanism in Thought and Action," delivered before the Phi Beta Kappa Society of Harvard University (June 29, 1870), in *Pages from an Old Life*, pp. 265, 293, 308, and 303.

132. Both before and after 1859, he was intrigued by cases of species variation; see, for example, his "Case of Malformation."

133. Mark A. DeWolfe Howe, "Dr. Holmes," p. 576; Holmes, "Mechanism in Thought and Action," *Pages from an Old Life*, p. 312; and Alice James, December 14, [1889], *Diary*, p. 69.

134. William James, review of Claude Bernard, *Rapport sur les progrès et la Marche de la physiologie générale en France* (1868), *Essays, Comments, and Reviews*, pp. 226–27. James was self-deprecating about his comments on Holmes, calling them

" 'gassy.' " In addition, in a letter to his brother, he praised his teacher on less scientific grounds: "The lecture tickled me to death by the perfection of its style." His father reassured him that his teacher approved of William's comments, but wholly skirted any mention of the scientific issues; Henry, Sr., wrote: "Holmes . . . is very much pleased with your notice of his pamphlet, which I have read, and I agree with you in thinking the style of it capital." See William to Henry James, Jr., February 12, 1868, *Correspondence of William James*, p. 30; and Henry, Sr., to William James, March 18, [1868], *TCWJ*, 1:97.

135. William to Henry James, Jr., June 12, 1869, *Correspondence of William James*, p. 82. Before taking the examination, James completed his thesis on the effects of cold on the body; see *TCWJ*, 1:289–302; and Bjork, *William James*, p. 86.

136. Charles Eliot was decisive in stiffening the requirements for the medical degree. See Brieger, *Medical America in the Nineteenth Century*, p. 6; and Henry Knowles Beecher and Mark Altschule, *Medicine at Harvard*, pp. 87–90.

137. William to Henry James, Jr., June 12, 1869, *Correspondence of William James*, p. 82; James's memory of Holmes's exam question is in Henry James III, *Charles William Eliot*, 1:275; and William James to Henry Bowditch, August 12, 1869, *LWJ*, 1:154.

138. Dupree, "Jeffries Wyman's Views on Evolution," p. 245.

139. James quoted in *TCWJ*, 1:228.

Part III Introduction

1. William James to Oliver Wendell Holmes, Jr., January 3, 1868, *TCWJ*, 1:508; also see discussion of conversation among club members in Wilson, *Transformation of American Philosophy*, p. 18.

2. Charles Peirce to Christine Ladd-Franklin [ca. 1904], in Ladd-Franklin, "Charles S. Peirce at the Johns Hopkins," p. 719 [Wiener, *Evolution and the Founders of Pragmatism*, p. 20]. Peirce remembered that "a knot of us young men in Old Cambridge, calling ourselves, half-ironically, half defiantly, 'The Metaphysical Club,'— for agnosticism was then riding its high horse, and was frowning superbly upon all metaphysics—used to meet, sometimes in my study, sometimes in that of William James"; see "Pragmatism" [ca. 1906], *CPCP*, 5.12 [Wiener, *Evolution and the Founders of Pragmatism*, p. 19]. The title seems borrowed from Auguste Comte's second great historical stage, the metaphysical, which, he argued, was currently being displaced by the scientific stage. Despite Comte's sharp contrast between metaphysics and science, the club had a decidedly scientific persuasion, especially among the leading figures, Wright and Peirce. Peirce offered a clue about the name as a note of defiance against a materialistic, antimetaphysical brand of science: he criticized the "positivist . . . habit of considering positivism and metaphysics as opposed species of philosophy"; see [Critique of Positivism], (1867–68), *WCP*, 2:127. This implies a hope to avoid the tendency to elevate scientific authority above metaphysics and an urge to find the metaphysical meaning of science. On the popularity of Comte and positivism in the 1860s and 1870s, see Cashdollar, *Transformation of Theology*.

3. Max Fisch has pieced together evidence from many sources to confirm that the

club existed as Peirce remembered it; see his essay, "Was There a Metaphysical Club?."

4. See Ladd-Franklin, "Peirce at the Johns Hopkins," p. 719; Edward H. Madden, *Chauncey Wright*, pp. 27 and 155; and Brent, *Charles Peirce*, pp. 67 and 84. James discusses the ideas of "C. S. Pierce" [*sic*] in Notebook 2, pp. 20–21, William James Papers. James refers directly to Peirce's discussion of his categories "I, IT, and THOU" in two essays written in Spring 1861, wcp, 1: 45–49. James critiqued Wright's antimetaphysical empiricism in the unpublished manuscript "Against Nihilism," in *Manuscript Essays and Notes*, pp. 150–55. Peirce read many drafts of logic papers, including his influential "Illustrations of the Logic of Science" series of essays (wcp, 3:242–338), to members of the club. Despite his differences with his son's friends, Henry James, Sr., also circulated collegially with these young men: he wrote to *North American Review* editor Charles Eliot Norton "at the instance of Mr. Wright to say that he [Wright] was disposed to relinquish the space accorded him in the forthcoming N. A. R." The elder James therefore wanted "to offer you my article on Faith & Science"; see Henry James, Sr., to Charles Eliot Norton, May 1, 1865, bMS Am 1088, Norton Papers. James did in fact publish "Faith and Science" in the *North American Review* later that year. Its spiritual science is in striking contrast to Wright's views; this brief window into its publication history is a marvelous example of the new approaches to science and religion emerging comfortably from the bosom of the old.

5. "Pragmatism" [ca. 1906], cpcp, 5.12. Also see Fisch, "Alexander Bain."

6. On the Metaphysical Club, see Fisch, "Chronicle of Pragmatism"; Wiener, *Evolution and the Founders of Pragmatism*; Mills, *Sociology and Pragmatism*; Thayer, *Meaning and Action*, pp. 79–83 and 488–92; John E. Smith, *Purpose and Thought*, pp. 195–97; and Kuklick, *Rise of American Philosophy*, pp. 46–103. On individual members, see "Nicholas St. John Green" (1877), in wcp, 3:208–10; Fisch, "Justice Holmes"; Higgins, "The Young John Fiske"; Ahlstrom and Mullin, *Scientific Theist*. The members of the club are significant not only for their later prominence but also for the diversity of their contributions: Wiener says that in the writing of his book, he became impressed with the "rich diversity of ideas in the history of but one school of American pragmatism," and he became convinced that "what was so loosely termed 'pragmatism' was not one coherent doctrine but, in fact, a whole congeries of ideas." So he regards his book as an examination of the "roots . . . [of] the history of American liberalism" in general; see "Lovejoy's Rôle in American Philosophy," pp. 170–71.

7. Mills, *Sociology and Pragmatism*, pp. 85 and 29.

8. See Fisch, "Philosophical Clubs"; and Flower and Murphey, *History of Philosophy in America*, pp. 401–514. Members of the Metaphysical Club also shared with their parents' generation an emphasis on character, which often emerged in their stress on morality; see Brooks, *Flowering of New England*, on the nature of character education (especially p. 34); and Peter Dobkin Hall, *Organization of American Culture*, on the continuity of character education throughout the nineteenth century.

9. Peirce, "Detached Ideas in General" (1898), cpcp, 1.662; and "Logic of Science" [Lowell Lectures of 1866], Lecture XI (November 1866), wcp, 1:499. Peirce was the major exception on the slavery issue: he was pro-Southern.

10. Quoted in Fisch, "Was There a Metaphysical Club?," p. 16.

11. See Gay, *Enlightenment*, especially vol. 1: *The Rise of Modern Paganism*.

12. Flower and Murphey, *History of Philosophy in America*, pp. 203–73 and 401–514; and Stevenson, *Scholarly Means to Evangelical Ends*.

13. Peirce, "Place of Our Age" (1863), WCP, 1:111 and 114. George Santayana characterized the moralism that was central to the club members' hope to compromise new thought with old as "gentility," and this trait prompted him to say that in their simultaneous moralism and unorthodoxy, they were "like clergy without church" (*Character and Opinion*, p. 43).

14. Wiener, *Evolution and the Founders of Pragmatism*, p. 27; Peirce, "Pragmatism" [ca. 1906], CPCP, 5.12; and Mills, *Sociology and Pragmatism*, p. 206.

15. Wiener, *Evolution and the Founders of Pragmatism*, p. 58; Mills, *Sociology and Pragmatism*, p. 115; and Kuklick, *Rise of American Philosophy*, pp. 25 and 21.

Chapter 6

1. Wright, "John Stuart Mill—A Commemorative Notice," 1873–74, PD, p. 415.
2. Charles Eliot Norton, "Biographical Sketch," PD, p. viii.
3. "Life" (1858), LCW, p. 6 [Edward H. Madden, *Chauncey Wright*, p. 4].
4. James Bradley Thayer's "Account of His Life," and Rufus Ellis to James Bradley Thayer, LCW, pp. 20, 18, and 20. Thayer solicited many reminiscences of Wright in putting together the *Letters of Chauncey Wright*; they appear below as letters to Thayer, and although not dated, they were all presumably written about 1875–78.
5. Wright, answers to the "mental photography" (questionnaire) of a friend [a Miss Shattuck], August 9, 1874, and Wright to Jane Norton, [September 1874], LCW, pp. 299 and 302.
6. E. W. Gurney to James Bradley Thayer, [1877], LCW, p. 364.
7. Addison Brown to James Bradley Thayer, LCW, p. 28.
8. Wright to Miss Shattuck, August 9, 1874, LCW, p. 299.
9. James Bradley Thayer quoted in LCW, pp. 24 and 22.
10. Wright quoted in LCW, p. 11n; and Norton quoted in LCW, p. 83.
11. Charles Eliot Norton, Wright to Jane Norton, March 1874, Wright to Grace Norton, March 25, 1870, Wright to Sara Sedgwick, December 18, 1874, Wright to Sara Norton, September 1, 1875, Wright to Jane Norton, February 26, 1870, Darwin Ware to James Bradley Thayer, LCW, pp. 83, 256, 178, 319, 353–54, 165, and 44.
12. Wright to Charles Eliot Norton, August 10, 1870, Wright to Jane Norton, February 15, 1869, Wright to Charles Eliot Norton, May 8, 1871, editorial comment of James Bradley Thayer, Wright to Frederick Wright, April 29, 1862, Wright to Grace Norton, January 13, 1870, and Wright to Grace Norton, July 16, 1870, LCW, pp. 192, 193, 144, 220, 38, 49, 159, and 186; and "Conflict of Studies" (1875), PD, p. 282. See Edward H. Madden, *Chauncey Wright*, pp. 63–69.
13. Wright to Grace Norton, July 25, 1875, LCW, p. 343; Edward H. Madden, *Chauncey Wright*, p. 5.
14. Wright quoted in J. J. Myers to James Bradley Thayer, LCW, p. 200.
15. Simon Newcomb to James Bradley Thayer, May 18, 1865, LCW, p. 70; Bruce, *Launching of Modern American Science*, p. 179; and Moyer, *Scientist's Voice in American Culture*, pp. 29–36 and 52–58.

16. "Winds and the Weather" and parts of "Philosophy of Herbert Spencer" (1865), *PD*, pp. 43–96. See Edward H. Madden, *Chauncey Wright*, pp. 10–11; and Edward H. Madden, "Cambridge Septem."

17. Charles Eliot to James Bradley Thayer, and Thayer's "Account of His Life," *LCW*, pp. 83 and 41.

18. Miss Howard to James Bradley Thayer, *LCW*, p. 121. Kuklick, in *Rise of American Philosophy*, reads this style as evidence that many of the ideas Wright propounded were "a pose" (p. 77). But it is more likely that he was saying what he believed while feeling the potently irreverent effect of his ideas on his audience. For example, when one friend lamented the challenge of geology to religion and cried, "if rocks go to pieces, what can you trust in?" Wright boldly and slyly replied, "Truth!" (*LCW*, p. 121).

19. E. L. Gurney to James Bradley Thayer, [1877], *LCW*, pp. 362 and 380.

20. Ibid., pp. 212–13 and 366; see p. 353 for a charming example of Wright's clear and simple scientific explanations to children. Also see Marcou, *Life, Letters, and Works*, 2:110.

21. Ladd-Franklin, "Charles S. Peirce at the Johns Hopkins," p. 719; Wiener, *Evolution and the Founders of Pragmatism*, p. 20.

22. Peirce, "Pragmatism" [ca. 1906], in *CPCP*, 5.12; and Wiener, *Evolution and the Founders of Pragmatism*, p. 19. The "corypheus" was the leader of the chorus in Greek drama.

23. Chauncey Wright, "Evolution of Self-Consciousness" (1873), *PD*, pp. 239–42; E. L. Gurney to James Bradley Thayer, [1877], and Wright to Miss Shattuck, August 9, 1874, *LCW*, pp. 363–70 and 299. Also see Edward H. Madden, *Chauncey Wright*, pp. 112–27, Flower and Murphey, *History of Philosophy in America*, pp. 535–53, Kuklick, *Rise of American Philosophy*, pp. 63–79, and Giuffrida, "Chauncey Wright's Theory of Meaning," p. 323. On Mill's critique of Hamilton, see Cashdollar, *Transformation of Theology*, pp. 145–46 and 154–56.

24. Chauncey Wright, "Natural Theology as a Positive Science" (1865), *PD*, p. 39. See Edward H. Madden, "Chauncey Wright: Forgotten American Philosopher," p. 27. Kuklick, in *Rise of American Philosophy*, holds a contrasting view, maintaining that "Wright hypothesized that . . . phenomenal knowledge of [God's] existence . . . would yield . . . knowledge." But even Kuklick recognizes that for Wright, "evidence of the supernatural in the phenomenal world . . . might not be enough to warrant a conclusion" (p. 67).

25. Edward H. Madden, *Chauncey Wright*, pp. 31–37; also see Wright to Francis Abbot, July 9, 1867, and Wright to Jane Norton, March 22, 1869, *LCW*, pp. 103 and 146; and Wilson, *Transformation of American Philosophy*, pp. 25–26. Wright's views closely coincide with the positivist critiques of religious knowledge of Auguste Comte and John Stuart Mill; see Cashdollar, *Transformation of Theology*.

26. Flower and Murphey, *History of Philosophy in America*, p. 540; and Chauncey Wright, "Evolution of Self-Consciousness" (1873), *PD*, p. 249; also see Wright to Grace Norton, June 6, 1871, and Wright to Francis Abbot, October 28, 1867, *LCW*, pp. 228 and 132.

27. Wright to Charles Darwin, August 1, 1871, Wright to Grace Norton, July 14, 1874, Wright to Grace Norton, August 12, 1874, and Wright to Charles Darwin, Sep-

tember 3, 1874, *LCW*, pp. 232, 271, 285, and 304; and Chauncey Wright, "Genesis of Species" (1871), *PD*, pp. 127 and 161.

28. Chauncey Wright quoted in Norton, "Biographical Sketch," *PD*, p. xvii. In twentieth-century terms, Wright was a philosopher of science rather than a practicing scientist. Mills makes a similar observation: "He did not feel the force of science in terms of its results, but as a method"; see *Sociology and Pragmatism*, p. 105.

29. Chauncey Wright, "Philosophy of Herbert Spencer" (1865), *PD*, p. 55; Robert Giuffrida, in "Chauncey Wright's Theory of Meaning," observes that according to Wright, "the justification of scientific theories . . . lie[s] in [their] usefulness . . . in the discovery of new facts" (p. 315).

30. Chauncey Wright, "Books Relating to the Theory of Evolution" (1875), *PD*, p. 395. Peirce expresses a similar distinction between Spencer and Darwin in "Early Nominalism and Realism" (1869), *WCP*, 2:314.

31. Chauncey Wright, "Philosophy of Herbert Spencer" (1865), *PD*, pp. 55–56.

32. Wright to Grace Norton, October 16, 1870, *LCW*, p. 203; also see Kennedy, "Pragmatic Naturalism of Chauncey Wright," p. 489; and Edward H. Madden, *Chauncey Wright*, pp. 77 and 136.

33. Chauncey Wright, "Physical Theory of the Universe" (1864), *PD*, p. 17.

34. Chauncey Wright, "Genesis of Species" (1871), *PD*, p. 137.

35. Chauncey Wright, "Evolution by Natural Selection" (1872), *PD*, p. 182; Wright's ridicule was directed at British anti-Darwinian St. George Mivart, but applied equally well to Agassiz.

36. Chauncey Wright, "Genesis of Species" (1871), *PD*, p. 142.

37. Ibid., p. 156.

38. Oliver Wendell Holmes, Jr., to Sir Frederick Pollock, August 30, 1929, Howe, ed., *The Holmes-Pollock Letters*, 2:122. On the application of pragmatic and probabilistic thinking to the law, see Katzenbach, "Holmes, Peirce, and Legal Pragmatism"; and Gigerenzer et al., eds., *Empire of Chance*, pp. 258–61.

39. Chauncey Wright, "Philosophy of Herbert Spencer" (1865), *PD*, p. 51. See Edward H. Madden, *Chauncey Wright*, p. 75.

40. Chauncey Wright, "Philosophy of Herbert Spencer" (1865), *PD*, p. 46. Wright's analysis here and in "Genesis of Species" (1871), ibid., p. 141, is similar to Peirce's in "Fixation of Belief" (1877), in *WCP*, 3:242–57.

41. Chauncey Wright, "Genesis of Species" (1871), and "Evolution by Natural Selection" (1872), *PD*, pp. 137 and 177. Edward Madden, in "Chauncey Wright and the American Functionalists," points out that in these situations of "causal complexity," Wright argues that "even when explanation is impossible, one can give a reasonable explanatory sketch" (p. 265).

42. Chauncey Wright, "Genesis of Species," *PD*, p. 131.

43. Chauncey Wright, "Evolution by Natural Selection" (1872), *PD*, p. 196.

44. Chauncey Wright, "Genesis of Species" (1871), *PD*, p. 141. See Edward H. Madden, *Chauncey Wright*, pp. 82–91; and Edward Madden, "Chance and Counterfacts," pp. 420–32.

45. Wright, note on Peirce's review of Berkeley, [1871], *WCP*, 2:489.

46. Chauncey Wright, "German Darwinism" (1875), *PD*, pp. 404 and 405.

47. "Pragmatism" [ca. 1906], in CPCP, 5.12.

48. Chauncey Wright, "Honey-Bees' Cells," p. 319; "Architecture of Bees"; "Arrangements of Leaves in Plants" (1871), PD, p. 311; and Wright to Grace Norton, July 29, 1874, LCW, p. 280.

49. Chauncey Wright, "Philosophy of Herbert Spencer" (1864), PD, pp. 9–10; also see "Genesis of Species" (1871), and "Evolution by Natural Selection" (1872), ibid., pp. 131 and 176–79; and Edward H. Madden, *Chauncey Wright*, pp. 87–89. See Burchfield, "Darwin," and *Lord Kelvin*.

50. Chauncey Wright, "Arrangements of Leaves in Plants" (1871), PD, pp. 296–328.

51. Chauncey Wright, "Evolution of Self-Consciousness" (1873), PD, pp. 199–266. See Edward H. Madden, *Chauncey Wright*, pp. 128–42; in "Chauncey Wright and the American Functionalists," Madden credits Wright with the founding of psychozoology (p. 273). This topic shows that Wright was already thinking in naturalistic terms even before reading Darwin: he had linked animal and human intelligence in a college essay of about 1852, "Whether the faculty of Brutes differ from those of men in kind or in degree only?," which is published in Edward H. Madden, *Chauncey Wright*, pp. 183–85.

52. Charles Darwin to Wright, October 23, 1871, LCW, p. 235. Wright was by no means alone in his eagerness to prove Darwinism right; see Fiske, *Darwinism*; and Plate, *Dinosaur Hunters*, which is a study of the investigations (and competitions for dramatic fossil finds) of paleontologists Othniel Marsh and Edward Cope.

53. William James, "Chauncey Wright" (1875), *Essays, Comments, and Reviews*, p. 16.

54. Wright to Charles Eliot Norton, March 21, 1870, LCW, p. 170.

55. Wright to Mrs. Peter Lesley [her husband was a Congregational minister and professor of geology at the University of Pennsylvania], February 12, 1860, LCW, p. 43 [Wiener, *Evolution and the Founders of Pragmatism*, p. 33].

56. Wright uses the words of British mathematician and philosopher Augustus De Morgan in a review of Alfred R. Wallace's *Contribution to the Theory of Natural Selection*; quoted in Wiener, *Evolution and the Founders of Pragmatism*, p. 61.

57. Wright to Charles Eliot Norton, August 18, 1867, Miss Howard to James Bradley Thayer, and Wright to Grace Norton, July 29, 1874, LCW, pp. 115, 121, and 274; "McCosh on Tyndall" (1875), and "Genesis of Species" (1871), PD, pp. 377 and 127.

58. Chauncey Wright, "Philosophy of Herbert Spencer" (1865), PD, p. 51; Edward H. Madden, *Chauncey Wright*, p. 75; Wright to Grace Norton, June 6, 1871, and Wright to Peter Lesley, January 19, 1865, LCW, pp. 227 and 70.

59. Wright to Francis Abbot, October 28, 1867, LCW, p. 133.

60. Peter Lesley to James Bradley Thayer [ca. 1876], and Wright to Grace Norton, July 29, 1874, LCW, pp. 66 and 275 [Wright, *Philosophical Writings*, pp. 56–57].

61. William James, "Chauncey Wright" (1875), in *Essays, Comments, and Reviews*, p. 16; Wright to Francis Abbot, December 20, 1864, LCW, p. 61; and William James, *Will to Believe*, p. 14. Similarly, Giuffrida observes, in "Chauncey Wright's Theory of Meaning," that "this agnosticism of Wright's, while denying that religious claims constitute knowledge, did not rule out the very possibility of their being true" (p. 317).

62. Wright to Miss Robbins, August 7, 1864, in Edward H. Madden, *Chauncey*

Wright, p. 155; and Wright to Grace Norton, July 18, 1875, LCW, pp. 341–43 [TCWJ, 1:530–32]. In the 1875 letter, Wright boasted that although James claimed the "right to believe," he had forced the younger man to "retract . . . the word 'duty.' " Showing their scientific affinity, they both agreed that "evidence is all that enforces the obligation of belief." Although they differed in emphasis and emotional tone, the structure of their arguments about belief are ironically similar; in addition, their reference to character shows the crucial place of their class affiliations in their theory of belief. By contrast, Edward Madden, in *Chauncey Wright*, argues that Wright was a severe check on James's religious impulses (pp. 43–50).

63. Chauncey Wright, "Natural Theology as a Positive Science" (1864), PD, p. 41; E. L. Gurney to James Bradley Thayer, LCW, p. 381; and Youmans, "Propagators of Atheism?," p. 367. Also see Edward H. Madden, *Chauncey Wright*, pp. 37, 49, and 37; and Lightman, in *Origins of Agnosticism*, argues that the British agnostics were so aggressive because they wanted to transform Christianity, not destroy it.

64. Rufus Ellis to James Bradley Thayer, LCW, p. 298.

65. Norton, "Biographical Sketch," PD, p. xii; Rev. Charles Grinnell quoted in Charles Salter to Charles Eliot Norton, August 10, 1870, Edward H. Madden, *Chauncey Wright*, p. 16.

66. Wright, "Philosophy of Mother Goose" (1856), LCW, pp. 39–40.

67. Wright to Francis Abbot, August 13, 1867, LCW, p. 112.

68. Wright to Charles Eliot Norton, August 18, 1867, LCW, p. 115; Edward H. Madden, *Chauncey Wright*, p. 42.

69. Chauncey Wright, "Philosophy of Herbert Spencer," PD, p. 69; Wright to Charles Eliot Norton, March 21, 1870, Wright to Grace Norton, March 25, 1870, and Wright to Grace Norton, July 29, 1874, LCW, pp. 171, 183, and 276. In *Sociology and Pragmatism*, Mills says of Wright's religion that he relegated it to the practical (p. 99). Edward Madden, in *Civil Disobedience and Moral Law*, argues that even Wright's view of morality was influenced by his Darwinism, with his proposition that "moral rules have been naturally selected" (p. 144). It is this part of Wright's philosophy that has most in common with Abbot and other advocates of "free religion" with a focus on morality and social improvement; see Peden, *Philosopher of Free Religion*.

70. Kloppenberg points out that philosophers who, in the 1860s to 1880s, "substituted an acceptance of contingency for the standard quest for certainty" (*Uncertain Victory*, p. 4) laid the groundwork for the political liberalism of the 1890s and 1900s. He mentions Wright only in passing, referring to his reputation for deterministic naturalism and his commitment to effective certainty in science (pp. 25, 38, and 64), but James plays a central role in Kloppenberg's analysis, and Wright's recognition of probabilities in Darwinism shows his kinship with the book's cast of characters.

71. Wright to Francis Abbot, July 9, 1867, LCW, p. 103 [Edward H. Madden, *Chauncey Wright*, p. 38].

72. Kuklick, in *Rise of American Philosophy*, makes this parallel, but sees the place of design in Wright's thought as evidence of broad kinship, rather than ironic similarity, with natural theology (pp. 68 and 77).

73. Wright to Grace Norton, July 12, 1875, TCWJ, 1:530; and William James, *Pragmatism*, p. 26. Despite the impact of Wright's positivist approach to facts, James's

empiricism was never itself positivistic because, as Josiah Royce said, for James, facts were "never mere data" (*William James*, p. 37).

74. Palmer, "William James," p. 33. James's attraction to Wright's empiricism coincided with his flirtation with Spencer and Büchner in the early to middle 1860s.

Chapter 7

1. "Family Record" (1864), MSCSP 79, Peirce Papers.
2. For years, there was no full-length biography of Charles Sanders Peirce, except for Joseph Brent's dissertation, "Life of Charles Sanders Peirce." Scholars relied on Eisele, "Charles S. Peirce"; Weiss, "Charles Sanders Peirce"; and Fisch, "Peirce as Scientist," in Ketner et al., eds., *Proceedings of the C. S. Peirce Bicentennial*. Although Kenneth Ketner is currently working on a major study, Brent has finally published an expanded version of his dissertation, *Charles Sanders Peirce*. The reasons for Brent's delay form a fascinating story that includes Harvard's embarrassment about "the legend of Peirce's immorality" (p. 9); also see Monaghan, "Strange Saga."
3. "Harvard Composition" (1856–57), MSCSP 1633, Peirce Papers.
4. "Every Man the Maker of his own Fortune" (1856–57), MSCSP 1629, Peirce Papers.
5. "Harvard Composition" (1856–57), MSCSP 1633, Peirce Papers.
6. "Harvard Composition" (1856–57), Peirce Papers. This quotation follows immediately after: "title: 'The alleged intolerant and persecuting conduct of the Pilgrim Fathers. Does it admit of any valid excuse?'"
7. "Harvard Composition" (1856–57), MSCSP 1633, Peirce Papers.
8. William James to his family, September 16, [1861], *LWJ*, 1:35; William to Henry James, May 3, 1903, *LWJ*, 2:191; [Notebook 2], (1862), Am1092.9 (4496), William James Papers; William James to Thomas Ward, December 16, 1868, in *TCWJ*, 1:290. Brent offers ample evidence of Peirce's actual violence of temper, and he suggests a medical explanation: like his father, he had trigeminal neuralgia (called facial neuralgia in the nineteenth century), which caused acute pain, disorientation, and depression (*Charles Sanders Peirce*, pp. 40–41).
9. William to Henry James, Jr., December 12, 1875, *Correspondence of William James*, p. 246.
10. Henry to William James, March 14, [1876], and December 3, [1875], *Correspondence of William James*, pp. 255 and 245.
11. This is the central biographical theme of Brent's *Charles Sanders Peirce*; Peirce commented on his ill-fated eccentricities in explaining that his left-handedness meant that "my brain must be different from the usual," and even drawing on a favorite pun, "*gauche*" (p. 44). Brent extends this poignant drama with a parallel analysis of his philosophy: Peirce was on a noble but tragic religious quest as the "wasp in the bottle," desperately attempting to penetrate to the real meaning behind the empirical signs of this world (especially pp. 322–47).
12. Melusina (Zina) Fay was a potent intellectual leader and political activist in her own right. Fisch suggests that she may have had a role in her husband's emphasis on triads with her argument about the Holy Spirit as a feminine element in the trinity;

see "Introduction," *WCP*, 1:xxx–xxxii. Peirce met Fay at Agassiz's School for Girls, which was across the street from the Peirce house, he dedicated many of his metaphysical writings "For Z. F.," and he wrote his "Views of Chemistry: Sketched for Young Ladies" (1861) for his wife and her sisters (*WCP*, 1:50–56). Fay was especially active in women's politics, particularly the movement for cooperative housework, and she authored some tracts to popularize her efforts, including *The Democratic Party* and *Co-Operative Housekeeping*. The only extensive study of Fay is Atkinson, "Zina Fay Peirce."

13. "Harvard Composition" (1856–57), MSCSP 1633, Peirce Papers.

14. The Coast Survey changed its name to Coast and Geodetic Survey in 1878. William James was such a good friend that Peirce even changed his middle name from Sanders to Santiago, the Spanish name for James. When Peirce slipped into total poverty toward the end of his life, James quietly started a fund to support him; see Brent, *Charles Sanders Peirce*, pp. 303–6.

15. MSCSP 632, Peirce Papers [Colapietro, *Peirce's Approach to the Self*, p. xiv]; [fragment] [ca. 1897], *CPCP*, 1.11 (italics in original); William James to Henry Bowditch, May 22, 1869, *TCWJ*, 1:296; and Peirce, "A Sketch of Logical Critic" [ca. 1911], *CPCP*, 6.184. Wright expressed similar views of Peirce: in a review of his essay on Berkeley, Wright stated, "We are afraid to recommend it to other readers, as Mr. Peirce's style reflects the difficulties of the subject, and is better adapted for persons who have mastered these than for such as would rather avoid them"; see Wright, [note on Peirce] (1871), *WCP*, 2:489.

16. [Draft of "Treatise on Metaphysics"] [ca. 1859], MSCSP 921, p. 14, Peirce Papers.

17. On Peirce's inconsistencies, see Goudge, *Thought of C. S. Peirce*; Murphey, *Development of Peirce's Philosophy*; and Wells, "True Nature of Peirce's Evolutionism," in Moore and Robin, *Philosophy of Charles Sanders Peirce*, pp. 304–22; for a forceful rejoinder, see Feibleman, *Philosophy of Charles S. Peirce*; and Corrington, *Introduction to C. S. Peirce*, attempts to resolve Peirce's realism and transcendentalism in the theme "ecstatic naturalism."

18. The first five volumes of *WCP* cover works through 1886. Also see Ketner, "Peirce as an Interesting Failure"; and Brent, *Charles Sanders Peirce* on Peirce's historical importance, theoretical contributions, and mania for system. Scholarship is immense and diverse. Helpful overviews include Knight, *Charles Peirce*; Feibleman, *Philosophy of Charles S. Peirce*; Freeman, ed., *Relevance of C. S. Peirce*; Hookway, *Peirce*; and Ketner, ed., *Peirce and Contemporary Thought*. For a sampling of studies on Peirce's many contributions to mathematics, see Charles S. Peirce, *New Elements of Mathematics*. For his influence on semiotics, see Fitzgerald, *Peirce's Theory of Signs*; Greenlee, *Peirce's Concept of Sign*; Eco, *Theory of Semiotics*; Tursman, *Peirce's Theory of Scientific Discovery*; Colapietro, *Peirce's Approach to the Self*; and Deledalle, *Charles S. Peirce*. For his achievements in philosophy of science, see Reilly, *Charles Peirce's Theory of Scientific Method*; and Skagestad, *Road of Inquiry*. For treatments of his pragmatism, see Thompson, *Pragmatic Philosophy of C. S. Peirce*; Murphey, *Development of Peirce's Philosophy*; Gallie, *Peirce and Pragmatism*; and Apel, *Charles S. Peirce*. For coverage of his philosophical realism, see Boler, *Charles Peirce and Scho-*

lastic Realism; and Potter, *Charles S. Peirce*. And for contributions to religious studies, see Orange, *Peirce's Conception of God*; and Raposa, *Peirce's Philosophy of Religion*.

19. See, for example, Robert J. Roth, "Is Peirce's Pragmatism Anti-Jamesian?," and John E. Smith, "Two Defenses of Freedom."

20. The faculty singled him out for praise; see Faculty and Administrative Board Minutes, Lawrence Scientific School (March 3, 1863).

21. Quoted in Fisch, "Was There a Metaphysical Club?," p. 16.

22. Fisch, introduction to *WCP*, 1:xviii. Charles Henry Peirce, who was a physician and assistant to Lawrence Scientific School chemistry professor Eban Norton Horsford, and Charlotte Elizabeth Peirce, whose German was better than Charles Peirce's, translated Stöckhardt's *Die Schule der Chemie* as *Principles of Chemistry, Illustrated by Simple Experiments*; see *WCP*, 1:xviii.

23. See "Tricks," MSCSP 1534, Peirce Papers, for a charming, but undated, example of Peirce's simultaneous enjoyment and earnest mathematical treatment of a card trick, where he sorts cards, looks for repeating patterns, and develops an equation to describe the pattern of what he has observed.

24. Peirce wrote this autobiographical fragment in memory of a conversation with his father in the spring of 1870; see Fisch, "Chronicle of Pragmatism," p. 451.

25. Fisch, "Peirce as Scientist," pp. 25 and 17–19.

26. [Fragment] [ca. 1897] and "Telepathy and Perception" (1903), *CPCP*, 1.3 and 7.597.

27. "What Pragmatism Is" (1905), *CPCP*, 5.411–12; "Lessons in Practical Logic," 1869–70, MSCSP 697, Peirce Papers; and [fragment] [ca. 1897], *CPCP*, 1.4.

28. [Fragment] [ca. 1897], *CPCP*, 1.4. For examples of Peirce's scientific research, see his *Photometric Researches*; and Lenzen, "Unpublished Scientific Monograph."

29. "Reply to the Necessitarians" (1893), *CPCP*, 6.604.

30. "Century's Great Men in Science," 1901, Peirce, *Charles S. Peirce*, p. 268.

31. "Harvard Composition" (1856–57), MSCSP 1633, Peirce Papers. He returned to this distinction between "scientific and literary men" in a lecture on "[William] Whewell" (November–December 1869), *WCP*, 2:337.

32. "Whewell" (November–December 1869), *WCP*, 2:337; and "Logic of Science" Lowell Lecture VI (October–November 1866), *WCP*, 1:465. He again referred to "Negroes" in a logical syllogism in "Forms of Induction and Hypothesis" (April–May 1865), *WCP*, 1:262.

33. "Harvard Composition" (1856–57), MSCSP 1633, Peirce Papers. The example from *Putnam's Magazine* (October 1854) is part of Richard Brown's argument about the expanding literary marketplace and the increasing role of persuasion in the dissemination of knowledge in a democracy (*Knowledge Is Power*, p. 232).

34. "My Life" (1859), and "Private Thoughts" (1860–88), *WCP*, 1:1–2 and 7.

35. David Pfeifer has discovered 325 references to religious topics in 40 different places throughout Peirce's works; see "Charles Peirce's Contribution to Religious Thought," in Ketner, ed., *Proceedings of the C. S. Peirce Bicentennial*, pp. 367–73.

36. "Science and Immortality," 1887 [Peirce, *Charles S. Peirce*, p. 348].

37. See Lightman, *Origins of Agnosticism*; Chadwick, *Secularization of the Euro-*

pean Mind; and Cashdollar, *Transformation of Theology*.

38. Hollinger, "Tonic Destruction." Similarly, Hoopes, in *Consciousness in New England*, argues that Peirce's mingling of materialist and mentalist views of nature constituted a via media in the contest between religious and secular visions of the world (pp. 226–27).

39. "Marriage of Science and Religion" (1893), Peirce, *Charles S. Peirce*, p. 351; and "Place of Our Age" (1863), WCP, 1:114.

40. For discussion of Peirce's often little-noticed religious side, see Mahowald, "Peirce's Concepts of God"; Orange, *Peirce's Conception of God*; Alexander, "Hypothesized God"; Raposa, *Peirce's Philosophy of Religion*; and Brent, *Charles Sanders Peirce*.

41. Quoted in Orange, *Peirce's Conception of God*, p. 3.

42. Ibid., pp. 3–4. Murphey (*Development of Peirce's Philosophy*, pp. 12–14) and Skagestad (*Road of Inquiry*, p. 38) even argue that Peirce's idealistic and religious interests are more important to his thought than his empirical and scientific commitments, which, they maintain, served as a mask which he needed for intellectual respectability.

43. Brent, *Charles Sanders Peirce*, pp. 345–47.

44. See Esposito, *Evolutionary Metaphysics*; and Raposa, *Peirce's Philosophy of Religion*. Similarly, Corrington, in *Introduction to C. S. Peirce*, argues that Peirce's religious impulses suggest an "ecstatic naturalism," in his awareness of nature's ability to point beyond itself and beyond what natural science can discover.

45. "Lessons from the History of Philosophy" (1903), CPCP, 1.20. On the way Peirce's realism involves idealism, see Boler, *Charles Peirce and Scholastic Realism*, p. 148; and Almeder, "Peirce on Scientific Realism." After demonstrating realist sympathies in the 1850s, Peirce did, however, veer away from realism briefly in the 1860s, likely under the influence of Chauncey Wright; see Fisch, "Peirce's Progress"; Deledalle, *Charles S. Peirce*, especially pp. 5–21.

46. Brent, *Charles Sanders Peirce*, pp. 33, 261, 46, and 345. Brent argues that this strain of thinking in Peirce was a source of his moral failings: a corollary to correspondence theory is that evil in the world has a positive story to tell in fostering the moral and spiritual growth of humanity, so it is not all bad; this corrupted Peirce, Brent argues, because it "cannot provide a way to distinguish good from evil" (p. 343). Peirce's family friend, the elder Henry James, met the same criticism for his Swedenborgianism. The critique came from a more orthodox disciple of the Swedish mystic: "[Henry James] seems to me always set on proving there is no difference between good and evil; indeed, if he has a preference it is for evil"; "a New York publisher" to William White, TCWJ, 1:117. As Brent himself implies, Peirce's poor moral handling of transcendental and Swedenborgian elements in his life does not detract from their importance in the construction of this thought.

47. On Peirce's religious affiliations, see Reilly, *Charles Peirce's Theory of Scientific Method*, pp. 3 and 158. On Peirce's triads, see "Lectures on Pragmatism" (1903), CPCP, 5.14–212; for succinct explanations, see Brent, *Charles Sanders Peirce*, pp. 62 and 331–33; and Knight, *Charles Peirce*, pp. 66–87.

48. There is some irony in these distinctions because Peirce was actually influenced, especially in the Swedenborgian leanings of his ideal-realism, by the elder James. See Krolikoswki, "The Peircean Vir"; and Taylor, "Peirce and Swedenborg" and "Peirce and James"; in addition, Orange has found evidence of Peirce's use of Swedenborgian terminology (*Peirce's Conception of God*, p. 5). By contrast, Trammel, in "Charles Sanders Peirce and Henry James," dismisses a strong connection between Peirce and either James or Swedenborg. Peirce assessed the elder James in a book review in which he noted that he gained "spiritual nutriment" from James, but that his book was "deficient in argumentation" ("Henry James's *The Secret of Swedenborg*" [1870], WCP, 2:438 and 436). This reveals that Peirce agreed with James—and with his own father—in his religious goal, but he could not agree with the earlier generation's methods of reconciling science and religion; for Peirce, deep inquiry into scientific method would be a first step to profound spiritual insight.

49. "Professor Peirce on Mathematics" (1858–59), MSCSP 1631, Peirce Papers; Benjamin Peirce quoted in Archibald, *Benjamin Peirce*, p. 5. Also see Archibald, "Benjamin Peirce"; and Peterson, "Benjamin Peirce." For a vivid account of his social and political views, see Benjamin Peirce, "National Importance."

50. "Table of Categories" (1860–62), and "Harvard Composition" (1856–57), MSCSP 1633, Peirce Papers.

51. Quoted in Skagestad, *Road of Inquiry*, p. 211.

52. [Draft of "Treatise on Metaphysics"] [ca. 1859], MSCSP 921, Peirce Papers; "Neglected Argument for the Reality of God" (1908), CPCP, 6.467; and "Table of Categories" (1860–62), MSCSP 922, Peirce Papers.

53. ["A Treatise on Metaphysics"] (1861–62), WCP, 1:78; he expressed the same idea in the unpublished "Table of Categories" (1860–62), MSCSP 922, Peirce Papers. James quoted the same idea in words he directly attributed to Peirce in his Notebook [2] (1862), bMS Am1092.9 (4496), William James Papers: "None succeed in leaving Faith entirely out. . . .—C. S. Pierce [sic]." James's misspelling of his friend's name may be an example of his general carelessness about proper spelling, which he called "the tyranny of the dictionary." Later in life, he told his colleague George Herbert Palmer, "Isn't it abominable that everybody is expected to spell in the same way?"; James quoted in Palmer, "William James," p. 32.

54. "Lessons from the History of Science" [ca. 1896], and "Drawing History from Ancient Documents" [ca. 1901], CPCP, 1.44 and 7.186.

55. "Vitally Important Topics" (1898), CPCP, 1.648.

56. "Some Consequences of Four Incapacities" (1868), WCP, 2:212. In another setting, Peirce revealed some of his "prejudices" toward morality: "We all know what morality is: it is behaving as you were brought up to behave" ("Vitally Important Topics" [1898], CPCP, 1.666).

57. "Scientific Method" [undated], CPCP, 7.54.

58. "Three Types of Reasoning" (1903), CPCP, 5.172.

59. "Fraser's Edition of *The Works of George Berkeley*" (1871), and "Drawing History from Ancient Documents" [ca. 1901], WCP 2:479 and 469; the second quotation is repeated with similar words in "Some Consequences of Four Incapacities" (1868), WCP, 2:239, and "Drawing History from Ancient Documents" [ca. 1901], CPCP, 7.186.

60. "Lessons from the History of Science" [ca. 1896], CPCP, 1.44.

61. "Logic" (1873), CPCP, 7.325. Peirce quoted parts of the poem, with slight paraphrasing, many times, thus suggesting a text he took to memory and considered vitally important; see "Minute Logic" (1902), CPCP, 1.217; and "How to Make Our Ideas Clear" (1878), WCP, 3:274. He attributed the poem to Alexander Pope not to Bryant.

62. "A Sketch of a Logical Critic" [ca. 1911]; review of Pearson, *The Grammar of Science* (1901); and "Telepathy and Perception" (1903), CPCP, 6.184, 8.136, and 7.598.

63. "Consequences of Four Incapacities" (1868), WCP, 2:239; and [fragment] [ca. 1897], CPCP, 1.10.

64. Family Record [ca. 1909], MSCSP 79, Peirce Papers; Peirce quoted in Eisele, "Peirce's Philosophy of Education," p. 56.

65. "Regenerated Logic" (1896), CPCP, 3.432; and "Fraser's Edition of *The Works of George Berkeley*," WCP, 2:469.

66. "Harvard Composition" (1856–57), MSCSP 1633, Peirce Papers.

67. "Ideals of Conduct" (1903), CPCP, 1.615. Peirce took this agenda so seriously that he conducted his philosophy with urgency—or "Peirce-istence"—as Brent astutely notices and places at the center of his biographical portrait (*Charles Sanders Peirce*, p. 298).

68. "Theory of Probable Inference" (1883), and "Nomenclature and Divisions of Triadic Relations" [ca. 1903], CPCP, 2.729 and 269.

69. Philosophers disagree on the soundness of his arguments: Laurens Laudan finds that Peirce offered "no cogent reason . . . for believing that most inductive methods are self-corrective" and instead relies on "an inarticulate faith in the ability of the mind somehow to ferret out the truth"; see his "Peirce and the Trivialization of the Self-Correcting Thesis," pp. 293 and 294. Skagestad (*Road of Inquiry*, pp. 195–99) and John W. Lenz ("Induction as Self-Corrective," in Moore and Robin, eds., *Philosophy of Charles Sanders Peirce*, pp. 151–62) believe that Peirce's claims are more modest, with self-correction applying to long-term cases of genuine inquiry.

70. "Evolutionary Love" (1893), CPCP, 6.293–95. On Peirce's evolutionism, see W. Donald Oliver, "The Final Cause and Agapism," and Thomas A. Goudge, "Peirce's Evolutionism," in Moore and Robin, eds., *Philosophy of Charles Sanders Peirce*, pp. 289–303 and 323–41. On his differences with Darwinism, see Feibleman, *Philosophy of Charles S. Peirce*, pp. 408–10; and Apel, *Charles S. Peirce*, pp. 150–53.

71. Benjamin Peirce quoted in Murphey, *Development of Peirce's Philosophy*, p. 13; Charles Peirce, "Table of Categories" (1860–62), MSCSP 922, Peirce Papers.

72. William James to Henry Bowditch, May 22, 1869, TCWJ, 1:269.

73. There has been a recent flourishing of scholarship: see Krüger et al., eds., *Probabilistic Revolution*; Theodore Porter, *Rise of Statistical Thinking*; Gigerenzer et al., eds., *Empire of Chance*; and Hacking, *Taming of Chance*. These works focus on technical questions in science and philosophy and on European developments and impacts—Peirce is one of the few Americans featured. I explore the intellectual and cultural history impacts of the probabilistic revolution, especially in relation to William James, in "From History of Science to Intellectual History."

74. See Turley, "Peirce on Chance"; also see Turley, *Peirce's Cosmology*.

75. [Draft of "Treatise on Metaphysics"] (1859), MSCSP 921, Peirce Papers.

76. Charles Sanders Peirce, "Theory of Probable Inference," Charles S. Peirce, ed., *Studies in Logic*, pp. 128 and 131.

77. "Of the Doctrine of Chances," [undated], MSCSP 1574, Peirce Papers.

78. ["A Treatise on Metaphysics"] (1861–62), *WCP*, 1:71. In an earlier draft of this essay, Peirce used the word "dogmatic" in place of "dialectic," which shows an even harsher critique of advocates of absolute certainty; see [draft of "Treatise on Metaphysics"] (1860), MSCSP 921, Peirce Papers.

79. "New List of Categories" (1867), *CPCP*, 1.549f.

80. See, for example, "Six Characters of Critical Common-Sensism" (1905), *CPCP*, 5.440.

81. "Doctrine of Necessity Examined" (1892), *CPCP*, 6.46–47.

82. "Laws of Nature and Hume's Argument against Miracles" (1901), Peirce, *Charles S. Peirce*, p. 302. Turley explains Peirce's different views of chance as phases in evolution over his lifetime through three distinct conceptions: chance is not real, but only a matter of human ignorance; chance plays a part in the real world and can be evaluated by scientific laws of probability; and the world was created with genuine chance, and since then things have been developing the habits of regular laws; see "Peirce on Chance."

83. Wiener, *Evolution and the Founders of Pragmatism*, p. 72.

84. "Architecture of Theories" (1891), *CPCP*, 6.33 [Wiener, *Evolution and the Founders of Pragmatism*, p. 84]. This quotation and many of the next few from the *Collected Papers* and from the Peirce manuscript papers can also be found in Wiener's book. But in his outstanding study of the place of Darwinism among the members of the Metaphysical Club, Wiener never notices the probabilistic nature of Darwin's theory and therefore records this perspective with genuine astonishment: "It is remarkable that Peirce took his mathematical analogy seriously as an illustration of his metaphysical generalization of Darwin's theory" (p. 82). To Wiener, Darwinism is empirical science, and Peirce's views are idiosyncratic misreadings.

85. "Architecture of Theories" (1891), *CPCP*, 6.33; also see Hoopes, *Consciousness in New England*, pp. 227–33.

86. "Evolutionary Love" (1893), *CPCP*, 6.297 [Wiener, *Evolution and the Founders of Pragmatism*, p. 78]. On the declining scientific prestige of Darwinism, see Bowler, *Eclipse of Darwinism*.

87. "Fixation of Belief" (1877), *WCP*, 3:244. On Maxwell's use of probabilistic thinking, see Garber, Brush, and Everitt, eds., *Maxwell on Molecules and Gases*; and Schweber, "Aspects of Probabilistic Thought."

88. "Why Should the Doctrine of Chances Raise Science to a Higher Plane?" (January 24, 1909), p. 15, Peirce Papers [Wiener, *Evolution and the Founders of Pragmatism*, p. 81].

89. "Concept of Probability" (January 23–30, 1909), MSCSP 706, Peirce Papers, p. 16 [quoted in part in Wiener, *Evolution and the Founders of Pragmatism*, p. 81]. For similar rephrasing of the nub of Darwin's argument in probabilistic language, see "Evolutionary Love" (1893), *CPCP*, 6.297.

90. "Concept of Probability" (January 23–30, 1909), MSCSP 706, Peirce Papers, pp. 13–15 [Wiener, *Evolution and the Founders of Pragmatism*, p. 82].

91. Hacking, *Taming of Chance*, p. 2.

92. Fisch, introduction to *WCP*, 3:xxi. Morris Cohen notes that Peirce's pendulum research strongly influenced many European scientists; Cohen, preface to *Charles S. Peirce*, pp. x–xi; and Lenzen calls Peirce's "Report on Gravity at the Smithsonian, Ann Arbor, Madison, and Cornell" "a monumental piece of work [which] testifies to Peirce's significant accomplishments as an able physicist in the nineteenth century"; Lenzen, "Unpublished Scientific Monograph," p. 5.

93. "On the Logic of Science," Harvard Lecture XI (1865), and "On the Logic of Science," Lowell Lecture I (1866), *WCP*, 1:302 and 358.

94. William to Alice James, November 14, 1866, *LWJ*, 1:80. James made strikingly similar comments about Peirce toward the end of his life. In the opening lecture of *Pragmatism*, after he credited his friend as "the founder of pragmatism," he said Peirce's talks on the topic were "flashes of brilliant light relieved against Cimmerian darkness! None of us, I fancy, understood *all* that he said"; *Pragmatism*, p. 10.

95. William James to Henry Bowditch, December 29, 1869, *TCWJ*, 1:321.

96. "On the Logic of Science," Harvard Lecture I (1865), *WCP*, 1:162; also see Harvard Lecture XI, ibid., 1:292.

97. "On the Logic of Science," Harvard Lecture IV (1865), *WCP*, 1:213; and [Critique of Positivism], (1867–68), *WCP*, 2:127; and Harvard Lecture II, [The Logic Notebook] (1865–66), and Harvard Lecture II, *WCP*, 1:178–79, 339, and 186. The incorrect spelling, "Compte," was very common among British and American commentators; see Cashdollar, *Transformation of Theology*, p. 118.

98. "On the Logic of Science," Harvard Lecture IV (1865), *WCP*, 1:208 and 223.

99. "On the Logic of Science," Harvard Lecture IV, Harvard Lecture X, Harvard Lecture XI, and Harvard Lecture VIII (1865), *WCP*, 1:219, 283, 302, and 258. On Peirce's critique of James's "will to believe," see his own letters to the younger philosopher: March 13, 1897, November 25, 1902, March 7, 1904, and July 23, 1905, *CPCP*, 8.249–63; also see Gallie, *Peirce and Pragmatism*, and Ayer, *The Origins of Pragmatism*.

100. "On the Logic of Science," Harvard Lecture IV (1865), and "Logic of Science," Lowell Lecture III (1866), *WCP*, 1:206 and 405.

101. Peirce, "Questions concerning Reality" (1868), *WCP*, 2:165; and [draft for "Lessons in Practical Logic"] [1869–70], MSCSP 697, Peirce Papers.

102. See Moyer, *Scientist's Voice in American Culture*. Despite this similarity, Newcomb was a constant professional enemy of Peirce; see Brent, *Charles Sanders Peirce*, pp. 152–55 and 198. Although Brent does not discuss this, it would be an interesting line of investigation to find out if their rivalry was caused by their similar, and perhaps competing, goals.

103. "Fixation of Belief" (1877), *WCP*, 3:245.

104. See Hutchison, *Transcendentalist Ministers*.

105. Peirce quoted in Fisch, "Was There a Metaphysical Club?," p. 13.

106. Peirce to his mother, April 20, 1872, quoted in Fisch, introduction to *WCP*, 3:xxii.

107. Fisch, "Was There a Metaphysical Club?," p. 5.

108. Ibid., pp. 6–7. In the 1870s, many popular magazines, including the *Atlantic*

Monthly, Appleton's Journal, Harper's, North American Review, and *Galaxy,* gave much increased attention to scientific subjects; in addition, *Popular Science Monthly* was founded in 1872. Unfortunately, magazine coverage tended toward what George Basalla has called "popular science" instead of "popularized science." See Cummings, *Mark Twain and Science*; and Basalla, "Pop Science."

109. Fisch, "Was There a Metaphysical Club?," p. 13.
110. Ibid., p. 15.
111. Fisch, "Chronicle of Pragmatism," pp. 456 and 460.
112. Fisch, "Was There a Metaphysical Club?," p. 15.
113. "Fixation of Belief" (1877), WCP, 3:242.
114. Perhaps Morris Cohen had found another line of argument in the essay, whose title appears misspelled as "The Taxation of Belief" [!] in the table of contents of his anthology of Peirce writings, *Charles S. Peirce,* p. v.
115. "Fixation of Belief" (1877), WCP, 3:244.
116. Sociologist C. Wright Mills is one of the few observers to think of this essay in these terms; *Sociology and Pragmatism*, p. 159.
117. "Fixation of Belief" (1877), WCP, 3:247.
118. Bain, *Emotions and the Will*, pp. 568 and 570.
119. "Fixation of Belief" (1877), WCP, 3:245; William James, *Principles of Psychology*, p. 125; and "Fixation of Belief" (1877), WCP, 3:245.
120. On the male ideal among early-nineteenth-century American intellectuals, see Leverenz, *Manhood and the American Renaissance*.
121. "Fixation of Belief" (1877), and "How to Make Our Ideas Clear" (1878), WCP, 3:247 and 261. These features of Peirce's theory also show the impress of Bain, who argued that "the real opposite of belief as a state of mind is not disbelief, but doubt, uncertainty"; belief is therefore a "thing of degree" and indicates "the highest point in the scale" which ranges from "certainty, through the stages of probability, down to the depths of total uncertainty"; Bain, *Emotions and the Will*, pp. 574, 580, and 591.
122. "Fixation of Belief" (1877), WCP, 3:248.
123. Ibid., 3:249–52. Stewart, in "Peirce on the Role of Authority," points out that Peirce does allow room for authority within the scientific community.
124. "Fixation of Belief" (1877), and "How to Make Our Ideas Clear" (1878), WCP, 3:253, 258–59, 253, and 255.
125. "Fixation of Belief" (1877), WCP, 3:253, 254, and 257. Fifteen years later, he expressed the same idea with even more passion for the importance of commitment and the limits of rational objectivity in belief formation: "Suppose, for example, that I have an idea that interests me. It is my creation. It is my creature; . . . I love it; and I will sink myself in perfecting it. It is not by dealing out cold justice to the circle of my ideas that I can make them grow, but by cherishing and tending them as I would the flowers in my garden"; see "Man's Glassy Essence" (1893), quoted in Brent, *Charles Sanders Peirce*, p. 22.
126. "How to Make Our Ideas Clear" (1878), WCP, 3:261 and 272.
127. Ibid., 3:263.
128. "Some Consequences of Four Incapacities" (1868), WCP, 2:212. Peirce made a similar critique of Kant, who, like Descartes, argued that "nothing which rests only

on what is inferential can be certain." Although he appreciated Kant's quest to make room for faith in the "practical reason," Peirce wanted to move beyond the mere appropriateness of faith by establishing more "validity for faith" as sure and sound beliefs than Kant (or Descartes) would allow; see ["Treatise on Metaphysics"] (1861–62), *WCP*, 1:76. At about the same time, James had a similar admiration for Kant, coupled with a critique of the weakness of his religion; in a notebook, James wrote, "Nihilism is Kant's logical end (and truly why does he affirm the existence of noumena at all?)," [Notes on Kant] [ca. 1860s], bMS 1092.9 (4448), William James Papers. Also see Hoopes, *Consciousness in New England*, pp. 197–98.

129. "How to Make Our Ideas Clear" (1878), *WCP*, 3:259 and 272–73. Hoopes, in *Consciousness in New England*, hails this line of thinking as Peirce's greatest contribution: he "rejected the traditional concept of consciousness," that is, "the notion of directly intuited experience within the self." In contrast with the traditional view of consciousness, which had prevailed in modern European thought since Descartes, Peirce regarded signs as the only source of ideas. Although the semiotic philosopher was an innovator, his skepticism about the ability of the mind to grasp ultimate truths harks back to his own New England religious tradition (pp. 198, 195, and 232).

130. "Questions Concerning Certain Faculties Claimed for Man" (1868), and "Some Consequences of Four Incapacities" (1868), *WCP*, 2:193 and 213. Peirce's insights would have a pioneering and profound influence on the field of semiotics. His most original contribution was to emphasize that signs are in a triadic relation, which includes the sign, the signified, and the interpreter. See Colapietro, *Peirce's Approach to the Self*, p. 4. Also see Fitzgerald, *Peirce's Theory of Signs*; Greenlee, *Peirce's Concept of Sign*; Eco, *Theory of Semiotics*; Tursman, *Peirce's Theory of Scientific Discovery*; and Charles Peirce, *Peirce on Signs*.

131. William James to Henry Bowditch, January 24, 1869, *LWJ*, 1:149.

132. "How to Make Our Ideas Clear" (1878), *WCP*, 3:266.

133. Ibid., 3:275.

134. "Doctrine of Chances" (1878), *WCP*, 3:277–78. Peirce frequently analyzed science for its method; for example, he uses Agassiz's collection of specimens and identification of species as an example of induction in operation, see "On the Logic of Science," Harvard Lecture IV (1865), *WCP*, 1:218).

135. "Doctrine of Chances" (1878), *WCP*, 3:278, 276, 278, and 280–81. See Theodore Porter, *Rise of Statistical Thinking*, pp. 40–192; and Gigerenzer et al., eds., *Empire of Chance*, pp. 37–69 and 141–62.

136. "Doctrine of Chances" (1878), *WCP*, 3:278.

137. Review of John Venn, *Logic of Chance* (1867), *WCP*, 2:98–102; and [Critique of Positivism] (1867–68), *WCP*, 2:125.

138. "Doctrine of Chances" (1878), *WCP*, 3:281, 284, and 285.

139. "Notes on the Doctrine of Chances" (1910), *CPCP*, 2.667.

140. "Probability of Induction" (1878), *WCP*, 3:291. Peirce's 1867 review of Venn's *Logic of Chance* is reprinted in *WCP*, 2:98–102. Also see Edward Madden, "Peirce on Probability," and Arthur Burks, "Peirce's Two Theories of Probability," in Moore and Robin, eds., *Philosophy of Charles Sanders Peirce*, pp. 122–40 and 141–50.

141. "Probability of Induction" (1878), *WCP*, 3:293–94 and 296. The Metaphysical

Club members were not alone in thinking about these distinctions within probabilities. For example, William Chauvenet, in *Method of Least Squares*, stated that the methods for reducing error from records of measurement—techniques which Peirce examined closely during his years of scientific work—are "designed to remove, as far as possible, every arbitrary consideration, and to furnish a set of principles which shall always guide us to the most probable results" (p. 473). In addition, their friend Simon Newcomb, in a report on the doctrine of probabilities in the *Proceedings of the American Academy of Arts and Sciences* (1860), criticized the conceptualist definition of "the probability of a proposition . . . as the amount of our belief in the truth of that proposition" (p. 433); like Peirce, he preferred the materialist definition, which relied on quantification. Daston identifies the conceptualist perspective as the epistemic, subjective approach to probabilities, which is linked to belief formation; and she associates the materialist position with the frequentist, objective approach, which contributed to the rise of statistics; she also points out that boundaries between them were not always firm, but that the conceptualist view predominated before the nineteenth century, and the materialist view since then; see *Classical Probability*. James helped to revive interest in the conceptualist approach to probabilities by spotlighting Blaise Pascal in *Will to Believe* (1895); also see O'Connell, *William James on the Courage to Believe*, and Graham, "William James and the Affirmation of God," especially pp. 210–41.

142. "Probability of Induction" (1878), WCP, 3:305. Newcomb agreed with Peirce's metaphysical certainty and was even more blunt in expressing it. In his report on the doctrine of probabilities, Newcomb declared, "The principle that every event which occurs is the result of law, and neither has or ever had any *absolute* uncertainty inherent in it, may be regarded as an induction almost as perfect as the laws of motion" (p. 343).

143. "Order of Nature" (1878), WCP, 3:307.

144. Ibid., 3:308, 312, 313, 317, 318, and 320.

145. Ibid., 3:321 and 322.

146. Peirce to Paul Carus [ca. 1910], CPCP, 8.227.

147. "Deduction, Induction, and Hypothesis" (1878), WCP, 3:328, 325, 326–27, and 326.

148. Ibid., 3:334 and 335–36.

149. Ibid., 3:331, 338, 330, and 338.

150. See Wilson, *Transformation of American Philosophy*.

151. [Critique of Positivism], (1867–68), WCP, 2:128.

152. "What Pragmatism Is" (1905), CPCP, 5.414.

Conclusion

1. Commenting on the British scene in the same era, Lightman points out that the agnostics "gloried in the sacredness of uncertainty" (*Origins of Agnosticism*, p. 30). James had a similar relish for uncertainty, but he was more optimistic than his British counterparts. According to Lightman, uncertainty presented British agnostics with an insoluble dilemma: They would "either . . . accept science and the agnosticism it apparently demands, thereby alienating [them]selves from the spiritual world of religion,

or . . . give up the search for knowledge and rush unthinkingly to embrace religion" (p. 2). As opposed to both the British agnostics and Wright, James sought a middle ground between certainty and uncertainty.

2. [Miscellaneous notes] (October 21, 1872), bMS Am 1092.9 (4473), William James Papers.

3. William James, "The Sentiment of Rationality," *Will to Believe*, p. 67. These quotations are from a portion of the essay first delivered as an address to the Harvard Philosophy Club in 1880 and later published as "Rationality, Activity, and Faith" in *Princeton Review* 2 (1882): 58–86.

4. Ibid., p. 70.

5. [Notebook 8] "Philosophizing" [ca. 1875], bMS Am 1092.9 (4502), William James Papers, pp. 2–3.

6. William James, *Will to Believe*, p. 20.

7. Lovejoy, *Thirteen Pragmatisms*, p. 55; and Palmer, "William James," p. 34.

8. Response to questionnaire of James B. Pratt (1904), William James Papers [*LWJ*, 2:214]. The questionnaire is reproduced as an appendix to Pratt's *Psychology of Religious Belief*, pp. 307–9; also see Pratt's "Religious Philosophy of William James."

BIBLIOGRAPHY

Dates in square brackets [ ] indicate, whenever possible, the first edition of the work cited.

Manuscript Sources

Cambridge, Massachusetts
  Gray Herbarium
    Asa Gray Papers
  Houghton Library, Harvard University
    Ralph Waldo Emerson Papers
    Henry James [Sr.] Papers
    William James Papers
    Charles Eliot Norton Papers
    Charles Sanders Peirce Papers
    Chauncey Wright Papers
  Harvard University Archives, Pusey Library
    Cambridge Scientific Club, General Folder
    Faculty and Administrative Board Minutes, Lawrence Scientific School
    Library Charging Lists
Washington, D.C.
  Smithsonian Institution
    Joseph Henry Papers

Primary Sources

Abbot, Francis E. *Organic Scientific Philosophy: Scientific Theism.* London: Macmillan, 1885.

Agassiz, Louis. "Address Delivered on the Centennial Anniversary of the Birth of Alexander von Humboldt." Boston: Boston Society of Natural History, 1869.

———. *Contributions to the Natural History of the United States.* 4 vols. Vol 1, *Essay on Classification.* Boston: Little, Brown and Co., 1857.

———. "Evolution and the Permanence of Type." *Atlantic Monthly* 33 (January 1874): 92–101.

———. *Geological Sketches.* Boston: J. R. Osgood, 1876.

———. *Methods of Study in Natural History.* Boston: Ticknor and Fields, 1863.

Agassiz, Louis, and Elizabeth Agassiz. *A Journey to Brazil.* Boston: Ticknor and Fields, 1868.

Agassiz, Louis, and Augustus A. Gould. *Principles of Zoology.* Boston: Gould, Kendall, and Lincoln, 1848.

Alcott, Bronson. *Observations on the Principles and Methods of Infant Instruction.* Boston: Carter and Hendee, 1830.

———. "Pestalozzi's Principles and Methods of Instruction." *American Journal of Education* 4 (March–April 1829): 97–107.
Bain, Alexander. *The Emotions and the Will.* London: John W. Parker, 1859.
Beecher, Henry Ward. *Evolution and Religion.* Boston: Pilgrim Press, 1885.
Bennett, Alfred. "The Theory of Natural Selection from a Mathematical Point of View." *Nature* 3 (1870): 30–33.
Blau, Joseph L. *American Philosophical Addresses, 1700–1900.* New York: Columbia University Press, 1946.
Boltzmann, Ludwig. "The Second Law of Thermodynamics." In *Theoretical Physics and Philosophical Problems: Selected Writings,* edited by Brian McGuinness. Boston and Dordrecht: D. Reidel Publishing Co., 1974.
Bowen, Francis. "Remarks on the Latest Form of the Development Theory." *Memoirs of the American Academy of Arts and Sciences,* n.s., 8 (1860): 98–107.
Brownson, Orestes. *Works of Orestes Brownson.* 20 vols. Edited by Henry F. Brownson. Vol. 9, *Containing the Spirit Rapper and Criticisms of Some Recent Theories in the Sciences.* Detroit: Thorndike Nourse Publisher, 1884.
Büchner, Ludwig. *Force and Matter: Empirico-Philosophical Studies.* Edited and translated by J. Frederick Collingwood. London: J. Trübner and Co., 1864. Originally published as *Kraft und Stoff: Empirisch-Naturphilosophische Studien* (Frankfurt: Meidinger, 1856 [1855]).
Burr, Enoch Fitch. *Pater Mundi; or, Doctrine of Evolution.* Boston: Noyes, Holmes, and Co., 1873.
———. *Pater Mundi; or, Modern Science Testifying to the Heavenly Father.* 3rd ed. Boston: Nichols and Noyes, 1869.
Bush, George. *Mesmer and Swedenborg; or, The Relation of the Developments of Mesmerism to the Doctrines and Disclosures of Swedenborg.* New York: John Allen, 1847.
———, ed. *The Memorabilia of Swedenborg; or, The Spirit World Laid Open.* New York: John Allen, 1846.
Bushnell, Horace. *Nature and the Supernatural.* [Dudleian Lectures, Harvard University, 1852.] 5th ed. New York: Scribner's, 1863.
Butler, Joseph. *Analogy of Reason* (1736), in *The Works of Joseph Butler,* edited by W. E. Gladstone. 2 vols. Oxford: Clarendon Press, 1896.
"A Catalogue of the Officers and Students of Harvard University for the Academic Year 1861–62." Cambridge: Sever and Francis, 1861.
[Chambers, Robert]. *Vestiges of the Natural History of Creation.* London: Churchill, 1844.
Chauvenet, William. *A Treatise on the Method of Least Squares, or The Application of the Theory of Probability in the Combination of Observations, being the Appendix to the Author's Manual of Spherical and Practical Astronomy.* Philadelphia: J. B. Lippincott and Co., 1868.
Child, Lydia Maria. *The Mother's Book.* Boston: Carter, Hendee, and Babcock, 1831.
Clifford, William K. *Lectures and Essays.* 2nd ed. Edited by Leslie Stephen and Frederick Pollock. New York: Macmillan, 1886.

Cole, Thomas. "Essay on American Scenery." *The American Monthly*, n.s., 1 (January 1836): 1–12.

Cooke, Josiah P., Jr. *Religion and Chemistry: A Re-Statement of an Old Argument*. Rev. ed. New York: Charles Scribner, 1880 [1864].

Dana, James Dwight. "Science and Scientific Schools." *American Journal of Education* 2 (1856): 345–74.

Darwin, Charles. *Charles Darwin's Natural Selection: being the Second Part of His Big Species Book, written from 1856 to 1858*. Edited by Robert C. Stauffer. London: Cambridge University Press, 1975.

———. *Charles Darwin's Notebooks, 1836–1844: Geology, Transmutation of Species, Metaphysical Enquiries*. Edited by Paul H. Barrett et al. London: British Museum [Natural History]; Ithaca: Cornell University Press, 1987.

———. *The Correspondence of Charles Darwin*. Edited by Frederick Burkhardt et al. 9 vols. to date. New York: Cambridge University Press, 1985– .

———. *Journal of Researches into the Geology and Natural History of the Various Countries Visited by "H. M. S. Beagle," under the Command of Captain FitzRoy, R.N., from 1832–36*. London: H. Colburn, 1839.

———. *The Life and Letters of Charles Darwin*. 2 vols. Edited by Francis Darwin. New York: D. Appleton and Co., 1888.

———. *More Letters of Charles Darwin*. Edited by Francis Darwin and A. C. Seward. New York: D. Appleton and Co., 1903.

———. *On the Origin of Species by Means of Natural Selection, or the Preservation of Favoured Races in the Struggle for Life*. London: John Murray, 1859; Cambridge: Harvard University Press, 1964.

Darwin, Charles, and Thomas Henry Huxley. *Autobiographies*. Edited by Gavin De Beer. New York: Oxford University Press, 1974.

Darwin, Charles, and Alfred Russel Wallace. *Evolution by Natural Selection*. Cambridge: Harvard University Press, 1958.

Darwin, Erasmus. *Zoonomia: or the Laws of Organic Life*. 2 vols. New York: AMS Press, 1974 [1794–96].

Dewey, John. *The Quest for Certainty*. In *John Dewey: The Later Works, 1925–1953*, edited by Jo Ann Boydston. Vol. 4. Carbondale: Southern Illinois University Press, 1984.

———. "Science and Free Culture." In *John Dewey: The Later Works, 1925–1953*, edited by Jo Ann Boydston, vol. 13, pp. 156–72. Carbondale: Southern Illinois University Press, 1988.

———. "William James." In *John Dewey: The Middle Works, 1899–1924*, edited by Jo Ann Boydston, vol. 6, pp. 91–97. Carbondale: Southern Illinois University Press, 1978.

Draper, John William. *History of the Conflict between Religion and Science*. New York: D. Appleton and Co., 1874.

Drummond, Henry. *Natural Law in the Spiritual World*. New York: A. L. Burt, 1883.

Du Bois, W. E. B. *Dusk at Dawn: An Essay toward an Autobiography of a Race Concept*. New York: Schocken Books, 1968 [1940].

Dupree, A. Hunter, ed. "Some Letters from Charles Darwin to Jeffries Wyman." *Isis* 42 (1951): 104–10.

Durand, Asher B. "Letters on Landscape Painting." *The Crayon* 1 (1855): 34–35, 97–98.

Eliot, Charles W. *Charles W. Eliot: The Man and His Beliefs*. Edited by William Allan Neilson. New York: Harper and Row, 1926.

———. "The New Education: Its Organization." *Atlantic Monthly* 23 (February 1869): 203–20.

[———]. "Popularizing Science." *Nation* 4 (1867): 33–34.

Eliot, Charles W., and Frank H. Storer. *A Manual of Inorganic Chemistry, arranged to facilitate the Experimental Demonstration of the Facts and Principles of the Science*. 3rd ed. New York: Ivison, Phinney, Blakeman, and Co., 1869.

Emerson, George B. "What We Owe to Louis Agassiz as a Teacher." Boston: Boston Society of Natural History, 1874.

Emerson, Ralph Waldo. *The Collected Works of Ralph Waldo Emerson*. Vol. 1, *Nature, Addresses, and Lectures*. Edited by Alfred R. Ferguson et al. Cambridge: Harvard University Press, 1971.

———. *The Conduct of Life*. Boston: Houghton Mifflin and Co., 1904.

———. *The Early Lectures of Ralph Waldo Emerson*. Vol. 3, *1838–1842*. Edited by Robert E. Spiller and Wallace E. Williams. Cambridge: Harvard University Press, 1972.

———. *Representative Men*. Edited by Joseph Slater et al. Cambridge: Harvard University Press, 1987.

Fay, Melusina. *Co-Operative Housekeeping, how not to do it and how to do it: A Study in Sociology*. Boston: J. R. Osgood, 1884.

——— [A. Political Zero, pseud.]. *The Democratic Party: A Political Study*. Cambridge: John Wilson and Son, 1875.

Finney, Charles Grandison. *Lectures on Revivals of Religion*. Edited by William McLoughlin. Cambridge: Harvard University Press, 1960 [1835].

Fiske, John. *Darwinism, and Other Essays*. Boston: Houghton Mifflin and Co., 1895 [1879].

———. *Outlines of Cosmic Philosophy Based on the Doctrine of Evolution with Criticism on the Positive Philosophy*. 2 vols. Boston: Houghton Mifflin and Co., 1889.

Fourier, Charles. *The Utopian Vision of Charles Fourier: Selected Texts on Work, Love, and Passionate Attraction*. Edited and translated by Jonathan Beecher and Richard Bienvenu. Boston: Beacon Press, 1971.

Frothingham, Octavius Brooks. *The Religion of Humanity*. New York: Asak Butts, 1873.

Gray, Asa. "Address of Professor A. Gray." *Proceedings of the Boston Society of Natural History* 17 (1875): 96–124.

———. "Analogy between the Flora of Japan and That of the United States." *American Journal of Science*, 2d ser., 2 (1846): 135–36.

———. *The Botanical Text-Book, for Colleges, Schools, and Private Students*. New York: Wiley and Putnam; Boston: Little, Brown and Co., 1842.

———. *Botany for Young People and Common Schools*. New York and Chicago: Ivison, Blakeman, Taylor, and Co., 1858.

———. *Darwiniana: Essays and Reviews Pertaining to Darwinism*. Cambridge: Harvard University Press, 1963 [1876].

———. *The Elements of Botany for Beginners and for Schools*. New York and Cincinnati: American Book Company, 1836.

———. *Field, Forest, and Garden Botany: A Simple Introduction to the Common Plants of the United States*. New York: Ivison, Phinney, Blakeman, and Co.; Chicago: S. C. Griggs, 1868.

———. *First Lessons in Botany and Vegetable Physiology*. New York: Ivison and Phinney, 1857.

———. *The Flora of North America, A Manual of the Botany of the Northern United States*. New York: Ivison and Phinney; Chicago: S. C. Griggs and Co., 1859.

———. "Harvard University Herbarium." *American Journal of Science*, 2d ser., 39 (March 1865): 225–26.

———. *How Plants Grow: A Simple Introduction to Structural Botany*. New York: Ivison and Phinney, 1859.

———. *The Letters of Asa Gray*. 2 vols. Edited by Jane Loring Gray. Boston: Houghton Mifflin and Co., 1893.

———. "Natural Selection and Natural Theology." *Nature* 27 (1883): 291–92 and 527–28.

———. Remarks on Darwin. *Proceedings of the American Academy of Arts and Sciences* 4 (April 10, 1860, May 1, 1860): 411–16 and 424–26.

———. Report on the botany of Japan. *Proceedings of the American Academy of Arts and Sciences* 4 (January 11, 1859): 131.

———. Review of *Flora Japonica*. *American Journal of Science* 39 (1840): 175–76.

———. *The Scientific Papers of Asa Gray*. 2 vols. Edited by Charles Sprague Sargent. Boston: Houghton Mifflin and Co., 1889.

———. "Statistics of the Flora of the Northern United States." *American Journal of Science*, 2d ser., 22 (November 1856): 204–32; and, 2d ser., 23 (May 1857): 62–84 and 369–403.

Hare, Robert. *Experimental Investigation of the Spirit Manifestations, Demonstrating the Existence of Spirits and Their Communion with Mortals*. New York: Partridge and Brittan, 1855.

Hempel, Carl. *Philosophy of Natural Science*. Englewood Cliffs, N.J.: Prentice-Hall, 1966.

Hempel, Charles Julius. *True Organization of the New Church as Indicated in the Writings of Emanuel Swedenborg and Demonstrated by Charles Fourier*. New York: William Radde, 1848.

Henry, Joseph. *The Papers of Joseph Henry*. Edited by Nathan Reingold et al. Washington, D.C.: Smithsonian Institution Press, 1972–.

———. *A Scientist in American Life: Essays and Lectures of Joseph Henry*. Edited by Arthur P. Molella et al. Washington, D.C.: Smithsonian Institution Press, 1980.

Herschel, John F. W. *A Preliminary Discourse on the Study of Natural Philosophy.* New York: Johnson Reprint Corporation, 1966 [1830].

Hitchcock, Edward. "The Study of Natural History." *Knickerbocker* 25 (1845): 283–96.

Hodge, Charles. *The Way of Life.* Edited by Mark A. Noll. New York: Paulist Press, 1987.

———. *What Is Darwinism?* New York: Charles Scribner, Armstrong and Co., 1874.

Holmes, Oliver Wendell, [Sr.]. *Border Lines of Knowledge in Some Provinces of Medical Science.* Boston: Ticknor and Fields, 1862.

———. *Boylston Prize Dissertations for the Years 1836 and 1837.* Boston: C. C. Little and J. Brown, 1838.

———. "A Case of Malformation." *Boston Medical and Surgical Journal* 34 (March 1847): 92–96.

———. "The Contagiousness of Puerperal Fever." *New England Quarterly Journal of Medicine and Surgery* 1 (April 1843): 503–30.

———. *Introductory Lecture.* Boston: David Clapp and Son, 1867.

———. *Pages from an Old Life: A Collection of Essays, 1857–1881.* Boston: Houghton Mifflin and Co., 1913 [1892].

———. *The Poetical Works of Oliver Wendell Holmes.* 3 vols. Boston: Houghton Mifflin and Co., 1908.

———. "Professor Jeffries Wyman, A Memorial Outline." *Atlantic Monthly* 34 (November 1874): 611–23.

Hopkins, William. "Physical Theories of the Phenomenon of Life." *Fraser's Magazine* 61 (1860): 739–52.

Howe, Mark DeWolfe, ed. *The Holmes-Pollock Letters: The Correspondence of Mr. Justice Holmes and Sir Frederick Pollock, 1874–1932.* 2nd ed. Cambridge: Harvard University Press, 1961 [1941].

Huxley, Thomas Henry. *Darwiniana.* New York: D. Appleton and Co., 1896.

———. *Evidence as to Man's Place in Nature.* Ann Arbor: University of Michigan Press, 1959 [1863].

———. *Science and Christian Tradition.* New York: D. Appleton and Co., 1894.

Jackson, James, Sr. *Memoir of James Jackson, Jr., M.D.* Boston: Hilliard, Gray and Co., 1836.

James, Alice. *The Diary of Alice James.* Edited by Leon Edel. New York: Dodd, Mead and Company, 1964.

James, Henry, Jr. *Autobiography.* Edited by Frederick W. Dupee. Princeton: Princeton University Press, 1983.

———. *The Letters of Henry James.* 2 vols. Edited by Percy Lubbock. New York: Charles Scribner's Sons, 1920.

———. *Notes of a Son and Brother.* New York: Charles Scribner's Sons, 1914.

———. *A Small Boy and Others.* New York: Charles Scribner's Sons, 1913.

James, Henry, [Sr.]. *Christianity, the Logic of Creation.* London: William White, 1857.

———. *Church of Christ not an Ecclesiasticism: A Letter of Remonstrance to a member of the Soi-Disant New Church*. 2nd ed. London: William White, 1856.

———. "Faith and Science." *North American Review* 101 (October 1865): 335–78.

———. "Fourier and Swedenborg." *Harbinger* 6 (1848): 132, 140–41.

———. *Lectures and Miscellanies*. New York: AMS Press, 1983 [1852].

———. *The Literary Remains of the Late Henry James*. Edited by William James. Boston: J. R. Osgood and Co., 1884.

———. "The Marriage Question." *New-York Daily Tribune* (September 18, 1852).

———. *Moralism and Christianity; or, Man's Experience and Destiny*. New York: J. S. Redfield, 1850.

———. *The Nature of Evil Considered in a letter to the Rev. Edward Beecher, D.D., Author of "The Conflict of Ages."* New York: D. Appleton and Co., 1855.

———. Preface to *Letters on Theron and Aspasio*, by Robert Sandeman. New York: John S. Taylor, 1838.

———. Preface to *Love in the Phalanstery*, by Victor Hennequin. New York: Dewitt and Davenport, 1849.

———. "A Scientific Statement of the Doctrine of the Lord, or Divine Man." *Massachusetts Quarterly Review* 3 (1850): 52–67.

———. *The Secret of Swedenborg: Being an Elucidation of his Doctrine of the Divine Natural Humanity*. Boston: Fields, Osgood and Co., 1869.

———. *Society the Redeemed Form of Man, and the Earnest of God's Omnipotence in Human Nature: Affirmed in Letters to a Friend*. Boston: Houghton, Osborn, 1879.

———. *Substance and Shadow: or Morality and Religion in their Relation to Life: An Essay Upon the Physics of Creation*. Boston: Ticknor and Fields, 1863.

James, William. *The Correspondence of William James*. Vol. 1, *William and Henry, 1861–84*. Edited by Ignas K. Skrupskelis and Elizabeth M. Berkeley. Charlottesville: University Press of Virginia, 1992.

———. *Essays, Comments, and Reviews*. The Works of William James, edited by Frederick H. Burkhardt. Cambridge: Harvard University Press, 1987 [1865–1909].

———. Introduction to *The Literary Remains of the Late Henry James*, by Henry James. Boston: James R. Osgood and Company, 1884.

———. *The Letters of William James*. Edited by Henry James. Boston: Atlantic Monthly Press, 1920.

———. *Manuscript Essays and Notes*. The Works of William James, edited by Frederick H. Burkhardt. Cambridge: Harvard University Press, 1988 [1870–1910].

———. *Manuscript Lectures*. The Works of William James, edited by Frederick H. Burkhardt. Cambridge: Harvard University Press, 1988 [1875–1908].

———. *A Pluralistic Universe*. The Works of William James, edited by Frederick Burkhardt. Cambridge: Harvard University Press, 1977 [1909].

———. *Pragmatism, A New Name for Some Old Ways of Thinking*. The Works of William James, edited by Frederick H. Burkhardt. Cambridge: Harvard University Press, 1975 [1907].

———. *The Principles of Psychology*. The Works of William James, edited by Frederick Burkhardt. Cambridge: Harvard University Press, 1981 [1890].

———. *The Varieties of Religious Experience* [Gifford Lectures on Natural Religion, 1901–2]. *The Works of William James*, edited by Frederick Burkhardt. Cambridge: Harvard University Press, 1985 [1902].

———. *The Will to Believe and Other Essays in Popular Philosophy*. *The Works of William James*, edited by Frederick H. Burkhardt. Cambridge: Harvard University Press, 1979 [1897].

———. *The Writings of William James: A Comprehensive Edition*. Edited by John J. McDermott. Chicago: University of Chicago Press, 1977.

Jordan, David Starr. "Agassiz at Penikese." *Popular Science Monthly* 40 (April 1892): 721–29.

Kant, Immanuel. *Critique of Practical Reason*. Translated by Lewis White Beck. Indianapolis: Bobbs-Merrill Educational Publishing, 1956 [1788].

———. *Religion within the Limits of Reason Alone*. Translated by Theodore M. Greene and Hoyt H. Hudson. New York: Harper and Row, 1960 [1793].

Lamarck, Jean Baptiste. *Zoological Philosophy*. Translated by Hugh Elliot. New York: Hafner, 1963 [1809].

Laplace, Pierre Simon. *The System of the World*. Translated by J. Pond. London: Richard Phillips, 1809 [1796].

LeConte, Joseph. "Agassiz and Evolution." *Popular Science Monthly* 32 (November 1887): 17–26.

———. *Evolution; its nature, its evidences, and its relation to religious thought*. 2nd ed. New York: D. Appleton and Co., 1905 [1888].

Leland, Charles Godfrey. *Memoirs*. New York: D. Appleton and Co., 1893.

Lyell, Charles. *Principles of Geology*. 3 vols. New York: Strechert-Hafner, 1970 [1830–34].

Lyman, Theodore. "Recollections of Agassiz." *Atlantic Monthly* 33 (February 1874): 221–29.

McCosh, James. *The Religious Aspects of Evolution*. New York: G. P. Putnam's Sons, 1888.

Madeley, Edward. *The Science of Correspondences Elucidated, the key to the Heavenly and True Meaning of the Sacred Scriptures*. 20th ed. Germantown, Pa.: Swedenborg Publishing Association, 1883 [1848].

Malthus, Thomas Robert. *An Essay on the Principle of Population as it Affects the Future Improvement of Society*. London: J. Johnson, 1798.

Munsell, Joel. *Collections on the History of Albany, from its Discovery to the Present Time, with Notices of its Public Institutions and Biographical Sketches of Citizens Deceased*. 4 vols. Albany: J. Munsell, 1865–71.

Newcomb, Simon. Report on the Doctrine of Probabilities. *Proceedings of the American Academy of Arts and Sciences* 4 (May 8, 1860): 433–40.

Norton, Charles Eliot. *The Letters of Charles Eliot Norton*. 2 vols. Edited by Mark DeWolfe Howe. Boston: Houghton Mifflin and Co., 1913.

Packard, A. S. *Memoir of Jeffries Wyman, 1814–1878*. Washington, D.C.: Judd and Detweiler, 1878.

Paige, Alonzo C. *Reports of Cases Argued and Determined in the Court of Chancery of the State of New York*. Vols. 4, 5, and 7. New York: Gould, Banks and Co., 1834, 1836, and 1839.

Paley, William. *Natural Theology, or, Evidences of the Existence and Attributes of the Deity, Collected from the Appearances of Nature.* New York: Evert Duckinck, 1814 [1802].

Peirce, Benjamin. "The National Importance of Social Science in the United States." An Address Delivered at the Opening Session of the American Social Science Association, at Cincinnati, May 18, 1878. Boston: Little, Brown and Co., 1878.

Peirce, Benjamin, et al. "Six Letters upon the Smithsonian Institution." *Boston Post* (1855).

Peirce, Charles Sanders. *Charles Sanders Peirce: Chance, Love, and Logic.* Edited by Morris Cohen. New York: Harcourt, Brace, and Co., 1923.

———. *Charles S. Peirce: Selected Writings.* Edited by Philip P. Wiener. New York: Dover Books, 1966 [1958].

———. *Collected Papers of Charles Sanders Peirce.* 8 vols. Vol. 1, *Principles of Philosophy.* Vol. 2, *Elements of Logic.* Vol. 3, *Exact Logic (Published Papers).* Vol. 4, *The Simplest Mathematics.* Vol. 5, *Pragmatism and Pragmaticism.* Vol. 6, *Scientific Metaphysics.* Edited by Charles Hartshorne and Paul Weiss. Cambridge: Harvard University Press, 1960 [1931–34]. Vol. 7, *Science and Philosophy.* Vol. 8, *Reviews, Correspondence, and Bibliography.* Edited by Arthur W. Burks. Cambridge: Harvard University Press, 1958.

———. *New Elements of Mathematics.* 4 vols. Edited by Carolyn Eisele. Atlantic Heights, N.J.: Humanities Press, 1976.

———. *Peirce on Signs: Writings on Semiotic by Charles Sanders Peirce.* Edited by James Hoopes. Chapel Hill: University of North Carolina Press, 1991.

———. *Photometric Researches, made in the years 1872–1875.* [Annals of the Astronomical Observatory of Harvard College, vol. 9.] Leipzig: Wilhelm Engelmann, 1878.

———. *The Writings of Charles Sanders Peirce: A Chronological Edition.* 5 vols. to date. Edited by Max H. Fisch et al. Bloomington: Indiana University Press, 1982–92.

———, ed. *Studies in Logic.* Boston: Little, Brown and Co., 1883.

Pestalozzi, Heinrich. *The Education of Man: Aphorisms.* Translated by Heinz Norden and Ruth Norden. New York: Philosophical Library, 1951.

———. *Leonard and Gertrude.* Translated by Eva Channing. Boston: D. C. Heath and Co., 1885 [1781–87].

Plato. *The Being and the Beautiful: Plato's Theaetetus, Sophist, and Statesman.* Translated by Seth Benardette. Chicago: University of Chicago Press, 1984.

Poe, Edgar Allan. "The Purloined Letter." In *The Collected Works of Edgar Allan Poe.* Vol. 3, *Tales and Sketches, 1843–1849.* Edited by Thomas Ollive Mabbott, pp. 972–97. Cambridge: Harvard University Press, 1978.

Popper, Karl. *The Logic of Scientific Discovery.* London: Hutchinson; New York: Basic Books, 1959.

Proceedings of the American Academy of Arts and Sciences 4 (1857–60).

Proceedings of the Boston Society of Natural History 7 (1859–61), 8 (1861–62), 9 (1862–64), 10 (1864–65), 11 (1866–68), 12 (1868–69), 13 (1869–70), 14 (1870–71).

Proceedings of the Botanical Section of the Academy of Natural Sciences of Philadelphia, In Memory of Dr. Asa Gray. February 13, 1888.

Putnam, F. W. "Jeffries Wyman." *Proceedings of the American Association for the Advancement of Science* 11 (1876): 495–505.

Quimby, Phineas P. *The Quimby Manuscripts: Showing the Discovery of Spiritual Healing and the Origin of Christian Science*. Edited by Horatio W. Dresser. New York: T. Y. Crowell and Co., 1921.

Romanes, George. Reply to Asa Gray. *Nature* 27 (1883): 362–64 and 528–29.

Royce, Josiah. *William James and Other Essays on the Philosophy of Life*. Freeport, N.Y.: Books for Libraries Press, 1911.

Santayana, George. *Character and Opinion in the United States*. New York: W. W. Norton, 1967 [1920].

Sargent, Mary Elizabeth, ed. *Sketches and Reminiscences of the Radical Club of Chestnut Street, Boston*. Boston: J. R. Osgood, 1880.

Shaler, Nathaniel Southgate. "Chapters from an Autobiography; II: A Pupil of Agassiz." *Atlantic Monthly* 103 (February 1909): 217–25.

Spencer, Herbert. *Illustrations of Universal Progress*. New York: D. Appleton and Co., 1864.

Stöckhardt, Julius A. *Principles of Chemistry, Illustrated by Simple Experiments*. Translated by Charles Henry Peirce and Charlotte Elizabeth Peirce. Cambridge: Bartlett, 1853.

Swedenborg, Emanuel. *A Compendium of the Theological Writings of Emanuel Swedenborg*. Edited by Samuel M. Warren. New York: Swedenborg Foundation, 1974.

——— . *The Essential Swedenborg: Basic Teachings*. Edited by Sig Synnestvedt. New York: Swedenborg Foundation, 1970.

Thoreau, Henry David. *Faith in a Seed: The Dispersion of Seeds and Other Late Natural History Writings*. Edited by Bradley P. Dean. Washington, D.C: Island Press, 1993.

Thornwell, James Henley. *The Collected Writings of James Henley Thornwell*. 4 vols. Edited by John B. Asger. Richmond: Presbyterian Committee of Publication, 1871–73.

Tocqueville, Alexis de. *Democracy in America*. Edited by J. P. Mayer and translated by George Lawrence. Garden City, N.Y.: Anchor Books, 1969 [1835].

Torrey, John, and Asa Gray. *The Flora of North America, Containing Abridged Descriptions of All Known Indigenous and Naturalized Plants Growing North of Mexico, Arranged According to the Natural System*. New York: Wiley and Putnam, 1838–43.

Townsend, Luther Tracy. *The Mosaic Record and Modern Science*. Boston: Howard Gannett, 1881.

Tyler, Samuel. *Discourse on the Baconian Philosophy*. Frederick City, Md.: Printed by E. Hughes, 1844.

——— . "The Influence of the Baconian Philosophy." *Princeton Review* 15 (1843): 481–506.

Tyndall, John. "The Belfast Address." [Presidential Address of the British Association for the Advancement of Science, 1874.] *Nature: A Weekly Illustrated Journal of Science* 10 (August 20, 1874): 308–19.

Wallace, Alfred Russel. *Contribution to the Theory of Natural Selection.* London: Macmillan, 1870.

———. "Note on the Passages of Malthus's 'Principle of Population' Which Suggested the Idea of Natural Selection to Darwin and Myself." In *Wallace on Natural Selection*, edited by H. Lewis McKinney, pp. 21–28. New Haven: Yale University Press, 1972.

Wayland, Francis. *Discourse on the Philosophy of Analogy.* Boston: Hilliard, Gray, Little, and Wilkins, 1831.

———. *Elements of Moral Science.* Edited by Joseph Blau. Cambridge: Harvard University Press, 1963 [1835].

Wendell, John L. *Reports of Cases Argued and Determined in the Supreme Court for the Correction of Errors of the State of New-York.* Vol. 16. Albany: William and A. Gould and Co., 1837.

Whewell, William. *History of the Inductive Sciences.* London: John W. Parker, 1837.

White, Andrew Dickson. *A History of the Warfare of Science and Religion within Christendom.* 2 vols. New York: D. Appleton and Co., 1896.

Wilder, Burt G. "Sketch of Dr. Jeffries Wyman." *Popular Science Monthly* 3 (January 1875): 355–60.

———. "What We Owe Agassiz." *Popular Science Monthly* 71 (July 1907): 5–20.

Winthrop, John. *A Short Story of the Rise, Reign, and Ruine of The Antinomians, Familists, and Libertines, that Infected the Churches of New England . . . and the lamentable death of Mrs. Hutchinson.* London: Ralph Smith, 1644.

Wright, Chauncey. "The Economy and Symmetry of the Honey-Bees' Cells." *Mathematical Monthly* (June 1860): 304–19.

———. *The Letters of Chauncey Wright.* Edited by James Bradley Thayer. Cambridge: Press of John Wilson and Son, 1878.

———. *Philosophical Discussions.* Edited by Charles Eliot Norton. New York: Henry Holt, 1877.

———. *The Philosophical Writings of Chauncey Wright: Representative Selections.* Edited by Edward H. Madden. New York: Liberal Arts Press, 1958.

———. "Remarks on the Architecture of Bees." *Proceedings of the American Academy of Arts and Sciences* 4 (May 8, 1860): 432–33.

———. "The Winds and the Weather." *Atlantic Monthly* 1 (1858): 272–79.

Wright, George Frederick. *Studies in Science and Religion.* Andover: Warren F. Draper, 1882.

Wyman, Jeffries. *Dear Jeffie: Being the Letters from Jeffries Wyman, first director of the Peabody Museum to his Son, Jeffries Wyman, Jr.* Edited by George E. Gifford, Jr. Cambridge: Peabody Museum Press, 1978.

———. "Notes on the Cells of the Bee." *Proceedings of the American Academy of Arts and Sciences* 7 (1865–68): 68–83.

———. "Observations on Crania." *Proceedings of the Boston Society of Natural History* 11 (April 15, 1868): 440–63.

———. Report on the Cells of the Hive Bee. *Proceedings of the Boston Society of Natural History* 10 (November 15, 1865): 234 and 278.

Youmans, Edward L. "Who Are the Propagators of Atheism?" *Popular Science Monthly* 5 (1874): 365–67.

Secondary Sources

Abzub, Robert. *Cosmos Crumbling: American Reform and the Religious Imagination*. New York: Oxford University Press, 1994.

Agassi, Joseph. *Faraday as a Natural Philosopher*. Chicago: University of Chicago Press, 1971.

Ahlstrom, Sydney E. *A Religious History of the American People*. New Haven: Yale University Press, 1972.

———. "The Scottish Philosophy and American Theology." *Church History* 24 (September 1955): 257–72.

Ahlstrom, Sydney E., and Robert B. Mullin. *The Scientific Theist: A Life of Francis Ellingwood Abbot*. Macon, Ga.: Mercer University Press, 1987.

Albanese, Catherine. *Corresponding Motion: Transcendental Religion and the New America*. Philadelphia: Temple University Press, 1977.

———. *Nature Religion in America*. Chicago: University of Chicago Press, 1990.

Alexander, Gary. "The Hypothesized God of C. S. Peirce and William James." *Journal of Religion* 67 (July 1987): 304–21.

Allen, Gay Wilson. *William James: A Biography*. New York: Viking Press, 1967.

Almeder, Robert. "Peirce on Scientific Realism." Paper presented at the Charles Sanders Peirce Sesquicentennial International Congress, Harvard University, September 6, 1989.

———. *The Philosophy of Charles Sanders Peirce: A Critical Introduction*. Oxford: Basil Blackwell, 1980.

Anderson, James William. "In Search of Mary James." *Psychohistory Review* 8 (1979): 63–70.

———. "Why Did William James Abandon Art?" *Emotions and Behavior Monographs* 4 (1987): 279–303.

———. "'The Worst Kind of Melancholy': William James in 1869." *Harvard Library Bulletin* 30 (October 1982): 369–86.

Apel, Karl-Otto. *Charles S. Peirce: From Pragmatism to Pragmaticism*. Translated by Michael Krois. Amherst: University of Massachusetts Press, 1981.

Appleby, Joyce. *Capitalism and the New Social Order: The Republican Vision of the 1790s*. New York: New York University Press, 1984.

———. "Republicanism in Old and New Contexts." *William and Mary Quarterly*, 3d ser., 43 (1986): 20–34.

Archibald, Raymond Clare. "Benjamin Peirce." In *Dictionary of American Biography*, edited by Dumas Malone, vol. 13, pp. 393–97. New York: Charles Scribner's Sons, 1934.

———. *Benjamin Peirce, 1809–1888: Biographical Sketch and Bibliography*. Oberlin, Ohio: Mathematical Association of America, 1925.

Atkinson, Norma P. "An Examination of the Life and Thought of Zina Fay Peirce, An American Reformer and Feminist." Ph.D. diss., Ball State University, 1983.
Axtell, James. "The Death of the Liberal Arts College." *History of Education Quarterly* 2 (1971): 339–52.
Ayer, A. J. *The Origins of Pragmatism: Studies in the Philosophy of Charles Sanders Peirce and William James.* San Francisco: Freeman, Cooper and Co., 1968.
Baatz, Simon. " 'Squinting at Silliman': Scientific Periodicals in the Early Republic, 1810–33." *Isis* 82 (1991): 223–44.
Bannister, Robert. *Social Darwinism: Science and Myth in Anglo-American Social Thought.* Philadelphia: Temple University Press, 1979.
Barlow, Thomas. *Pestalozzi and American Education.* Boulder: Este Es Press, 1977.
Barzun, Jacques. *A Stroll With William James.* New York: Harper and Row, 1983.
Basalla, George. "Pop Science: The Depiction of Science in Popular Culture." In *Science and Its Public: The Changing Relationship*, edited by Gerald Holton and William A. Blanpied, pp. 261–78. Boston and Dordrecht: D. Reidel Publishing Co., 1976.
Bates, Ralph. *Scientific Societies in the United States.* 2nd ed. New York: Columbia University Press, 1958.
Beatty, John. "Speaking of Species: Darwin's Strategy." In *The Darwinian Heritage*, edited by David Kohn, pp. 265–81. Princeton: Princeton University Press, 1985.
———. "What's in a Word?: Coming to Terms in the Darwinian Revolution." *Journal of the History of Biology* 15 (1982): 215–39.
Beecher, Henry Knowles, and Mark Altschule. *Medicine at Harvard: The First Three Hundred Years.* Hanover: University Press of New England, 1977.
Beecher, Jonathan. *Charles Fourier: The Visionary and His World.* Berkeley: University of California Press, 1987.
Beisner, Robert L. *Twelve Against Empire: The Anti-Imperialists, 1898–1900.* New York: McGraw-Hill, 1968.
Bell, Ian F. A. "Divine Patterns: Louis Agassiz and American Men of Letters." *Journal of American Studies* 10 (1976): 349–81.
Bell, Millicent. "Jamesian Being." *Virginia Quarterly Review* 52 (Winter 1976): 115–32.
Bendall, D. S., ed. *Evolution from Molecules to Men.* New York: Cambridge University Press, 1983.
Benjamin, Walter. *Illuminations.* Edited by Hannah Arendt and translated by Harry Zohn. New York: Schocken Books, 1969 [1968].
Berger, Peter L. *The Sacred Canopy: Elements of a Sociological Theory of Religion.* New York: Doubleday and Co., 1967.
Bernstein, Richard. *Beyond Objectivism and Relativism: Science, Hermeneutics, and Praxis.* Philadelphia: University of Pennsylvania Press, 1988.
Berthoff, Rowland. "Independence and Attachment, Virtue and Interest: From Republican Citizen to Free Enterpriser, 1787–1837." In *Uprooted Americans*, edited by Richard Bushman et al., pp. 99–123. Boston: Little, Brown and Co., 1979.
Bixler, Julius Seelye. *Religion in the Philosophy of William James.* Boston: Marshall Jones Co., 1926.

Bjork, Daniel W. *The Compromised Scientist: William James in the Development of American Psychology*. New York: Columbia University Press, 1983.

———. *William James: The Center of His Vision*. New York: Columbia University Press, 1988.

Blake, Ralph M., Curt J. Ducasse, and Edward H. Madden, eds. *Theories of Scientific Method: The Renaissance through the Nineteenth Century*. Seattle: University of Washington Press, 1960; New York: Gordon and Breach, 1989.

Blum, Ann Shelby. *Picturing Nature: American Nineteenth-Century Zoological Illustrations*. Princeton: Princeton University Press, 1993.

Boler, John F. *Charles Peirce and Scholastic Realism: A Study of Peirce's Relation to John Duns Scotus*. Seattle: University of Washington Press, 1963.

Bowden, Henry. *Church History in the Age of Science*. Chapel Hill: University of North Carolina Press, 1971.

Bowlby, John. *Charles Darwin: A New Life*. New York: W. W. Norton, 1991.

Bowler, Peter J. *Charles Darwin: The Man and His Influence*. London: Basil Blackwell, 1990.

———. *The Eclipse of Darwinism: Anti-Darwinian Evolutionary Theories in the Decades around 1900*. Baltimore: Johns Hopkins University Press, 1983.

———. *Evolution: The History of an Idea*. Berkeley: University of California Press, 1984.

———. *The Mendelian Revolution: The Emergence of Hereditarian Concepts in Modern Science and Society*. Baltimore: Johns Hopkins University Press, 1989.

———. *The Non-Darwinian Revolution: Reinterpretation of a Historical Myth*. Baltimore: Johns Hopkins University Press, 1988.

———. "Scientific Attitudes to Darwinism in Britain and America." In *The Darwinian Heritage*, edited by David Kohn, pp. 641–81. Princeton: Princeton University Press, 1985.

Boydston, Jeanne. *Home and Work: Housework, Wages, and the Ideology of Labor in the Early Republic*. New York: Oxford University Press, 1990.

Bozeman, Theodore Dwight. *Protestants in an Age of Science: The Baconian Ideal and Antebellum American Religious Thought*. Chapel Hill: University of North Carolina Press, 1977.

Bradford, Miles Gerald. "Practical Theism and Pantheism: Two Approaches to God in the Thought of William James." Ph.D. diss., University of California, Santa Barbara, 1977.

Brent, Joseph L. *Charles Sanders Peirce, A Life*. Bloomington: Indiana University Press, 1993.

———. "A Study of the Life of Charles Sanders Peirce." Ph.D. diss., University of California at Los Angeles, 1960.

Brieger, Gert H., ed. *Medical America in the Nineteenth Century: Readings from the Literature*. Baltimore: Johns Hopkins University Press, 1972.

Brock, Erland J., et al., eds. *Swedenborg and His Influence*. Bryn Athyn, Pa.: Academy of the New Church, 1988.

Brooks, Van Wyck. *The Flowering of New England: Emerson, Thoreau, Hawthorne and the Beginnings of American Literature, 1815–65*. New York: E. P. Dutton, 1936.

Brown, Chandos Michael. *Benjamin Silliman: A Life in the Young Republic*. Princeton: Princeton University Press, 1989.

———. "A Natural History of the Gloucester Sea Serpent: Knowledge, Power, and the Culture of Science in Antebellum America." *American Quarterly* 42 (September 1990): 402–36.

Brown, JoAnne. *The Definition of a Profession: The Authority of Metaphor in the History of Intelligence Testing, 1890–1930*. Princeton: Princeton University Press, 1992.

———. "Professional Language: Words That Succeed." *Radical History Review* 34 (1986): 33–51.

Brown, Richard D. *Knowledge Is Power: The Diffusion of Information in Early America, 1700–1865*. New York: Oxford University Press, 1989.

Browning, Don S. *Pluralism and Personality: William James and Some Contemporary Cultures of Psychology*. Lewisburg, Pa.: Bucknell University Press, 1980.

Bruce, Robert V. *The Launching of Modern American Science, 1846–1876*. New York: Alfred A. Knopf, 1987.

Buckley, Michael J. *At the Origins of Modern Atheism*. New Haven: Yale University Press, 1987.

Bulhof, Ilsen. *The Language of Science: A Study of the Relation between Literature and Science in the Perspective of Hermeneutical Ontology, with a Case Study of Darwin's* Origin of Species. New York: E. J. Brill, 1992.

Burchfield, Joe D. "Darwin and the Dilemma of Geological Time." *Isis* 65 (1974): 301–21.

———. *Lord Kelvin and the Age of the Earth*. New York: Science History Publications, 1975.

Burkhardt, Richard. *The Spirit of System: Lamarck and Evolutionary Biology*. Cambridge: Harvard University Press, 1977.

Burnham, John C. *How Superstition Won and Science Lost: Popularizing Science and Health in the United States*. New Brunswick: Rutgers University Press, 1987.

Bush, Clive. *Halfway to Revolution: Investigation and Crisis in the Work of Henry Adams, William James, and Gertrude Stein*. New Haven: Yale University Press, 1991.

Bushman, Richard. *From Puritan to Yankee: Character and Social Order in Connecticut, 1690–1765*. Cambridge: Harvard University Press, 1967.

———. *The Refinement of America: Persons, Houses, Cities*. New York: Alfred A. Knopf, 1992.

Butler, Jon. *Awash in a Sea of Faith: Christianizing the American People*. Cambridge: Harvard University Press, 1990.

Byrd, Gibson. "The Artist-Teacher in America: His Changing Role in Our Institutions." *Art Journal* 23 (Winter 1963–64): 130–36.

Campbell, John Angus. "Scientific Discovery and Rhetorical Invention: The Path to Darwin's *Origin*." In *The Rhetorical Turn: Invention and Persuasion in the*

Conduct of Inquiry, edited by Herbert W. Simons, pp. 58–90. Chicago: University of Chicago Press, 1990.

Cannon, Susan. *Science in Culture: The Early Victorian Period*. New York: Science History Publications, 1978.

Cantor, Geoffrey. *Michael Faraday: Sandemanian and Scientist: A Study of Science and Religion in the Nineteenth Century*. New York: St. Martin's Press, 1991.

Carey, Alex. "Reshaping the Truth: Pragmatists and Propagandists in America." In *American Media and Mass Culture*, edited by Donald Lazere, pp. 35–41. Berkeley: University of California Press, 1987.

Carnes, Mark C., and Clyde Griffen, eds. *Meanings for Manhood: Constructions of Masculinity in Victorian America*. Chicago: University of Chicago Press, 1990.

Carter, Paul A. *The Spiritual Crisis of the Gilded Age*. De Kalb: Northern Illinois University Press, 1971.

Cashdollar, Charles D. *The Transformation of Theology, 1830–1890: Positivism and Protestant Thought in Britain and America*. Princeton: Princeton University Press, 1989.

Chadwick, Owen. *The Secularization of the European Mind in the Nineteenth Century*. New York: Cambridge University Press, 1975.

Chase, Franklin H. *Syracuse and Its Environs: A History*. 3 vols. New York: Lewis Historical Publishing Co., 1924.

Chittenden, Russell Henry. *History of the Sheffield Scientific School of Yale University, 1846–1922*. 2 vols. New Haven: Yale University Press, 1928.

Clark, Hubert Lyman. "Jeffries Wyman." In *Dictionary of American Biography*, edited by Dumas Malone, vol. 20, pp. 583–84. New York: Charles Scribner's Sons, 1936.

Clebsch, William A. *American Religious Thought: A History*. Chicago: University of Chicago Press, 1973.

Cohen, Morris. Preface to *Charles S. Peirce: Chance, Love, and Logic*. New York: Harcourt, Brace, and Co., 1923.

Colapietro, Vincent M. *Peirce's Approach to the Self: A Semiotic Perspective on Human Subjectivity*. Albany: State University of New York Press, 1989.

Collier, Katherine Brownell. *Cosmogonies of Our Fathers: Some Theories of the Seventeenth and Eighteenth Centuries*. New York: Octagon Books, 1968.

Commager, Henry Steele. *The American Mind: An Interpretation of American Thought and Character Since the 1880s*. New Haven: Yale University Press, 1950.

Conkin, Paul. *Puritans and Pragmatists: Eight Eminent American Thinkers*. New York: Dodd, Mead and Co., 1968.

Conser, Walter H., Jr. *God and the Natural World: Religion and Science in Antebellum America*. Columbia: University of South Carolina Press, 1993.

Coon, Deborah. "Courtship with Anarchy: The Socio-Political Foundations of William James's Pragmatism." Ph.D. diss., Harvard University, 1988.

Corrington, Robert S. *An Introduction to C. S. Peirce: Philosopher, Semiotician, and Ecstatic Naturalist*. Lanham, Md.: Rowman and Littlefield Publishers, 1993.

Corti, Walter Robert, ed. *The Philosophy of William James*. Hamburg: Meiner, 1976.

Cortissoz, Royal. *John La Farge: A Memoir and a Study*. Boston: Houghton Mifflin and Co., 1911.

Cotkin, George. *Reluctant Modernism: American Thought and Culture, 1880–1900*. New York: Twayne, 1992.

———. *William James, Public Philosopher*. Baltimore: Johns Hopkins University Press, 1990.

Cott, Nancy F. *The Bonds of Womanhood: "Woman's Sphere" in New England, 1780–1835*. New Haven: Yale University Press, 1977.

Coulson, Thomas. *Joseph Henry: His Life and Times*. Princeton: Princeton University Press, 1950.

Cremin, Lawrence A. *American Education: The National Experience, 1783–1876*. New York: Harper and Row, 1980.

Croce, Paul Jerome. "From History of Science to Intellectual History: The Probabilistic Revolution and the Chance-Filled Universe of William James." *Intellectual History Newsletter* 13 (1991): 11–32.

———. "James's Early Scientific Education." *History of the Human Sciences* 8 (1995): 9–27.

———. "Money and Morality: The Life and Legacy of the First William James." *New York History* 68 (April 1987): 174–90.

———. "A Scientific Spiritualism: The Elder James's Adaptation of Emanuel Swedenborg." In *Swedenborg and His Influence*, edited by Erland J. Brock et al., pp. 251–62. Bryn Athyn, Pa.: Academy of the New Church, 1988.

———. "William James in Search of an Audience: Psychology Texts, the Popularization of Professionalism, and the 'Men of Science.'" Unpublished manuscript.

Crosby, Alfred W. *The Columbian Exchange: Biological and Cultural Consequences of 1492*. Westport, Conn.: Greenwood Press, 1972.

———. *Germs, Seeds, and Animals: Studies in Ecological History*. New York: M. E. Sharpe, 1993.

Crowther, J. A. *The Life and Discoveries of Michael Faraday*. New York: Macmillan, 1920.

Crunden, Robert M. *Ministers of Reform: The Progressives' Achievement in American Civilization, 1889–1920*. New York: Basic Books, 1982.

Cummings, Sherwood. *Mark Twain and Science: Adventures of a Mind*. Baton Rouge: Louisiana State University Press, 1988.

Danes, Gibson. "William Morris Hunt and His Newport Circle." *Magazine of Art* 43 (April 1950): 144–50.

Daniels, George H. *American Science in the Age of Jackson*. New York: Columbia University Press, 1968.

———, ed. *Darwinism Comes to America*. Waltam, Mass.: Blaisdell Publishing Co., 1968.

Danziger, Kurt. *Constructing the Subject: Historical Origins of Psychological Research*. New York: Cambridge University Press, 1990.

Daston, Lorraine. *Classical Probability in the Enlightenment*. Princeton: Princeton University Press, 1988.

David, F. D. *Games, Gods, and Gambling: The Origins and History of Probability and Statistical Ideas from the Earliest Times to the Newtonian Era.* New York: Hafner, 1962.

Dean, Bradley. "Henry D. Thoreau and Horace Greeley Exchange Letters on the 'Spontaneous Generation of Plants.'" *New England Quarterly* 66 (1993): 630–38.

De Beer, Gavin. *Charles Darwin: A Scientific Biography.* Garden City, N.Y.: Doubleday and Co., 1965.

Deck, Raymond H., Jr. "The Vastation of Henry James, Sr.: New Light on James's Theological Career." *Bulletin of Research in the Humanities* 83 (Summer 1980): pp. 216–47.

Deetz, James. *In Small Things Forgotten: The Archeology of Early American Life.* Garden City, N.Y.: Anchor Books, 1977.

Deledalle, Gérard. *Charles S. Peirce: An Intellectual Biography.* Translated by Susan Petrilli. Philadelphia: John Benjamins Publishing Co., 1990.

Desmond, Adrian. *The Politics of Evolution: Morphology, Medicine, and Reform in Radical London.* Chicago: University of Chicago Press, 1989.

Diamond, Jared. "The Arrow of Disease." *Discover* 13 (October 1992): 64–73.

Dickson, R. J. *Ulster Migration to Colonial America, 1718–1775.* London: Routledge and Kegan Paul, 1966.

Diehl, Carl. *Americans and German Scholarship, 1770–1870.* New Haven: Yale University Press, 1978.

Diggins, John Patrick. *The Promise of Pragmatism: Modernism and the Crisis of Knowledge and Authority.* Chicago: University of Chicago Press, 1994.

Dobbs, Betty Jo Teeter. *The Janus Faces of Genius: The Role of Alchemy in Newton's Thought.* New York: Cambridge University Press, 1991.

Dobzhansky, Theodosius. *Genetics and the Origin of Species.* New York: Columbia University Press, 1941.

Dolan, Jay P. *The American Catholic Experience: A History from Colonial Times to the Present.* Garden City, N.Y.: Doubleday and Co., 1985.

Donnelly, Margaret E., ed. *Reinterpreting the Legacy of William James.* Washington, D.C.: American Psychological Association, 1992.

Dooley, Patrick K. *Pragmatism as Humanism: The Philosophy of William James.* Chicago: Nelson-Hall, 1974.

Douglas, Ann. *The Feminization of American Culture.* New York: Alfred A. Knopf, 1977.

Doyle, David N., and Owen Dudley Edwards, eds. *America and Ireland, 1776–1976: The American Identity and the Irish Connection.* Westport, Conn.: Greenwood Press, 1980.

Ducasse, Curt J. "Francis Bacon's Philosophy of Science." In *Theories of Scientific Method: The Renaissance through the Nineteenth Century*, edited by Ralph M. Blake et al., pp. 50–74. New York: Gordon and Breach, 1989.

———. "John F. W. Herschel's Methods of Experimental Inquiry." In *Theories of Scientific Method: The Renaissance through the Nineteenth Century*, edited by Ralph M. Blake et al., pp. 153–80. New York: Gordon and Breach, 1989.

———. "William Whewell's Philosophy of Scientific Discovery." In *Theories of Scientific Method: The Renaissance through the Nineteenth Century*, edited by

Ralph M. Blake et al., pp. 185–217. New York: Gordon and Breach, 1989.

Dupree, A. Hunter. *Asa Gray: American Botanist, Friend of Darwin*. Baltimore: Johns Hopkins University Press, 1988 [1959].

———. "Christianity and the Scientific Community in the Age of Darwin." In *God and Nature: Historical Essays On the Encounter Between Christianity and Science*, edited by David C. Lindberg and Ronald L. Numbers, pp. 351–68. Berkeley: University of California Press, 1986.

———. "Jeffries Wyman's Views on Evolution." *Isis* 44 (1953): 243–46.

Early Science at Harvard: Innovators and Their Instruments, 1765–1865. Exhibit catalog. Cambridge: Fogg Art Museum, Harvard University, 1969.

Eco, Umberto. *A Theory of Semiotics*. Bloomington: Indiana University Press, 1976.

Eco, Umberto, and Thomas A. Sebeok, eds. *The Sign of Three: Dupin, Holmes, Peirce*. Bloomington: Indiana University Press, 1983.

Edel, Leon. *The Life of Henry James*. Vol. 1, *The Untried Years, 1843–1870*. New York: Avon Books, 1953.

Edie, James. *William James and Phenomenology*. Bloomington: Indiana University Press, 1987.

Eisele, Carolyn. "Charles S. Peirce." In *Dictionary of Scientific Biography*, edited by Charles C. Gillespie, vol. 10, pp. 482–88. New York: Charles Scribner's Sons, 1974.

———. "Peirce's Philosophy of Education in His Unpublished Mathematics Textbooks." In *Studies in the Philosophy of Charles Sanders Peirce*, edited by Edward C. Moore and Richard S. Robin, pp. 51–75. Amherst: University of Massachusetts Press, 1964.

Eisendrath, Craig. *Unifying Moments: The Psychological Philosophy of William James and Alfred North Whitehead*. Cambridge: Harvard University Press, 1971.

Elbert, Sarah. *A Hunger for Home: Louisa May Alcott and Little Women*. Philadelphia: Temple University Press, 1984.

Emerson, Edward Waldo. *The Early Years of the Saturday Club, 1855–1870*. Boston: Houghton Mifflin and Co., 1918.

Epstein, Barbara Leslie. *The Politics of Domesticity: Women, Evangelism, and Temperance in Nineteenth-Century America*. Middletown, Conn.: Wesleyan University Press, 1981.

Esposito, Joseph L. *Evolutionary Metaphysics: The Development of Peirce's Theory of Categories*. Athens: Ohio University Press, 1980.

Farrell, Betty G. *Elite Families: Class and Power in Nineteenth-Century Boston*. Albany: State University of New York Press, 1993.

Febvre, Lucien. *The Problem of Unbelief in the Sixteenth Century: The Religion of Rabelais*. Translated by Beatrice Gottlieb. Cambridge: Harvard University Press, 1982 [1942].

Fee, Elizabeth, and Daniel M. Fox. *AIDS: The Burdens of History*. Berkeley: University of California Press, 1988.

Feibleman, James K. *An Introduction to the Philosophy of Charles S. Peirce, Interpreted as a System*. Rev. ed. Cambridge: MIT Press, 1969 [1946].

Feinstein, Howard. *Becoming William James*. Ithaca: Cornell University Press, 1984.

———. "The Double in *The Autobiography* of the Elder Henry James." *American Imago* 31 (Fall 1974): 293–315.
Field, Michael, and Martin Golubitsky. *Symmetry in Chaos: A Search for Pattern in Mathematics, Art, and Nature*. New York: Oxford University Press, 1993.
Fisch, Max H. "Alexander Bain and the Genealogy of Pragmatism." *Journal of the History of Ideas* 15 (1954): 413–44.
———. "Justice Holmes, the Prediction Theory of the Law, and Pragmatism." *Journal of Philosophy* 39 (1942): 85–97.
———. "Peirce as Scientist, Mathematician, Historian, Logician, and Philosopher." In *Proceedings of the C. S. Peirce Bicentennial International Congress*, edited by Kenneth L. Ketner, pp. 13–31. Lubbock: Texas Tech Press, 1981.
———. "Peirce's Progress from Nominalism toward Realism." *Monist* 51 (1967): 159–78.
———. "Philosophical Clubs in Cambridge and Boston." *Coranto* 2 (Fall 1964): 12–23; 2 (Spring 1965): 12–25; and 3 (Fall 1965): 16–29.
———. "Supplement: A Chronicle of Pragmatism, 1865–1879." *Monist* 48 (1964): 441–66.
———. "Was There a Metaphysical Club in Cambridge?" In *Studies in the Philosophy of Charles Sanders Peirce*, edited by Edward C. Moore and Richard S. Robin, pp. 3–32. Amherst: University of Massachusetts Press, 1964.
Fisher, R. A. *The Genetic Theory of Natural Selection*. Oxford: Clarendon Press, 1930.
Fitzgerald, John J. *Peirce's Theory of Signs as Foundation for His Pragmatism*. The Hague: Mouton, 1966.
Fleming, Donald. *John William Draper and the Religion of Science*. Philadelphia: University of Pennsylvania Press, 1950.
Flournoy, Theodore. *The Philosophy of William James*. Translated by Edwin B. Holt and William James, Jr. London: Constable and Co., 1917. Originally published as *La Philosophie de William James* (Saint-Blaise: Foyer Solidariste, 1911).
Flower, Elizabeth, and Murray G. Murphey. *A History of Philosophy in America*. New York: Capricorn Books, 1977.
Fontinell, Eugene. *Self, God, and Immortality: A Jamesian Investigation*. Philadelphia: Temple University Press, 1986.
Ford, Marcus P. *William James's Philosophy: A New Perspective*. Amherst: University of Massachusetts Press, 1982.
Fox, Richard W., and T. J. Jackson Lears, eds. *The Power of Culture: Critical Essays in American History*. Chicago: University of Chicago Press, 1993.
Fox-Genovese, Elizabeth. *Within the Plantation Household: Black and White Women of the Old South*. Chapel Hill: University of North Carolina Press, 1988.
Frankenberry, Nancy. "Pragmatism, Truth, and Objectivity." *Soundings* 74 (Fall/Winter 1991): 509–24.
Fredrickson, George M. *The Black Image in the White Mind: The Debate on Afro-American Character and Destiny, 1817–1914*. New York: Harper and Row, 1971.

———. *The Inner Civil War: Northern Intellectuals and the Crisis of the Union.* New York: Harper and Row, 1968 [1965].

Freeman, Eugene, ed. *The Relevance of C. S. Peirce.* LaSalle, Ill.: Hegeler Institute, 1983.

Frei, Hans. *The Eclipse of Biblical Narrative: A Study in Eighteenth- and Nineteenth-Century Hermeneutics.* New Haven: Yale University Press, 1974.

Friedlander, Max J. *On Art and Connoiseurship.* Translated by Tancred Borenius. Boston: Beacon Press, 1960 [1942].

Fuller, Robert C. *Alternative Medicine and American Religious Life.* New York: Oxford University Press, 1989.

———. *Americans and the Unconscious.* New York: Oxford University Press, 1986.

Fuller, Steve. *Philosophy, Rhetoric, and the End of Knowledge.* Madison: University of Wisconsin Press, 1993.

———. *Social Epistemology.* Bloomington: Indiana University Press, 1988.

Fullinwider, S. P. "William James's Spiritual Crisis." *Historian* 38 (1975): 39–57.

Furner, Mary O. *Advocacy and Objectivity: A Crisis in the Professionalization of American Social Science, 1865–1905.* Lexington: University Press of Kentucky, 1975.

Gale, Barry G. *Evolution without Evidence: Charles Darwin and* The Origin of Species. Brighton, England: Harvester Press, 1982.

Galison, Peter L. "History, Philosophy, and the Central Metaphor." *Science in Context* 2 (1988): 197–212.

Gallie, W. B. *Peirce and Pragmatism.* Westport, Conn.: Greenwood Press, 1966.

Garber, Elizabeth, Stephen G. Brush, and C. W. F. Everitt, eds. *Maxwell on Molecules and Gases.* Cambridge: MIT Press, 1986.

Gavin, William Joseph. *William James and the Reinstatement of the Vague.* Philadelphia: Temple University Press, 1992.

Gay, Peter. *The Enlightenment: An Interpretation.* 2 vols. New York: Alfred A. Knopf, 1967.

Geertz, Clifford. *The Interpretation of Cultures: Selected Essays.* New York: Basic Books, 1973.

Ghiselin, Michael T. *The Triumph of the Darwinian Method.* Berkeley: University of California Press, 1969.

Gibian, Peter Andrew. "Oliver Wendell Holmes in the Conversation of His Culture." Ph.D. diss., Stanford University, 1987.

Giere, Ronald N., and Richard Westfall, eds. *Foundations of Scientific Method: The Nineteenth Century.* Bloomington: Indiana University Press, 1973.

Gigerenzer, Gerd, et al., eds. *The Empire of Chance: How Probability Changed Science and Everyday Life.* New York: Cambridge University Press, 1989.

Gilbert, James B. *Work without Salvation: America's Intellectuals and Industrial Alienation, 1880–1910.* Baltimore: Johns Hopkins University Press, 1977.

Gillespie, Neal C. *Charles Darwin and the Problem of Creation.* Chicago: University of Chicago Press, 1979.

Gillispie, Charles C. *Genesis and Geology: A Study in the Relation of Scientific*

Thought, Natural Theology, and Social Opinion in Great Britain, 1790–1850. New York: Harper and Row, 1959.

Ginzburg, Carlo. "Clues: Roots of an Evidential Paradigm." In *Myths, Emblems, Clues,* translated by John Tedeschi and Anne C. Tedeschi, pp. 96–125. London: Hutchinson Radius, 1990.

Giuffrida, Robert. "Chauncey Wright's Theory of Meaning." *Journal of the History of Philosophy* 16 (1978): 313–24.

Gladish, Robert W. *Swedenborg, Fourier, and the America of the 1840s.* Bryn Athyn, Pa.: Swedenborg Scientific Association, 1983.

Gladstone, J. H. *Michael Faraday.* New York: Chautauqua Press, 1872.

Gleick, James. *Chaos: Making a New Science.* New York: Penguin Books, 1987.

Glick, Thomas F., ed. *The Comparative Reception of Darwinism.* Austin: University of Texas Press, 1974.

Gottschalk, Stephen. *The Emergence of Christian Science in American Religious Life.* Berkeley: University of California Press, 1973.

Goudge, Thomas A. *The Thought of C. S. Peirce.* Toronto: University of Toronto Press, 1950.

Gould, Stephen Jay. "Darwin's Delay." In *Ever Since Darwin.* New York: Norton, 1977.

———. *The Mismeasure of Man.* New York: W. W. Norton, 1981.

Graham, George P. "William James and the Affirmation of God." Ph.D. diss., New York University, 1988.

Grattan, Clinton Hartley. *The Three Jameses: A Family of Minds, Henry James, Senior, William James, and Henry James.* New York: Longmans, Green and Co., 1932.

Green, E. R. R. "Ulster Emigrants' Letters." In *Essays in Scotch-Irish History,* edited by E. R. R. Green, pp. 88–100. London: Routledge and Kegan Paul; Atlantic Heights, N.J.: Humanities Press, 1969.

Green, Harvey. *The Light of the Home: An Intimate View of the Lives of Women in Victorian America.* New York: Pantheon Books, 1983.

Green, Ronald M. "Kant's Philosophy: An Overview." In *Kant and Kierkegaard: The Hidden Debt,* pp. 33–74. Albany: State University of New York Press, 1992.

Greene, John C. *Darwin and the Modern World View.* Baton Rouge: Louisiana State University Press, 1961.

Greenlee, Douglas. *Peirce's Concept of Sign.* The Hague: Mouton, 1973.

Grohskopf, Bernice. "'I'll Be a Farmer': Boyhood Letters of William James." *Virginia Quarterly Review* 66 (Fall 1990): 585–600.

Gross, Alan G. "The Origin of Species: Evolutionary Taxonomy as an Example of the Rhetoric of Science." In *The Rhetorical Turn: Invention and Persuasion in the Conduct of Inquiry,* edited by Herbert W. Simons, pp. 91–115. Chicago: University of Chicago Press, 1990.

———. *The Rhetoric of Science.* Cambridge: Harvard University Press, 1990.

Gruber, Howard E. *Darwin on Man.* New York: E. P. Dutton, 1974.

Guarneri, Carl J. *The Utopian Alternative: Fourierism in Nineteenth-Century America.* Ithaca: Cornell University Press, 1993.

Gunn, Giles. *Thinking across the American Grain: Ideology, Intellect, and the New Pragmatism*. Chicago: University of Chicago Press, 1992.

———, ed. *The Bible and American Arts and Letters*. Philadelphia: Fortress, 1983.

Guralnick, Stanley M. "Geology and Religion before Darwin: The Case of Edward Hitchcock, Theologian and Geologist (1793–1864)." *Isis* 63 (1972): 529–43.

———. *Science and the Ante-Bellum American College*. Philadelphia: American Philosophical Society, 1975.

Habegger, Alfred. *Henry James and the "Woman Business."* New York: Cambridge University Press, 1989.

Hacking, Ian. *The Emergence of Probabilities: A Philosophical Study of Early Ideas about Probability, Induction, and Statistical Inference*. New York: Cambridge University Press, 1975.

———. "Nineteenth-Century Cracks in the Concept of Determinism." *Journal of the History of Ideas* 4 (1983): 455–75.

———. *The Taming of Chance*. New York: Cambridge University Press, 1990.

Hall, David D. "The Victorian Connection." In *Victorian America*, edited by Daniel Walker Howe, pp. 81–94. Philadelphia: University of Pennsylvania Press, 1976.

Hall, Peter Dobkin. *The Organization of American Culture, 1700–1900: Private Institutions, Elites, and the Origins of American Nationality*. New York: New York University Press, 1982.

Hallengren, Anders. *The Code of Concord: Emerson's Search for Universal Laws*. Stockholm: Almqvist and Wiksell International, 1994.

Halttunen, Karen. "'Through the Cracked and Fragmented Self': William James and *The Turn of the Screw*." *American Quarterly* 40 (December 1988): 472–90.

Handy, Robert T. *A Christian America: Protestant Hopes and Historical Realities*. Rev. ed. New York: Oxford University Press, 1984.

Harlow, Virginia. *Thomas Sergeant Perry: A Biography*. Durham: Duke University Press, 1950.

Haskell, Thomas. *The Emergence of Professional Social Science: The American Social Science Association and the Nineteenth-Century Crisis of Authority*. Urbana: University of Illinois Press, 1977.

———, ed. *The Authority of Experts: Studies in History and Theory*. Bloomington: Indiana University Press, 1984.

Hastings, Katharine. "William James of Albany, N.Y. and His Descendants." *The New York Genealogical and Biographical Record* 55 (April 1924): 101–19.

Hatch, Nathan O. *The Democratization of American Christianity*. New Haven: Yale University Press, 1989.

Hatch, Nathan O., and Mark A. Noll, eds. *The Bible in America: Essays in Cultural History*. New York: Oxford University Press, 1982.

Hawkins, Hugh. *Between Harvard and America: The Educational Leadership of Charles W. Eliot*. New York: Oxford University Press, 1972.

Heilenberger, Michael, et al., eds. *Probability since 1800: Interdisciplinary Studies of Scientific Development*. Bielefeld: B. Kleine, 1983.

Herbert, Sandra. "Darwin, Malthus, and Selection." *Journal of the History of Biology* 4 (1971): 209–18.

Higgins, John E. "The Young John Fiske, 1842–1874." Ph.D. diss., Harvard University, 1960.
Higham, John, and Paul Conkin, eds. *New Directions in American Intellectual History*. Baltimore: Johns Hopkins University Press, 1979.
Himmelfarb, Gertrude. *Darwin and the Darwinian Revolution*. New York: W. W. Norton, 1962.
Hislop, Codman. *Eliphalet Nott*. Middletown, Conn.: Wesleyan University Press, 1971.
Hodge, M. J. S. "Law, Cause, Chance, Adaptation, and Species in Darwinian Theory in the 1830s, with a Postscript on the 1930s." In *Probability since 1800: Interdisciplinary Studies of Scientific Development*, edited by Michael Heilenberger et al., pp. 287–329. Bielefeld: B. Kleine, 1983.
———. "Natural Selection as a Causal, Empirical, and Probabilistic Theory." In *The Probabilistic Revolution*. Vol. 2, *Ideas in Science*, edited by Lorenz Krüger et al., pp. 233–66. Cambridge: MIT Press, 1987.
Hoffert, Sylvia D. *Private Matters: American Attitudes toward Childbearing and Infant Nurture in the Urban North, 1800–1860*. Champaign: University of Illinois Press, 1989.
Hofstadter, Richard. *Social Darwinism in American Thought*. Rev. ed. Boston: Beacon Press, 1955.
Hollinger, David A. "Justification by Verification: The Scientific Challenge to the Moral Authority of Christianity in Modern America." In *Religion and Twentieth-Century American Intellectual Life*, edited by Michael J. Lacey, pp. 116–35. New York: Cambridge University Press, 1989.
———. "Tonic Destruction: The Ethics of Science in Modern United States History." Paper for the Conference on Religion and the History of American Intellectual Life, Woodrow Wilson Center, Washington, D.C., March 13–14, 1986.
———. "The Problem of Pragmatism in American History." *Journal of American History* 67 (June 1980): 88–107.
———. "William James and the Culture of Inquiry." In *In the American Province*, pp. 3–22. Bloomington: Indiana University Press, 1985.
Hookway, Christopher. *Peirce*. London: Routledge and Kegan Paul, 1985.
Hoopes, James. *Consciousness in New England: From Puritanism and Ideas to Psychoanalysis and Semiotic*. Baltimore: Johns Hopkins University Press, 1989.
———. "Objectivity *and* Relativism Affirmed: Historical Knowledge and the Philosophy of Charles S. Peirce." *American Historical Review* 98 (1993): 1545–55.
Hoover, Dwight W. *Henry James, Sr. and the Religion of Community*. Grand Rapids: William B. Eerdmans Publishing Co., 1969.
Horsman, Reginald. *Race and Manifest Destiny: The Origins of American Anglo-Saxonism*. Cambridge: Harvard University Press, 1981.
Houghton, Walter E. *The Victorian Frame of Mind, 1830–1870*. New Haven: Yale University Press, 1957.
Hovenkamp, Herbert. *Science and Religion in America, 1800–1860*. Philadelphia: University of Pennsylvania Press, 1978.

Howe, Daniel Walker, ed. *Victorian America*. Philadelphia: University of Pennsylvania Press, 1976.

Howe, Mark A. DeWolfe. "Dr. Holmes, the Friend and Neighbor." *Yale Review*, n.s., 7 (April 1918): 562–78.

Hull, David L. *Darwin and His Critics: The Reception of Darwin's Theory of Evolution by the Scientific Community*. Chicago: University of Chicago Press, 1973.

———. *Philosophy of Biology*. Englewood Cliffs, N.J.: Prentice-Hall, 1974.

Hunt, William Morris. *On Painting and Drawing*. New York: Dover, 1976. Reprint of *Talks on Art*. 2 vols. Boston: Houghton Mifflin and Co., 1896, 1898.

Hurth, Elizabeth. *In His Name: Comparative Studies in the Quest for the Historical Jesus*. New York: Peter Lang, 1989.

Hutchison, William. *The Modernist Impulse in American Protestantism*. Cambridge: Harvard University Press, 1976.

———. *The Transcendentalist Ministers: Church Reform in the New England Renaissance*. New Haven: Yale University Press, 1959.

———, ed. *Between the Times: The Travail of the Protestant Establishment in America, 1900–1960*. New York: Cambridge University Press, 1989.

Huxley, Julian. *Evolution: The Modern Synthesis*. New York: Harper and Brothers, 1943.

Imbrie, John, and Katherine Palmer Imbrie. *Ice Ages: Solving the Mystery*. Short Hills, N.J.: Enslow Publishers, 1979.

James, Henry, III [William James's son]. *Charles William Eliot: President of Harvard University, 1869–1909*. 2 vols. Boston: Houghton Mifflin and Co., 1930.

James, Mary Ann. *Elites in Conflict: The Antebellum Clash over the Dudley Observatory*. New Brunswick: Rutgers University Press, 1987.

Jensen, Joan M. *Loosening the Bonds: Mid-Atlantic Farm Women, 1750–1850*. New Haven: Yale University Press, 1986.

Johnson, Paul E. *A Shopkeeper's Millennium: Society and Revivals in Rochester, New York, 1815–1837*. New York: Hill and Wang, 1978.

Jones, Maldwyn A. "Ulster Migration, 1783–1815." In *Essays in Scotch-Irish History*, edited by E. R. R. Green, pp. 47–68. London: Routledge and Kegan Paul; New York: Humanities Press, 1969.

Jones, William J. *Christ in the Camp: or, Religion in Lee's Army*. Richmond: B. F. Johnson and Co., 1887.

Jonsson, Inge. *Emanuel Swedenborg*. Translated by Catherine Djurklou. New York: Twayne Publishers, 1971.

Juster, Susan. "'In a Different Voice': Male and Female Narratives of Religious Conversion in Post-Revolutionary America." *American Quarterly* 41 (March 1989): 34–62.

Kaestle, Carl F. *Pillars of the Republic: Common Schools and American Society, 1780–1860*. New York: Hill and Wang, 1983.

Kasson, John F. *Civilizing the Machine: Technology and Republican Values in America, 1776–1900*. New York: Penguin Books, 1976.

Katzenbach, Nicolas deB. "Holmes, Peirce, and Legal Pragmatism." *Yale Law Review* 84 (April 1975): 1123–40.

Keeney, Elizabeth B. *The Botanizers: Amateur Scientists in Nineteenth-Century America*. Chapel Hill: University of North Carolina Press, 1992.

Kellert, Stephen H. *In the Wake of Chaos: Unpredictable Order in Dynamical Systems*. Chicago: University of Chicago Press, 1993.

Kelley, Cornelia Pulsifer. *The Early Development of Henry James*. Rev. ed. Urbana: University of Illinois Press, 1965.

Kelley, Mary. *Private Woman, Public Stage: Literary Domesticity in Nineteenth-Century America*. New York: Oxford University Press, 1984.

Kennedy, Gail. "The Pragmatic Naturalism of Chauncey Wright." In *Studies in the History of Ideas*, edited by the Philosophy Department of Columbia University, vol. 3, pp. 477–503. New York: Columbia University Press, 1935; New York: AMS Press, 1970.

Kenney, Alice P. *The Gansevoorts of Albany*. Syracuse: Syracuse University Press, 1969.

Kessler-Harris, Alice. "Cultural Locations: Positioning American Studies in the Great Debate." *American Quarterly* 44 (September 1992): 299–312.

Ketner, Kenneth Laine. *Peirce and Contemporary Thought: Philosophical Inquiries*. New York: Fordham University Press, 1994.

———. "Peirce as an Interesting Failure." In *Proceedings of the C. S. Peirce Bicentennial International Congress*, edited by Kenneth Laine Ketner et al., pp. 55–58. Lubbock: Texas Tech Press, 1981.

Ketner, Kenneth Laine, et al., eds. *Proceedings of the C. S. Peirce Bicentennial International Congress*. Lubbock: Texas Tech Press, 1981.

King, John Owen. *The Iron of Melancholy: Structures of Spiritual Conversion in America from the Puritan Conscience to Victorian Neurosis*. Middletown, Conn.: Wesleyan University Press, 1983.

Kloppenberg, James T. *Uncertain Victory: Social Democracy and Progressivism in European and American Thought, 1870–1920*. New York: Oxford University Press, 1986.

Knight, Thomas S. *Charles Peirce*. New York: Twayne, 1965.

Kohlstedt, Sally Gregory. *The Formation of the American Scientific Community: The American Association for the Advancement of Science, 1848–1860*. Urbana: University of Illinois Press, 1976.

———. "The Nineteenth-Century Amateur Tradition: The Case of the Boston Society of Natural History." In *Science and Its Public: The Changing Relationship*, edited by Gerald Holton and William A. Blanpied, pp. 173–90. Boston and Dordrecht: D. Reidel Publishing Co., 1976.

———. "Parlors, Primers, and Public Schooling: Education for Science in Nineteenth-Century America." *Isis* 81 (September 1990): 425–45.

Kohn, David. "Darwin's Principle of Divergence as Internal Dialogue." In *The Darwinian Heritage*, edited by Kohn, pp. 245–57. Princeton: Princeton University Press, 1985.

———. "Theories to Work By: Rejected Theories, Reproduction, and Darwin's Path

to Natural Selection." *Studies in the History of Biology* 4 (1980): 67–170.
———, ed. *The Darwinian Heritage*. Princeton: Princeton University Press, 1985.
Kottler, Malcolm Jay. "Charles Darwin's Biological Species Concept and Theory of Geographic Speciation: The Transmutation Notebooks." *Annals of Science* 35 (1978): 275–97.
Krolikoswki, Walter P. "The Peircean Vir." In *Studies in the Philosophy of Charles Sanders Peirce*, 2d ser., edited by Edward C. Moore and Richard S. Robin, pp. 257–70. Amherst: University of Massachusetts Press, 1964.
Krüger, Lorenz, et al., eds. *The Probabilistic Revolution*, 2 vols. Vol. 1, *Ideas in History*. Vol. 2, *Ideas in Science*. Cambridge: MIT Press, 1987.
Kuhn, Thomas. *The Structure of Scientific Revolutions*. 2nd ed. Chicago: University of Chicago Press, 1962.
Kuklick, Bruce. *Churchmen and Philosophers: From Jonathan Edwards to John Dewey*. New Haven: Yale University Press, 1985.
———. *The Rise of American Philosophy: Cambridge, Massachusetts, 1860–1930*. New Haven: Yale University Press, 1977.
Kuritz, Hyman. "The Popularization of Science in Nineteenth-Century America." *History of Education Quarterly* 21 (Fall 1981): 259–74.
Ladd-Franklin, Christine. "Charles S. Peirce at the Johns Hopkins." *The Journal of Philosophy, Psychology, and Scientific Methods* 13 (December 1916): 715–22.
Larrabee, Harold A. "The Flight of Henry James the First." *New England Quarterly* 10 (December 1937): 774–75.
———. "The Jameses: Financier, Heretic, Philosopher." *American Scholar* 1 (1932): 401–13.
The Late Landscapes of William Morris Hunt. Exhibit catalog, University of Maryland Art Gallery, January 15–February 22, and Albany Institute of History and Art, March 13–April 25, 1976. College Park: University of Maryland Press, 1976.
Laudan, Laurens. "Peirce and the Trivialization of the Self-Correcting Thesis." In *Foundations of Scientific Method in the Nineteenth Century*, edited by Ronald Giere and Richard Westfall, pp. 275–306. Bloomington: Indiana University Press, 1973.
Law, John, and R. J. Williams. "Putting Facts Together: A Study of Scientific Persuasion." *Social Studies of Science* 12 (1982): 535–58.
Lears, T. J. Jackson. *No Place of Grace: Anti-Modernism and the Transformation of American Culture, 1880–1920*. New York: Pantheon Books, 1981.
Leary, David E. "William James and the Art of Human Understanding." *American Psychologist* 47 (February 1992): 152–60.
Lee, Gerald. *Joseph Neef: The Americanization of Pestalozzianism*. Tuscaloosa: University of Alabama Press, 1978.
Lenoir, Timothy. "The Göttingen School and the Development of Transcendental Naturphilosophie in the Romantic Era." In *Studies in the History of Biology*, edited by William Coleman and Camille Limoges, vol. 6, pp. 148–61. Baltimore: Johns Hopkins University Press, 1981.
Lentricchia, Frank. *Ariel and the Police: Michel Foucault, William James, Wallace Stevens*. Madison: University of Wisconsin Press, 1988.

———. "On the Ideologies of Poetic Modernism, 1890–1913: The Example of William James." In *Reconstructing American Literary History*, edited by Sacvan Bercovitch, pp. 220–49. Cambridge: Harvard University Press, 1986.

———. "The Return of William James." *Cultural Critique* 4 (Fall 1986): 5–31.

Lenzen, Victor. "An Unpublished Scientific Monograph by C. S. Peirce." *Transactions of the Charles S. Peirce Society* 5 (Winter 1969): 5–24.

Leverenz, David. *Manhood and the American Renaissance*. Ithaca: Cornell University Press, 1989.

Levinson, Henry S. *The Religious Investigations of William James*. Chapel Hill: University of North Carolina Press, 1981.

———. *Science, Metaphysics, and the Chance of Salvation: An Interpretation of the Thought of William James*. Missoula, Mont.: Scholars Press, 1978.

Lewis, R. W. B. *The American Adam: Innocence, Tragedy, and Tradition in the Nineteenth Century*. Chicago: University of Chicago Press, 1955.

———. *The Jameses: A Family Narrative*. New York: Farrar, Straus, and Giroux, 1991.

Leyburn, James G. *The Scotch-Irish: A Social History*. Chapel Hill: University of North Carolina Press, 1962.

Lightman, Bernard. *The Origins of Agnosticism: Victorian Unbelief and the Limits of Knowledge*. Baltimore: Johns Hopkins University Press, 1987.

Limerick, Patricia Nelson. *The Legacy of Conquest: The Unbroken Past of the American West*. New York: W. W. Norton, 1987.

Lindberg, David C., and Ronald L. Numbers, eds. *God and Nature: Historical Essays on the Encounter between Christianity and Science*. Berkeley: University of California Press, 1986.

Livingston, James. *Pragmatism and the Political Economy of Cultural Revolution, 1850–1940*. Chapel Hill: University of North Carolina Press, 1994.

Livingstone, David N. *Darwin's Forgotten Defenders: The Encounter between Evangelical Theology and Evolutionary Thought*. Grand Rapids: William B. Eerdmans, 1987.

———. *Nathaniel Southgate Shaler and the Culture of American Science*. Tuscaloosa: University of Alabama Press, 1987.

Love, James Lee. *The Lawrence Scientific School in Harvard University, 1847–1906*. Burlington, N.C.: n.p., 1944.

Lovejoy, Arthur O. "Milton and the Paradox of the Fortunate Fall." In *Essays in the History of Ideas*. Baltimore: Johns Hopkins University Press, 1948.

———. *The Thirteen Pragmatisms and Other Essays*. Baltimore: Johns Hopkins University Press, 1963.

Lurie, Edward. *Louis Agassiz: A Life in Science*. 2nd ed. Baltimore: Johns Hopkins University Press, 1988 [1960].

McCardell, John. *The Idea of a Southern Nation: Southern Nationalists and Southern Nationalism, 1830–1860*. New York: W. W. Norton, 1979.

McCaughey, Robert A. "The Transformation of American Academic Life: Harvard University, 1821–1892." *Perspectives in American History* 8 (1974): 237–332.

McDannell, Colleen. *The Christian Home in Victorian America, 1840–1900.* Bloomington: Indiana University Press, 1986.

McDermott, John J. *The Culture of Experience: Philosophical Essays in the American Grain.* New York: New York University Press, 1976.

———. *Streams of Experience: Reflections on the History and Philosophy of American Culture.* Amherst: University of Massachusetts Press, 1986.

McGiffert, Michael. "Christian Darwinism: The Partnership of Asa Gray and George Frederick Wright, 1874–1881." Ph.D. diss., Yale University, 1958.

McKinney, H. Lewis. *Wallace and Natural Selection.* New Haven: Yale University Press, 1972.

Madden, Edward H. "The Cambridge Septem." *Harvard Alumni Bulletin* 57 (1955): 310–15.

———. "Chance and Counterfacts in Wright and Peirce." *Review of Metaphysics* 9 (1956): 420–32.

———. "Chauncey Wright and the American Functionalists." In *Theories of Scientific Method: The Renaissance through the Nineteenth Century,* edited by Ralph M. Blake et al., pp. 263–81. Seattle: University of Washington Press, 1960; New York: Gordon and Breach, 1989.

———. *Chauncey Wright and the Foundations of Pragmatism.* Seattle: University of Washington Press, 1963.

———. "Chauncey Wright: Forgotten American Philosopher." *American Quarterly* 4 (Spring 1952): 25–34.

———. *Civil Disobedience and Moral Law in Nineteenth-Century American Philosophy.* Seattle: University of Washington Press, 1968.

Madden, Marian C., and Edward H. Madden. "The Psychosomatic Illness of William James." *Thought* 54 (December 1979): 367–92.

Maher, Jane. *Biography of Broken Fortunes: Wilkie and Bob, Brothers of William, Henry, and Alice James.* Hamden, Conn.: Archon Books, 1986.

Mahowald, Mary B. "A Majority Perspective: Feminine and Feminist Elements in American Philosophy." *Cross Currents* 36 (1953): 410–17.

———. "Peirce's Concepts of God and Religion." *Transactions of the Charles S. Peirce Society* 12 (1976): 367–77.

Manier, Edward. *The Young Darwin and His Cultural Circle: A Study of the Influences which Shaped the Language and Logic of the Theory of Natural Selection.* Boston: D. Reidel, 1977.

Marcell, David. *Progress and Pragmatism: James, Dewey, and Beard, and the American Idea of Progress.* Westport, Conn.: Greenwood Press, 1974.

Marcou, Jules. *Life, Letters, and Works of Louis Agassiz.* 2 vols. New York: Macmillan, 1895.

Marsden, George M. *The Evangelical Mind and the New School Presbyterian Experience.* New Haven: Yale University Press, 1970.

———. *Fundamentalism and American Culture: The Shaping of Twentieth-Century Evangelicalism, 1870–1925.* New York: Oxford University Press, 1980.

Martin, David. *A General Theory of Secularization.* New York: Harper and Row, 1978.

Martin, Terence. *The Instructed Vision: Scottish Common Sense Philosophy and the Origins of American Fiction.* Bloomington: Indiana University Press, 1961.
Marty, Martin E. *The Modern Schism: Three Paths to the Secular.* New York: Harper and Row, 1969.
Matthiessen, F. O. *The James Family: A Group Biography.* New York: Vintage Books, 1980 [1947].
Mayr, Ernst. *Animal Species and Evolution.* Cambridge: Harvard University Press, 1963.
———. "Darwin and Natural Selection: How Darwin May Have Discovered His Highly Unconventional Theory." *American Scientist* 65 (1977): 321–77.
Mayr, Ernst, and William Provine. *The Evolutionary Synthesis.* Cambridge: Harvard University Press, 1980.
Mechling, Jay, ed. "Special Section: William James and the Philosophical Foundations for the Study of Everyday Life." *Western Folklore* 44 (October 1985): 301–32.
Merz, John Theodore. *A History of European Thought in the Nineteenth Century.* 4 vols. Edinburgh: William Blackwood and Sons, 1896–1914.
Meyer, Donald H. *The Instructed Conscience: The Shaping of the American National Ethic.* Philadelphia: University of Pennsylvania Press, 1972.
Midgley, Mary. *Evolution as a Religion: Strange Hopes and Stranger Fears.* New York: Methuen, 1985.
Miller, Howard S. *Dollars for Research: Science and Its Patrons in Nineteenth-Century America.* Seattle: University of Washington Press, 1970.
Miller, Kerby A. *Emigrants and Exiles: Ireland and the Irish Exodus to North America.* New York: Oxford University Press, 1985.
Miller, Larry. "William James and Twentieth-Century Ethnic Thought." *American Quarterly* 31 (Fall 1979): 533–55.
Miller, Perry. *The New England Mind: The Seventeenth Century.* New York: Macmillan, 1939.
Millet, Frank D. "Mr. Hunt's Teaching." *Atlantic Monthly* 46 (August 1880): 189–92.
Mills, C. Wright. *Sociology and Pragmatism: The Higher Learning in America.* Edited by Irving Louis Horowitz. New York: Paine-Whitman Publishers, 1964.
Mitchell, W. J. T., ed. *Against Theory: Literary Studies and the New Pragmatism.* Chicago: University of Chicago Press, 1985.
Molella, Arthur P., and Nathan Reingold. "Theorists and Ingenious Mechanics: Joseph Henry Defines Science." *Science Studies* 3 (1973): 323–51.
Monaghan, Peter. "The Strange Saga of the Biography of a Brilliant Man." *Chronicle of Higher Education* 39 (March 3, 1993): A6–A7 and A14.
Monroe, Will S. *History of the Pestalozzian Movement in the United States.* New York: Arno Press, 1969.
Moore, Edward C., and Richard S. Robin, eds. *Studies in the Philosophy of Charles Sanders Peirce*, 2d ser. Amherst: University of Massachusetts Press, 1964.
Moore, James R. *The Post-Darwinian Controversies: A Study of the Protes-*

tant Struggle to Come to Terms with Darwin in Great Britain and America, 1870–1900. New York: Cambridge University Press, 1979.
Moore, James R., and Adrian J. Desmond. *Darwin: The Life of a Tormented Evolutionist*. New York: Warner Books, 1992.
Moore, R. Laurence. "Insiders and Outsiders in American Historical Narrative and American History." *American Historical Review* 87 (April 1982): 390–412.
———. *Religious Outsiders and the Making of Americans*. New York: Oxford University Press, 1986.
Morgan, Robert, with John Barton. *Biblical Interpretation*. New York: Oxford University Press, 1988.
Morrison, Samuel Eliot. *The Development of Harvard University since the Inauguration of President Eliot, 1869–1929*. Cambridge: Harvard University Press, 1930.
———. *Three Centuries of Harvard, 1636–1936*. Cambridge: Harvard University Press, 1936.
Morse, John Torrey, Jr. *The Life and Letters of Oliver Wendell Holmes*. 2 vols. Boston: Houghton, Mifflin and Co., 1896.
Moyer, Albert E. *A Scientist's Voice in American Culture: Simon Newcomb and the Rhetoric of Scientific Method*. Berkeley: University of California Press, 1992.
Murphey, Murray G. *The Development of Peirce's Philosophy*. Cambridge: Harvard University Press, 1961.
Murphy, John P. *Pragmatism: From Peirce to Davidson*. Boulder: Westview Press, 1990.
Myers, Gerald E. *William James: His Life and Thought*. New Haven: Yale University Press, 1986.
Neuhaus, Richard J. *The Naked Public Square: Religion and Democracy in America*. Grand Rapids: William B. Eerdmans, 1984.
Niebuhr, H. Richard. *Christ and Culture*. New York: Harper and Row, 1951.
Noll, Mark A. "Common Sense Traditions and American Evangelical Thought." *American Quarterly* 37 (Summer 1985): 217–38.
———, ed. *The Princeton Theology: Scripture, Science, and Theological Method from Archibald Alexander to Benjamin Breckinridge Warfield, 1812–1921*. Grand Rapids: Baker Books, 1983
Novak, Barbara. *American Painting of the Nineteenth Century: Realism, Idealism, and the American Experience*. New York: Harper and Row, 1979.
Numbers, Ronald L. *Creation by Natural Law: Laplace's Nebular Hypothesis in American Thought*. Seattle: University of Washington Press, 1977.
———. "George Frederick Wright: From Christian Darwinist to Fundamentalist." *Isis* 79 (December 1988): 624–45.
O'Connell, Robert J. *William James on the Courage to Believe*. New York: Fordham University Press, 1984.
Oleson, Alexandra, and Sanborn Brown, eds. *The Pursuit of Knowledge in the Early Republic: American Scientific and Learned Societies from Colonial Times to the Civil War*. Baltimore: Johns Hopkins University Press, 1976.

Olin, Doris, ed. *William James: "Pragmatism" in Focus*. New York: Routledge, Kegan and Paul, 1992.

Olsen, Rodney. *Dancing in Chains: The Youth of William Dean Howells*. New York: New York University Press, 1991.

Orange, Donna M. *Peirce's Conception of God: A Developmental Study*. Lubbock, Tex.: Institute for Studies in Pragmaticism, 1984.

Ospovat, Dov. *The Development of Darwin's Theory: Natural History, Natural Theology, and Natural Selection, 1838–1859*. Cambridge: Cambridge University Press, 1981.

Palmer, George Herbert. "William James." *Harvard Graduates' Magazine* 29 (September 1920): 29–34.

Parker, Gail T. *The History of the Mind Cure in New England*. Hanover: University Press of New England, 1975.

Peden, W. Creighton. *The Philosopher of Free Religion: Francis Ellingwood Abbot*. New York: Peter Lang, 1992.

Pelikan, Jaroslav. *Spirit versus Structure: Luther and the Institutions of the Church*. New York: Harper and Row, 1968.

Perry, Lewis. *Boats against the Current: American Culture between Revolution and Modernity, 1820–1860*. New York: Oxford University Press, 1993.

Perry, Ralph Barton. "Religion versus Morality according to the Elder Henry James." *International Journal of Ethics* 42 (1932): 289–303.

———. *The Thought and Character of William James*. 2 vols. Boston: Little, Brown and Co., 1935.

———. *The Thought and Character of William James, Briefer Version*. New York: Braziller, 1954 [1948].

Perry, Ronald W., Michael K. Lindell, and Marjorie Green. "Threat Perception and Public Response to Volcano Hazard." *Journal of Social Psychology* 116 (April 1982): 199–204.

Persons, Stow. *Free Religion: An American Faith*. New Haven: Yale University Press, 1947.

Peterson, Sven Richard. "Benjamin Peirce: Mathematician and Philosopher." *Journal of the History of Ideas* 16 (1955): 89–112.

———. "William James: The Formative Years, 1842–1884." Ph.D. diss., Columbia University, 1954.

Pfeifer, Edward. "United States." In *The Comparative Reception of Darwinism*, edited by Thomas F. Glick. Austin: University of Texas Press, 1974.

Plate, Robert. *The Dinosaur Hunters: Othniel C. Marsh and Edward D. Cope*. New York: D. McKay, 1964.

Poirier, Richard. *Poetry and Pragmatism*. Cambridge: Harvard University Press, 1992.

Porter, Charlotte M. *The Eagle's Nest: Natural History and American Ideas, 1812–1842*. University: University of Alabama Press, 1986.

Porter, Theodore. *The Rise of Statistical Thinking, 1820–1900*. Princeton: Princeton University Press, 1986.

Posnock, Ross. *The Trial of Curiosity: Henry James, William James, and the Challenge of Modernity*. New York: Oxford University Press, 1991.
Potter, Vincent G. *Charles S. Peirce: On Norms and Ideals*. Amherst: University of Massachusetts Press, 1967.
Pratt, James Bissett. *The Psychology of Religious Belief*. New York: Macmillan, 1907.
———. "The Religious Philosophy of William James." *Hibbert Journal* 10 (1911): 225–34.
Priebe, Cedric Joseph, III. "William James's Application of Darwinian Theory to Consciousness and Emotion in the *Principles*." Senior thesis, Harvard University, 1984.
Provine, William. *The Origins of Theoretical Population Genetics*. Chicago: University of Chicago Press, 1971.
Prucha, Francis Paul. *American Indian Policy in Crisis: Christian Reformers and the Indian, 1865–1900*. Norman: University of Oklahoma Press, 1976.
———, ed. *Americanizing the American Indians: Writings of the "Friends of the Indian," 1880–1900*. Cambridge: Harvard University Press, 1973.
Rabinowitz, Richard. *The Spiritual Self in Everyday Life: The Transformation of Personal Religious Experience in Nineteenth-Century New England*. Boston: Northeastern University Press, 1989.
Raboteau, Albert J. *Slave Religion: The "Invisible Institution" in the Antebellum South*. New York: Oxford University Press, 1978.
Ramsey, Bennett. *Submitting to Freedom: The Religious Vision of William James*. New York: Oxford University Press, 1993.
Raposa, Michael L. *Peirce's Philosophy of Religion*. Bloomington: Indiana University Press, 1989.
Reilly, Francis E. *Charles Peirce's Theory of Scientific Method*. New York: Fordham University Press, 1970.
Reingold, Nathan. "Joseph Henry." *The Dictionary of Scientific Biography*, edited by Charles C. Gillispie, vol. 6, pp. 277–81. New York: Charles Scribner's Sons, 1972.
———. "The New York State Roots of Joseph Henry's National Career." *New York History* 54 (1973): 133–44.
———, ed. *Science in Nineteenth-Century America: A Documentary History*. Chicago: University of Chicago Press, 1964.
———, ed. *The Sciences in the American Context: New Perspectives*. Washington, D.C.: Smithsonian Institution Press, 1979.
Riasanovsky, Nicholas V. *The Teaching of Charles Fourier*. Berkeley: University of California Press, 1969.
Richards, Leonard L. *"Gentlemen of Property and Standing": Anti-Abolitionist Mobs in Jacksonian America*. New York: Oxford University Press, 1970.
Richards, Robert J. *Darwin and the Emergence of Evolutionary Theories of Mind and Behavior*. Chicago: University of Chicago Press, 1987.
———. "Why Darwin Delayed, or Interesting Problems and Models in the History of Science." *Journal of the History of the Behavioral Sciences* 19 (1983): 45–53.

Richardson, Robert J., Jr. *Thoreau: A Life of the Mind*. Berkeley: University of California Press, 1986.

Rivinus, E. F., and E. M. Youssef. *Spencer Baird of the Smithsonian*. Washington, D.C.: Smithsonian Institution Press, 1992.

Roberts, Jon. *Darwinism and the Divine in America: Protestant Intellectuals and Organic Evolution, 1859–1900*. Madison: University of Wisconsin Press, 1988.

Rockmore, Tom, and Beth J. Singer, eds. *Antifoundationalism Old and New*. Philadelphia: Temple University Press, 1992.

Rodgers, Andrew Denny. *John Torrey: A Story of North American Botany*. Princeton: Princeton University Press, 1942.

Rodgers, Daniel. "Republicanism: The Career of a Concept." *Journal of American History* 79 (June 1992): 11–38.

Rorabaugh, W. J. *The Alcoholic Republic: An American Tradition*. New York: Oxford University Press, 1979.

Rorty, Richard. *Consequences of Pragmatism (Essays: 1972–1980)*. Minneapolis: University of Minnesota Press, 1982.

———. *Contingency, Irony, and Solidarity*. New York: Cambridge University Press, 1989.

Rosenberg, Charles. *The Cholera Years: The United States in 1832, 1849, and 1866*. Chicago: University of Chicago Press, 1987.

Rosenberg, Rosalind. *Beyond Separate Spheres: The Intellectual Roots of Modern Feminism*. New Haven: Yale University Press, 1982.

Ross, Dorothy. *The Origins of American Social Science*. New York: Cambridge University Press, 1991.

Rossiter, Margaret. "Benjamin Silliman and the Lowell Institute: The Popularization of Science in Nineteenth-Century America." *New England Quarterly* 44 (1971): 602–26.

———. "Louis Agassiz and the Lawrence Scientific School." Undergraduate thesis, Radcliffe College, 1966.

Roth, John K. *Freedom and Morality: The Ethics of William James*. Philadelphia: Westminster Press, 1969.

Roth, Robert J. *British Empiricism and American Pragmatism: New Directions and Neglected Arguments*. New York: Fordham University Press, 1993.

———. "Is Peirce's Pragmatism Anti-Jamesian?" *International Philosophical Quarterly* 5 (December 1965): 541–63.

Rowley, William E. "The Irish Aristocracy of Albany, 1798–1878." *New York History* 52 (July 1971): 275–84.

Rudolph, Frederick. *The American College and University: A History*. New York: Vintage Books, 1962.

Rudwick, Martin. *The Meaning of Fossils: Episodes in the History of Palaeontology*. 2nd ed. New York: Science History Publications, 1976.

Ruf, Frederick J. *The Creation of Chaos: William James and the Stylistic Making of a Disorderly World*. Albany: State University of New York Press, 1991.

Ruse, Michael. "Charles Darwin's Theory of Evolution: An Analysis." *Journal of the History of Biology* 8 (Fall 1975): 219–42.

———. "Darwin and Artificial Selection." *Journal of the History of Ideas* 36 (1975): 339–50.

———. *The Darwinian Revolution: Science Red in Tooth and Claw.* Chicago: University of Chicago Press, 1979.

———. *Darwinism Defended: A Guide to the Evolution Controversies.* Reading, Mass.: Addison-Wesley, 1982.

———. "Darwin's Debt to Philosophy: An Examination of the Influence of the Philosophical Ideas of John F. W. Herschel and William Whewell on the Development of Charles Darwin's Theory of Evolution." *Studies in the History and Philosophy of Science* 6 (1975): 159–81.

Russett, Cynthia Eagle. *Darwin in America: The Intellectual Response, 1865–1912.* San Francisco: W. H. Freeman and Co., 1976.

Ryan, Mary P. *Cradle of the Middle Class: The Family in Oneida County, New York, 1790–1865.* New York: Cambridge University Press, 1981.

Saarinen, Thomas F., and James L. Sell. *Warning and Response to the Mount St. Helen's Eruption.* Albany: State University of New York Press, 1985.

Schrager, Amy. *Prophetic Woman: Anne Hutchison and the Problem of Dissent in the Literature of New England.* Berkeley: University of California Press, 1987.

Schull, Jonathan. "Selection—James's Principal Principle." In *Reinterpreting the Legacy of William James*, edited by Margaret E. Donnelly, pp. 139–51. Washington, D.C.: American Psychological Association, 1992.

Schwartz, Sanford. *The Matrix of Modernism: Pound, Eliot, and Early Twentieth-Century Thought.* Princeton: Princeton University Press, 1985.

Schweber, Silvan S. "Aspects of Probabilistic Thought in Great Britain during the Nineteenth Century: Darwin and Maxwell." In *Probability since 1800: Interdisciplinary Studies of Scientific Development*, edited by Michael Heilenberger et al., pp. 41–96. Bielefeld: B. Kleine, 1983.

———. "The Origin of the *Origin* Revisited." *Journal of the History of Biology* 10 (1977): 229–316.

Schwehn, Mark S. "Making the World: William James and the Life of the Mind." *Harvard Library Bulletin* 30 (October 1982): 426–54.

Scott, Joan W. *Gender and the Politics of History.* New York: Columbia University Press, 1988.

Seelye, John. " 'Rational Exultation': The Erie Canal Celebration." *Proceedings of the American Antiquarian Society* 94 (October 1984): 241–67.

Seigfried, Charlene Haddock. *Chaos and Context: A Study in William James.* Athens: Ohio University Press, 1978.

———. "Extending the Darwinian Model: James's Struggle with Royce and Spencer." *Idealistic Studies* 14 (September 1984): 259–72.

———. "Poetic Invention and Scientific Observation: James's Model of 'Sympathetic Concrete Observation.' " *Transactions of the Charles S. Peirce Society* 26 (1990): 115–30.

———. *William James's Radical Reconstruction of Philosophy.* Albany: State University of New York Press, 1990.

———, ed. "Special Issue: Feminism and Pragmatism." *Hypatia: A Journal of Feminist Philosophy* 8 (Spring 1993).

Shalhope, Robert E. "Republicanism and Early American Historiography." *William and Mary Quarterly*, 3d ser., 39 (1982): 334–56.

———. "Toward a Republican Synthesis: The Emergence of an Understanding of Republicanism in American Historiography." *William and Mary Quarterly*, 3d ser., 29 (1972): 49–80.

Shannon, Martha A. S. *Boston Days of William Morris Hunt*. Boston: Marshall Jones, Co., 1923.

Sharples, S. P. "Some Reminiscences of the Lawrence Scientific School." *Harvard Graduate's Magazine* 26 (June 1918): 532–40.

Sheets-Pyenson, Susan. *Cathedrals of Science: The Development of Colonial Natural History Museums during the Late Nineteenth Century*. Montreal: McGill-Queen's University Press, 1988.

Shilts, Randy. *And the Band Played On: People, Politics, and the AIDS Epidemic*. New York: St. Martin's Press, 1987.

Showalter, Elaine. Introduction to *Alternative Alcott*, by Louisa May Alcott. New Brunswick: Rutgers University Press, 1988.

Simons, Herbert W., ed. *The Rhetorical Turn: Invention and Persuasion in the Conduct of Inquiry*. Chicago: University of Chicago Press, 1990.

Sinclair, Bruce. "Americans Abroad: Science and Cultural Nationalism in the Early Nineteenth Century." In *The Sciences in the American Context: New Perspectives*, edited by Nathan Reingold, pp. 35–53. Washington, D.C.: Smithsonian Institution Press, 1979.

Skagestad, Peter. *The Road of Inquiry: Charles Peirce's Pragmatic Realism*. New York: Columbia University Press, 1981.

Sklar, Kathryn Kish. *Catharine Beecher: A Study in American Domesticity*. New York: W. W. Norton, 1973.

Skocpol, Theda. *Protecting Soldiers and Mothers: The Politics of Social Provision in the United States, 1870s to 1920s*. Cambridge: Harvard University Press, 1992.

Slotten, Hugh Richard. *Patronage, Practice, and the Culture of American Science: Alexander Dallas Bache and the United States Coast Survey*. New York: Cambridge University Press, 1994.

Small, Miriam Rossiter. *Oliver Wendell Holmes*. New York: Twayne, 1962.

Smith, Carleton Sprague. "William James in Brazil." In *Four Papers Presented in the Institute for Brazilian Studies, Vanderbilt University*, pp. 97–138. Westport, Conn.: Greenwood Press, 1951.

Smith, Crosbie, and M. Norton Wise. *Energy and Empire: A Biographical Study of Lord Kelvin*. New York: Cambridge University Press, 1989.

Smith, Gary Scott. *The Seeds of Secularization: Calvinism, Culture, and Pluralism in America, 1870–1915*. Grand Rapids: Christian University Press; William B. Eerdmans Publishing Co., 1985.

Smith, Harriette Knight. *The History of the Lowell Institute*. Boston: Lamson, Wolffe and Co., 1898.

Smith, John E. *America's Philosophical Vision*. Chicago: University of Chicago Press, 1992.
——— . *Purpose and Thought: The Meaning of Pragmatism*. New Haven: Yale University Press, 1978.
——— . "Two Defenses of Freedom: Peirce and James." In *The Idea of Freedom in American Philosophy*, edited by Donald Lee, pp. 51–64. New Orleans: Tulane University Press, 1987.
Sontag, Susan. "Scenes from a Play: Alice in Bed." *New Yorker* 69 (May 31, 1993): 142–49.
Spalding, John Howard. *Introduction to Swedenborg's Religious Thought*. New York: Swedenborg Publishing Association, 1966.
Spears, Monroe K. "William James as Cultural Hero." In *American Ambitions: Selected Essays on Literary and Cultural Themes*, pp. 10–25. Baltimore: Johns Hopkins University Press, 1987.
Spicer, Edward. *Cycles of Conquest: The Impact of Spain, Mexico, and the United States on the Indians of the Southwest, 1533–1960*. Tucson: University of Arizona Press, 1976.
Stanton, William R. *The Leopard's Spots: Scientific Attitudes toward Race in America, 1815–1859*. Chicago: University of Chicago Press, 1960.
Stevenson, Louise. *Scholarly Means to Evangelical Ends: The New Haven Scholars and the Transformation of Higher Learning in America, 1830–1890*. Baltimore: Johns Hopkins University Press, 1986.
Stewart, W. Christopher. "Peirce on the Role of Authority in Science." *Transactions of the Charles S. Peirce Society* 30 (Spring 1994): 297–326.
Stoever, William. *A Faire and Easie Way to Heaven: Covenant Theology and Antinomianism in Early Massachusetts*. Middletown, Conn.: Wesleyan University Press, 1978.
Story, Ronald. *The Forging of an Aristocracy: Harvard and the Boston Upper Class, 1800–1860*. Middletown, Conn.: Wesleyan University Press, 1980.
Strickland, Charles. "A Transcendentalist Father: The Childrearing Practices of Bronson Alcott." *Perspectives in American History* 3 (1969): 5–71.
Strouse, Jean. *Alice James: A Biography*. Boston: Houghton Mifflin Co., 1980.
Strout, Cushing. "William James and the Twice-Born Sick Soul." In *The Veracious Imagination: Essays on American History, Literature, and Biography*, pp. 199–222. Middletown, Conn.: Wesleyan University Press, 1981.
Suckiel, Ellen K. *The Pragmatic Philosophy of William James*. Notre Dame: University of Notre Dame Press, 1982.
Sulloway, Frank J. "Darwin's Early Intellectual Development: An Overview of the 'Beagle' Voyage (1831–1836)." In *The Darwinian Heritage*, edited by David Kohn, pp. 121–54. Princeton: Princeton University Press, 1985.
Taylor, Eugene I. "Peirce and James Reconsidered." Paper presented at the Charles Sanders Peirce Sesquicentennial Congress, Harvard University, September 4, 1989.
——— . "Peirce and Swedenborg." *Studia Swedenborgiana* 6 (June 1986): 25–51.
——— . "The Swedenborgian and Transcendentalist Roots of William James's Reli-

gious Perspective." Division 6, American Psychological Association meeting, Los Angeles, Calif., August 1981.

———. "William James on Darwin: An Evolutionary Theory of Consciousness." *Annals of the New York Academy of Science* 602 (September 1990): 7–33.

———. *William James on Exceptional Mental States: The 1896 Lowell Lectures.* New York: Charles Scribner's Sons, 1983.

Teller, James David. *Louis Agassiz: Scientist Teacher.* Columbus: Ohio State University Press, 1947.

Tharp, Louise Hall. *Adventurous Alliance: The Story of the Agassiz Family of Boston.* Boston: Little, Brown and Co., 1959.

Thayer, Horace Standish. *Meaning and Action: A Critical History of Pragmatism.* Indianapolis: Bobbs-Merrill, 1968.

Thomas, John L. *Alternative America: Henry George, Edward Bellamy, Henry Demarest Lloyd and the Adversary Tradition.* Cambridge: Harvard University Press, 1983.

Thomas, Keith. *Religion and the Decline of Magic: Studies in Popular Beliefs in Sixteenth and Seventeenth Century England.* New York: Charles Scribner's Sons, 1971.

Thompson, Manley H. *The Pragmatic Philosophy of C. S. Peirce.* Chicago: University of Chicago Press, 1953.

Thornton, Tamara Plakins. *Cultivating Gentlemen: The Meaning of Country Life among the Boston Elite, 1785–1860.* New Haven: Yale University Press, 1989.

Tilton, Eleanor M. *Amiable Autocrat: A Biography of Oliver Wendell Holmes.* New York: Henry Schuman, 1947.

Toulmin, Stephen. *Human Understanding: The Collective Use and Evolution of Concepts.* Princeton: Princeton University Press, 1972.

Trammel, Richard Louis. "Charles Sanders Peirce and Henry James the Elder." *Transactions of the Charles Sanders Peirce Society* 9 (Fall 1973): 202–20.

Trobridge, George. *Swedenborg: Life and Teaching.* New York: Swedenborg Foundation, 1944.

Turley, Peter T. "Peirce on Chance." *Transactions of the Charles S. Peirce Society* 5 (Fall 1969): 243–54.

———. *Peirce's Cosmology.* New York: Philosophical Library, 1977.

Turner, Frank M. *Between Science and Religion: The Reaction to Scientific Naturalism in Late Victorian England.* New Haven: Yale University Press, 1974.

Turner, James. *Without God, without Creed: The Origins of Unbelief in America.* Baltimore: Johns Hopkins University Press, 1985.

Tursman, Richard. *Peirce's Theory of Scientific Discovery: A System of Logic Conceived as Semiotic.* Bloomington: Indiana University Press, 1987.

Tyler, Alice Felt. *Freedom's Ferment: Phases of American Social History from the Colonial Period to the Outbreak of the Civil War.* Minneapolis: University of Minnesota Press, 1944.

Vanden Burdt, Robert J. *The Religious Philosophy of William James.* Chicago: Nelson-Hall, 1981.

Van Dusen, Wilson Miles. *The Presence of Other Worlds: The Psychological/*

Spiritual Findings of Emanuel Swedenborg. New York: Harper and Row, 1974.

Verano, John W., and Douglas Ubelaker, eds. *Disease and Demography in the Americas.* Washington, D.C.: Smithsonian Institution Press, 1992.

Veysey, Laurence R. *The Emergence of the American University.* Chicago: University of Chicago Press, 1970.

Vorzimmer, Peter. "Darwin, Malthus, and the Theory of Natural Selection." *Journal of the History of Ideas* 30 (1969): 527–42.

Warren, Austin. *The Elder Henry James.* New York: Macmillan, 1934.

Watts, Steven. *The Republic Reborn: War and the Making of Liberal America, 1790–1820.* Baltimore: Johns Hopkins University Press, 1989.

Weeks, Edward. *The Lowells and Their Institute.* Boston: Little, Brown and Co., 1966.

Weiss, Paul. "Charles Sanders Peirce." In *Dictionary of American Biography*, edited by Dumas Malone, vol. 14, pp. 398–403. New York: Charles Scribner's Sons, 1934.

Wells, Harry K. *Pragmatism: Philosophy of Imperialism.* New York: International Publishers, 1954.

Welter, Barbara. "The Cult of True Womanhood, 1820–1860." *American Quarterly* 18 (Summer 1966): 151–74.

West, Cornel. *The American Evasion of Philosophy: A Genealogy of Pragmatism.* Madison: University of Wisconsin Press, 1989.

Westbrook, Robert. *John Dewey and American Democracy.* Ithaca: Cornell University Press, 1991.

Westfall, Richard S. *Science and Religion in Seventeenth-Century England.* Ann Arbor: University of Michigan Press, 1973 [1957].

White, William. *The Life of Emanuel Swedenborg, together with a Brief Synopsis of his Writings, both Philosophical and Theological.* Philadelphia: Lippincott, 1879.

Wiener, Philip P. *Evolution and the Founders of Pragmatism.* Cambridge: Harvard University Press, 1949.

———. "Lovejoy's Rôle in American Philosophy." In *Studies in Intellectual History*, edited by the Johns Hopkins History of Ideas Club, pp. 161–73. Baltimore: Johns Hopkins University Press, 1953.

Wild, John. *The Radical Empiricism of William James.* Garden City, N.Y.: Doubleday and Co., 1969.

Wilkins, Walter J. *Science and Religious Thought: A Darwinian Case Study.* Ann Arbor: UMI Research Press, 1987.

Wilshire, Bruce. *William James's Phenomenology: A Study of "The Principles of Psychology."* Bloomington: Indiana University Press, 1968.

Wilson, Daniel J. *Science, Community, and the Transformation of American Philosophy, 1860–1930.* Chicago: University of Chicago Press, 1990.

Winsor, Mary P. *Reading the Shape of Nature: Comparative Zoology at the Agassiz Museum.* Chicago: University of Chicago Press, 1991.

Wolf, Eric. *Europe and the People without History.* Berkeley: University of California Press, 1982.

Wood, Allen W. *Kant's Moral Religion.* Ithaca: Cornell University Press, 1970.

Wood, Gordon S. *The Creation of the American Republic, 1776–1787.* Chapel Hill: University of North Carolina Press, 1969.

———. *The Radicalness of the American Revolution.* New York: Alfred A. Knopf, 1992.

Woodrow, James. "Evolution." In *American Philosophical Addresses, 1700–1900,* edited by Joseph L. Blau, pp. 491–513. New York: Columbia University Press, 1946.

Woodward, William R. "James's Evolutionary Epistemology: 'Necessary Truths and the Effects of Experience.'" In *Reinterpreting the Legacy of William James,* edited by Margaret E. Donnelly, pp. 153–69. Washington, D.C.: American Psychological Association, 1992.

Wyatt-Brown, Bertram. *Southern Honor: Ethics and Behavior in the Old South.* New York: Oxford University Press, 1982.

Yeazell, Ruth Bernard. *The Death and Letters of Alice James.* Berkeley: University of California Press, 1981.

Young, Frederic. *The Philosophy of Henry James, Senior.* New York: Bookman Associates, 1951.

Young, Robert M. "Darwin's Metaphor: Does Nature Select?" In *Darwin's Metaphor: Nature's Place in Victorian Culture,* pp. 79–125. Cambridge: Cambridge University Press, 1985.

———. "The Historiographic and Ideological Contexts of the Nineteenth-Century Debate on Man's Place in Nature." In *Changing Perspectives in the History of Science,* edited by M. Teich and R. M. Young. London: Heinemann, 1973.

INDEX

Abbot, Francis Ellingwood, 152, 170–71, 285 (n. 69)
Academy of Natural Sciences, 260 (n. 4)
African-Americans, 20, 139–40, 185–86, 240 (n. 44), 277 (n. 113)
Agassiz, Alexander, 124
Agassiz, Elizabeth Carey, 114, 119, 162, 271 (n. 6)
Agassiz, Louis, xii, 79, 87, 91, 97–99, 102, 112–25 passim, 130, 133, 136, 138, 139, 142, 164, 165, 202, 227, 252 (n. 33), 261 (n. 16), 267 (n. 67), 271 (n. 6), 276 (n. 95), 295 (n. 134); on Darwinism, 111, 121–24, 126, 129, 134, 140, 143, 145–46, 147, 273–74 (n. 43), 274 (nn. 46, 48); and plans of creation, 115, 116–17, 272 (n. 20); early career, 115–16; glacial theory, 116–17, 117–18, 120, 122–23, 123, 128, 272 (nn. 17, 19); move to the United States, 117–18; and special creation, 118, 139–40; and Museum of Comparative Zoology, 118–19, 120, 121, 123, 138, 272 (n. 28), 274 (n. 51); as teacher, 119–20, 124, 126, 143, 162, 273 (n. 31), 274 (n. 51); as public figure, 119–20, 272 (n. 25), 273 (n. 34); as popularizer, 120, 122
Agnosticism, 107–8, 134, 152, 163, 170, 172, 175, 228, 268 (n. 80), 296–97 (n. 1)
AIDS, 8
Albanese, Catherine, 244 (n. 23)
Alcott, Abigail May, 246 (n. 40)
Alcott, Bronson, 246 (n. 40), 247 (n. 48)
Alcott, Louisa May, 246 (n. 40)
Allen, Gay Wilson, 40, 43

Amateur science, 89, 96, 135, 260 (n. 8), 263 (n. 30)
Amazon River. *See* Brazil
American Academy of Arts and Sciences, 128, 138, 161, 202
American Association for the Advancement of Science, 120
American Journal of Science, 89, 260 (n. 8)
Analogy, arguments based on, 91, 101, 103, 111, 122, 129, 131, 261 (n. 17), 265 (n. 50), 266 (n. 57)
Anatomy, 138, 144
Anderson, James William, 246 (n. 41), 247 (n. 45), 255 (n. 1), 259 (n. 50)
Anthropology, 139
Antinomianism, 55, 70, 250 (n. 4), 252 (n. 24)
Antireligious beliefs. *See* Secularism
Appleton, W. H., 206
Appleton Chapel, 229
Astronomy, 167
Atheism, 107, 132, 133
Atlantic Monthly, 112, 161, 294 (n. 108)

Bache, Alexander Dallas, 91, 119–20, 261 (n. 16)
Baconianism, 90–91, 102, 120, 127, 139, 140, 141, 168, 260 (n. 11), 261 (n. 16),
Bain, Alexander, 152, 208–9, 294 (n. 121)
Basalla, George, 292 (n. 108)
Bee cells, 139, 141, 277 (n. 112), 278 (n. 115)
Beecher, Henry Ward, 236–37 (n. 13)
Bentham, Jeremy, 152
Berra, Yogi, 11
Bjork, Daniel, 238 (n. 24), 248 (nn. 54,

64), 256 (n. 1), 257 (nn. 25, 29), 258–59 (n. 49), 274 (n. 53)
Boltzmann, Ludwig, 100, 102
Boston elites, 95–96, 112–14, 117–18, 120–21, 122, 126, 152, 153, 158–60, 177, 178, 181, 263 (n. 30), 270–71 (n. 2), 271 (n. 5)
Boston Society of Natural History, 139, 141
Botany, 96, 101, 114, 125–27, 263 (n. 30)
Boulogne, France, 46, 68
Bowen, Francis, 102, 132
Bowler, Peter, 259 (n. 2)
Boydston, Jeanne, 246 (n. 37)
Brazil, 116, 123–24, 143
Brent, Joseph, 286 (nn. 2, 8, 11), 289 (n. 46), 291 (n. 67)
Brewster, David, 261 (n. 14)
Brooks, Van Wyck, 280 (n. 8)
Brown, Richard, 288 (n. 33)
Bryant, William Cullen, 192, 291 (n. 61)
Büchner, Ludwig, 108, 137, 270 (nn. 82, 83), 286 (n. 74)
Buckley, Michael, 239 (n. 38)
Burnham, John, 275 (n. 65)
Bushnell, Horace, 276 (n. 93)
Butler, Jon, 248 (n. 59)
Butler, Joseph, 261 (n. 17)

Calvinism, 144–45, 246 (n. 42), 250 (n. 8), 251 (n. 15), 278 (n. 130)
Cambridge Scientific Club, 128
Capitalism, 28–29
Carey, Elizabeth. *See* Agassiz, Elizabeth Carey
Carter, Paul, 11
Cashdollar, Charles, 236 (n. 11), 238 (nn. 25, 30), 239 (n. 42), 261 (n. 18), 279 (n. 2), 282 (n. 25), 293 (n. 97)
Catastrophism, 116, 122, 272 (n. 17). *See also* Agassiz, Louis: glacial theory
Certainty, 3, 4, 7, 13, 14–15, 16, 19, 32, 36, 48, 50, 55, 57, 86, 91, 94, 96, 102, 106, 107–10, 123, 129, 131, 132, 137, 138, 142, 143, 153, 154, 165–68, 169, 174, 175, 183, 190, 196–97, 203, 205, 210, 212, 213, 216, 219–23, 225–26, 228–30, 235 (n. 6), 237–38 (n. 23), 285 (n. 70), 292 (n. 78), 296 (n. 142)
Chadwick, Owen, 238 (n. 25)
Chambers, Robert, 93, 129, 273–74 (n. 43)
Chance, 7, 9, 131, 166, 167, 195, 198, 200, 218, 237–38 (n. 23), 292 (n. 82)
Chaos, 7
Character education, 280 (n. 8), 285 (n. 65)
Chauvenet, William, 296 (n. 141)
Chemistry, 134–38, 184, 186, 276–77 (nn. 99, 100)
Chichester, Mrs., 251–52 (n. 22)
Cholera, 35–36
Christian Darwinism, 132–33. *See also* Science and religion: harmony between
Civil War (American), 87, 118, 152, 179, 225, 230, 258 (n. 36)
Clifford, W. K., 12, 172
Clubs, intellectual and social. *See* Boston elites
Coast and Geodetic Survey, the United States, 120, 181, 201, 287 (n. 14)
Cohen, Morris, 293 (n. 92), 294 (n. 114)
Coigniet, Leon, 77
Cole, Thomas, 78 (n. 33)
Colleges, antebellum, 244 (n. 26), 245 (n. 29)
Commager, Henry Steele, 11
Common Sense philosophy, 90, 92, 154, 162, 260–61 (n. 12), 262 (n. 19)
Comte, Auguste, 62, 187, 203, 238 (n. 30), 279 (n. 2), 282 (n. 25), 293 (n. 97)
Conchology, 114

Congress, United States, 120, 273 (n. 34)
Consensus history, 11
Conser, Walter, 259–60 (n. 3), 260 (n. 9), 262 (nn. 19, 21)
Conversion experiences, 53
Convictions. See Religion: convictions
Coon, Deborah, 240 (n. 50)
Cope, Edward, 284 (n. 52)
Corrington, Robert, 287 (n. 17), 289 (n. 44)
Cosmic Evolutionism, 107, 268–69 (n. 74)
Cotkin, George, 237 (n. 14)
Cott, Nancy, 246 (n. 37)
Cranch, C. P., 113
Crunden, Robert, 249 (n. 78)
Cultural biography, xi, 18
Cultural epistemology, 21
Cultural history, 3, 10, 11, 18–19, 20, 236 (n. 7)
Cuvier, Georges, 115–16, 125, 271–72 (n. 15), 272 (n. 17)

Dana, James Dwight, 92, 97, 142
Darwinism, xii, 10, 62, 85–88, 89, 93, 93, 99–110 passim, 111, 112, 139–48, 152, 155, 157, 160, 163, 164, 168–70, 197, 198–201, 226–27, 237–38 (nn. 23, 24), 252 (n. 33), 255 (n. 59), 259–60 (nn. 2, 3), 283 (n. 30), 284 (n. 51), 285 (n. 69); persuasiveness of, 99–104, 110, 264 (n. 44); scientific responses to, 100, 101–2, 105–6, 109, 119, 121–25, 130–31, 135, 142, 143, 145–46, 148, 264–65 (nn. 46, 47), 273 (n. 31), 274 (nn. 46, 48), 292 (n. 86); as deterministic, 100, 102; as argued in *Origin of Species*, 100–101, 104, 105–6, 120, 122, 140; methods of, 100–105, 110, 115–16, 168, 199–201, 204, 215–16, 221, 259 (n. 2), 263–64 (n. 40), 265 (nn. 47, 49), 266 (nn. 52, 53, 57), 267 (n. 63); use of analogy in, 101, 103, 265 (n. 50), 266 (n. 57); as developed before *Origin of Species*, 103–4, 127–29, 142, 264 (n. 43), 266–67 (n. 58), 267 (nn. 59, 60, 63); denial of morality in, 104, 143, 267 (n. 64); neglect of religion in, 104–5, 107, 143; probabilistic arguments of, 105–6, 127–29, 142, 155, 165–68, 198–200, 227, 265 (nn. 47, 49), 267 (n. 65), 268 (n. 72), 285 (n. 70); and neo-Darwinism, 106, 130–31, 166, 199, 268 (nn. 70, 72), 273 (n. 31), 275–76 (n. 80); religious responses to, 107–10, 110; evidence for species development in, 139, 140–41, 278 (nn. 115, 132). See also Agassiz, Louis: on Darwinism; Gray, Asa: on Darwinism; James, William: on Darwinism
Daston, Lorraine, 7, 296 (n. 141)
Delacroix, Eugène, 77, 257 (n. 29)
Democratic Republicans, 88
De Morgan, Augustus, 284 (n. 56)
Descartes, René, 211, 213, 214, 235 (n. 6), 294–95 (nn. 128, 129)
Design theory, 174–75. See also Natural theology
Determinism, 7, 17
Dewey, John, ix, 5, 17
Dewey, Orville, 15, 88–89
Dom Pedro II, 124
Draper, John, 187
Du Bois, W. E. B., 241 (n. 57)
Dudley Observatory, 263 (n. 32)
Dupin, C. Auguste, 1–2, 3
Dupree, A. Hunter, 126, 259 (n. 2)
Durand, Asher B., 258 (n. 33)

Economic laws, 167
Edel, Leon, 249 (n. 69)
Eliot, Charles W., xii, 98, 113, 134–38, 147, 202, 227, 263 (nn. 37, 39), 276 (nn. 95, 96), 276–77 (n. 99), 277 (n. 100), 279 (n. 136)

Ellis, Rufus, 158, 172
Embryology, 101, 141
Emerson, Edward Waldo, 40, 44
Emerson, Ralph Waldo, 40, 52, 56, 57, 60, 79, 112, 113, 114, 205, 249 (n. 73), 253 (n. 37), 254–55 (n. 56), 271 (n. 11)
Empiricism, 100–103, 136–37, 138–42. *See also* Baconianism
Enlightenment, the European, 92, 94, 108, 153–54, 252 (n. 24), 262–63 (n. 28)
Episcopalian church, 143, 189
Erie Canal, 28–30, 243 (n. 10)
European expansion, 2, 14–15
Evangelical religion, 11, 15, 56–57, 93–95
Everett, Edward, 158
Evolution. *See* Darwinism
Experts. *See* Professionalism

Fact gathering, scientific. *See* Baconianism; Empiricism
Fairfield Academy, 125
Faraday, Michael, 51, 76, 257 (n. 27)
Fay, Harriet Melusina (Zina), 181, 189, 286–87 (n. 12)
Febvre, Lucien, 239 (n. 37)
Federalists, 88
Feinstein, Howard, 242 (n. 1), 244 (n. 24), 245 (nn. 33, 35), 247–48 (nn. 51, 54), 249 (n. 70), 251 (n. 19), 255–56 (n. 1), 257 (nn. 25, 29)
Finney, Charles Grandison, 56
Fisch, Max, 286–87 (n. 12)
Fiske, John, 102, 152, 274 (n. 46)
Florida, 118, 122
Forbes, Edward, 116
Fortunate fall, 59–60, 253 (n. 46)
Fourier, Charles, 46, 60–61, 70, 253–54 (n. 50), 254 (nn. 51, 52)
Fox, Richard Wightman, 236–37 (n. 13)
French Revolution, 88
Froissy, Juliette, 181
Fuller, Steve, 241 (n. 60)

Galton, Francis, 216, 265 (n. 49)
Geertz, Clifford, 3
Genetics, 130–31
Geography, 101
Geology, 92, 101
German idealism, 89, 154, 162, 260 (n. 9), 262 (n. 19)
Ghiselin, Michael, 265 (n. 47)
Gibbes, Lewis, 90
Gillespie, Neal, 264 (n. 40)
Giuffrida, Robert, 283 (n. 29), 284 (n. 61)
God, 171, 174, 179, 186–87, 188, 189, 190, 194, 196, 204, 218–19, 229; of the gaps, 130; as creator, 132–33, 136. *See also* Agassiz, Louis: and special creation; James, Henry, Sr.: theory of creation
Goethe, Johann Wolfgang von, 115, 271 (n. 11)
Graduate education, 98, 119, 135. *See also* Agassiz, Louis: as teacher; Lawrence Scientific School
Gray, Asa, xii, 93, 98, 124–34, 136, 138, 139, 140, 163, 273 (n. 37), 273–74 (n. 43), 276 (n. 95), 277 (n. 112); on the flora of Japan, 111, 127–29, 275 (nn. 69, 71, 72); on the neutrality of science and religion, 125, 133–34, 136, 227, 276 (n. 93); early career, 125–27, 278 (n. 66); as teacher, 126–27; and natural system of classification, 127; as public figure, 127–29, 134; support of Darwinism, 127–31, 140, 141, 147; criticism of Darwinism, 131–33
Gray, Jane Loring, 126
Great Awakenings, 93–94, 179
Greek drama, 282 (n. 22)
Green, Nicholas St. John, 152
Gurney, E. W., 159, 161, 162, 172

Habegger, Alfred, 246 (n. 39), 251 (n. 15), 253 (n. 47), 254 (n. 52), 255 (n. 1)

Hacking, Ian, 7, 200
Hall, David, 271 (n. 2)
Hall, Peter Dobkin, 238 (n. 30), 280 (n. 8)
Hallengren, Anders, 253 (n. 37)
Hamilton, William, 162–63, 282 (n. 23)
Hampton-Sidney College, 138
Hare, Robert, 261 (n. 14)
Harmonial piety. *See* New Thought
Hart, Albert Bushnell, 241 (n. 57)
Harvard Medical School, 138, 146–47, 279 (n. 136)
Harvard University, 152, 153, 158–59, 161, 162, 178, 181, 189, 201, 202, 241 (n. 57). *See also* Graduate Education; Harvard Medical School; Harvard University Herbarium; Lawrence Scientific School
Harvard University Herbarium, 274 (n. 56)
Hawthorne, Nathaniel, 179
Henry, Joseph, 51, 62–65, 90, 91, 95, 120, 261 (n. 16)
Herbert, Sandra, 265 (n. 50)
Herod, 32
Herschel, William, 105, 135, 266 (nn. 52, 53, 57)
Higher criticism, 94
Himmelfarb, Gertrude, 263 (n. 40)
History of science, 6–10, 16–17
Hitchcock, Edward, 92
Hodge, M. J. S., 268 (n. 72)
Hollinger, David, 11–12, 16, 187
Holmes, Abiel, 144–45
Holmes, Oliver Wendell, Jr., 146, 152, 166, 283 (n. 38)
Holmes, Oliver Wendell, Sr., xii, 113, 114, 123, 134, 138, 139, 144–47, 227, 278 (n. 130), 278–79 (n. 134)
Hoopes, James, 239 (n. 38), 289 (n. 38), 295 (n. 129)
Horses, structural development of, 141
Horsford, Eban Norton, 288 (n. 22)
Hovenkamp, Herbert, 239 (n. 39)

Howells, William Dean, 55, 247 (n. 48)
Hull, David, 264 (nn. 40, 46), 265 (n. 47), 266 (n. 53)
Humbolt, Alexander von, 115, 271 (n. 12)
Hunt, William Morris, 73–74, 77–81, 113, 258 (n. 45)
Hutchinson, Anne, 250 (n. 4)
Huxley, Thomas Henry, 12, 100, 145, 172
Hypothesis formation, 90, 98, 101–4, 121–22, 130, 137, 141, 142, 164, 168, 183, 197, 201, 204, 220–22, 227
Hypothetico-deductive method, 103, 266 (n. 57)

Illinois, 28
Induction, 100, 102, 121, 129, 164, 166, 193, 195, 203, 217, 218, 219–22, 266 (n. 53), 295 (n. 134), 296 (n. 142)
Intellectual history, 11, 15
Irish immigration, 28, 30, 242–43 (n. 4), 243 (n. 12)

Jackson, James, Sr., 144
James, Alice, 18, 25, 45, 202, 247 (n. 50), 249 (n. 70), 249–50 (n. 82), 278 (n. 127)
James, Augustus, 245 (n. 32)
James, Catherine Barber, 30, 31, 35
James, Garth Wilkinson, 25, 44, 112, 258 (n. 36)
James, Henry, Jr., 25, 26, 27, 39, 42, 44, 45, 47, 54, 67, 67–69, 77, 79, 112, 147, 157, 180–81, 249 (n. 69), 256 (n. 6), 258 (n. 36)
James, Henry, Sr., x, xii, 17, 140; philosophy, 25, 52, 55–60, 69, 74; child rearing, 25–26, 35, 37–38, 39–49, 58–59, 67, 72–75, 77, 78–79, 85, 137, 144, 226, 242 (n. 1), 247 (n. 48), 248 (n. 57), 255–56 (n. 1); childhood, 27, 32, 39, 50, 242 (n. 1),

244 (n. 24), 247–48 (n. 51), 248 (n. 64); spiritualism, 31, 32–33, 35, 37, 40, 41, 42–43, 47–48, 49–66 passim, 87, 120, 145, 164, 188, 189, 227, 242 (n. 1), 246 (n. 39), 289 (n. 46), 290 (n. 48); use of alcohol, 33; rebelliousness, 33–34, 170; inheritance, 34–35, 36, 47, 51; vocation, 35, 36; on marriage, 37, 254 (n. 52); scientific interests, 49–50, 55–59, 62–65, 85–88, 92–93, 94–95, 97, 98, 99, 104, 105, 106, 108, 109, 114, 117, 124, 130, 133, 143–44, 278–79 (n. 134), 280 (n. 4); theory of creation, 59–60, 52–53, 65, 251 (n. 15); on the self, 60, 61, 253 (n. 47), 255 (n. 65); on reform, 60–62, 69–70, 227; on art, 78; crisis, 246 (n. 38)

James, Mary Ann, 263 (n. 32)

James, Mary Walsh, 25, 37–39, 44, 47, 55, 70, 246 (n. 41), 247 (n. 45), 251–52 (n. 22), 255–56 (n. 1)

James, Robertson, 25, 44, 112, 242 (n. 1), 258 (n. 36)

James, Rev. William, 245 (n. 34)

James, William: in cultural canon, ix; youth, ix, 17, 25–26, 39–40, 42–48, 52, 179, 192, 230, 247 (n. 45), 247–48 (n. 51), 249 (n. 69), 255–56 (n. 1); scholarly study concerning, ix, 21, 234–35 (nn. 1, 2); and uncertainty in science and religion, x, xi, 9, 17, 109–10, 124–25, 147–48, 174, 195, 197, 198, 201, 224, 226, 227, 228–30; intellectual circle around, x–xi, 17–18, 21, 134, 146, 148, 153–56, 157, 161, 169, 170, 171–72, 175–76, 180–83, 183, 191, 193, 197, 201, 210, 214, 222, 223–24, 226, 227–29, 230, 235–36 (n. 6), 253 (n. 44), 285 (n. 65), 287 (n. 14), 290 (n. 53); education in science, xii, 17–18, 49–50, 62, 65, 67, 71–73, 81, 85–88, 89, 95, 97, 99, 106, 108, 109, 111, 134, 136–44, 153, 226–27, 229, 230–31; *Principles of Psychology*, 2, 209, 238–39 (n. 35), 240 (n. 48), 258–59 (n. 49); and probabilistic revolution, 9–10, 131, 217–18, 227, 291 (n. 73), 295–96 (n. 141); belief without certainty, 10, 17, 153, 154, 175, 223–24, 225, 226, 229–31, 235–36 (n. 6), 293 (n. 99), 297 (n. 1); politics, 18, 240 (n. 46); as elite, 20; moralism, 31, 76, 173, 224; vocational choice, 41–42, 47, 48, 67, 69–81, 124, 147–48, 230, 247–48 (n. 51), 255 (n. 1); schooling, 43–44, 45–47; language learning, 43–46, 72, 78; crises, 53, 65, 109, 230, 251 (n. 19), 257 (n. 25); on his father, 55, 73–74, 153, 189, 226, 229, 230, 248 (n. 54); artistic study, 67, 68, 73, 74, 77–81, 258–59 (nn. 49, 50); scientific interests, 67–69, 71, 108–9, 146–47, 155, 165, 269–70 (nn. 81, 82), 279 (nn. 134, 135), 285–86 (n. 73); ideas of fate, 75; diaries and notebooks, 75–77, 180, 228, 229, 290 (n. 53); psychological interests, 76, 230, 257 (n. 29), 259 (n. 49), 270 (n. 84), 274 (n. 53); religious interests, 109, 125, 137, 138, 143, 162, 175, 229–30; on Darwinism, 109–10, 142, 147, 153, 169, 176, 200, 215, 226–27, 229, 270 (n. 84); study with Agassiz, 115, 116, 120, 121, 124, 129, 143, 202, 274 (n. 53); study with Eliot, 136–38; study with Wyman, 138–43; "Will to Believe," 171–72, 229, 230, 285 (n. 65); on Charles Peirce, 202, 202–3, 205, 212, 214, 222–24, 228, 293 (n. 94); "Sentiment of Rationality," 228–29; personality, 241 (n. 57), 290 (n. 53); on Immanuel Kant, 294–95 (n. 128)

James, William (William of Albany):

business activity, 28; as elite, 28–31, 113; religion, 30–31, 32, 36, will, 34–35, 245 (nn. 32, 33, 35)
James family, 17, 43, 113
Jenkin, Fleeming, 274 (n. 48)
Jesus Christ, 60, 94, 173, 179, 194
Johns Hopkins University, 181
Jordan, David Starr, 119, 272 (n. 20)
Journal of Speculative Philosophy, 214
Juster, Susan, 246 (n. 38)

Kant, Immanuel, 3, 8, 163, 190, 236 (n. 8), 294–95 (n. 128)
Kelley, Mary, 244 (n. 17)
Kelvin, Lord, 169, 268 (n. 68)
Kessler-Harris, Alice, 20, 241 (n. 58)
King, John Owen, 251 (n. 19)
Kloppenberg, James, 12–14, 16, 249 (n. 78), 285 (n. 70)
Kuhn, Thomas, 122, 274 (n. 49)
Kuklick, Bruce, 155, 282 (nn. 18, 24), 285 (n. 72)

La Farge, John, 80, 81
Laplace, Pierre-Simon, 91–92, 261–62 (n. 18)
Lauden, Laurens, 291 (n. 69)
Lawrence, Abbott, 97–98, 117, 118
Lawrence Scientific School, 64, 74, 85–86, 95, 97–99, 111, 112, 113, 117, 134, 135, 138, 151, 184, 227, 252 (n. 33), 256 (n. 4), 263 (n. 39), 276 (n. 95), 288 (n. 22)
Lears, Jackson, 249 (n. 78)
Lee, Robert E., 87
Leland, Charles Godfrey, 88
Lenz, John, 291 (n. 69)
Lenzen, Victor, 293 (n. 92)
Lesley, Peter, 171
Levinson, Henry S., 237–38 (n. 23), 248 (n. 59), 270 (n. 83)
Lewis, R. W. B., 60, 245 (nn. 33, 34), 259 (n. 50)
Liberal religion. *See* Modernists, religious

Lightman, Bernard, 238 (n. 25), 269 (n. 80), 285 (n. 63), 296–97 (n. 1)
Limerick, Patricia, 241 (n. 55)
Linnaean system of classification, 127
Livingston, James, 241 (n. 52)
Livingstone, David, 263 (n. 39)
Locke, John, 239 (n. 38)
Lovejoy, Arthur, 229
Lowell, James Russell, 138–39
Lowell, John Amory, 97, 117, 263 (n. 30)
Lowell, John, Jr., 95–96
Lowell Institute, 95–96, 117, 121, 123, 138, 139, 180, 185, 202, 204
Luther, Martin, 250 (n. 4)
Lyceums. *See* Amateur science
Lyell, Charles, 93, 120, 272 (n. 17), 283 (n. 68)
Lyman, Ann, 158

McCaughey, Robert, 263 (n. 37)
McCosh, James, 170
McDermott, John, 242 (n. 60)
Madden, Edward, 283 (n. 41), 285 (n. 69)
Malaria, 145
Malthus, Robert, 104, 267 (n. 61)
Manifest Destiny, 94
Marsh, Othniel, 284 (n. 52)
Masculinity, 53, 74, 113, 209, 240 (n. 46), 247 (n. 50), 251 (n. 16), 270–71 (n. 2); white males, 18, 20
Massachusetts Institute of Technology, 123, 277 (n. 100)
Materialism. *See* Naturalism
Mathematics, 159, 178, 191, 192, 195, 207
Maxwell, James Clerk, 199, 268 (n. 72), 292 (n. 87)
Mayr, Ernst, 265 (n. 50)
Medicine, 144–47, 278 (n. 130), 279 (n. 136)
Medieval Europe, 14
Mendel, Gregor, 130–31, 199, 275 (n. 80)

Mental photography, 281 (n. 5)
Metaphysical Club, xii, 151–56, 157, 162, 172, 173, 201, 205, 206, 209, 210, 279–80 (nn. 2, 3, 4), 280 (n. 6), 292 (n. 84), 295–96 (n. 141)
Meteorology, 167
Michelangelo, 190
Michigan, University of, 125–26
Mill, John Stuart, 157, 163, 168, 198, 282 (nn. 23, 25)
Millet, Jean-François, 80, 258 (n. 47)
Mills, C. Wright, 152–53, 155, 283 (n. 28), 285 (n. 69), 294 (n. 116)
Modernists, religious, 107, 268–69 (nn. 74, 76)
Moore, James R., 263 (n. 39), 264 (n. 40), 268 (n. 74)
Moore, R. Laurence, 241 (n. 55)
Morality, moralism, xii, 30, 32, 35, 41, 80, 112, 281 (n. 13)
Morphology, 101, 141
Multiculturalism, 18–21, 240 (n. 50)
Murphey, Murray, 289 (n. 42)
Myers, Gerald, 249 (n. 70)

National Academy of Sciences, 202
Native American history, 2, 15, 18, 19, 235 (n. 4)
Naturalism, 91–93, 99, 104–5, 107–10, 131–32, 135, 137–38, 145, 147–48, 152, 154, 164, 167, 171, 174, 187, 189, 227, 263 (n. 40), 268–69 (n. 74), 269 (n. 80), 276–77 (n. 99)
Natural selection. *See* Darwinism
Natural theology, 15, 57, 132–34, 174, 218, 227, 252 (n. 30)
Naturphilosophie, 115, 271 (n. 11)
Nautical Almanac, 151, 161, 205
Nebular hypothesis, 91–92, 169, 261–62 (n. 18)
Nentuig, Juan, 15
Neo-Lamarckianism, 266 (n. 57), 273 (n. 31)
Neuchâtel, 116, 117, 272 (n. 22)

Newcomb, Simon, 161, 205, 295–96 (nn. 141, 142)
New historicism, 12
New religions, 94, 248 (n. 59)
New Thought, 107, 268–69 (nn. 74, 78)
Newton, Isaac, 99, 264 (n. 44)
New York City, 28
New York Lyceum of Natural History, 125
North American Review, 161, 205–6, 294 (n. 108)
North Carolina, 128
Norton, Charles Eliot, 60, 143, 147–48, 157, 160, 161, 172, 280 (n. 4)
Norton, Grace, 171
Norton, Sara, 160
Nott, Eliphalet, 30, 33, 244 (n. 27)
Nott, Josiah, 140, 277 (n. 113)
Novak, Barbara, 258 (n. 45)

Oken, Lorenz, 115, 271 (n. 11)
Owen, Richard, 102, 142

Palaeontology, 92, 141
Paley, William, 56, 132, 252 (n. 30)
Palmer, George Herbert, 175, 229
Paris, 68
Pascal, Blaise, 296 (n. 141)
Paul, St., 63, 174
Peabody Museum, 138
Peirce, Benjamin, 113, 159, 177, 184, 188–89, 194, 201, 202, 262 (n. 18), 273 (n. 34), 276 (n. 95), 286 (n. 8), 290 (nn. 48, 49)
Peirce, Charles Henry, 288 (n. 22)
Peirce, Charles Sanders, xi, xii, 19–20, 21, 113, 131, 136, 151–55, 157, 162, 165, 167–68, 175–76, 177–224, 227, 253 (n. 44), 270 (n. 81), 279 (n. 2), 280 (n. 4), 283 (nn. 30, 40); confidence in science, 176, 177, 185, 188, 191–93, 197, 203, 207, 212–13, 215–24; on uncertainty of science, 176, 177, 192–201, 203, 216, 217, 219, 223–24, 227–28;

enthusiasm for logic and science, 177, 180, 183–88, 190, 193, 194, 201–4, 208–9, 212, 219, 222, 227, 288 (n. 23), 294 (nn. 123, 125); ambivalence, 177, 182, 183, 190, 197, 200, 207, 212, 214, 216, 217, 218, 219, 220, 222, 223, 224, 287 (n. 17); early years of, 177–87; political views of, 178–79, 185–186, 194; pro-Southern sympathies of, 179, 185; on morality, 179–81, 190, 191, 194, 196, 209, 220; personality, 180–81, 286 (n. 8), 291 (n. 67); scientific work, 181, 197, 201–2, 205, 212, 215–16, 218; writing style, 181–82, 202, 206, 207, 214, 215, 222, 287 (n. 15), 293 (n. 94); "Illustrations of the Logic of Science" series, 183, 201, 206, 207–22 passim; on uncertainty in philosophy, 185, 190, 192, 195, 203, 205, 210–11, 213–14, 221, 295 (n. 129); on literature, 185–86, 288 (n. 31); on religion, 187–91, 195–96, 204, 218–19, 220, 222, 289 (n. 42), 292 (n. 78), 294–95 (nn. 128, 129); idealism, 188–94, 202, 203, 219, 222; on long-term thinking, 190, 192–95, 197, 198, 200, 214, 217, 218, 291 (n. 69); on agapism, 194, 198; on tychism, 195, 198; on probabilities, 195–97, 198–201, 216–18, 220, 224, 291 (n. 73), 292 (nn. 78, 82, 84, 89), 296 (nn. 141, 142); on synechism, 198; on Darwinism, 198–201, 204, 215–16, 221, 222, 292 (nn. 84, 89); on logic of science, 202–22 passim; on abduction, 204, 220–21; on William James, 204, 293 (n. 99); hopes to influence the public, 204–7, 208–11, 214, 220, 222, 223; on belief formation, 204–15 passim, 217, 218, 221–22, 224, 228; on habits, 208–12, 221, 223, 224; on signs, 214

Peirce, Charlotte Elizabeth, 288 (n. 22)
Peirce, Elizabeth, 177
Peirce, Thomas, 177
Pelikan, Jaroslav, 250 (n. 4)
Perry, Lewis, 240 (n. 47)
Perry, Ralph Barton, 44
Perry, Thomas Sargeant, 205–6, 259 (n. 6)
Pestalozzi, Heinrich, 249 (n. 72)
Phyllotaxis, 169
Physics, 159, 184, 293 (n. 92)
Physiological psychology, 146–47
Physiology, 138, 144
Plato, 78, 257 (n. 31)
Poe, Edgar Allan, 1–2
Polygenesis, 139–40, 277 (nn. 112, 113)
Pope, Alexander, 291 (n. 61)
Popularization, 4, 5–6, 8–9, 16, 19, 21–22, 56, 87–91, 95–96, 120, 127, 135, 137, 155, 182, 185, 204–15 passim, 236 (n. 11), 239 (n. 42), 275 (nn. 64, 65)
Popular Science Monthly, 206–7, 294 (n. 108)
Porter, Theodore, 7
Positivism, 4, 10, 62, 154, 163, 187, 203, 227, 236 (n. 11), 238 (nn. 25, 30), 239 (n. 42), 255 (n. 59), 262 (n. 18), 279 (n. 2), 282 (n. 25), 286 (n. 74)
Potter, Alonzo, 143
Pragmatism, 12, 21, 152, 157, 165, 182, 205, 206, 208, 214, 223, 237 (n. 23), 241 (n. 58), 253 (n. 44), 270 (n. 84), 280 (n. 6), 283 (n. 38), 293 (n. 94)
Pratt, James, 297 (n. 8)
Presbyterian Church, 30, 32, 50, 124, 125, 134, 245 (n. 34)
Princeton Theological Seminary, 50, 94, 170, 250 (n. 5)
Probabilities, xii, 5, 6–10, 12, 36, 99, 102, 105–6, 122, 128–30, 131–32, 142, 152, 165–68, 173, 174, 175,

183, 195–200, 215–18, 227, 237
(n. 16), 254 (n. 53), 254–55 (n. 56),
265 (n. 47), 267 (n. 65), 268 (n. 72),
283 (n. 38), 291 (n. 73), 292 (n. 87),
294 (n. 121), 296 (nn. 141, 142)
Professionalism, xii, 4–6, 8, 16, 19,
21–22, 88, 89–91, 94–99, 129–30,
134–36, 144, 166, 184, 236 (nn. 10,
12)
Progressive Evolutionism. *See* Cosmic Evolutionism
Progressives, 12–13, 174, 285 (n. 70)
Protestant Reformation, 14, 50, 93,
250 (n. 4), 252 (n. 24)
Protoplasm, 145
Psychozoology, 284 (n. 51)
Puerperal fever, 145
Puritanism, New England, 179, 295
(n. 129)

Quetelet, Adolphe, 216, 255 (n. 56)

Ramsey, Bennett, 240 (n. 49)
Religion: convictions, x, 4, 5, 8, 11, 35,
93–95, 96; churches, 11, 50–51, 57,
144–45, 248 (n. 59); doubt concerning, 14–16, 94, 262–63 (n. 28);
belief in, 15–16, 136; privatization
of, 94, 95; tonic destruction of, 135,
172, 187. *See also* Great Awakenings; Presbyterian Church; Protestant Reformation; Religious history;
Roman Catholicism; Sabbath Day
restrictions; Science and religion
Religion and Science. *See* Science and Religion
Religious history, 3–4, 8, 10–11,
14–16, 17, 42
Rensselaer Institute, 97
Republicanism, 6, 28–30, 31, 34, 178,
243–44 (n. 16)
Revivals of religion. *See* Great Awakenings
Richards, Robert, 265 (n. 50)
Roberts, Jon, 239 (n. 42)

Rockmore, Tom, 235 (n. 6)
Rogers, William Barton, 123
Roman Catholicism, 239–40 (n. 44),
252 (n. 24)
Romanes, George, 132
Romanticism, 32, 39, 47, 55, 56, 188,
244 (n. 23), 249 (n. 72), 252 (n. 22),
262 (n. 19)
Rosenberg, Rosalind, 235 (n. 3)
Rosenthal, Sandra, 235 (n. 6)
Ross, Dorothy, 238 (n. 30)
Royal Society, 261 (n. 14)
Royce, Josiah, 286 (n. 73)
Ruf, Frederick, 240 (n. 49)
Ruse, Michael, 265 (n. 47, 50), 266
(nn. 52, 57)
Rush, Benjamin, 33
Ruskin, John, 129–30
Ryan, Mary, 246 (n. 37)

Sabbath Day restrictions, 30–31, 80
Sanborn, Franklin, 112
Sandemanianism, 51–52, 250 (nn. 7,
8, 9)
Santayana, George, 281 (n. 13)
Saturday Club, 79, 112–14, 126, 144,
146, 153, 278 (n. 127)
Say, Thomas, 262 (n. 23)
Science, social authority of, x, 3–5
Science and religion: harmony between,
13, 15, 35–36, 64, 56, 81, 85, 90–
93, 94–99, 107, 108, 112, 117,
124–25, 136, 153–54, 172, 174,
190, 194, 210, 230, 259 (n. 3), 262
(n. 21), 263 (n. 30), 268 (n. 74),
270–71 (n. 1), 276 (n. 93); separation of, 88–99 passim, 107, 125,
133–34, 136, 163–65, 187–88,
190–91, 194, 227, 268–69 (nn. 74,
79); conflict between, 99–100, 222,
263 (n. 39), 268–69 (n. 74)
Science before 1860, xii, 61–62, 86–99
passim, 227, 260 (n. 4)
Science of society, 60–62
Scientific naturalism. *See* Naturalism

Index

Scientific schools, 97–99
Scott, Joan, 235 (n. 3)
Scottish Common Sense. *See* Common Sense philosophy
Secularism, 10–17, 36, 91–92, 93, 108, 238 (nn. 25, 30), 257 (n. 24), 262 (n. 28), 289 (n. 38)
Seelye, John, 243 (n. 10)
Seigfried, Charlotte Haddock, 235 (n. 6), 240 (n. 49)
Semiotics, 182, 214
Sentimentalism, 94, 135, 153
Shakespeare, William, 159, 161
Shaler, Nathaniel Southgate, 263 (n. 39)
Sheffield Scientific School, 97
Showalter, Elaine, 246 (n. 40)
Silliman, Benjamin, 260 (n. 8)
Skagestad, Peter, 289 (n. 42), 291 (n. 69)
Skocpol, Theda, 235 (n. 3)
Slavery, 18, 88, 139–40, 153
Smith, Gary Scott, 11
Smith, John E., 242 (n. 60)
Smithsonian, 96, 120
Social Darwinism, 194
Social history, 10–11, 263 (n. 37)
Sociology of knowledge, 208, 294 (n. 116)
South, the American, 18
Species, fixity of, 93, 116–17, 128, 165–66, 262 (n. 23), 272 (n. 20)
Species development. *See* Darwinism
Spencer, Herbert, 12, 102, 137, 164, 165, 270 (nn. 81, 83), 283 (n. 30), 286 (n. 74)
Spiritualism, 261 (n. 14)
Statistics, 7, 8, 128–29, 196, 199, 237 (n. 23), 265 (n. 49). *See also* Probabilities
Stefen, Leslie, 187
Stevenson, Robert Louis, 46
Stewart, Christopher, 294 (n. 123)
Stoicism, 173
Storer, Frank H., 136, 277 (n. 100)

Strouse, Jean, 246 (n. 42), 247 (n. 50)
Strout, Cushing, 255 (n. 1)
Swedenborg, Emanuel, 42, 53–55, 59–60, 63, 107, 145, 188–89, 247 (n. 48), 251 (nn. 21, 22), 252 (n. 24), 253 (nn. 40, 41), 254 (n. 51), 289 (n. 46), 290 (n. 48); vastations, 52–55; correspondence, theory of, 58–59, 65, 253 (n. 41)

Taylor, Eugene, 253 (n. 44)
Teaching, 19–20, 119–20, 126–27, 138, 182
Thayer, James Bradley, 159, 281 (n. 4)
Thayer, Nathaniel, 123
Thomas, John, 241 (n. 56)
Thomas, Keith, 262 (n. 28)
Thoreau, Henry David, 56, 161, 252 (n. 33)
Thornwell, James Henley, 92
Tilton, Elizabeth, 236–37 (n. 13)
Tocqueville, Alexis de, 4, 235 (n. 10)
Torrey, John, 125–26
Town and Country Club. *See* Saturday Club
Turley, Peter, 292 (n. 82)
Turner, Frank, 263 (n. 39), 269 (n. 80)
Turner, James, 14–16
Tyler, Samuel, 91, 261 (n. 16)
Tyndall, John, 12, 100

Uncertainty, 5–6, 10, 13, 17, 19, 20, 21–22, 35–36, 47–48, 70, 75, 81, 85–86, 110, 167, 183, 195–98, 204, 205, 210–12, 213, 216, 219–22, 223–24, 225–31, 235 (n. 6), 236 (nn. 10, 11), 237 (n. 23), 294 (n. 121); in science, x–xii, xiii, 3, 4–5, 7–8, 12–13, 16, 88, 102, 104, 105, 107, 121, 128, 129, 131–32, 164, 165, 166, 175, 197, 203–4, 237 (n. 23), 259 (n. 2), 267 (n. 65); in religion, x–xii, xiii, 3, 4–5, 8, 10–11, 13, 14–17, 21, 43, 107, 147–48, 163, 189–90, 196

Uncle Tom's Cabin, 185, 186
Uniformitarianism, 116, 272 (n. 17). *See also* Catastrophism; Darwinism; Lyell, Charles
Union College, 28, 33–34, 70, 72–73, 74
Unitarian Church, 136, 152, 158, 173, 188, 189
Upham, Charles, 273 (n. 34)
Utilitarianism, 173

Van Winkle, Edgar B., 69–75, 256 (n. 7)
Venn, John, 217

Wallace, Alfred Russel, 103–4, 267 (nn. 59, 61)
Ward, Samuel, 113
Warner, John, 152
War of 1812, 27
Wayland, Francis, 91, 261 (n. 17)
Welter, Barbara, 239 (n. 37)
Westfall, Richard, 239 (n. 38)
Whewell, William, 102, 260 (n. 6), 266 (nn. 52, 53), 272 (n. 17)
Wiener, Philip, 155, 198, 280 (n. 6), 292 (n. 84)
Wilkins, Walter, 269 (n. 74)
Women's studies, 2, 18, 20, 94, 172, 235 (n. 3), 241 (n. 57), 244 (n. 17), 246 (nn. 37, 38, 39, 40, 41), 247 (n. 50), 249–50 (n. 82), 254 (n. 52)

Wood, Gordon, 243–44 (n. 16)
Woodrow, James, 133, 276 (n. 91)
Woolsey, Theodore Dwight, 56
Wright, Chauncey, xii, 1, 21, 136, 151–52, 155–56, 157–76 passim, 181, 187, 205, 270 (n. 81), 279 (n. 2), 280 (n. 4), 293 (n. 102); and the neutrality of science and religion, 134, 163–65, 169–71, 172, 174, 175, 276 (n. 93), 282 (n. 24); early life, 158–63; relations with children, 160, 173, 282 (n. 20); political views, 160–61; as a teacher, 162; on scientific method, 164–66, 170, 173, 175–76, 227–28, 286 (n. 74); on probabilities, 166–68, 217; on cosmic weather, 167, 216–17; on religion, 170–76, 297 (n. 1); as influence on William James, 171–72, 223–24; on morality, 173, 228
Wright, George Frederick, 133, 276 (n. 91)
Wyman, Jeffries, xii, 98, 113, 134, 138–43, 147–48, 163, 168, 227, 276 (n. 95)

Youmans, Edward, 119, 172
Young, Robert, 265 (n. 50)

Zoology, 101, 115, 138, 141
Zurich, 115